Passageways

By the Same Author

Waiting for the Party: The Life of Frances Hodgson Burnett
(Frances Hodgson Burnett: Beyond the Secret Garden)
Edmund Gosse: A Literary Landscape
A.A. Milne: His Life
The Brilliant Career of Winnie-the-Pooh
Emily Tennyson: The Poet's Wife
Glimpses of the Wonderful: The Life of Philip Henry Gosse
My Oxford (edited)
Portraits from Life by Edmund Gosse (edited)

Books for Children include

The Young Traveller in Japan
The Camelthorn Papers
Tracks
The Ashton Affair
Home and Away
The Travelling Tooth
The Only Treasure
The Day with the Duke
Pennies for the Dog
The Chatterbox
Gilbert and the Birthday Cake
The Horse at Hilly Fields
Allsorts 1 to 7 (edited)

Passageways

the story of a
New Zealand family

ANN THWAITE

OTAGO

Published by Otago University Press

PO Box 56/Level 1, 398 Cumberland Street, Dunedin, New Zealand

Fax: 64 3 479 8385

Email: university.press@otago.ac.nz

Website: www.otago.ac.nz/press

First published 2009

ISBN 978 1 877372 67 4

Cover image: The Harrop children, David and Ann, Cornwall, England, 1939

Editors: Richard Reeve and Wendy Harrex

Editorial assistant: Taryn Tait

Cover and book design: Fiona Moffat

Printed through Condor Production Ltd, Hong Kong

Contents

Family passages 6
Acknowledgements 7
Family tree showing descent from my great-grandparents 10
Introduction: The jigsaw puzzle of the past 11

PART ONE: DISCOVERING OUR ROOTS
Family tree: my father's mother's family 14
1 Mainly about the Campbells and the Browns 15
Family tree: my father's father's family 34
2 Mainly about the Harrops 35
3 Despair and hope in Hokitika and Waitaki 61
Family tree: my mother's mother's family 88
4 Mainly about the Hoggs, the Olivers and the Jefcoates 89
Family tree: my mother's father's family 112
5 Mainly about the Valentines and the Maxwells 113
Family tree: my mother's own family 136
6 The headmaster's daughter 137
7 Choosing partners 163

PART TWO: TOGETHER, APART, TOGETHER
8 Remembering, not forgetting, New Zealand 201
9 A strenuous pair 227
10 Out of harm's way 259
11 The last lap 289
Afternote 319

Notes 321
Bibliography 333
List of Illustrations 337
Index 341

FAMILY PASSAGES

Date	Passengers	Ship	From	To
c. 1815	Our great-great-great grandparents, Margaret & Alexander MacKay	?	Rogart, Sutherland, Scotland	Nova Scotia
c. 1823	Johanna née Mackay & John Campbell, Alexander (3), Merrion (1)	?	Rogart, Sutherland, Scotland	Pictou, Nova Scotia
1849?	James & Helen (Ellen) Maxwell, James (9), Mary (6), George (1)	?	Alloa, Stirlingshire, Scotland	Co. Cavan, Ireland
19.11.1851–1.3.1852	John & Catherine Maxwell, George (9), Ellen (5)	Agra	London, England	Wellington, NZ
18.9.1852–9.2.1853	Angus Campbell & Jane (1st wife and cousin) née Mackay, and children Margaret Jane and John	Aurora	Nova Scotia	Port Phillip, Melbourne, Australia
30.4.1853–14.8.1853	Adam & Barbara Brown, Elizabeth (19), Bethia Jane (17), James (15) twins Janet and Barbara (11), John (7), Thomas (5)	Catherine Glen	Glasgow, Scotland	Port Phillip, Melbourne, Australia
23.6.1858–23.9.1858	James & Helen Maxwell, James (18), Mary (15), George (9), William (7), John (5) & Archibald Valentine, crew	Jura	Glasgow, Scotland	Port Chalmers, NZ
4.7.1863–10.10.1863	James & Sarah Harrop	Lancashire Witch	London, England	Timaru, NZ
25.8.1864–4.1.1865	Thomas & Janet Jefcoate, son born on voyage	Eastern Empire	London, England	Lyttelton, NZ
c. 1865	Angus Campbell & Angus MacKay	Claud Hamilton	Port Phillip, Melbourne, Aus.	Auckland, NZ
c. 1868	Bethia Campbell, Elizabeth (7), John Adam (3), Angus James (1)	?	Port Phillip, Melbourne, Aus.	Greymouth?, NZ
1868?	Archibald & Charlotte Valentine, Jane (Jeannie) (19)	?	Montrose, Fife, Scotland	Port Chalmers?, NZ
17.10. 1873	Bethia Campbell, Elizabeth (12), John Adam (8), Angus James (5), Bethia Jane (3) – after a visit to Melbourne	Alhambra	Port Phillip, Melbourne, Aus.	Greymouth, NZ
1891	Thomas & Janet Jefcoate – return visit to England and Scotland	?	?	?
1907	Thomas & Janet Jefcoate – return visit to England	?	?	?
1921–1922	Win Valentine – return visit to North America and Europe	Niagara Maunganui	Auckland, NZ Vancouver?, Canada	Vancouver, Canada Auckland?, NZ
14.7.1923	Angus John Harrop	Remuera	Wellington, NZ	Southampton, England
26.5.1926	Hilda Mary Valentine	Marama to Sydney Beltana via South Africa	Wellington, NZ	London, England
1928	Jim & Nellie Valentine – return visit to UK and Europe	Marama to Sydney Bendigo to UK Cathay to Sydney	Wellington, NZ	Southampton, England
1934	Angus & Hilda Harrop, David (3), Ann Barbara (1½) – return visit to New Zealand	Akaroa Tamaroa	Southampton, England Napier, NZ	Wellington, NZ Southampton?, England
1940	Hilda Harrop, David (9), Ann Barbara (7)	Ceramic, Viceroy of India Themistocles, Larg's Bay, Aorangi	Liverpool, England	via South Africa & Australia, Auckland, NZ
1942	Hilda Harrop	Akaroa	Wellington, NZ	via Panama Canal, Halifax, Nova Scotia, Belfast & London
Nov. 1944–Mar. 1945	Angus Harrop – to Australia and NZ via USA, Mexico and Panama Canal Zone	Aquitania Coptic ?	Liverpool, England Panama Australia	New York Australia NZ
June 1945	Angus Harrop, David (14), Ann Barbara (12)	Empire Grace	Auckland, NZ	Liverpool, England

Acknowledgments

Most of my material, as will become obvious throughout the book, comes from family papers. I am particularly grateful for the three unpublished memoirs by my mother, her father, J.A. Valentine, and her aunt, W.A. Valentine, and for the pages entitled 'Discovering the Jefcoates' by my cousin, the late Helen Davidson. I would also like to acknowledge the support of other cousins, including Judy Mertzlin and Gill Poulier of Melbourne, Ruth McDonald of Auckland and Janet Hanna of both Henley-on-Thames in England and Auckland. It was a great help that they were all insistent that I should write whatever I wanted to write, without worrying about how they would feel. Janet and Richard Hanna exemplify in my own generation the way our family continues to have loyalties on both sides of the world and, in their case, in a way that would have amazed our grandparents.

My main debt is to my brother, David Harrop of New Plymouth. His research (in the midst of an extremely busy life) has been remarkable and I could not have written the book without it. On the family history tour he organised, we visited nineteen museums and libraries, where the staff were unfailingly helpful. I would like to mention individually Mary Rooney at the West Coast Historical Museum at Hokitika and Anna Blackman at the Hocken Library, University of Otago, Dunedin. I must also thank the following institutions: the Alexander Turnbull Library and Archives New Zealand in Wellington, the Black's Point Museum at Reefton, the Ross Goldfields Information Centre, the Conservation Centre at Arthur's Pass, Land Information New Zealand (L.I.N.Z.) in Christchurch, the Canterbury Museum Research Centre, the Macmillan Brown Library at Canterbury University, the South Canterbury Museum, Timaru, the Waikouaiti Museum, the Otago Museum and the Otago Settlers Museum.

I would like to thank more distant family connections, whose own interest in genealogy was extremely useful: Ursula Furkert of Wellington, John Campbell of Melbourne, Helen Bannan of Auckland, Ruth Brockbank of Waikouaiti and Graham Jefcoate, whom I met fortuitously when I was working at the British Library in London. I am grateful too for help from my Marsden friends, Gaye Law, Sue Fetherston, Winty Fysh and the late Barbara Yaldwyn. I am only sorry Holly did not live to read what I have written.

Other friends whose interest and support have meant a great deal to me include Margery and Gary Blackman of Dunedin, Judith and Llyn Richards of Wellington and, in England, Jan Martin of Halesworth and Gill Frayn of Greenwich, with whom I explored unfamiliar parts of London where my great-grandparents had lived.

The photographs and ephemera, my father's cuttings books and the tens of thousands of words I read – in the letters and diaries my mother had kept and handed on to me – remain for the most part in my house in Norfolk, but some are now in the archives of the Imperial War Museum in London. A number of the remainder should certainly at some point find their way back to New Zealand. I would be glad to hear from any library interested in acquiring the material.

I must conclude by thanking the readers of the first printout, all of whom helped me to improve the final text. They were David and Margaret Harrop (my brother and his wife), Michael Millgate, Karl and Kay Stead, Anthony Thwaite and our daughters, Alice and Lucy. Their readings were made possible (as so much else is made possible) by the brilliant technology and skill of Hilary Tulloch, who has been dealing with my difficult manuscripts now for over twenty years. The enthusiasm of Hilary and her husband, Dick, as she dealt with each chapter in turn, made a tremendous difference to the whole enterprise. I intend this to be the last time I write a book and my gratitude is particularly heartfelt as I write these words. This time our intensive final work on the text was in Dublin and I thank them for their hospitality as well as so much else. Throughout everything, my agent, Camilla Hornby of Curtis Brown in London, has also given me vital support, for which I am extremely grateful.

ANN THWAITE
Norfolk, England
December 2008

For David, Margaret and Anthony,
and for our children
and theirs
on both sides of the world

'There is nothing to write which is better than life itself.'
The novelist Julian Barnes in *Staring at the Sun*

'I never can get interested in things that didn't happen to people who never lived.'
The reader Helène Hanff in *84 Charing Cross Road*

'How to make all this into something true?'
The poet Alan Jenkins in *A Shorter Life*

Family Tree showing descent from my great-grandparents

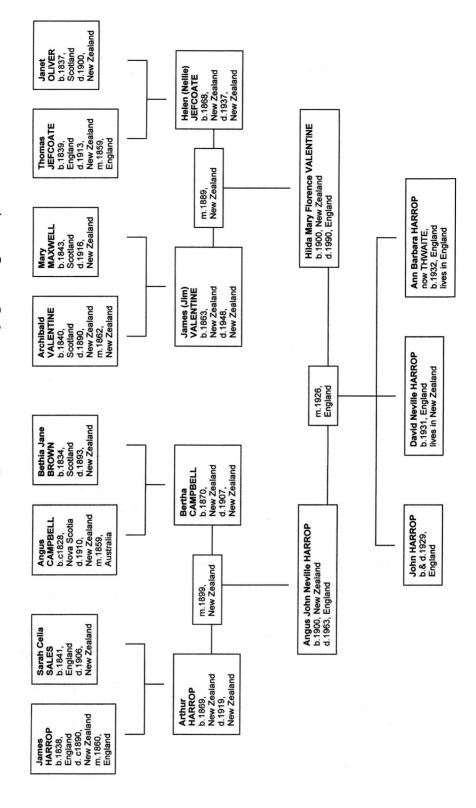

James HARROP
b.1838,
England
d. c1890,
New Zealand
m.1860,
England

Sarah Celia SALES
b.1841,
England
d.1906,
New Zealand

Angus CAMPBELL
b.c1828,
Nova Scotia
d.1910,
New Zealand
m.1859,
Australia

Bethia Jane BROWN
b.1834,
Scotland
d.1893,
New Zealand

Archibald VALENTINE
b.1840,
Scotland
d.1890,
New Zealand
m.1862,
New Zealand

Mary MAXWELL
b.1843,
Scotland
d.1916,
New Zealand

Thomas JEFCOATE
b.1839,
England
d.1913,
New Zealand
m.1859,
England

Janet OLIVER
b.1837,
Scotland
d.1900,
New Zealand

m.1899,
New Zealand

Arthur HARROP
b.1869,
New Zealand
d.1919,
New Zealand

Bertha CAMPBELL
b.1870,
New Zealand
d.1907,
New Zealand

m.1889,
New Zealand

James (Jim) VALENTINE
b.1863,
New Zealand
d.1948,
New Zealand

Helen (Nellie) JEFCOATE
b.1868,
New Zealand
d.1937,
New Zealand

m.1926,
England

Angus John Neville HARROP
b.1900, New Zealand
d.1963, England

Hilda Mary Florence VALENTINE
b.1900, New Zealand
d.1990, England

John HARROP
b. & d.1929,
England

David Neville HARROP
b.1931, England
lives in New Zealand

Ann Barbara HARROP
now THWAITE,
b.1932, England
lives in England

The jigsaw puzzle of the past

In her introduction to a collection of early colonial women's writing, *Married and Gone to New Zealand* (1960), Alison Drummond wrote of the value of letters. 'Seemingly trivial details and explanations are of incalculable value, even a century later. They supply the researcher with those small but important pieces that help to solve the jigsaw puzzle of the past.' I have myself often used the image of the jigsaw puzzle when talking or writing about biography. With well-known people, their lives played out on some sort of public stage, the pieces of the puzzle are numerous, often so numerous that the biographer has to leave some out, not because they are not part of the picture, but simply to confine the book to a reasonable length.

With some of my nineteenth-century forebears, the immigrants to New Zealand, the problem is that nearly all the interesting pieces that made up their lives have been lost and can never be found, however hard one looks. The letters and diaries, if such there were, have been thrown away by impatient clearers-up, unable to imagine our curiosity. This is a common regret among people trying to discover a family history. The challenge then is to construct some sort of story from the evidence that remains: certificates of birth, marriage and death, census records, electoral rolls, and such things as local newspapers and trade directories.

Both my parents were born in 1900, to parents who had themselves also been born in New Zealand. The background of my father, Angus Harrop, was mysterious and almost totally unknown to us before my brother David and I began the research for this book. But the family of my mother, Hilda Valentine, is as fully documented as any biographer could wish. She always found it difficult to throw away anything that was in the least interesting, an attitude I share myself. The cupboards she left behind were crammed full of letters, postcards, diaries – the earliest of these an unrestrained notebook she began in 1916. Some of her own letters written from New Zealand during World War II to her closest friend, Moyra Todd, had been returned to her on Moyra's death and provided me with a recent first reading that told me many things about myself of which I had no memory. Letters to my father, in London during the Blitz, and his letters to her, also told me a great deal I did not know. My mother wrote her own memoirs – and so did both her father and an aunt, who took their family's story back to the arrival in Dunedin in 1858.

We have much less from my father's side, though I did find some useful pages of reticent autobiography (unpublished) and a few personal passages in his published books. By beginning the book with my father's side of the family I have hoped to redress the balance to some extent. Our experience with the history of that side, the Campbells, the Browns and the Harrops, may be more typical than the experience we had in following the history of my mother's side, the Jefcoates, the Maxwells and the Valentines. And I should say at this point that, when I say 'our' and 'we' and 'us', I am referring always to my brother and myself. I am grateful for the huge amount of research he has done, for the numerous letters to archivists and librarians, for his time on the internet and for setting up the family history tour we did together with Margaret his wife. I realise David would have dealt with some of this material very differently, if he had been writing the book himself, and that he originally had some reservations about making public some of the more private – and painful – material. A great deal of the material comes from within the family. As well as letters, diaries and memoirs, covering a long period, there is an extraordinarily detailed account of our childhood, recorded as it happened by my mother. So this book is not weighed down with Sources, as my recent biographies have been. I have actually never felt the need for every phrase to have a reference 'as if it were applying for a job' – as one of my friends once put it. But this story is – as Edmund Gosse notoriously and inaccurately claimed in *Father and Son* – as much of a document, as 'scrupulously true' as I can make it. I have left out, in the second section of the book particularly, many things I know, but I have not made up anything I did not know. Everything is based on evidence.

I may well have got some things wrong, writing, as I am, on the other side of the world. If any readers have corrections, I hope they will write to me. I will always be interested to hear from readers whose own family stories touch on mine, if they can add to and illuminate what I have written.

PART ONE

Discovering Our Roots

My father's mother's family: the Campbells and the Browns

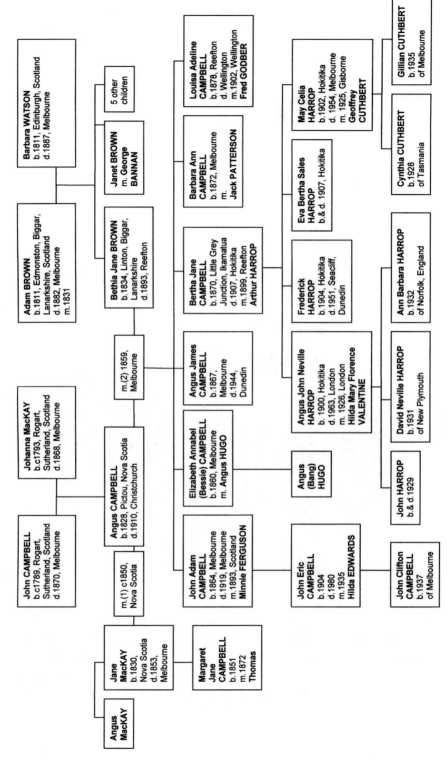

CHAPTER 1

Mainly about the Campbells and the Browns

A small boy is standing on the verandah of a little wooden house at the ends of the earth. He is wearing a sailor collar and a large straw hat, though the sun may not be shining. His face is too small for me to tell whether he is smiling. I don't think he is. He has been told by the photographer to stand very still, not to move, and he has tried to do what he was told.

The photograph was given to the boy in a lavish album, filled with scenes of his father out and about on his job as a surveyor on the West Coast of New Zealand. We can see this recognisable man among tree ferns above Lake Brunner, with a dog on the rocks in the bed of the Hohonu River, trudging along the road at Barrytown. The album has the boy's name on the front page in fancy lettering: Angus John Neville Harrop. Below it are the place and the date: Hokitika, 1907. It is his

seventh birthday and he is alone on the verandah of the house in Fitzherbert Street. Less than two months earlier, his mother has died after childbirth. Somewhere in the house, I suppose, beyond the open door, are the other children named on the death certificate: May Celia, aged four and three quarters, Frederick, two, and the baby Eva, who survived long enough to learn to smile but who would die a month after her older brother's birthday.

That boy was my father, the woman who died my grandmother, the mother he never mentioned. May became an aunt living in Australia – the only sibling we knew my father had. There is a photo of them, the two of them, a studio photo, very different from the one of the boy on the verandah, though it could be the same hat. They are lovely children, beautifully dressed.

They both look the photographer straight in the eye. Angus is solemn, but May is very nearly smiling. One of her pretty shoes is pointed in the air, as if she would like to be dancing. This photograph belongs to an entirely different time, a happy time before Frederick's birth. It hangs on the wall in my living room on the other side of the world. The photo of the boy on the verandah is in the album in a cupboard. It is too sad for framing. The other two children, my uncle and my aunt, Frederick and Eva, are the disappeared. Why do I think about them when my father obviously wanted me never to know of their existence?

The impetus to write not another biography but my own family's story certainly came from looking at that photo in my father's album, a photo of a small boy on a verandah in Hokitika, a photo I never remember seeing when my parents were alive. Their generation (born in 1900) have all gone now; there is no one left to answer any questions. But the cupboards are stuffed with things they left behind. I realised looking at the photo how little I knew about my own family. I had spent the last thirty-five years immersed in other people's lives. I knew much less about my own background than I did about the backgrounds of Frances Hodgson Burnett and A.A. Milne, the Gosses (Philip Henry and Edmund, father and son), the Tennysons and the Sellwoods (Emily Tennyson's family).

I knew very little about my family history beyond the fact that all four of my grandparents had been born in New Zealand. I assumed – how could it not be so? – that all my great-grandparents had travelled there at some point in the nineteenth century, looking for a better life. That was what emigrants did, and in New Zealand everyone is an immigrant of one sort or another. Michael King, that much lamented historian (who died not long before I was expecting to meet him), summed up 'the basic need driving human history' as 'the search for secure places in which to live'. To live means 'to eat, shelter, reproduce and practise cultural or spiritual values'. It is easy enough to know that my ancestors, arriving in New Zealand, ate, found shelter and reproduced. There is an abundant family to prove it. What is much more difficult is to find evidence of those cultural and spiritual values.

'The search for secure places in which to live' interests me, that search which drove my ancestors to make that long journey to the other side of the world. In Britain one looks at human history in a different way. In the part of England where I live – south Norfolk – there are many people who see history not as a search for anything (for they have always been in 'a secure place'), but as something that has happened both elsewhere and around them. They, like their ancestors before them, are not going anywhere. Many of my neighbours' families have 'always lived in Norfolk' just as my husband's family had 'always lived in Yorkshire'.

But no one has 'always lived in New Zealand'. Only the birds – the tuis, the fantails, the bell-birds – might make that claim. (There is that singular lack of any native land mammals – except a couple of bats, which – along with the insects – hardly count.) In New Zealand today we can listen to the surviving descendants of the birds who woke Joseph Banks with the 'most melodious wild musick' he had ever heard, as he lay on his bunk in Captain Cook's *Endeavour*, a quarter of a mile offshore in 1770. We can know the birds sang those songs when there was no one there to hear them.

Historians assume that there had been early visitors: Polynesian travellers who did not survive and left no trace. James Belich suggests the earliest continuous settlements were in 'the Far North and Coromandel', perhaps in the eleventh century, but Michael King insisted no evidence exists of a human occupation of New Zealand earlier than the thirteenth century, and evidence of those early days is limited. Famous for their carving on wood, bone, ivory and greenstone, these Polynesian settlers made no pottery, though there was abundant clay, and found no metal, though 600 years later it would be gold that would bring a flood of new adventurers.

'Though one of the parts of the earth best fitted for man, New Zealand was probably about the last of such lands occupied by the human race', William Pember Reeves wrote in his history published in 1898. The Maori, and indeed the Moriori, shared with their European fellow settlers that search over many miles of sea for a secure place to live. In one of his own books, my father quoted Te Rangi Hiroa, the anthropologist (otherwise known as Peter Buck), as drawing the parallel. All 'migrations of peoples are caused by a push from behind or an alluring prospect in front.' The push could be poverty, over-population, combined with a sense of adventure. The prospect ahead was a land (though not yet, at that period, flowing with milk and honey) that was rich in possibility and extraordinarily beautiful.

If the land was perhaps 680 million years in the making (the estimate is, of course, not mine), the human arrivals were remarkably close together. It is this feeling of a shared land – a once-uninhabited potential Paradise – that has at different times encouraged both Maori and Pakeha to imagine New Zealand could escape the racial problems that beset other once colonial countries.

My parents at school in New Zealand in the early years of the twentieth century were brought up on what has been called 'the great New Zealand myth'. They were told stories of the arrival of Kupe and his family, straining their eyes after many long days at sea, until they saw in the distance what appeared to be at first a long white cloud, a cloud that turned out to be the land of their dreams and that they were said to have called Aotearoa. The land of 'the Long White Cloud' gained wide currency as the title of Pember Reeves' history I quoted from. Fifty years after it was written, my father was given the rather daunting task of bringing it up to date with additional chapters.

We were told Kupe's story too and another one – more obviously a myth – of Maui fishing up New Zealand from the depths of the sea, his hook Cape Kidnappers, known in Maori as Matau-a-Maui. There were other stories of the 'coming of the Fleet', of the seven canoes, in what could have been the fourteenth century. These stories became lodged in the imaginations of both Maori and Pakeha. As King put it, the story of the arrival of the canoe was a happy metaphor for Kotahitanga, the fundamental unity of Maori origins and aspirations, over and above the tribal divisions we hear so much about.

In the later part of the twentieth century there was a good deal of debunking of these stories we had all enjoyed. 'Alas and again', King wrote, 'as in the case of Kupe's deeds, the Great Fleet story proved to be without verifiable Maori foundations.' But he came round to seeing, as others had done before him, that though Kupe and the Fleet may never have existed, their stories have indeed played a part in the history of the country.

Certainly the boy on the Hokitika verandah had those stories in his head and they helped to turn Angus Harrop into the writer he became. Story, history, became something that took him away from the harsh reality of daily life. That his situation was harsh after his mother's death there is no doubt, but it is also clear from what he wrote that all his life he looked back to the West Coast with deep affection. My brother David, who must also play a major part later in this book, remembers how proud Angus Harrop was of his roots in Hokitika, how he would amuse us with his own version of the haka. How well its strange name lent itself to the chant: 'Hokitika – he! Hokitika – ha!' with the appropriately menacing grimace.

But I think that our father always knew he had to get away from Hokitika if he were to make anything of his life. I think he felt, even as a small boy in Fitzherbert Street, that everything that mattered was on the other side of the mountains or across the sea. Hokitika had sprung up in the 1860s on a plain between the mountains and the Tasman Sea on that West Coast of the South Island. 'As we walked to school', he once wrote, 'we walked towards the long range of the Southern Alps and learned gradually the names of the main peaks which stood out so boldly on the clear, bright mornings which follow night rain on the Coast.' He early learnt the height of Mt Cook, 12,349 feet, and taught it to us when we were small. If only it had been four feet shorter! How neat that would have been. He must also have learnt in those early days that England, from which Captain Cook had sailed, was as many miles away on the other side of the world.

When young Angus walked in the other direction, with the mountains behind him, the river to his left, he would come to the beach beyond Revell Street, black sand littered with driftwood, bleached like bones. The sea was often so rough that the children were forbidden to swim in it and had to make do with the river. Looking out to sea, did he know that his mother's family, the Campbells, had made a remarkable journey beginning in 1820 from Rogart in Sutherland in the far north of Scotland to Nova Scotia, then on to Melbourne and eventually across the Tasman Sea to Greymouth, not far north of Hokitika? Both Greymouth and Hokitika were in the 1860s major ports for arrivals from

Australia, though it is difficult to believe that now. Greymouth is still a fishing port, but in Hokitika only a mural on the side of a warehouse bears witness to the time at the height of the gold rush when fifty ships might be lined up along the quay. You have to go into the museum to get any idea of Hokitika's vivid past.

Angus Harrop carried his Campbell grandfather's Christian name and must have known, I think, that his mother's ancestry was entirely Scottish, though his Campbell great-grandparents (John and Johanna née MacKay) were buried in Melbourne and the generation before that lie at Pictou in Nova Scotia. My father's maternal grandmother, Bethia Jane, was born a Brown, not a very distinguished name, but it was her father, Adam Brown (also buried in Melbourne), born at Edmonston near Biggar in Lanarkshire in 1811, who was the only one of my great-great-grandparents who claimed to be a 'gentleman'.

The estate there and the fortified farm house, known as Edmonston Castle, were in the Brown family for over 150 years. Little of the castle still stands but, touring Scotland recently, we were entertained to sherry by the present owner, Harold Whitson, in the house (baronial, castellated, built in 1812) where my great-great-grandfather grew up. Both Harold Whitson and the local historian,

Brian Lambie, were well aware of these ancestors of ours. Lambie spoke of Adam Brown's departure from Edmonston as if it had happened only a few years ago, suggesting it was for his health rather than merely to seek his fortune that Adam left for Australia.

He arrived with his family at Port Philip in 1853. One of the few things his granddaughter, Bertha Campbell Harrop, left to her first-born, my father, was an impressive document, apparently drawn up in 1837, the year Victoria came to the throne, which traces Adam Brown's ancestry (and therefore also my own) on separate lines back to James II of Scotland, to Sir William Wallace, to a large number of 'Sir William Baillies of Hoprig and Lamington', to the Sempils of Cathcart Castle and the Lawsons of Cairnmuir and Sir John Clerk of Pennycuik. There are altogether, often following the female line, a remarkable number of titles: knights and baronets litter the page and even the odd Duke and Earl, a long time back. Then with Adam Brown, born a fourth surviving son, it is downhill all the way.

What is remarkable about that curious piece of boasting (similar trees, I believe, were concocted for many nineteenth-century families) is that the present John Campbell of Melbourne, the grandson of my grandmother Bertha's brother, had no such family trees passed on to him, but was recently found to have tracked down exactly the same genealogy through hundreds of hours of independent research. I saw his huge family tree when I was in Australia not long ago and was amazed.

James Belich characterises immigrants as consisting of 'two insecure groups': 'those who hoped to rise and those who feared to fall.' In my family the great majority of my ancestors travelled to the other side of the world hoping to rise and most of them certainly did. I'm not even sure they were 'insecure'; they might rather have been confident in their optimism, based on tales of a land of opportunity without the class distinctions that so oppressed them in Britain. Almost all these early emigrants found and made for themselves worlds which were preferable to those they left behind. To some extent they brought 'Home' with them, in the sense of their race, nationality and religion. All their lives my ancestors went on thinking of themselves as British.

In my family only the Browns of Edmonston were in the category of those who 'feared to fall'. When Adam Brown's daughter, Bethia, my great-grandmother, married Angus Campbell in her father's house in 'Bouverie Street, North Melbourne' in 1859, Adam described himself no longer as a 'gentleman', but as a 'merchant'. Bethia herself was a 'dressmaker', not a young lady of fashion. The bridegroom, Angus Campbell, described as a 'painter', was undoubtedly one of those who hoped to rise.

It was Angus Campbell, my father's grandfather, who travelled ahead of his family to New Zealand in 1866, hoping to find gold. He makes two fleeting appearances in letters from his first wife's brother, Angus MacKay. The MacKays and the Campbells had travelled from Nova Scotia together. Jane, the first wife, had died soon after their arrival in Melbourne – it was said to have been from an infection caught while helping others who were sick on the voyage. If she had survived, I would not exist, at least in the form I know myself today. This is the sort of sobering reflection that often strikes people as they work on family history. How easily things might have been otherwise than the way they are.

I mentioned Angus MacKay's letters. He was writing to his brother back in Nova Scotia. As a biographer I love letters; I have always relied on them to help me tell my stories – and there will be plenty of them in the later chapters of this book. But it was painful to realise how very few survive in my family from the nineteenth century. The lack is partly because my people were often on the move and when they were static were likely to be short of space and inclined (as I have never been) to throw things out; and partly perhaps because they were not – as many of their descendants became – compulsive writers. They were nearly all literate. I have come across, on all the certificates I've seen, only two Xs instead of a signature, one the mark of one of my mother's great-grandmothers, Hannah Jefcoate, and the other merely the mark of a witness at another family marriage in England in 1840.

Angus MacKay wrote on 15 March 1873: 'Angus Campbell and his family are still residing at Reefton West Coast. Margaret Jane, his daughter and our niece, got married twelve months ago to a Mr Perry, a storekeeper.' Margaret Jane was the daughter of Angus Campbell's first wife Jane and so was the half-sister of my grandmother and really of no significance in this story. But any evidence relating to my father's side of the family in the nineteenth century (apart from certificates of birth, marriage and death) is so rare that I received from John Campbell copies of MacKay's two letters with what I can only describe as joy.

MacKay's letters to Nova Scotia emphasise how much more equable the climate of New Zealand was and make it obvious that Canadian weather was one reason the families had left on that five-month voyage round the Cape of Good Hope, initially to Australia. There is also a definite suggestion, though no actual evidence, that gold had something to do with it. As John Campbell wrote to my brother: 'After Jane's death Angus became hard to trace. I fancy he probably went to the gold digging as did jolly nearly all the young males in the colony at that time.' Angus Campbell eventually turned up at the Rose, Shamrock and Thistle Hotel (the proprietor obviously wanting to have a wide appeal) at 176 Elizabeth Street, Melbourne. At 174, next door, was Miss Healey's dressmaking establishment where young Bethia Jane Brown worked.

They were married according to the rites of the 'Free Presbyterian Church'. MacKay's letters suggest what steady God-fearing people these were. His letter of 23 September 1877 ends: 'May the great and merciful Creator so direct and guide us all, that if we will not meet here in this world of trial, that by His grace we may be so fitted as to meet in the sure and better world.' It may not be expressed with great originality but it seems sincere. Angus MacKay was living by then in New Zealand, in Napier, 'a healthy and rather smart little place', and went on to become Mayor of Dannevirke.

The second reference to my grandmother's family is in that 1877 letter. MacKay wrote: 'I have not heard from Angus Campbell for some time. He stated in his last note that he was doing pretty well in Reefton as the Diggings were very promising.' This is the only suggestion that my Campbell great-grandfather was actually involved in the gold rush. Whether he was ever *digging* himself we don't know but he certainly prospered on the miners' trade.

The birth certificate of my grandmother, Bertha Jane Campbell, shows that she was born at Little Grey Junction, now known by its original Maori name as Ikamatua, on 7 March 1870. It was a tiny settlement where the Little Grey River meets the Grey, on the direct route from Greymouth up to the diggings in the Reefton area. The birth place was rather a surprise as my brother had already uncovered Bertha's arrival, as a child of three, at Greymouth on board the *Alhambra*, which left Melbourne on 16 October 1873. She travelled with her mother, Bethia Jane Campbell, her brothers, John Adam aged eight and Angus James aged five, her sister Elizabeth, known as Bessie and then aged twelve, and an unmentioned babe-in-arms, Barbara Ann. John Adam would eventually, after some time for better schooling with the Browns in Melbourne, go to Edinburgh to train as a doctor, return to Melbourne and become his namesake John Campbell's grandfather. On this 1873 voyage from Melbourne to Greymouth, the father of the family, Angus Campbell, was not travelling with them.

Since the records tell us the new baby, Barbara Ann, was born in Melbourne – unlike her sisters (older and younger) – it must be that my great-grandmother returned to her own family for the birth and then joined her husband again when he had established himself in Reefton. The baby was named after her Brown grandmother, born in Edinburgh in 1811 as Barbara Watson. I myself carry both the names of this great-aunt, though the other way round. As my mother, throughout the fifty-eight years of our shared life, always used both my names, Ann Barbara, I discovered Barbara Ann with particular interest. The journey was difficult enough for the family, travelling from Ikamatua to the Coast, but there were regular sailings between Greymouth and Melbourne. Some indeed thought of the West Coast as an 'appanage' of Australia and it was said to be quicker to go to Melbourne than to travel north to Auckland.

My grandmother had been born at Ikamatua because, at that point, her father owned a miners' store there in partnership with another brother-in-law, George Bannan (the husband of Bethia's sister Janet), who had established Bannan's Little Grey Hotel at the junction as early as 1866 and had presumably encouraged Campbell to join him.

Travelling to Ikamatua recently with my brother and his wife, I found there was very little to see apart from a small hotel. It carries an apparently permanent VACANCY sign, presumably because few nowadays have any reason to stay there. It is an easy distance by car to either Reefton in the hills or Greymouth on the coast. In the 1860s and 1870s it was, of course, a different matter. It was then just the right place for horses and their riders to take a rest, and indeed many of the miners in their search for gold were walking from the coast to the goldfields and would have needed more than one stop on the way.

We stopped in Ikamatua, wondering where exactly the Campbell-Bannan store had been and whether anyone knew anything about it. A woman came out of the hotel and of course we got talking. She didn't know anything, but she thought she knew someone who might. She would be happy to telephone for us. Everywhere we went we found people interested in our research and wanting to help. But here the first woman phoned knew nothing either. It was all so long ago. Indeed, it was over 130 years since my grandmother's birth in that remote place. And soon after she was born there had been what seemed a disaster at the time, but subsequently turned out to be quite the reverse. In February 1872 the Grey River had flooded and washed away both the store and Bannan's original hotel. It was then that my great-grandmother Bethia, pregnant with her fifth child, took the children to her parents in Australia and Angus Campbell moved up to Reefton just at the time of its transition from a mining camp into a substantial township. Two banks were moving in – the National Bank and the Bank of New Zealand (with gold-smelting facilities) – and it now had its own police force of two alert constables. A Government school opened on 2 June 1873 on the corner of Bridge Street and Broadway.

The Bannans stayed in the Ikamatua area. Advertisements in two local papers show that George Bannan opened splendid new premises in the winter of 1872. 'Offering superior accommodation for Visitors and Travellers, the hotel is situated on the main road from Greymouth to the Inangahua and Little Grey quartz and alluvial goldfields and within an easy stage of one day from the Seaport.' Moreover there were, attached to the hotel, 'Wheelwrights, Waggon-builders and General Blacksmiths' shops where repairs are promptly executed'. Saddlery and Harness could be repaired or made to order and goods packed and dispatched to all parts of the goldfields.

On our recent visit the name 'Bannan' did mean something. Another phone call was made. Our helpful acquaintance led us in her car to an isolated homestead in a pleasant valley where we found, living alone, Iris Didham, aged eighty-two, glad of the chance to talk about the Bannans to whom she was related by marriage. It rather spoils the story to admit that the sad tale she told us we had already heard from a remote relation, Helen Booth, born a Bannan, who shared our Brown great-great-grandparents and with whom my brother David had had contact after seeing her Brown family contribution on the 'FamilySearch' website. George Bannan, in the end, had not done 'pretty well'. His superior accommodation had not attracted the customers he expected. As the gold rush died down and the miners no longer streamed up from the coast but settled in the towns, there was not enough work for the wheelwrights and blacksmiths he employed. George Bannan took out loans to keep afloat and when in 1890 the creditors foreclosed, Bannan killed himself with a shot in the head.

This suicide was well over a hundred years ago, but in a country area stories get handed on over the cups of tea which you cannot get on the internet. The family story suggested the creditors had been unreasonable, with a devastating outcome. If there were other darker reasons for Bannan's death they would hardly have been passed down in the family.

In Reefton, as Angus MacKay reported to Nova Scotia, my great-grandfather Angus Campbell did indeed do 'pretty well'. He went on to own two hotels, first the Washington and then the more substantial Southern Cross, and a good deal of other property. He became a major shareholder (listed in the launch advertisement) in a public company 'formed for the purpose of importing and selling General Merchandise'. He also had shares in both the Progress Mine at Devil's Creek and the Argosy Gold Mining Company. 'Reefton was the place to be in the 1870s', we were told by the curator at the Black's Point museum just outside the town. In 1872 and 1873 there was a huge influx of men eager to work in the mines. Extracting the gold from the quartz meant mines with 'crushing batteries' and a great deal of speculation. Alluvial gold, the panning for it in rivers, continued as a one-man adventure. But most of the effort went into gold *mining* which was developing as a highly organised industry.

'The wealth was here from the gold,' the museum curator said, adding optimistically, 'And it still is.' When we were there, there was little sign of wealth in Reefton, but we were told (and we had heard a similar story in Ikamatua) that a Perth-based company, Oceana Gold, is due to re-open at least one of the gold mines in the area – ending years of false starts and crushed optimism. The museum, housed in the Old Wesleyan Methodist Church (built in 1876, not long after the Campbells arrived), was the usual rather charming clutter of rusting farm and kitchen tools, commemorative china, portraits of local worthies and decaying photographs and newspapers. It looked badly in need of an injection of Oceana Gold.

When the Campbells arrived, things were different. 'The people who made money were the shop-keepers and the hotel-owners', we were told. Lots of the miners spent as much as they earned. As Charlie Douglas, the explorer, wrote not long afterwards: 'Fortunately the digger was not a saving being; he dug wealth out of the country and recklessly spent it.' There was inevitably a lot of drinking. (What else was there to do when the day's work was done?) Supplies were naturally expensive, having come so far. At one point the diggers were paying one shilling a pound for flour – when four years later a shilling could buy four times as much.

Reefton makes much of the fact that the booming 1880s brought electricity to the town. Dawson's Hotel on Broadway – the main street which today bears as little resemblance to its counterpart in Manhattan as a flea does to a butterfly – became the first building in the southern hemisphere to be permanently illuminated by electricity. And Reefton's Broadway itself was apparently lit only about six years after Thomas Edison's company began to light the streets of New York. But the 1880s also brought a stockmarket crash and the failure of many companies floated on the gold rush boom. Even so, local publicity estimates that, by the end of the nineteenth century, Reefton's 'quartz lodes had yielded over two million pounds'.

Now the town feels like the back of beyond. The Raggedy Repairman has closed his shop and gone off on a day's 4WD expedition, leaving a note to that effect. Who can blame him? We see St Stephen's church where our grandparents were married – its corrugated iron roof wonderfully red against the blue sky – and the wooden Court House, recently reprieved from demolition and prettily painted in shades of blue. The museum curator had found us a photo with a glimpse of the Southern Cross Hotel on the corner of Broadway and Walsh Street, white weatherboard, with a railed balcony on the first floor and a shady verandah over the street. It has gone now. It was here that my great-grandmother died.

Bethia Jane Campbell's death notice in the *Inangahua Herald*, the local paper, shows she died, aged fifty-nine, on 2 February 1893 in the Southern Cross Hotel, which was her home, 'after a long and painful illness … a beloved wife, deeply regretted'. The illness, of course not publicly announced, was 'cancer of the uterus'. I can imagine, in the months of her dying, she would have heard, night after night, the wild uproar of the roistering gold diggers, fewer now but still roistering. My father once quoted a West Coast poet who died young, Cornelius O'Regan:

What days of cheerful toiling, what wild uproarious nights,
What happy days, what glorious nights were then;
Such mirth and merry-making, such drinking and such fights –
Old mate, such times they never come agen.

Writing to England not long before this (5 November 1886) a traveller called Robert Paulin had condemned 'the drink of the colony of New Zealand' as 'really the most abhorrent, noxious trash, whether taken in the form of beer, wine or spirits. All are more or less chemical compounds, having but a slight acquaintance with the hop, the grape or the malt.' I hate to think that my great-grandfather served such stuff in the Southern Cross at Reefton, but I have to suppose that he did. I also hate to think of his dying wife and her grieving daughters unable to shut out the merrymaking and the fighting. I met two of my grandmother's sisters, Bessie and Louisa, fifty years later when I was a child in Wellington during World War II. But I did not think (children usually don't) to ask them any questions about those Reefton days and the times that never came again.

As the Reefton connection was so strong (my grandmother having evidently lived there for most of her life until her marriage), I looked the town up in the index to my father's first book *The Romance of Westland*, written as his M.A. thesis and published in 1923 by Whitcombe and Tombs to coincide with the British and Inter-Colonial Exhibition held at Hokitika that December. Reefton was not in the index. It was only when I checked in the original thesis (packed with far more illustrative material than the subsequent book) that I realised from his map that Reefton is *not* in Westland but in the province of Nelson, though, in those early days, as far away from 'the comparative comfort of colonial town life' as anywhere on the Coast. The River Grey, just south of Ikamatua, is the boundary of Westland.

I wanted my father's own description of Reefton at that gold rush time, but will instead have to use some of his more general paragraphs. Angus Harrop was writing of a time not very long before he was born in Hokitika, a time which must often have been talked about in his hearing when he was a boy. He writes of the thousands of diggers who had made the same journey his mother's father had made from Australia to New Zealand in the mid 1860s. As he wrote of the dead, I think he was also thinking of his father's father, James Harrop, whose story will be told in my next chapter.

But there was no royal road to wealth in Westland – in fact there was no real road at all in those early days when the first few hundred prospectors dispersed over the country. Westland was unique among centres of gold discovery. The miner in Nelson fields was only a few miles away from the comparative comfort of colonial town life, but in Westland the seeker after gold was faced with a succession of hardships – enough to deter all but the very stoutest hearts. The country was well nigh impassable, while natural food supplies were practically non-existent, for even the Maoris found fernroot hardly sufficient to sustain them in the inhospitable forest and mountain regions.

Risks and accidents were the daily fare of the adventurer who sought the precious metal in Westland. Death reaped a plentiful harvest and the names of his victims are legion. These pioneers of Westland could say with Captain Scott, a pioneer of another sphere and of a later age: 'We took risks, we knew we took them.' Many of them perished as did he, far from home and friends. In their life and in their death they remind the world that the bodies of pioneers are the bridges that join the settled world to the wilderness.

But even the grim face of Death could not arrest the eager flow of diggers pressing on to gather the golden harvest. When there was definite information of the extent of the gold discoveries, no natural obstacles could impede the flow of men. Many perished in the rivers or died of starvation in the trackless forests and some returned to civilisation, but the great majority pressed on. To the Waimea first, then to the Totara, swarmed the rush of eager, excited diggers. Somebody would hear a whisper of gold being located in a certain creek, next day a thousand men would leave an assured rich reward for the prospect of one a little richer. Disappointments were many and the really rich rewards fell only to the favoured few.

The rushes at first naturally followed the courses of the many rivers, for the forests were a death trap and the rivers kept the digger aware of his bearings. The rush to the Arahura was phenomenally successful, but rumours of finds at Lake Kanieri and in the Kokatahi district drew away many hundreds of diggers. Every river and every creek was tried, and almost every one yielded rich returns. As more men came from oversea and overland more discoveries were made, and the newcomers were rewarded with returns which brought further thousands in their train. It was the old, old story of the lure of gold. As it had been with every previous rush so it was with this one. Clerks dropped their pens; farm labourers abandoned the plough-reins; the waiters left the hotels and the blacksmith deserted his forge. Teachers too had heard the voice of adventure. But those who had thought that wealth was to be gained without great effort were quickly disillusioned. They returned as quickly as they had come, and only the hardy faced the forests and the floods. Poor and rich, educated and uneducated, strove together, and no man was better than his neighbour. A glorious opportunity for one and all, and a testing time for character, resource, and grit!

My father was only twenty-two when he wrote that, and I think his excitement was justified. He goes on to say how much it must thrill the successors of the pioneers to think of what was achieved in that brief time. With such a heredity and such an environment, surely, he thought, New Zealanders should be inspired to 'high deeds and noble service'. We don't say such things nowadays, but they are still worth reading.

My grandmother, Bertha, was twenty-three when her mother died. Her youngest sister, Louisa, was still only fifteen, though she had left school two years before, 'destined home duties', as the Reefton School records have it; her older brother, Angus James Campbell had been 'destined to trade'. That Angus was obviously the sort of respectable young man who was able to find an appropriate niche in that wild place. Do banks count as trade? I suppose they do. My father's uncle found his niche as the Bank of New Zealand's clerk-in-charge, its Agent, at Lyell.

Lyell happens to be a rather interesting place in a negative way. It certainly has an interesting history. It is now a tourists' stopping place for picnics on the road between Murchison and Inangahua. We duly stopped there and marvelled at the fact that Lyell no longer exists. There was a fire in 1896 and later an earthquake and now there is nothing but a plateau of green grass, high above the Buller River, with various signs telling the visitor that there were once, in gold rush times, five hotels and a great deal else.

This was in spite of the fact that in its early days the only land contact with Inangahua and thence to the coast was a foot-track on the other side, the south side, of the Buller. And this track was perilous as in many places the bank was unstable; men with heavy swags were in danger of falling into the river and horses of losing their footing. Publicans' licenses in Lyell could require them to provide a boat for the crossing there (or, later, to maintain the bridge) and, in some cases, to keep the track clear of fallen timber between, say, Deep Creek and the Eight Mile Creek on the way to Westport.

My great-uncle's job was not without its possible perils, even in the 1880s, though things had calmed down a good deal in the twenty years since the following notice appeared on 11 October 1865:

> Mr Walmsley of the Bank of New South Wales attacked and robbed about 12 o'clock in the day by 4 or 5 armed men between No Town and the Twelve-Mile on the Grey River Goldfields in the Province of Nelson, about 14 miles distant from the Grey mouth in the Province of Canterbury, of 821 ounces of Gold Dust and about £1000 in Bank-Notes.

There were other hazards besides robbers. Another bank official, George Preshaw, recorded conditions when he carried gold, bought on the diggings, to safe-keeping in the Bank. 'I always slept in my clothes, boots, hat and all; the saddle-bags containing gold dust, gold and silver coin, under my headpillow; the notes about my person, inside my Crimean shirt; my revolver by my side.' When he could, he travelled along the coast and slept on the beach, 'just above the high water mark. I chose this airy situation to escape these pests – the sandflies, mosquitoes and bush rats.'

Angus James Campbell, my great-uncle, stayed with the Bank all his life and eventually moved south to Otago, not dying until 1944. He is buried in Anderson's Bay cemetery, Dunedin, not far from the grave of his nephew Frederick. I can see there are too many Anguses in this chapter. Angus MacKay, the letter-writer, we can now forget. My father, never to be forgotten, was Angus Harrop; his grandfather and this uncle were both Angus Campbell and his Aunt Bessie (born Elizabeth Campbell) married Angus Hugo and was the mother of another Angus.

You have already heard that my Great-Aunt Louisa, the youngest in her family, was 'destined' to help at home, even before her mother's death. But what of her older sister, the grandmother I never knew? The Reefton School records are silent and her marriage certificate, as was customary with women at this period (indeed it is so on my own, fifty-six years later), is blank in the space for 'occupation', as if women were always expected to be idle. Often it is simply because they have given up work to marry. Bertha's mother's Melbourne marriage certificate is unusual in having 'dressmaker' in that space.

As my grandmother, Bertha, was twenty-nine at the time of her marriage and it was her younger sister, Louisa, who was performing the 'home duties', it is reasonable to suppose Bertha had been working. As a girl, she had surely taken her turn behind the bar at the Southern Cross Hotel, an occupation which would of course have been unmentionable on a marriage certificate. Later she may have worked as a dressmaker; she would certainly have been trained by her mother to make her own clothes and may have made other people's as well.

But I think it most likely that she was what was called a 'pupil teacher', like her future husband, as he studied to become a surveyor, and like both our other grandparents. It was the common fate of bright pupils to stay on at school and teach the younger children what they themselves had so recently learned. And there is no date in the school records for her leaving school.

Bertha certainly looks bright in the one surviving photograph of her. I have in front of me as I write two photographs taken in a Reefton studio by W. Sherlock, the photographer responsible for the magnificent panoramic view of Reefton in its prime that can be seen in the museum at Black's Point. The one of Bertha as a young woman, taken not long before her marriage in 1899, I find extraordinarily moving. She looks sad and sensitive and even wary. I have to remind myself how still the photographer would, I am sure,

have required her to be. I see something of my father in her face and I know, as I look at her, how little time she had left and what pain the few years would bring. Her high lace collar is pretty – a word inadequate to describe the young woman herself.

There is an abundance of lace in the other Reefton studio portrait. It is of my father, undated; he is perhaps eight or nine months old. I can see he is his mother's pride and joy. I think she made his lacy, beribboned gown herself, and put the silver rattle in his little hand, whether it was his own or merely a photographer's prop. I am sure she was not responsible for the stiff, ugly flower arrangement behind the baby's left shoulder. I wish I had known her.

At some point between his wife's death and his daughter's wedding six years later, Angus Campbell had stopped being a hotel-keeper; the father of the bride is now described as a 'Carriage Painter', which seems a step down, whatever way you look at it.

He was almost back to where he had started in Melbourne; 'painter' is on his own marriage certificate. His successful doctor son, John Adam Campbell, marrying in Glasgow in the year of his mother's death, fancifully described his father as a 'stockbroker'. It would seem likely they were his own stocks and shares he was selling.

This great-grandfather – with his hotels, his property and land titles, his shares in mining and importing companies – had surely not been one of those (in the Belich phrase) who feared to fall. But fall he undoubtedly did. The gold rush days were soon over. Reefton was already becoming, long before the end of the nineteenth century, somewhere more like the quiet town we visited in the early twenty-first. Angus Campbell lived until 1910 and is buried in Christchurch, described as a 'contractor' – a term that can mean almost anything.

There was one obvious place for us to stay in Reefton, not an obvious town to want to stay in. My brother had booked us in at Reef Cottage, a Bed and Breakfast on the main street, Broadway – just across from the Raggedy Repairman. At the bottom of this street our father's grandfather, Angus Campbell, had served hundreds of thirsty miners at the Southern Cross Hotel. Reef Cottage, I discovered on my arrival, reading the 'Information for Visitors', had for many years been the office of the town's lawyer, a man called Patterson. The moment I came into the room where I was to sleep I noticed a heavy door, perhaps five inches thick, leading to a smaller windowless room, now transformed into the ubiquitous 'en suite'. There was a circular brass badge on the door, bearing the words

Fire and Burglar Proof
Strong room doors and safes
J. Mann & Co
Makers. Dunedin

The name Patterson was familiar. My grandmother's sister, Barbara Ann, had married a Jack Patterson, and surely we had seen the name recently, looking through the family papers we had with us? We were carrying a copy of our father's father's will and there it was with Isaac Patterson's letterhead. (We assume he was Jack's brother.) It reads

Barrister and Solicitor,
PO Box no 53
Reefton
Telephone no. 16

I was to sleep in the very room where my Harrop grandfather's will had been drawn up and to take my shower in the strong room where long ago a copy had been lodged for the twelve years from his wife's death until his own.

So now it seems time to bring this grandfather into the story, to leave the Browns and the Campbells, remembering their impressive travels from Lanarkshire and from Sutherland, to Nova Scotia, to Melbourne and eventually to the South Island of New Zealand. But before we leave Reefton I need to record, without knowing how they met, that my grandfather, Arthur Neville Harrop, aged thirty, married my grandmother Bertha Jane Campbell, aged twenty-nine, at the Anglican Church of St Stephen's, Reefton, on a late autumn day, 24 May 1899. Just over nine months later on 7 March 1900, his mother's birthday, my father, Angus John Neville Harrop, was born in Hokitika, not so far away, on the coast.

My father's father's family: the Harrops and the Sales

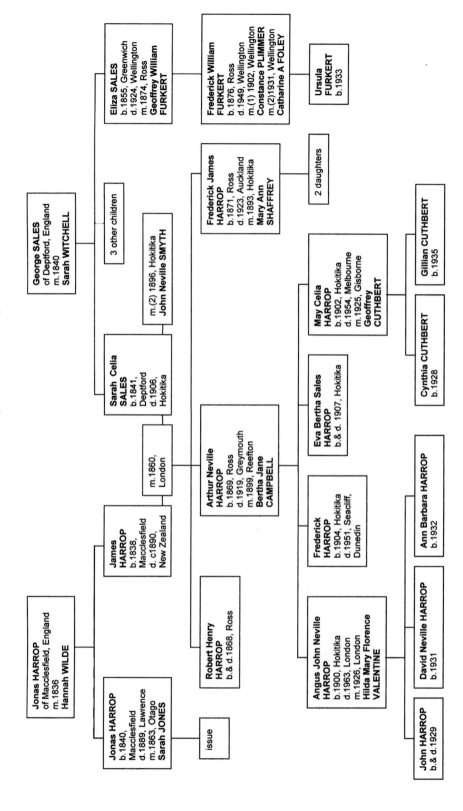

Jonas HARROP
of Macclesfield, England
m.1836
Hannah WILDE

George SALES
of Deptford, England
m.1840
Sarah WITCHELL

3 other children

Eliza SALES
b.1855, Greenwich
d.1924, Wellington
m.1874, Ross
Geoffrey William FURKERT

Frederick William FURKERT
b.1876, Ross
d.1949, Wellington
m.(1) 1902, Wellington
Constance PLIMMER
m.(2)1931, Wellington
Catharine A FOLEY

Ursula FURKERT
b.1933

m.(2) 1896, Hokitika
John Neville SMYTH

Sarah Celia SALES
b.1841,
Deptford
d.1906,
Hokitika

m.1860,
London

Frederick James HARROP
b.1871, Ross
d.1923, Auckland
m.1893, Hokitika
Mary Ann SHAFFREY

2 daughters

James HARROP
b.1838,
Macclesfield
d. c1890,
New Zealand

Jonas HARROP
b.1840,
Macclesfield
d.1889, Lawrence
m.1863, Otago
Sarah JONES

issue

Robert Henry HARROP
b. & d.1868, Ross

Arthur Neville HARROP
b.1869, Ross
d.1919, Greymouth
m.1899, Reefton
Bertha Jane CAMPBELL

May Celia HARROP
b.1902, Hokitika
d.1954, Melbourne
m.1925, Gisborne
Geoffrey CUTHBERT

Eva Bertha Sales HARROP
b. & d. 1907, Hokitika

Frederick HARROP
b.1904, Hokitika
d.1951, Seacliff,
Dunedin

Angus John Neville HARROP
b.1900, Hokitika
d.1963, London
m.1926, London
Hilda Mary Florence VALENTINE

Cynthia CUTHBERT
b.1928

Gillian CUTHBERT
b.1935

Ann Barbara HARROP
b.1932

David Neville HARROP
b.1931

John HARROP
b. & d.1929

CHAPTER 2

Mainly about the Harrops

By the time of his marriage in 1899 my grandfather, Arthur Harrop, had managed to establish himself as a professional man, a qualified surveyor. It had not been easy. We know very little about his parents, Sarah and James Harrop, but it is certain that they had compelling reasons to leave London in 1863. James was born in Canal Street, Macclesfield, in the north-west of England in March 1838. The occupation of his father, Jonas Harrop, on James's birth certificate is given as 'wharfinger', which means he was either the owner or the manager of a wharf on the Macclesfield Canal, once busy with the silk trade. James went south at a time of deep depression, following the decline of the silk industry.

James was not a weaver, but everyone was affected in a town which depended almost entirely on a single luxury product. On his marriage certificate in 1860 James's occupation is given as a 'cabinet-maker', but it was probably as a carpenter (the occupation he gives on the shipping list a few years later) that he first sought work in Deptford, a congested area of London, on the south bank of the Thames, packed since Elizabethan times with people largely employed, in one way or another, in the dockyards. It was the site of Henry VIII's great naval yard. The picture on the next page, engraved at the time, gives some idea of what anyone might see walking along the river towards London Bridge.

It is too fanciful to imagine that James was attracted to the area by the fact that Grinling Gibbons, probably the most famous woodcarver ever, was born there. The reredos of the church of St Nicholas, where Sarah's parents were married, was the marvellous work of Gibbons' hands. It is more relevant that it was in the Deptford dockyards that two of Captain Cook's ships, *Resolution* and *Discovery*, were fitted out for his last voyage. Stories of Cook's adventures in the South Seas were still heard from time to time in the Deptford taverns seventy-five years after his death.

Deptford was somewhere that work was likely to be found. It was there that James met Sarah, daughter of George Sales, a 'cordwainer' or shoemaker, whose father worked, like James, as a carpenter. George Sales had married Sarah Witchell at St Nicholas on 16 February 1840. In the graveyard of this church lies the body of Christopher Marlowe, killed by a dagger in a drunken brawl in a Deptford tavern in 1593. It is a nice coincidence that Marlowe's father was also a Kentish shoemaker, but it is doubtful that my great-great-grandparents were aware of this peripheral connection with Shakespeare's brilliant contemporary. I assume that it was in Deptford that James and Sarah met. It was her birthplace and James gives 'Kent' as his place of origin on the shipping list, an entirely misleading suggestion as he was born in Macclesfield and Kent makes one think not of Deptford, where he had lived, but of orchards, oasthouses, the great cathedral of Canterbury and the white cliffs of Dover.

Deptford *is* in Kent, but its present postal designation as London SE gives a more accurate impression of that crowded place, its pre-Victorian housing, both its slums and its fine houses, largely demolished by Nazi bombs and replaced by unimpressive post-war rebuilding. Little trace remains of Waterloo Place, St Paul's, where Sarah Witchell was living at the time of her marriage. From a quiet back street, it has been transformed into Watson's Street, a cluttered, vibrant thoroughfare, just north of New Cross Road. My Victorian map shows that already, when her daughter Sarah Sales was born in 1841, Deptford had easy access by rail to central London, its own dockyards, and was within walking distance of more extensive docks with their exotic names (Russia, Greenland, Norway and so on) reminding everyone of the possibilities of travel. Across Deptford Creek, very close at hand, was Greenwich with the Royal Naval School and the Royal Hospital where work might be found.

However, at the time of their marriage at St Pancras, 'the district church of Camden Town', on 10 April 1860, Sarah Sales and James Harrop moved right into London. On the certificate, as is usually the case, Sarah is said to have no occupation. She was still a 'minor' – she was nineteen. James' father, Jonas Harrop, a wharfinger at the time of his birth, is now described as a 'contractor', again that particularly unrevealing job description. James, himself, is trying to make a living as a 'cabinet-maker': the grand houses of Regent's Park and St John's Wood are close at hand. Both bride and groom give their address as 78 Bayham Street, just east of the Park and of Camden High Street and not very far north of Tottenham Court Road, which was already the centre of the furniture trade in London. From the census records I know that the Bayham Street address was of a lodging-house, crammed with four families.

That was in 1861. Ten years earlier there had been the Great Exhibition, celebrating industrial prosperity, creativity and resourcefulness, with a dazzling display of 100,000 different objects, including, from Auckland, a model pa made from beeswax, Kauri gum and examples of different woods for furniture making. The Exhibition did not reflect the conditions of working Britain at this period: the squalor, the unemployment, the almost unbearable long hours and pitiful pay of the thousands who slaved in mill and mine, dock and factory and in a myriad of little workshops in the cities. The expansion of the railways had brought a rapid increase in London's population, with so many thinking that things must be better somewhere else than where they had come from.

A.R. Wallace (Darwin's co-theorist on selective evolution), writing in 1898 in *The Wonderful Century*, gave frightening figures for the increase in infant mortality as London's population grew, and there was a similar increase in numbers dying in the workhouse. As the rich got richer and paraded in Hyde Park, 'one third of the population of London', Wallace wrote, 'are living miserable, poverty-stricken lives, the bulk of them with grinding, hopeless toil, only modified by the still worse condition of want of employment, with its accompaniments of harassing anxiety and partial starvation.' It has been said that there was no revolution in England at this period only because the poor were too exhausted by their daily struggle. It seems Sarah Harrop's parents (the cordwainer and his wife) were in dire straits themselves by now as Sarah's youngest sister Eliza (of whom we shall hear more) was born in the workhouse at Greenwich.

It seems likely that it was a fear of unemployment, if not unemployment itself, which made James Harrop start thinking about emigration. Henry Mayhew looks directly at cabinet-makers in his extraordinarily detailed *London Labour and the London Poor*, with its scenes of 'squalor, misery, dirt, vice, ignorance and discontent'. Mayhew shows that, in spite of '200 miles of new streets' and the thousands of new houses erected in the capital, the lot of a cabinet-maker (a term which covered the making of any sort of furniture) was particularly unfortunate.

The trade in the middle of the nineteenth century was in a bad way. Skilled craftsmen were being tempted to do poor work with cheaper materials as the large furniture dealers (Mayhew says there were just 'two large houses') gave lower and lower payment for the chairs and tables and cupboards they were offered as they tried to appeal to a wider market. Mayhew tells a number of sad stories of which I will quote from just one, which gives us a clear indication of why James Harrop determined to seek a better life in New Zealand:

> I have been out of work a twelvemonth, as near as I can reckon .... When I first joined the trade there was plenty of work to do. For this last twelvemonth I have not been able to get anything to do, not at my own trade. I have made up one dozen mahogany chairs on my own account. The wood and labour of them cost me £1.5s, I had to pay for a man to do the carving of them, and I had to give £1 for the wood. I could get it much cheaper now, but then I didn't know anything about the old broken ship-wood that is now used for furniture. The chairs I made I had to sell at a sacrifice. I was a week making them, and got only £2 for the dozen when they were done .... There are two large houses in London that are making large fortunes in this manner. About a fortnight after I found out that I couldn't possibly get a living at this work, and as I didn't feel inclined to make the fortunes of the large houses by starving myself, I gave up working at chair-making on my own account. I then made a few clothes-horses. I kept at that for about six months. I hawked them in the streets, but I was half-starved by it. Some days I sold them, and some I was without taking a penny .... At last I became so reduced by the work that I was not able to buy any more wood, and the week after that I was forced to quit my lodging. I owed three weeks' rent, at 1s.6d a week, and was turned out in consequence. I had no things for them to seize, they had all gone long before. Then I was thrown upon the streets .... I was sleeping about anywhere I could. I used to go and sit at the coffee-houses where I knew my mates were in the habit of going, and they would give me a bit of something to eat, and make a collection to pay for a bed for me. At last this even began to fail me, my mates could do no more for me .... I was a whole week walking in the streets without ever lying to rest. I used to go to Billingsgate to get a nap for a few minutes, and then I used to have a doze now and then on a door-step and under the railway arches. At this time I had scarcely any food at all, not even bread .... I applied at St Luke's, and told them I was starving. They advised me to apply at the Houseless Poor Asylum. I did so, and was admitted directly. I have been four nights in the Asylum already, and I don't know what I shall do when I leave. My tools are all gone; they are sold, and I have no money to buy new ones. There are hundreds in the trade like me, walking about the streets with nothing to do and no place to put their heads.

This poor fellow I quote ended up in an Asylum for the Houseless Poor. My great-grandfather was obviously determined that that should not be his own fate and it seems natural that he and Sarah, and thousands like them, were beguiled by the posters and advertisements encouraging them to think about emigration. It is even possible that someone lent them *The Emigrant's Guide*, which went into many editions.

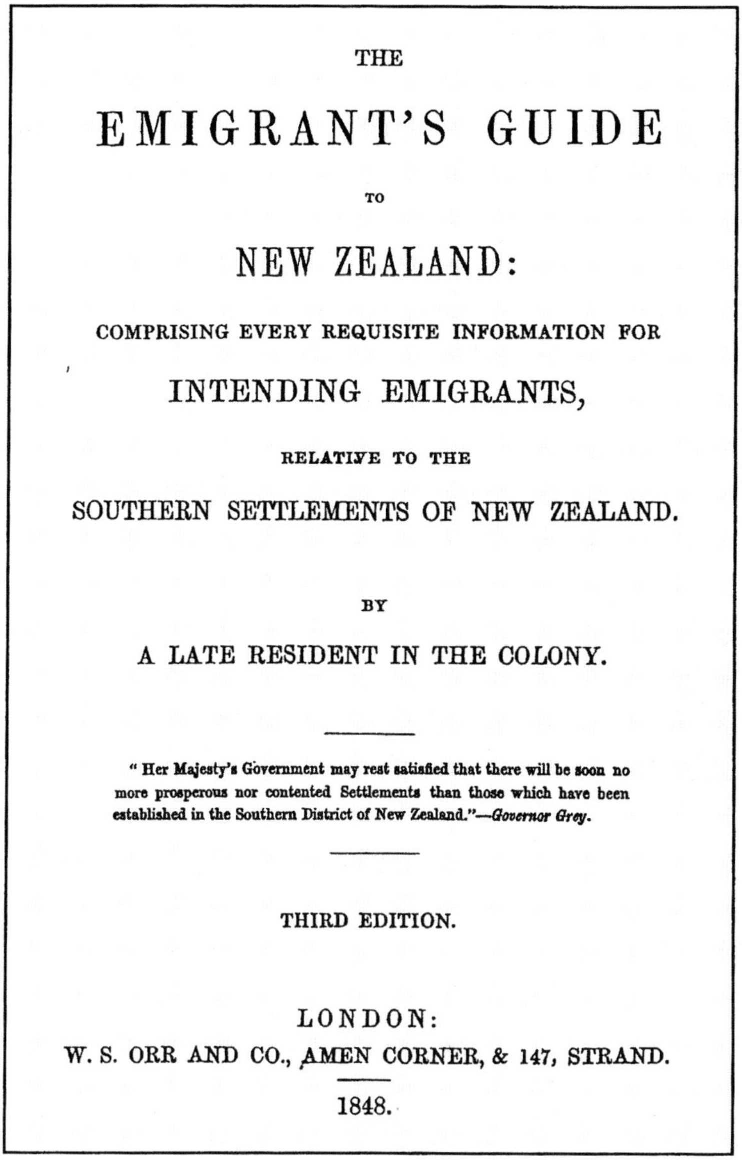

THE

EMIGRANT'S GUIDE

TO

NEW ZEALAND:

COMPRISING EVERY REQUISITE INFORMATION FOR

INTENDING EMIGRANTS,

RELATIVE TO THE

SOUTHERN SETTLEMENTS OF NEW ZEALAND.

BY

A LATE RESIDENT IN THE COLONY.

———

" Her Majesty's Government may rest satisfied that there will be soon no more prosperous nor contented Settlements than those which have been established in the Southern District of New Zealand."—*Governor Grey.*

———

THIRD EDITION.

LONDON:
W. S. ORR AND CO., AMEN CORNER, & 147, STRAND.
———
1848.

Readers were enticed by descriptions of a climate 'even in its coldest parts greatly milder than the south of France, which is in the same latitude' – not, of course, that any of these young people had had any chance to experience the climate of the south of France.

The Britain of the South, a book published in 1857, was full of promises of the delights in store for those enterprising enough to cross the world. New Zealand was a land free not only of snakes and insect pests ('the wire-worm, turnip fly and the devouring locust' being entirely unknown), but offered all social classes 'opportunities for their mutual betterment'. It was continually remarked that New Zealand had no 'lurking tigers' or other savage beasts, and that trouble with the Maori was unlikely if not unmentionable. The English newspapers carried reports of 'the picturesqueness, the mountain grandeur, and the forestial wealth of this truly wonderful country' and this was *before* the discovery of that other sort of wealth, before the papers reported excitedly that gold, in vast quantities, was to be found in many parts of New Zealand.

It is surely relevant that another Jonas Harrop (with the same name as my great-great-grandfather), born in Macclesfield in 1840, came from Victoria to Tuapeka – in Otago, west of Dunedin – just at the time gold was discovered there. He developed a business as a pharmaceutical chemist and flourished on the trade of the gold-diggers. He became a thoroughly fine citizen, Justice of the Peace, serving on the local school committee and taking his turn as Mayor of Lawrence. Moreover he passed on his skills and knowledge to his daughter, who became in May 1890 one of the first women in New Zealand to qualify as a pharmacist. Many of the New Zealand Harrops are descended from this Jonas Harrop, who had two sons as well as the daughter. He was a younger brother of James, my great-grandfather. It seems certain that Jonas wrote from Tuapeka to James in 1862, encouraging James and Sarah to make the 12,000-mile journey under sail to the other side of the world. It was to the Tuapeka area that the Harrops would go when they first arrived.

However bad the conditions in Victorian London, however limited the chance of any sort of prosperity, it still required a huge amount of courage to make the decision to leave England. The long journey itself, always uncomfortable and sometimes dangerous, was enough to put most people off – at least if they realised what it entailed. And then there was the strong likelihood that the emigrants would never see again the family and friends who stayed at home.

Once Sarah and James Harrop had made their decision to apply for assisted passages, James had to provide testimonials to the Canterbury agent in London. When approved (and carpenters were much in demand), half the passage money would be paid for them and James had to sign a 'promissory note' agreeing eventually to pay the remaining £26.12s in Canterbury to the

Provincial Government. The ship they were allocated was the *Lancashire Witch*, a full-rigged sailing vessel, built in Québec not long before and chartered by Shaw Savill and Co., a shipping line whose name has been familiar to me all my life, so often has our family crossed the world in its ships.

The journey between England and New Zealand, by sea or air, remains the longest journey it is possible to make by regular transport. In 1863, in a sailing ship, there was always the fear (in ignorant passengers' minds) that the winds might blow the ship off course, make it miss New Zealand and be swept on to Antarctica or miss the desired destination and start coming back again. Everyone knew that the world was round and that New Zealand was not only on the other side but as far as you can go without coming back. Some ships never caught sight of land until they reached New Zealand; most of the emigrants spent nearly three months without walking on dry land. It could be more if things went wrong and the ship spent a long time becalmed. Friends and relatives at home might hear nothing for the best part of a year, though sometimes the captain would be able to hail a ship passing in the opposite direction and hand over a bag of mail.

Emigrants were encouraged to write diaries as well as letters. Three have survived from the voyage of the *Lancashire Witch*, from fellow passengers of my great-grandparents. The dullest, with far too much about latitudes and longitudes and daily distances sailed, followed the guidelines for diaries published in the *Emigrant Voyagers' Manual* in 1850, which also gave advice about what to take with you. The other two vivid diaries, both now online, were written by Arthur Price, who travelled with his wife in a second-class cabin, and David Carr, who was in the single men's steerage area, adjoining the family quarters where the Harrops were, in the middle of the ship.

Carr, who was twenty-seven, a year or two older than James, claimed to be a 'farm labourer', as did most of the assisted emigrant men (apart from a few carpenters like James and the odd blacksmith or shepherd); many of the women described themselves as 'domestic servants', though most of them would not remain as such for long. Agricultural labourers and domestic help were in huge demand in the new colony, but we know the labourers anyway were very often not what they claimed to be. One of them, Richard Pelvin, another fellow passenger on the *Lancashire Witch*, was actually a soldier who had been a guard on a convict ship going out to Sydney years before and had also seen service in India, Malta and Ireland. It is thanks to his memoirs (written much later) that we know that the doctor on board the *Lancashire Witch* was 'a thorough gentleman. I have known him send his dinner from the cabin table to some of the sick ones (we had 26 deaths on the voyage) to see if he could tempt any of them to eat.' When we know what happened on this ship it is some comfort to know there was at least a sympathetic doctor, though there was so often little that he could do and many of the sick children were too small or weak to be tempted by the crumbs from the rich man's table.

There was a medical examination before the emigrants went on board, but it was not as thorough as it might have been. Only 'one family has been put on shore with the whooping cough', David Carr wrote. Later he would write: 'Truly this is an ill-fated ship.' But that was many weeks away – on 23 September.

My great-grandparents, Sarah and James Harrop, boarded the *Lancashire Witch* when she lay in the East India Dock, across the Thames from Deptford, on Wednesday, 1 July 1863, and went downriver with a steam tug to Gravesend the following day, finally leaving at noon on Saturday, 4 July. They must have been dismayed at their accommodation – the cramped double berth with only a curtain for privacy. There were a great many wailing children and it was difficult to find a moment's quiet

It was possible to see exactly what the quarters were like when we visited the Otago Settlers' Museum in Dunedin. The area was essentially a converted cargo space (cargo – mostly wool – would fill it on the return journey), windowless (no port-holes), with eight double bunks on each side, long tables with shelves above them right down the middle, clothes lines draped from side to side. I wrote 'exactly' but of course we had to imagine the fug, the stench, the men and women crowded in, with the bewildered children under their feet. 'We pulled together and that is how we got on,' one woman said. And that was the only way, but it was hard to get on with everyone nauseated by the rolling and pitching of the ship.

Sea-sickness is one thing. There was plenty of that, especially at the beginning before people found their sea-legs. But it is not life threatening in adults. The first death was on Sunday, 19 July – a small girl, aged two and a half, from 'gastric fever', it was said. That was the first, and it was the first death the diary

writer, Arthur Price, had ever seen. He wrote about it at length and went to the ship's hospital early the next morning:

> I helped the sailmaker sew the little thing up. We placed two large pieces of chain at the feet to make it sink. Lissy and myself went on deck and it was a most splendid morning, the sun was just rising, everything so calm and still, not a ripple on the sea, the sails set straight, not going more than two knots, everything seemed just beautiful. They layed the corpse on a board and covered it with a Union Jack, two sailors carried it to the side of the deck, and rested its feet upon the side. The father and mother and eldest daughter followed and stood behind crying. The schoolmaster read the burial service, and when he came to the part 'we commit this body to the deep' they raised the head, and the body slipped off into the sea with a sudden splash, and sank immediately to rise no more till that day when the sea shall give up its dead unto Him who gave life. The cry of the mother at the moment the body fell was dreadful. The father standing behind the mother and daughter with his arms around both, all crying. It was indeed a pitiful sight – the first time I witnessed a funeral at sea, and I hope the last, but I fear not as there are more on board very ill.

The bell tolled for that child's death, David Carr's diary added. I myself saw such a funeral once on board a liner in the Red Sea, with the coffin covered in a Union Jack. On the *Lancashire Witch* there were so many deaths that they stopped having funerals and slipped the bodies overboard at dead of night, trying to diminish the alarm. They were mainly very small bodies; there were twenty-six deaths altogether and only four were adults. Long afterwards, when she was herself a great-grandmother, one of the children whose playmate had died in the night said she had all her life remembered the sound of 'the splash as the little one's body was committed to the deep'.

There were also nine births on board the ship and these must have caused fear and noise as well as joy. The Harrops would have been well aware of the disastrous experience of the Goodman family travelling in the same quarters. John Goodman, a farm labourer from Nottinghamshire, and his wife, Ellen, started the voyage with four children: Thomas, Benjamin, Mary Elizabeth and John Henry, all under six. On 9 August a new daughter was born; ten days later little John Henry died and two days after that, Mary Elizabeth. It seemed that the *Lancashire Witch*, like the *Mooltan* fourteen years earlier (where cholera was the killer), travelled with a 'dread pestilence on board'. Carr reported that even a number of the strong young men had 'not been out of bed for some weeks'.

When the ship, diverting from its normal route, anchored in False Bay, off Simonstown on the Cape of Good Hope, with Table Mountain in sight, no one was allowed on shore while medicines and fresh food (including four live sheep) were brought out to the ship, as it flew the yellow quarantine flag. The infections were named as scarlet fever and whooping cough.

Of course deaths, births and sickness were not the whole story of the voyage. David Carr commented at one point how easily most of the passengers managed to ignore what was going on, dancing on deck, playing cards or the concertina (even on Sundays to his Scottish amazement), while others lay desperately ill. 'So is human life callous and indifferent (in general) of anything but what affects themselves', he wrote. Carr was a thoughtful man, a reader too. One day he wrote that he had been 'busy engaged in reading Walter Scott's poems and sometimes so wrapped up in them that I forgot I was on the sea.' When they were becalmed he quoted Coleridge: 'as idle as a painted ship upon a painted ocean.'

The steerage passengers were kept pretty busy, preparing their own meals, even making their own bread, keeping their quarters clean for the regular inspections, swilling out the latrines with salt water, airing their bedding, washing their clothes. All the time the weather was a constant source of interest and sometimes distress. On 27 July it was so hot that it was intolerable below and the Captain said that they must have all their meals on deck where the tar melted even under the sail awning.

Towards the end of the voyage, on 22 September, there was the worst gale they had had. 'Hail and snow enough to frighten the women.' It was impossible to sleep. 'We sometimes go for four or five days without a wink', Price wrote. 'After living here I am quite sure we can live anywhere. I have been trying to have my tea, but very little can I get … I can assure you' (he told his diary) 'it's fearful, but bear up it cannot last forever. That's what I tell them.'

Both Price and Carr, these two diarists, had admirable temperaments, or at least wanted to give that impression. Some of the other passengers and crew were less agreeable and there were, from time to time, dramatic quarrels and fights. There were drunken incidents, a steward ordered to the forecastle with the sailors for beating some small boys, a Quartermaster put in irons and locked up in the Second Mate's room, a passenger punished for striking the ship's cook, who had removed a pot of his food from the furnace, a couple of bored lads tied to the mast and fined four shillings for scaling the rigging.

But most of the long days were without incident and tedious as the passengers went about their tasks and passed the rest of the time as best they could. One passenger wrote: 'Nothing worth mentioning except sky and water, water and sky.' On the good days the ship seemed like 'a snug little village', on the worst it was more like 'a floating prison'. Fourteen Sundays made a regular break in the routine when two services were held on deck and somehow the passengers managed to appear rather cleaner than usual. But there was nowhere to go,

David Carr regretted, 'to retire by one's self to hold communion with God.'

At last, on 11 October 1863, the fifteenth Sunday since they left England, the *Lancashire Witch* arrived in Timaru where Sarah and James Harrop disembarked after a voyage they would never forget. 'Small place, beautiful country, splendid mountains', Arthur Price wrote as the ship left Timaru for its final port, Lyttelton. I have no idea what friends the Harrops made on board, but it is interesting that there are names on the passenger list that would become familiar to many New Zealanders: Holland, Shipley, Hight. The boy who became my father's beloved teacher and eventually Sir James Hight was born seven years after his parents shared accommodation with my father's Harrop grandparents. I wonder whether this frail travelling coincidence was discovered and discussed. I like to think it was. All these passengers were on assisted passages in steerage.

James Belich has suggested that it was mainly the early 'genteel' immigrants who eventually turned tail and left New Zealand. Wellington, he tells us, had kept only 85 of the original 436 'capitalists' by 1848. 'That is, Wellington had a maximum approval rating of 20 per cent among those who had the power to vote with their feet.' One knows that this did not necessarily mean complete disillusionment or dislike of the new colony. There could be many reasons, alongside a basic home-sickness, that made people abandon their new lives. Reading again recently Lady Barker's classic account of early days in Canterbury, *Station Life in New Zealand*, first published in 1870, I felt amazed that they did give up. Their courage and spirit of adventure are so obvious that it is difficult to believe the devastating snowstorm and floods of 1867 were enough to make them abandon a place where, in Mary Anne's own words she had been 'so *very* happy'. Certainly the few Maori in the area had prophesied the storm, but said when it came that they had no legend of anything like it ever happening before.

For most of these early immigrants there was no chance of going home, even if they could have faced the possible horrors of another 100-day sea-voyage. There is no evidence that any of my great-grandparents showed any inclination to give up. Certainly for Sarah and James Harrop it would have been out of the question whatever befell them.

By 1865 James was a shareholder in a gold-mining claim in Wetherstones, north of Tuapeka, a few miles from Gabriel's Gully, the site of the first discovery of Otago gold. One of his partners was a Dubliner called John Neville Smyth, who had arrived in New Zealand as third officer on the ship *Electric*. Alongside his gold-digging activities, James Harrop ran a book agency 'and was likewise agent for the *Otago Witness* and other papers', according to the *Tuapeka Times*.

By the time of the 1867 floods in South Canterbury, Sarah, James and J.N.

Smyth were all already in Westland. Ross, where they first settled, was, like Hokitika and Reefton, a gold rush town just coming into being in these years immediately after the Harrops' arrival. On a fine, detailed 'Emigration Map of Nelson, Marlborough and Canterbury', engraved in Edinburgh in 1865, there are *no* towns on the West Coast, no visible settlements between Cascade Point and Cape Farewell. There are plenty of headlands and river mouths (named from the sea). Inland, as far north as the Grey River, nothing is named except the Lakes Brunner and Pokerua, between the Southern Alps (Line of Perpetual Snow) and the sea.

How the Harrops and Smyth got to Ross we have no idea, but it must surely have been stories of more gold that encouraged them to make the journey, difficult as it was, by land or sea. Most came to Ross from Hokitika. On 9 August 1865 the *West Coast Times* gave clear directions for the journey on foot. There was as yet no road:

> The best route to this lately discovered goldfield is to follow the sea beach to Totara, on arriving at which – 12 miles from Hokitika – it will be necessary to cross in the boat; and after proceeding two miles along its banks … another crossing must be made in a boat, which lands about 300 yards up the river …. On leaving the boat follow up the bed of the Totara to its junction with Donnellys Creek, follow up the latter for 3½ miles towards the range which looks like the Pyrenees in Victoria. A path to the right up a steep pitch of blue slate brings you on to a track cut by Mr McGee, 1½ miles up which is situated the new rush – Jones' Creek as it is called by some of the residents, he being the first to apply for a prospecting claim.

We know the Harrops were in Ross by 1868 – five years after the *Lancashire Witch* docked in Timaru on the other side of the South Island – because in that year their son, Robert Henry, was born and died there, aged only eight months. There is an announcement in the *West Coast Times* of his death and a brief invitation on 10 August 1868: 'The friends of Mr and Mrs Harrop are invited to attend the funeral of their son at Ross this day.' It was eight years since Sarah and James were married in St Pancras and, with the lack of contraception and their apparent fertility – for two more sons would soon follow the death of this baby – it would seem to suggest a series of miscarriages, if not stillbirths, in the early years of their marriage. If, as seems likely, one reason for their emigration had been to give a better chance to future children, Robert Henry's death must have been an appalling blow. The good news is that my grandfather, Arthur Neville Harrop, was born on 8 May 1869, almost exactly nine months after his brother's early death.

If the names Robert, Henry and Arthur seem to have been chosen for no particular reason but simply because their parents liked them, the name Neville given to this new son comes to have some significance. One of the three sponsors or godparents at his baptism – along with the two parents – was John Neville Smyth, from whom the baby obviously took his second name. Smyth was then twenty-nine, and practising as a surveyor. He must have been a tower of strength, a close friend in those early days in Ross. In time my father would also carry two of his names as Angus John Neville Harrop, and my brother would be David Neville. It seemed obviously a family name, going back several generations, David thought, giving it to his second son, Christopher Neville. And now it turns out to have come from this man Smyth, of whom we had never heard. It may occur to the reader that there is a possibility that we are not really Harrops at all, that Smyth was the father of Sarah's children.

If it was gold that brought James Harrop to Ross, it would seem he did not have much success. Ross existed for gold. There was not much else going on. We don't know if James paid his thirty shillings for a miner's licence. He must have been tempted to try his luck, though there would have been plenty of work going for a carpenter, the trade he had given on the shipping list. Ross, like Reefton, had complicated mines. It was not like Kaniere or Kokatahi where the only way to find the gold was through individual effort, digging and washing and sifting, panning and cradling in the beds of streams. Ross, unlike Reefton, had no quartz mines but the only example in New Zealand of deep-level alluvial mining. And that meant elaborate wooden constructions: waterwheels, flumes on stilts to carry water from the river to the hillside claims, slabs to shore up the shafts, beams and cross-bars and platforms of planks for the windlasses to stand on.

There were houses too, of course, as the miners saw that Ross was *not* a flash in the pan, but somewhere to stay. There were churches as well (Wesleyan Methodist, Roman Catholic, Anglican and Presbyterian within four years) and schools, hotels and stores. By 1868, the year the Harrop baby died, the town had its own hospital, newspaper, cricket club, volunteer fire brigade, German Association, Scandinavian Society and a local militia.

In April 1871 a report from Ross in the *West Coast Times* gives some idea of Ross's immediate past and the reason why Sarah Harrop may have preferred John Smyth's company to that of the women of the town. The Resident Magistrate had declared that there were to be no more licences issued for dancing:

> Although we have been unusually fortunate here in having well conducted dance-houses … we hope to see women brought here who are capable and have some better idea of the duties of life than shuffling about on a dance-floor, and tempting men to drink till early morn.

The following year Sarah encouraged her sister to come out from England, perhaps on the death of their parents. Sarah must have hoped Eliza would be someone who would have some 'better idea of the duties of life'. Eliza Sales was only eight years old in the summer of 1863 when her sister sailed on the *Lancashire Witch* and was still, at seventeen, a minor when she emigrated herself. As a single woman she was offered a free passage (more women were badly needed in the colony) but, as a minor, she needed sponsorship from Sarah and James.

That story seems to have ended happily. Emigrants were advised that a wife was 'something prettier and more fruitful', more useful indeed, 'than patent plough, thrashing-mill or thorough-bred'. But hundreds of men arrived in New Zealand alone and found far too few women to go around, and those who were around not always the sort of woman a discerning man would want to marry. Eliza married Geoffrey Furkert, who had arrived on the West Coast for the gold but was now prospering as a butcher and cattle dealer. Their only surviving son, Frederick William, became eventually Engineer-in-Chief of the Public Works department in Wellington and the writer of a book, *Early New Zealand Engineers*. It was his daughter, Ursula, who provided me with the results of her research into our shared Sales ancestors, the Deptford cordwainer and his wife, James Harrop's parents-in-law.

By the time the Harrops moved away from Ross in 1879, the town had less than half the population it had when they arrived more than ten years earlier. But the town would never disappear, as did other gold rush towns on the Coast. In 1993 a geologist at the Ministry of Commerce calculated that the site of Ross itself, which has never been exploited (the mines lying just outside the town), contains gold with a current value of about 700 million dollars.

With all the building work going on in the late 1860s there was obviously plenty of work for a carpenter, if not for a cabinet-maker. But in 1869, on my grandfather's birth certificate and again on that of his younger brother, Frederick James, their father is described as a 'bailiff'. That same year, 1871, James Harrop appears on the 'List of Officers of the Provincial and County Governments of New Zealand' as 'Bailiff to the Warden's and Resident Magistrate's Court' in Ross, earning £150 a year. This may not sound a great deal and, indeed, was only the same as the wage for a 'Lunatic Attendant' on the female ward in the hospital and less than that for the 'Inspector of Nuisances' for the Borough Council in Hokitika. But it compares very well with the Ross miner's average annual earnings from gold at that time. This is said to have been one-third greater than 'the average of gold miners in the colony' and was calculated as £132.2s 6d. How such a calculation can be arrived at I have no idea. But the figure makes it seem that James should have been satisfied with his salary.

Involving, admittedly, some lunatics and a good many nuisances, the job of bailiff was less strenuous physically than that of the miners. However it was not without its dangers.

Crime in Ross was largely the result of what we would now call binge-drinking, then thought of as 'drunken sprees' or 'benders', resulting in mugging and brawling. But there were sometimes more dangerous characters in the area and James Harrop, as a bailiff, was apparently not confined to the court house. He had powers of arrest and distraint and had to get out and about in the course of his duties. One of the early diggers, a man called A.H. Wylde, told of an incident in the Ross area when he and the bailiff, walking in single file through dense bush, climbing over the fallen tree-ferns that sometimes blocked the path, suddenly found themselves challenged by a couple of bushrangers – one was in front of them on the track and one behind. '"Stand," said the one in front. Immediately a voice called out from behind my friend and said "Hello, Mr Bailiff, shell out!" So we were then in between the two bushrangers,' Wylde recalled long afterwards. They were robbed of everything they carried with them. Burgess, the leader of the gang, was later hanged in Nelson. In his confession he said that Wylde and the Ross bailiff were 'the last two they let go alive'.

It may have been incidents like this that made the Harrops leave Ross in 1879. There is evidence that the two boys, Arthur and Frederick, were at school in Hokitika that year, and living in Fitzherbert Street, the very place where my story started twenty-eight years later. Arthur was ten and Frederick eight and their father's name, James Harrop, is on the school records. But there is no other trace of him in Hokitika. It is possible that, as Sarah and the two boys went north, James went in the opposite direction, for the next sign of him is in 1882 on the electoral roll in Haast, 176 difficult miles away from Hokitika, south of the glaciers and most easily reached in those days by sea. His occupation is given as 'chain-man'.

The chain-man has, fortunately, nothing to do with chain gangs. He is not bound by a chain but in charge of one – the chain that was a vital piece of equipment for a surveyor. A chain, as some of us learnt at school, is twenty-two yards long. My Oxford dictionary says 'a chain is a measuring line, used in land-surveying, formed of one hundred iron rods called links jointed together by eyes at their ends.' 'At first', the dictionary goes on, 'chains of varying lengths were used, but that described by Gunter in 1624 is the one now adopted; it measures 66 feet.'

Gunter's chain was eventually replaced by a steel band, lighter and easier to use, but the word 'chain' persisted and so did the chain-man, whose job it was to use it as the surveyor directed. In the Otago Settlers' Museum I saw an actual chain such as I had never imagined when I learnt the measurement (along with acres, gills, bushels and pecks) sixty years ago.

In Christchurch in 1853 Edward Gibbon Wakefield ('the great coloniser', as Belich called him) commented on 'the luxurious independence of the common people'. He was perfectly happy with 'the democratic ways of a carpenter who addressed Henry Sewell without the Mister' and admired the fact that there was 'absolutely no servility'. New Zealand seemed the ideal place for a working man, with intelligence and skills but no capital, to make a decent life for himself and his family. What went wrong for James Harrop it is impossible to discover. Things did go wrong, just as they did for Wakefield himself, who spent the last seven years of his life as a recluse in his Wellington house, with visits only from two bulldogs and his niece, Alice, who will appear again in a later chapter. It seems likely that Sarah Harrop might have echoed a question in Priscilla Wakefield's diary: 'Why should the misconduct of those we love destroy the happiness they might share with us?'

Sarah and James Harrop had been through so much together. They had survived that terrible voyage from England and the death of at least one child, perhaps more. They lived together for around twenty years. But at some point, for some reason, they separated. Did James gamble and drink too much? Did he dally with the dancing women while his wife sat at home with the little boys? Did Sarah nag and compare him unfavourably with their friend the surveyor, John Neville Smyth? Or was James an upright irreproachable fellow who simply moved on when he discovered his wife no longer loved him best?

I have already mentioned Smyth as the godfather of my grandfather, Arthur Neville Harrop, the older of the two small boys. There is no way to tell whether Smyth was responsible for the separation. That he was involved is obvious. In

August 1884, when my grandfather was sixteen and presumably about to be confirmed, it is his godfather, J.N. Smyth, who makes a 'correct copy' of the baptismal entry, even if he cannot spell 'Diocese'.

In 1893 when Frederick James, the younger brother aged twenty-two, is married to Mary Ann Shaffrey in Hokitika it is J.N. Smyth, surveyor, who is one of the witnesses; there is no sign of the bridegroom's father, James Harrop, described on the certificate not as cabinet maker, carpenter, bailiff or chain-man, but as a 'labourer'. How could they say that that was his 'rank or profession'? He had, in fact, disappeared. No one knew where he was or what he was doing, whether he was alive or dead.

When David and I were in Ross years ago, on our first visit, we knew at that time nothing much more about our grandfather, Arthur Harrop, than the fact that he had been born in Ross. So, one sunny day, we walked around the cemetery, thinking we might find his parents' graves. There is now a forty-minute walkway taking visitors up from the town, alongside old water-races, to the graves on a hillside with views over to the sea. We thought our great-grandparents might lie under one of the illegible gravestones. There were many we could not read, their inscriptions obliterated by time and the stones themselves buried under a tangle of brambles and tussock. Now we know that the only Harrop grave we might have found in Ross was that of the infant Robert Henry. What happened to James Harrop remains a mystery.

I think that, on one of those surveying expeditions as a chain-man from Haast, he drowned, as so many did, and that his body was never found. 'Many perished in the rivers', I quoted in my first chapter from my father's first book. Even if the bodies were found, there was a good case for burying them where they were. Carrying a corpse many miles through the bush, down mountainsides, fording more dangerous rivers, was too much to expect from even the toughest survey party. Charlie Douglas, the explorer and surveyor, reckoned not being able to swim saved his life many times; he wouldn't tackle the rivers or those 'dark brown bush creeks' swimmers often tried to cross. Douglas told stories of too many corpses in makeshift coffins 'carried out by well-meaning friends who got drunk at every stopping place' and used the top of the box for a picnic table and the thirsty bearers' beer. 'I think most of us who love the mountains would prefer to be quietly buried there', Douglas wrote. I imagine James Harrop's bones undisturbed among the 'mountain grandeur' he had travelled so far to find.

Frederick Harrop, James and Sarah's younger son, was now, in the mid-1890s, married and working as a clerk in the Lands and Survey department office in Hokitika. There is a group photograph of him standing on the right just

behind Charlie Douglas, who is bearded and quizzical, his arm resting on the end of the studio settee. This great-uncle of mine, aged twenty-four, looks short and extremely neat and tidy and enough like my father to make me smile.

This is almost the last we will hear of this Frederick. I never met him; he died long before I was born. He had gone into the department as a cadet immediately on leaving school, but his older brother, my grandfather, took a different path. Arthur decided to earn some sort of living as a pupil teacher while he worked to fulfil his ambition to become a fully qualified surveyor. He was encouraged surely by that devoted friend of the family, J.N. Smyth, and by his mother. His father, James Harrop, was no longer in the race, but Arthur was determined to make proper use of his brains and skills. For years he was employed as a teacher, first in Hokitika and then in Kokatahi, studying in the evenings for his exams. Kokatahi was now a small settlement, no longer the tented encampment it had been twenty-five years earlier when hundreds of men desperate for gold ate stews of wild birds and fouled the manuka groves. By 1892 Arthur is listed on the electoral roll at Kokatahi as both teacher and postmaster. He had been appointed at the age of twenty to run the local Post Office – presumably out of school hours – a useful supplement to his teacher's pay.

That same year Arthur Harrop's name appears in the 'declaration book' at Canterbury College; the date is 14 April 1892. There is no signature for he had enrolled and made his promise by post. 'I do solemnly promise that I will faithfully obey the Regulations of Canterbury College as far as they apply to me.' A librarian at the university (its campus now at Ilam in Christchurch) brought the big volume up from the archives for us to see because we had found to our surprise – folded at the back of one of our father's scrapbooks – a faded receipt for three guineas for the 1892 College Annual Examination. This was our only clue to this earlier connection to the college where both our parents graduated thirty years later. That huge sum (three guineas was probably more than Arthur earned in a week) allowed him to take the exams he needed to take and exempted him from attending lectures. It was only this year, 1892, that the Land Act finally recognised the need for 'standardisation of land boundary surveying' in New Zealand. It was 1896 before he was able to take his final examinations as the 'Regulations for the Examination of Surveyors' were only gazetted on 5 March of that year.

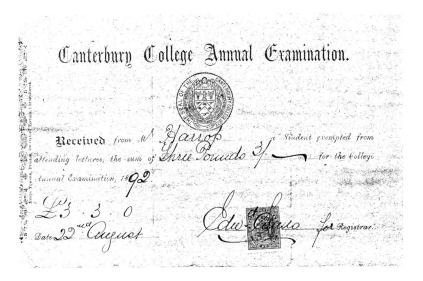

Arthur Harrop benefited from extra-mural education and distance learning long before the phrases had been invented. In these early days a large number of the students were part-time, but there were some who never got near the place at all. The university college on the other side of the Southern Alps was almost as inaccessible to the young man in Kokatahi as if it had been in England. The book in Christchurch had been signed in 1891, just the year before his own name was first entered, by Ernest Rutherford, James Hight and Apirana Ngata – none of whom my grandfather had the chance to meet, but all of whom my father came to know in the years ahead: the nuclear scientist on the other side of the world, his Professor of History, and the Minister for Native Affairs.

James Belich calls getting on 'the great colonial game for individuals and families'. One of the ways to get on was to own land, to farm, to become your own master. Another passport to respectability was further education, education which would qualify you for a profession: teaching itself, law, medicine, banking, or surveying, which was, of course, a very different matter in the new colony from its practice in England. Belich writes: 'Some marginally genteel professions were upwardly revalued in the new land …. Surveying was a profession whose status increased.' There was a lot of surveying still to be done. Surveyors were vital recorders of vital information, their task not just to lay out and design new towns, but to measure and map much of the hinterland that had still not been explored. Surveyors had been encouraged to come to New Zealand for many years and ten surveyors' apprentices travelling out in 1841 had been contractually guaranteed cabin passages and to be treated as gentlemen. It was only in 1876, on the abolition of the separate provincial governments, that New Zealand had a unified system of survey throughout the country.

In the early days surveyors were often also both engineers and architects and there was no clear division between them. But by the 1890s, when my grandfather, Arthur Harrop, was taking his exams, the legal system of land registration meant that only a Licensed Surveyor could put a signature to a plan from which a title could be issued. At the offices of LINZ (Land Information New Zealand) in Christchurch, it is possible to see some of the town plans my grandfather drew with his neat signature at the bottom. The most beautiful is for Runanga (just north of Greymouth) at the scale of two chains to an inch. It is dated 25 November 1903. Runanga was a mining town, but for coal not gold. We went there and admired the newly refurbished Miners' Hall with its bold, challenging slogans: 'World's Wealth for World's Workers' and 'United we stand, Divided we fall'. Not far away was a signposted walk to Coal Creek Falls, one of the subjects in my father's 1907 photograph album, unspoilt and totally recognisable nearly a hundred years later.

James Harrop had dropped out of the game, had perhaps never had sufficient urge to 'get on' after making the great effort to get to the other side of the world. James Harrop had never been really 'respectable', but John Neville Smyth as a surveyor had always seemed so. In 1896 he married my great-grandmother Sarah Celia Harrop in the Church of All Saints, Hokitika. She is described on the marriage certificate as a 'Widow' since 'about 1890'. If James really had drowned, or at least disappeared, in 1890, with some witness able to swear that he was dead, it is surprising that Sarah and John Smyth waited so long to marry. Smyth was fifty-six and Sarah a year younger; they had been friends – and perhaps more – for over twenty years. If there was no such witness, the date of 1890 is surprising. One would expect 1889. Rules about bigamy were the same as in England. One had to wait for seven years of 'continual absence', without any evidence of the missing spouse being alive during that time, before remarriage. That husbands (if not wives) did quite regularly disappear is suggested by the fact that the rules on bigamy are printed in the information section of a diary belonging to my Valentine grandmother.

Sarah Harrop, later Smyth, remains a shadowy figure. The only other thing I know about her is that both she and her sister, now Eliza Furkert, signed one of the suffrage petitions, along with about 30,000 other women (perhaps nearly a quarter of the adult female population of New Zealand). The petitions urged the Government to adopt measures to enable women to vote at the next general election in 1893, pointing out the 'grievous wrong' of denying women what had already been admitted by Parliament to be a just right. As it was, women had found themselves classed with 'juveniles, lunatics and criminals'. Only fourteen years after there was universal suffrage for men, New Zealand became the first country in the world to grant women the vote.

This would become one of the most celebrated achievements of Dick Seddon's Liberal Government, but, in fact, Seddon had only reluctantly and eventually (after years of opposition) allowed the Bill to pass. Seddon, 'King Dick', who had come to the West Coast for the gold and loved to speak of New Zealand as 'God's own country', became something of a hero to my father, not least because of his connection with the Coast. Pember Reeves, who knew him well, might acknowledge Seddon's 'political vulgarity' and point out that he became 'respectability's favourite butt and bête noir'. But Reeves also hugely admired 'the daring man', imagining him after death arriving on the banks of the Styx and 'commenting promptly on the inferiority of Stygian river-scenery to that of the sunlit streams of romantic New Zealand' – and then urging Charon, the aged ferryman, to retire and take advantage of the Old Age Pension. Seddon died – still Premier – in 1906 and my father's early memories included hearing the tolling of the church bells in Hokitika for his passing and the erection of the fine statue in Sewell Street four years later.

Another of my father's local heroes was Charlie Douglas, the great surveyor who could not swim. In the last quarter of the nineteenth century it was Douglas who 'made a systematic survey of the rivers of South Westland and investigated the possibilities of practicable passes across the Alps.' Angus Harrop remembered that he had often, as a child in Hokitika, heard the name of 'this remarkable man when other surveyors were talking with my father.' Douglas was particularly remarkable, among all the early explorers of the West Coast, for leaving behind copious journals and letters, as well as the detailed field books with plans and sketches that all the surveyors had to keep.

Douglas was a maverick, a loner, outside the system, but wonderfully included in it. In the early days he was rarely in Hokitika, spending most of his time in the field, in the bush and on the mountains. He had no home and as he got older, especially in the winter months, he was given a bach at the back of the office. When he was in town himself, my grandfather must have seen Douglas at work on the huge mile-to-the-inch geological maps of Westland. There were two of them, each eighteen feet long and five across – an extraordinary achievement.

The first field book of Arthur Harrop's which survives at LINZ is dated 1898. One of the archivists in Christchurch handed me a pile, fourteen altogether, covering the work of nine years. They are neat black notebooks, eight inches long and five and a half inches across, labelled clearly, black on white:

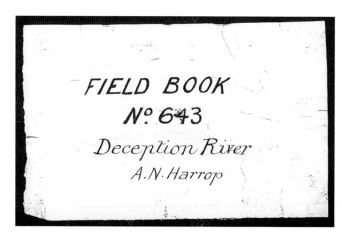

The sketches and measurements and locations inside the notebooks are as legible and vivid as the day my grandfather drew them, although only one of them still has the black elastic band which would at the time have held it carefully shut. The book would also probably have been wrapped in oilcloth and even possibly kept in a tin box. Months of work could have been lost in a moment if a field book went astray or got soaked. The field book was irreplaceable. The centenary history of surveying in New Zealand makes the point that

> The surveyor's field book … is unique among records prepared by professional men. For a solicitor's diary is generally not evidence after his death, he being under no duty to write it, nor is a doctor's case book for the same reason. But it was the surveyor's legal obligation to enter measurements and observations as he made them.

When I looked at the books, marvelling at the skill and concentrated effort that they demonstrated, I was, in fact, rather sad that my grandfather was so totally professional unlike some of his fellow surveyors. There are no sketches of his companions or of longed-for young women, no scribbled exclamations about mosquitoes, no recipes or signs of fried duck staining the pages. In the open he drew carefully and intensely in pencil. This section of an area by the Taipo River gives some idea of the painstaking work involved. The survey would show precisely how things were at one particular moment in time. Obviously the river beds, and much else, changed as snow melted and rain poured.

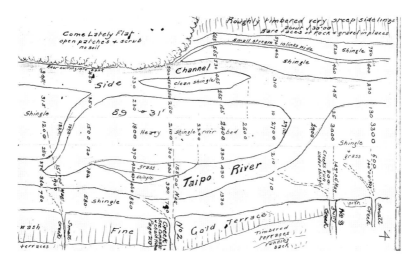

Sometimes there are 'General Notes' and rough sketches with less punctilious measurements, which give some idea of tougher experiences above the valleys. On one occasion Arthur wrote, beneath a sketch of 'pinnacled peaks':

> River ends in large snowfield at the bottom and on the sides of an impassable mountain range. The soft snow being all off we found it impossible to climb over the pinnacled range at the back of the snow basin. There was still a very large quantity of snow left on the snowfields – frozen hard. The River was easily fordable almost throughout on our second visit. There is over 2 miles of the very roughest travelling from ½ mile below 1st junction up – tremendous boulders – all waterworn (different to the Whitcombe).

Just occasionally in the evening Arthur drew the view from the camp. The next picture includes the camp itself. He drew well enough but had no claim to be a fine artist as some of the surveyors were and, in any case, the sketch is rather spoiled by the printed guide lines which run across the middle of each

from peg x – looking up Hohonu River
Greenstone Road

page of the field book. 'Peg X' in the caption reminds me that pegging was the prime business of the surveyor. As the surveyors' historian, Nola Easdale, put it: 'All the trig surveys, the reconnaissance journeys, all the humping of theodolite, chains, pegs, slashers, tents, food and other gear by the survey party had but one ultimate purpose – the driving in of the landmarks, the pegs.' To remove survey pegs was a criminal offence 'the gravity of which it is impossible to exaggerate' as the magistrate told a youth who had done just that. Easdale, telling this story, went on to show this was no new idea by quoting the Bible, recalling that Moses said 'Cursed be he that removeth his neighbour's landmark.'

There were few neighbours in the hinterland where Arthur Harrop spent most of his time in his early years as a surveyor. The only people he saw on these expeditions were the other members of his gang. He would have three or four men with him, including the chain-man, in charge of running out the chain for measuring (as we have seen) and a cook responsible for making sure everyone had something to eat. What they took with them from Hokitika was supplemented by what the cook could procure from the land (by now teeming with imported mammals) and the rivers: venison, wild pork, duck, native pigeon, eels and fresh fish.

'The hardest worked man on a surveyor's staff', W.B.D. Murray wrote in 1896, 'is undoubtedly the surveyor himself.' Therefore he advised

> make as much use of horse service as you can. It sometimes takes say three hours hard tramping to get to a trig station, you are from four to six hours working at the instrument and you have the trek back to camp. This goes on

from day to day and unless you assist yourself in some way, you are bound to break down sooner or later. Your men have many chances of a spell … and when they get to camp their work is done.

As for the surveyor himself, 'I may say his work is never done, day or night, wet or dry, he has always duties to perform.' In his tent by candlelight he could be seen 'diving into logs, sines, tangents etc etc in connection with the plan, or inking in the day's work in the field book, and then laying out the work for the following day.'

There are good photos in the archives of the West Coast Historical Museum in the old library in Hokitika of these surveying gangs and one, taken at Frosty Creek, on the Main South Road to Ross includes, I feel sure, my grandfather on horseback. No names are given, but one of the other men in the photo is possibly Joe Pfahlert, whose great-nephew, Denis, we were able to meet when we were

in the museum. Joe Pfahlert definitely appears in front of Arthur Harrop and the theodolite in another camp photograph, equally interesting and with all the names supplied. Another of the group is a moustached and hatted Shaffrey, Arthur's brother-in-law. The cook, Fred Martin, identifies himself clearly with

not only an apron, but a plate and mug. If you look closely you can also see a small cat in the hands of the youngest member of the party. Survey gangs often travelled with cats to keep down the bush rats which would otherwise attack the stores. Denis Pfahlert, a man of my age, had his own stories of life in the bush, recalling trapping and skinning 3500 possums in one winter alone. As he spoke, it seemed to me how little some things had changed over the years. The bush could be just as thick, the creeks just as wet. It was impossible to travel very far without having to cross a river or a creek and wet boots were still as difficult to put on next morning.

The surveyor himself had no privileges in the field. He had the knowledge of a larger pay packet when he got to town, but he shared the camp conditions with the men. None of them took account of the eight-hour day, which was campaigned for so vigorously in the new colony from the earliest times. But the surveyor himself needed to have not only the skills of a bushman and mountaineer, as they all did, but those of a meteorologist, an astronomer, and a mathematician. The use of the theodolite required great skill. The sketch maps and the figures in the field books had to yield exact results. Measurements included not just chains but complicated calculations involving fixing points astronomically and using trigonometrical connections between them.

After the camaraderie and the rigours of the camps in the bush, Arthur must have felt he needed a place of his own to go home to. After years of struggle and study, at thirty he must have felt he could afford to marry and have a family. I wish I knew something of his meeting and courting my grandmother, Bertha Campbell. She must have found him rather different from the sort of men she had been accustomed to meet in the Southern Cross Hotel. They made their vows to each other in St Stephen's Church, Reefton, on 24 May 1899. The words in the marriage service, about not being separated until death did them part, must have seemed something of a mockery. For Bertha must have known how much Arthur would be away, even as she waited for my father's birth, so soon after the marriage. Mary Sturge wrote a verse that rather crudely sums up what lay ahead for my grandmother:

> Surveyor's wives! Oh listen while I state
> What is their dreary melancholy fate;
> And pause ye fair, e'er entering on the life
> That still awaits a Land Surveyor's wife.
> What though your husband may his partner love,
> And prize her company all else above,
> It matters not, because so much he'll roam
> That he will hardly be at home!

CHAPTER 3

Despair and hope in Hokitika and Waitaki

The small house in Hokitika where my father grew up is a typical early New Zealand house. It is the house in the photograph at the beginning of this book. Thousands like it were built in the nineteenth century and some of them survive today. As early as 1857 Charles Hursthouse described one in his book encouraging emigration to *The Britain of the South*:

> We are apt to picture a 'wooden cottage' as a sort of flimsy, make-shift, band-box dwelling. But in such a climate as New Zealand's, these cottages are wind and weather proof; neither hot, cold nor draughty; and neatly painted, backed by a clump of trees and embowered in gardens – their eaves and verandahs covered with jessamine, rose, peach and vine – they present an air of rustic elegance and sparkling beauty to which the plastered 'bell-and-brass-knocker' deformities of our [English] streets and villages can make no possible pretensions.

Hursthouse gives the dimensions of these 'verandah cottages' as 32-foot square with two front rooms (14' x 18') and two back rooms, with a kitchen and wash house area behind. He declared such a place to be 'amply large enough for a family of six'.

The Harrops' house in Fitzherbert Street, Hokitika, was sadly lacking in jessamine, rose, peach or vine clambering over the verandah. And in the photograph it does seem flimsy and may well have let in the driving West Coast rain. My father remembered that rain 'lively enough on the iron roof' and so much of it that he said it 'might well be reckoned in feet rather than inches'. We went to look for the house, not very optimistically, and found it had long since disappeared, the site (now with a large palm tree) becoming part of the garden of the house next door.

We were staying not far away in a house that *has* survived from the nineteenth century – the bed and breakfast place opposite the museum in Hamilton Street: Teichelmann's. We found ourselves having breakfast in the very room where Dr. Ebenezer Teichelmann must have had reason, over and over again, to write up his notes and sigh over the family in Fitzherbert Street.

Dr Teichelmann was their family doctor, but he was not a commonplace G.P. He was an explorer, a mountaineer and a photographer. Trained in England, the son of a German father, he had arrived from Australia just two years before my father was born and shared the duties of a G.P. with those of Surgeon-General at the Westland District Hospital. Between 1905 and 1907 he made a sequence of ascents hardly paralleled in early New Zealand climbing, including lugging a 20kg full-plate camera to the top of Mount Cook and taking some most remarkable photographs. It was always possible that he would be up a mountain when he was most needed, but he was certainly there to sign my grandmother's death certificate.

She died five days after the birth of her daughter, Eva. I like to think Dr Teichelmann fought particularly hard during the five days of 'cardiac debility' to try to save her life, for he knew the circumstances of the family and the dire situation she would leave behind on her death.

With the fatal syncope on 14 January 1907, Bertha Jane Harrop, née Campbell, aged thirty-six, left behind four children, the oldest of them my father, not yet seven. Their ages are given like this, as is the way on New Zealand death certificates:

> Age of each daughter 4, 5 days
> Age of each son 6, 2

As I suggested on the opening page of this book, when my father was alive I knew only that he had had one sister, May, now also long dead. My mother, my brother and I stayed with her and her family briefly in Melbourne on our way from England to New Zealand in 1940, at the beginning of the war. After my father died, my mother told me that there had been a great sadness in his life that I did not know about. He had not wanted us to know. Ever. As we grew up it was partly, I think, to protect us from the fear of having such a child ourselves. Over many years, on the other side of the world, an instinct for self-preservation had led him to try to forget a younger brother, born in November 1904, when Angus was not yet five. It must have been one of his earliest memories, Frederick's birth and the sadness that filled the house when there should have been joy. For Frederick was what we used to call 'handicapped', what we might now disguise with euphemisms – he had learning difficulties; he was disabled. In the blunt language of the time he was labelled an 'Imbecile' – a word familiar to me from the census description of Alfred Tennyson's younger brother, Edward, who was put away in a 'small and comfortable lunatic asylum' in York in 1832. It is not, I discover, quite as damning a description as 'Idiot', which was used in an early census to describe the occupant of our local manor house in Norfolk, with 'servant to the Idiot' next down in the column of 'occupations'.

My mother remembered the damaged boy, my father's brother, and wrote in her old age: 'Angus's mother died when he was six, the new baby born with such difficulty she died and Fred, the baby, was spastic.' The baby was indeed badly damaged and suffered, it would seem, from what we would now call cerebral palsy. All the symptoms described in the doctors' notes over the years seem to fit that diagnosis.

But my mother did not know the whole story, so reluctant was my father to talk about these hard painful memories. My mother knew nothing of the birth of the fourth child – baptised as Eva Bertha Sales Harrop – whose birth had actually brought about her mother's death. When the baby herself died three months later, the remaining children, Angus, May and Frederick, had lost in less than a year their grandmother, their mother and their baby sister. They were left with their distraught father, whose work as a surveyor often took him away from the family for weeks at a time.

The grandmother – their father's mother – had always been an intimate member of the family group. Sarah Celia Smyth née Sales was present at my father's birth, as it says on the certificate when she registered it. She must, I'm sure, have been delighted that this first grandson, though named Angus after his maternal grandfather, Angus Campbell, also carried the Christian names of her own second husband, John Neville Smyth. The next child carried Sarah Celia's second name as her own second name. Frederick had the name of his uncle, Sarah's other son, and the new baby, for the brief time she was alive, carried the name Sales as well as her mother's name. Nothing could demonstrate more clearly than this naming how central this grandmother was.

I guess that after J.N. Smyth's death late in 1901 the family had moved from Bealey Street, round the corner, to join Sarah in Fitzherbert Street. Certainly May was born there and probably shared her grandmother's bedroom. Sarah must have been a great support to Bertha in those first years of the new century when Arthur's field books show that he was constantly away in the bush. And now they were both dead – Sarah in May 1906, aged sixty-five, just eight months before her daughter-in-law.

After Bertha's death, her younger sisters, Barbara and Louisa, offered to take one of the children each; they would be happy to have May and Angus. Both aunts were married. Louisa Godber was living in Wellington and Barbara

Patterson in Opawa, near Christchurch, both long journeys away. Arthur could not bear to lose his children as well as his wife. And of course no one wanted poor Frederick. No one but his father could contemplate caring for a little boy who twitched and slobbered and grimaced and made strange noises as he struggled to make himself understood. The family stayed together in Fitzherbert Street and got what help they could. May, aged not quite five, joined Angus at school in April 1907, the very month their baby sister died.

I did not know that as a little boy my father had known his grandmother. There is very little that I did know. In those days James Harrop's disappearance, his wife's second marriage, the existence of this step-grandfather, John Neville Smyth – these things were intimate secrets, not the sort of thing to tell the world, or even your own children. My father never talked about his childhood; I was surprised to find that there is far more about his early life than I had remembered in his books, though he wrote always about the good things, not the pain: the view of the snowy Alps as he walked to school, the camping in the bush, the birds, the train that puffed its way slowly from Hokitika to Greymouth ('The 24-mile journey timed to take an hour and three-quarters.'). From it they 'got as much pleasure as if it were the latest silver and blue express from London to Scotland'.

His sister, May, told my mother bitter tales of a slatternly house-keeper who used to take their food to her alcoholic parents. My mother, wanting to forgive Arthur for employing such a person, said: 'Hokitika was a very small town and there was not much choice of a house-keeper.' My cousin, Gill Poulier, thought that this unnamed woman might well have been the same person whose arrival on board ship in Melbourne many years later caused her mother such agitation that her husband thought the encounter and its reminders might have been responsible for the severe and eventually fatal stroke May suffered shortly after the woman's departure.

By that time May had already proved to be sadly damaged herself. She had apparently no idea how to be a loving mother, having no memory of having had one. My cousin Cynthia, Gill's older sister, wrote to me five years ago from Tasmania where she now lives:

> I was reminded of you the other day when I heard Anthony at, I think, the Cheltenham Festival, reading a letter, written to him by Philip Larkin, on our ABC Radio National. The 1971 letter contained a poem written (I presume as a joke) for you to include in a book of poems for children you were editing at the time. It began 'They f..k us up, our mum and dad' and went on for 2 verses in that lovely lilting metre to conclude with something like 'and vow to have no kids at all'.

The poem that struck Cynthia so forcibly and which she misquoted so enthusiastically is perhaps the most famous of Larkin's poems, but it would seem she had not come across it before. This is the last stanza:

> Man hands on misery to man.
>> It deepens like a coastal shelf.
> Get out as early as you can,
>> And don't have any kids yourself.

Cynthia went on:

> For me it summed up perfectly the hazards of family life as experienced in all their horror by my sister and me for 20 years until our mother was laid low by a serious stroke. For whatever reason she was a very angry, very violent, domineering and cruel woman and Geoffrey had no hope of protecting us from her. Not that he tried, having been crushed himself in the confidence department as only child of a domineering wealthy widow. He was concentrating on trying to save himself. That poem said it all. Between genetics and psychoses the next generation has no hope unless by a fluke. I know it certainly mangled my capacity as a mother.

Cynthia has no contact with her daughter, Jane, 'by mutual agreement' and told me she has not spoken to her sister since 1983. So women too can hand on misery to women. I can only think with sadness of them all, admiring the different ways they have coped with depression, separation, regret.

There were three things that saved my father in the early days after his mother's death. First, and most important, was his father's love and concern, his pride in this boy's bright ability that was always so obvious in that dark home. There was not much chance for the two of them, father and son, to spend time alone together. But there were expeditions into the bush when Arthur took Angus along with him. After his wife's death (as the dates in the Field Books indicate), Arthur Harrop worked mainly in the office, first as Chief Draughtsman and then, eventually, as District Surveyor. My father wrote of 'the old wooden Survey Office' he 'knew so well' – he must have gone down there sometimes after school, reluctant to go back to Fitzherbert Street. In one of his books my father wrote:

> I went camping occasionally with the survey parties …. There comes back to me the delicious aroma of the evening meal, blended with the smoke from the wood in the camp oven, which came to us after long days with the chainmen

in the forest. Some of the days I spent fishing in the streams for what we called mountain trout …. Imagine a clear stream making its way through forest probably traversed by not more than a dozen men since the beginning of time. Above the stream a section of blue sky framed by the green tops of the tall trees. A few yards from the edge of the stream, no trace of the sky. We walk about as in some immense natural conservatory carpeted with delicate ferns, decked with clematis and a host of other creepers. Occasionally we come to a clearing made by the fall of some giant tree, whose trunk the ferns and mosses quickly clothe with green. Here, perhaps, we sit to share the midday sandwich with the bright-eyed tom-tits who know no fear, to admire the flitting fantails and to listen to the bell-birds calling from their tree towers. This to me is the essential New Zealand, the part of her which no other country can completely duplicate, and the part of her which, despite the pressure of crowds, the hunger for timber and the fumes of petrol, can still be found by those who look for it.

My father was writing for an English publisher, mainly for an English readership and, presumably because of that, uses the word 'forest', rather than 'bush', which comes more naturally to me when thinking about New Zealand – though, I am told, the word 'rainforest' is now quite generally in use. Angus ended that passage by regretting the fact that he was, on those early surveying expeditions, too young to appreciate quite how lucky he was. That he did appreciate the bush and the camping and show an interest in his father's work is proved by the album I mentioned on the first page of this book – the collection given to him in 1907 with the brilliant photographs by the camp cook, J.C. Martin, of a score of places young Angus might have visited with his father. There were the rivers, Taramakau, Arnold, Hohonu, the friends in the remote settlements, Corbetts and Martins and many more, and there were the gorges and waterfalls and lakes.

To me it was particularly poignant to find a loose copy of one of the photographs, evidently used as a greetings card for Christmas 1906. My

grandfather, Arthur, is smoking a pipe, sitting on a rock with a companion, his nephew Angus Hugo (nicknamed Bang), a dog nearby. The inscription on the back reads: 'COMPLIMENTS OF THE SEASON *Self and Bang*' and underneath are the initials of my grandparents: A.N.H., B.J.H.

Three weeks after that Christmas, B.J.H., my grandmother, was dead – and A.N.H. left to find as much consolation as he could from the love and achievements of his eldest child, with his seventh birthday just weeks away.

The second thing that saved my father in these early days was the library, the splendid Hokitika Free Public Library, one of the grandest of the eighteen libraries throughout New Zealand endowed by the millionaire philanthropist Andrew Carnegie, a Scot who had made a fortune in America. He had offered to donate a library to any town in the English-speaking world that would give a site and guarantee annual maintenance costs from public funds.

Angus was six when the foundation stone was laid, not long before his mother's death, and eight on the joyful occasion of its opening in the winter of 1908. It is an amazing building with its Corinthian columns and triangular pediments, its huge windows and ornamented balustrades. Now the home of the West Coast Historical Museum (with its Archives where we spent some happy time), it has been called 'the finest building architecturally' on the Coast and has been restored quite recently to its former glory. Standing there in 1908 in Hamilton Street, opposite Dr Teichelmann's consulting rooms, totally out of scale and style with everything else around, it must have made a huge impression on young Angus Harrop, who had seen nothing like it before. I am sure it had a good deal to do with turning him into the compulsive reader and writer that he became.

The third thing that made a great difference to my father's life, and the one for which there is more evidence, was sport – an enthusiasm he shared with both his father and his uncle, and with practically everyone else in Hokitika. I said my father never talked about his childhood, but sometimes referred to it in his books with a good deal of reticence and self-censorship. Once he wrote about it at greater length. Some pages survive of a sort of autobiography he began to write in 1940, presumably just after he found himself in London without a family when we sailed off to the other side of the world, out of harm's way. He was writing on the back of the typescript of his *England and the Maori Wars*. The numbering is such that it is clear that, at some point, he destroyed a good many pages – again reflecting, I think, that there were things he never wanted us to know. It seems that, in those dangerous times, when death must have seemed quite likely, he started to write the story of his life but then changed his mind, reserved as he naturally was, and turned the book into a more general study – never finished – to be called *A New Zealander on London Bridge*, echoing Macaulay.

Most of the Hokitika material in the early pages that survive is about sport. From 'a very tender age', perhaps soon after his mother's death, Angus said he elected himself 'a supporter of the Excelsior Club' and began a lifetime's career of rugby watching. Cass Square, only a short walk from Fitzherbert Street, was the scene of Homeric battles between the local clubs. In the summer there was cricket – apparently played on a concrete pitch because of all the rain that West Coasters were always keen to claim fell mostly in the night. There were a good many exciting matches and there was always a crowd of little boys hovering near the boundaries, hoping to have the chance to pick up the ball as it raced over the line and dreaming of the possibility of catching a full toss that had gone for six. Later, when he was himself playing, he used to like 'fielding at point, about five yards or so from the wicket …. You have to keep wide awake when you are as close as that, of course,' he once told my brother.

But tennis was the game that was most important to Angus, from that same 'very tender age' when he cheered on the Excelsior Club. He said how much his outlook on life was coloured by the 'quite accidental circumstance' that his headmaster at his Hokitika school – an elegant man called Hugh Wake – was an enthusiastic tennis player, though there were no grass courts in the town. Mr Wake himself played at the local club after school, nearly every day in the summer, with an admiring crowd of children peering through the wire netting. He was eventually West Coast champion in both Singles and Doubles, the best tennis player on the Coast. Then the amazing thing was that he managed to get a court laid down for the children at the primary school, long before such things were common even in the District High Schools.

Watching Mr Wake and the older children at school, Angus learnt how to score and had a good idea of tactics by the time he was in Standard IV and at last allowed to play himself. 'As soon as I was qualified I entered the lists with an inherited racquet some ounces too heavy for me, but quite good enough to send me into the seventh heaven of delight. When not playing at school I spent hours volleying on the verandah at home.' He was ten years old. He thought of the years of enjoyment that followed, 'the strenuous days in the sun'. He never ceased to be grateful to this headmaster. Years later they played some sets together on the courts in Lincoln's Inn Fields in London and remembered Hokitika. What my father did not say, in this piece he wrote about the joys of tennis, was what a part it had played in securing for himself, eventually, a partner in his life who could cope with the demons that ruined his sister's.

Writing to Angus in 1941, when they were on opposite sides of the world, my mother told him she had been talking in Wellington to his aunts. 'I was much interested,' she said, telling him not to get ruffled by what she was saying, 'to hear at different times from Aunts Barbara and Louisa how difficult you were as a small boy. L. stresses the fact that she understood you and she never had any trouble with you, but with people who didn't understand you, you could be very troublesome.' It seems to me that she was talking of house-keepers – there was probably a series of them, trying to cope with the difficult small motherless boy and girl and their helpless brother, before poor Arthur had to settle for the slatternly one with the alcoholic parents. My mother wrote of the anger that used to 'boil over' when things did not go as Angus hoped they would or when she tried to question him about things that he did not want to think about. For the most part, she understood him and respected his wish to put the past, the painful childhood days, behind him. Even as she wrote her letter she could imagine him 12,000 miles away 'all hot and angry – but why? The reason I write this is because if *only* you'll admit the tendency which you never can bear to do – you are half-way to avoiding the actual boiling over.' She assured him she had never asked the aunts one thing, but 'Aunt Barbara *loves* to talk about you when you were small and Aunt Louisa hardly less so.' 'However', she added reassuringly, 'don't worry as I'm not seeing them very often.'

This is an important letter for understanding the anger Angus and May felt from this early stage in their lives. It seems my mother was able to cope and understand, whereas Geoffrey, May's husband, was not able to help her. It is very interesting to me that in this letter my mother says nothing about any possible reasons why Angus might have been a troublesome, difficult child. She makes no mention of the dead mother or the 'spastic' brother, who was still alive at that point in 1941, though I think she did not know it. They remained unmentionable, a source of sadness and guilt so painful that it could never be explored.

I don't think, in fact, that the aunts had seen a great deal of the Hokitika children. They were a long way away. Angus made just one journey to the North Island in the days before he went to boarding school. Wellington was his first city and the shock of his first sight of it stayed with him for the rest of his life. He had taken the coastal steamer *Arahura* from the West Coast to the capital and back. 'Crossing the bar at Greymouth', he wrote thirty years later, 'was a sufficiently vivid reminder of what the pioneers put up with in even smaller craft.' Had he heard of his mother's journey from Melbourne to Greymouth as a child in 1873? Travelling to Wellington, Angus said, they spent hours ashore in Westport and Nelson before crossing Cook Strait and spotting Pelorus Jack, the famous dolphin protected by Order of Council:

> I shall never forget the beauty of Wellington by night, as seen after that first voyage, the circle of hills around the harbour illuminated by thousands of lights. Most exciting of all were the moving lights, for to me an electric tram was the last word in modern locomotion and the thought of a journey in one was almost too exciting to be borne. The child of today, gazing at airliners from his cradle, may never be able to realise what I felt when I saw the lights of Wellington's trams. Beside this transition from Hokitika, with its two or three thousand people, to the wonders of the metropolis, the contrast between the two ends of a later journey – from Wellington to London – was comparatively insignificant.

Hokitika in 1910 was certainly not the vibrant, tumultuous place it had been in Gold Rush times, when the 1866 Directory listed 102 hotels. It was now a small quiet town, but my father remembered it still having 'that first wild flavour of freedom from convention which life had in a new land, where sites for towns were carved out of the forest' and settlers were inclined to be 'those who had found irksome the class distinctions and snobbery of older lands'. But nothing could emphasise more clearly how remote, how rural (ten minutes' walk and you could be in deep bush) and how limited Hokitika must have seemed than the fact that Wellington, in my father's eyes, appeared to be the most dazzling, the most modern, the most amazing of capital cities, having more in common with London than it did with Hokitika.

This was Katherine Mansfield's Wellington, though Kathleen Beauchamp herself (to give her her real name) was, by the time my father came for his holiday, already in London. Her father's background was very similar to his mother's, though Hal Beauchamp became a great deal more successful than Angus Campbell. Our slight connection with New Zealand's most famous writer – whom I grew up admiring as much as any writer I read – is an odd one. My father's Aunt Louisa, with whom he stayed on this early visit to Wellington, had married Frederick Godber in 1902; Godber's was the most admired confectioners and caterers in Wellington.

Early in 1890, when Fred Godber was fifteen and already working for his father, there were huge celebrations to mark the fiftieth anniversary of the Treaty of Waitangi, already to some people 'contentious and problematic', but seen as the occasion of the founding of the Colony of New Zealand. The Wellington *Evening Press* reported that the hundreds of schoolchildren at the Basin Reserve were each presented with a paper bag containing two sorts of cake, a handful of lollies and some biscuits, all 'done at a cost of five pence farthing per head by Mr J. Godber of Cuba Street'.

Godber's Artcraft shop and kitchens, by then opposite the Parliament Buildings, were the caverns of delight my father entered as a boy and which my brother and I enjoyed, in our turn, thirty years later. In 1907 Mrs Beauchamp's garden party in Tinakori Road – not far from the Godbers' own similar house and garden in Glenmore Street – was naturally catered for by Godber's. In the story by her daughter, Katherine Mansfield, 'The Garden Party', it is Godber's man who arrives with the cream puffs and tells the tale of the 'horrible accident' on which the story depends.

Compared with Wellington, Hokitika might seem quiet and dull. Even so, it was a good place to grow up in and to come back to from boarding school. A farewell evening for Arthur's brother and his wife (following a promotion to the Lands and Survey Office in Napier) suggests a supportive community with a good deal going on. The *West Coast Times* gave a lot of space to the party in Preston's Tea Rooms. The Harrops were the sort of people Hokitika and, specifically, St Mary's Church 'could ill afford to lose'. Mrs Harrop was presented with a solid silver biscuit barrel and tribute was paid to the couple's involvement in amateur dramatics, 'all branches of sport' and any 'charitable object' that arose. The evening naturally ended with the singing of 'For They are Jolly Good Fellows'.

I have mentioned boarding school. It was inevitable, I think, that Arthur Harrop would want for Angus the best secondary school that he could find, though it would have been hard for him to let him go. Neither Arthur nor the boy himself would have liked to think that what they were looking for was an 'élite education'. 'Gentility' and 'élitism', favourite words in Belich's view of New Zealand history, were definitely suspect in Hokitika. 'Free, secular and compulsory' primary education had been established in 1877. In 1900, the year my father was born, very few children went on to secondary school. Belich gives a figure of 'fewer than ten per cent', which increased to thirty-seven per cent by 1917. But it was still not free of charge. Hokitika had had its own District High School since 1891, but it had no sixth form. There was less likelihood of going on from there to university. In 1914 May would gain an Education Board scholarship, which entitled her to a free place at the High School. But one can imagine how she must have longed to get away, like her brother.

It was in 1912 that Angus sat the examinations, hoping to win a Junior National Scholarship, competed for by children all over New Zealand. From March of that year, just after his twelfth birthday, there survives a postcard to 'dear Angus' from his father, apparently attending some sort of surveyors' meeting in Timaru. The photograph on the card is of St Mary's Church, Timaru, built (in some sense) by Archdeacon Harper, the man who had baptised Arthur in 1869. Arthur wrote:

Claremont
via Timaru
20/3/12

Dear Angus,

How are you getting on. It seems a long time since I heard from you all. The church on this P.C. was built by Archdeacon Harper Church of England. It is the finest Church in New Zealand except the Cathedrals. I like it better than Christchurch Cathedral. It has a beautiful soft tone inside – all the windows & columns are lovely. I was all over it with Mr Brodrick the Chief surveyor here. There is a grand view from the tower. From here we look down on Timaru below us. At night when the lights are lit it is just like a great illumination for fireworks. I hope you are getting on well with the scholarship work now. How are the drawing & writing getting on? How is tennis? Will Lawrence Gooch beat Chalk in the championships? He might you know. How would that do? With love to all

D.A.D.

One can hear something of the sort of conversations they must have had in those remarks about tennis. The scholarship enquiry seems more routine. I think Arthur was confident that Angus was 'getting on well'. What moves me is the way my grandfather signed off: D.A.D. This was exactly the way Angus signed the letters and cards he wrote to me, though he never mentioned that it had been his father's habit too.

The eminent doctor, Truby King, had published a strongly-worded paper on 'The Evils of Cram' six years earlier. He attributed the mental breakdown of a number of the patients in his hospital at Seacliff, near Dunedin, to the stresses and strains of the education system. Breakdown could be the devastating result of 'our modern system of strenuous, compulsory cramming and examination, with rewards and temptations in the way of prizes, scholarships, displays and public praise for the winners.' Six years later Truby King's opposition had had no effect on what went on. My father wrote about it like this, looking back to 1912 nearly thirty years later in those unpublished memoirs:

> We were, of course, in the deadly grip of the examination system at the Hokitika school – the system which we now know, because it has been scientifically proved, made our lives a misery and turned us all out into an unsympathetic world with a store of knowledge completely useless for all practical purposes. I must confess that I do remember extra classes after ordinary school for scholarship candidates. But the teacher who took them, the same Miss Ward who had initiated us into the mysteries of the alphabet and who was now in charge of the other end of the school, must have had some mysterious power. The only feeling about those classes that remains with me through the years is one of sympathy for her in what must have been a formidable labour, though one of love. When the smoke of battle cleared away, I found myself in possession of a scholarship.

The first cutting in a small scrapbook Angus began to keep at this time comes from the local paper.

Scholarship Results. Wellington, Jan 14, 1913:
Following is the list of the Hokitika candidates at the Education Department examinations of November and December last …. The names are arranged in the order of merit with the total marks gained by the candidate, out of the possible 800

Angus Harrop   549

He was at the top of the Hokitika list, though it was not a remarkable mark – less than seventy per cent. He made no comment; he was probably just relieved it was over and there would be more time for tennis. There may have been some 'public praise'. On the Honours Board with him there are two exotic names, Erle Schroder and Jules Malfroy, who also crossed the Southern Alps for their further education and were particular friends of my father. They were familiar names to me as a child, loving their sound.

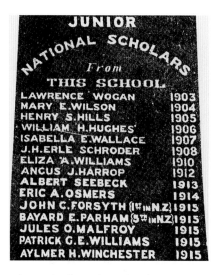

Where should Angus go now? He remembered that

To our remote corner of New Zealand the fame of a young and vigorous headmaster had penetrated, and, when my father's telegram of inquiry was answered, I found myself consigned to Waitaki School and the care of Frank Milner, who had been its head for six years.

I suspect that Arthur Harrop had heard talk of Milner when he was in Timaru the year before, had perhaps even gone a little further south and taken a look at the school in Oamaru. (He would have been impressed with Waitaki and with Oamaru itself and its astonishing white stone buildings, which make even the Carnegie library in Hokitika look dull.) Whether Arthur Harrop saw the school or not, he made an excellent decision. If the love of his father, the library and sport had saved my father from anger and despair in Hokitika, it was now Frank Milner who took over and gave him what, in Milner's own words, would prove to be 'a glorious chance'.

But first Angus had to get there. This would always be an adventure, however many times he made the journey over the years. It was a case of taking the train to Otira and then crossing the Alps by Arthur's Pass in one of Cobb and Co.'s coaches, pulled by five horses which had an uncanny sense of the width of that narrow road – so that though there were moments when it seemed the coach would plunge hundreds of feet to the river, it never did. The road along the Gorge was entirely cut out of the rock. Imagine a ledge with hairpin bends along a cliff. In many places the rocks hung over the road, threatening to crash down and crush the coach and horses, but somehow they never did. Looking out of the coach, glimpsing the white foaming Otira River, the boy could have dropped a pebble into the water 500 feet below, just by holding out his arm, so near were they to the edge.

Often Angus got to ride on the box beside the driver, with the reek of sweat and dust and horseflesh in his nostrils and the clatter of iron-rimmed wheels and hooves in his ears. That was even more exciting, if also more alarming. On the boy's very first journey to school the Waimakariri was in flood, so the excitement wasn't over, even when they came down from the mountains. The horses had to swim dragging the coach behind them, the water well over its axles.

Anyone who has visited the Information Centre at Arthur's Pass will have seen a Cobb and Co. coach and read the amazing claim that 'only one life was lost during the coaching era. A baby was killed when thrown from an overturned coach above the Otira zigzag in 1907.' In the Centre you can also read a nice piece of light verse by Tremayne Curnow, father of the more famous Allen. It includes these lines:

> The driver tries to calm my fears
> As round a hairpin bend he steers.
> 'There's been no accident for years'
>   He hastens to assure me ….
> I'm no seeker after thrills.
> I'd rather travel under hills
> Than over them in rain and chills
>   In constant trepidation ….

The Otira rail tunnel was finally opened in 1923 just before Angus left New Zealand, at last making the West Coast more easily accessible. As the only Hokitika man on the Christchurch *Press*, he would make that earliest journey through the tunnel, now a regular tourist route. But he was always glad he had been born early enough to 'savour the joys of box-seat travel behind horses whose intelligence and sure-footedness in negotiating hairpin bends in snowstorms on Arthur's Pass was a constant wonder and delight.' Now there is the elegant viaduct to make the drive across the Alps safe, tame and swift, but still beautiful. Having crossed it, on our way to Christchurch, we paused at the Death's Corner look-out point where the keas potter and peck among the parked cars and boulders, hoping someone has ignored the notices telling visitors NOT to feed them. It was October and bleak; there was still a lot of snow around. I could see that parts of the old road have practically disappeared beneath a slope of scree.

Angus Harrop began at Waitaki Boys' High School, Oamaru, in February, 1913. This photo shows a Hansom cab and a group of boys in front of the school in that very year. Waitaki was certainly on its way to being, if not already, one of the best schools in New Zealand. My father spent a lifetime grateful for what it gave him during the six years he was there.

It may be true that Waitaki, and schools like it, had more in common with English public schools than the 'egalitarian myth' would like. It has been claimed that such schools 'taught gentility', that 'they featured fags, prefects, corporal punishment and Arnoldian principals trained at Charterhouse and Trinity and known as "the Man".' Frank Milner was indeed known as 'the Man', but he had never been near Charterhouse and Trinity and the last thing he taught at Waitaki was 'gentility'.

Milner's background was totally New Zealand. He had been educated at

Nelson and at Canterbury University College alongside Ernest Rutherford. When he took his first class degree in languages and literature (Latin and English) he headed the list for the whole country – Canterbury in those days being a part of the University of New Zealand. Milner had a passion for literature and an extraordinary memory. He was able to quote long passages, not only of poetry but of prose, and to speak without a note for hours. He knew every boy in his school and wanted to bring out the best in each one.

Milner thought that passing examinations, if regrettably necessary, was 'of little moment'. The primary concern of education was rather the development of the whole personality – moral, intellectual, aesthetic and physical – so that the boy would be fitted as an adult to play a part in making a better world. Milner was an idealist and, educationally, a radical. He was also both an Imperialist and an internationalist, seeing no contradiction between the two. His views should never be confused with those of his namesake Alfred Milner, who was at least partly responsible for the Boer War. But they shared a belief in the British Empire as 'the supreme political creation of all time'.

Frank Milner's rebellious son Ian (whom my husband and I got to know when he taught in Prague) could detect in his father 'an inner sturdy fibre of New Zealand democratic feeling', even if he saw him also as 'Canute trying to hold back the waves of New Zealand nationalism'. Frank Milner always saw Britain as the centre of the world, the Mother Country, to whom New Zealand owed some sort of debt. This was a debt being paid daily, through most of the time Angus was at school, in a war that posed no immediate threat to New Zealand's security. Masters and Old Boys were wounded and dying at Gallipoli, on the Somme, at Beaumont-Hamel, and at Bapaume. One hundred and twenty Waitakians were killed in World War I, including Katherine Mansfield's beloved only brother. Another 300 were wounded. My father's commonplace books – five substantial notebooks, with carefully written out chunks of poetry and prose – are full of war poems. Kipling, Rupert Brooke and Julian Grenfell gave way to the stark and moving realism of Wilfrid Gibson's

> *Two rows of cabbages,*
> *Two of curly-greens,*
> *Two rows of early peas,*
> *Two of kidney-beans.*
>
> That's what he keeps muttering,
> Making such a song,
> Keeping other chaps awake
> The whole night long.

Both his legs are shot away,
And his head is light,
So he keeps on muttering
All the blessed night:

Two rows of cabbages,
Two of curly-greens,
Two rows of early peas,
Two of kidney-beans.

In 1917 the five new open-air dormitories – with nothing between the boys and the night air but canvas blinds – were named Anzac Cove, Lone Pine, Quinn's Post, Chunuk Bair and Sari Bair; from them, my father said, 'went boys to fill the places of men left on the deadly peninsula', Gallipoli. Angus wrote out in his notebook a poem by C. Fox Smith called 'The Evacuation', which includes these lines:

But some there are will never quit this bleak and bloody shore,
And some that marched and fought with us will fight and march no more,
Their blood has bought till judgment day the slopes they stormed so well,
And we're leaving them, leaving them, sleeping where they fell.

The chill the boys felt as they went to sleep in their narrow beds was not only from the night air.

Waitaki was full of remarkable boys who would become remarkable men in their different ways. My father kept in touch with many of them all his life and at least two of them will come in later in this book as important players in this story: Eric Baume and Reuel Lochore. The boys endured what might seem a Spartan regime with its emphasis on healthy minds in healthy bodies – but the school was also unusually liberal, tolerant and wide-ranging. Certainly no English public school offered wool-classing as a subject, had an experimental farm or had boys dressed in the typical New Zealand uniform of dark shorts and open-necked grey shirts. It also made a huge difference to the school that it offered a free education to any boy who had won a Junior National Scholarship, like my father, whose fees only had to cover boarding costs.

There were examinations for Senior National Scholarships, three years later, taken by most of the boys late in the year before they turned sixteen. Frank Milner sent a telegram from Nelson where he was on holiday:

CONGRATULATIONS ON YOUR SCHOLARSHIP
SECOND PLACE FOR OTAGO AND SIXTH FOR NEW ZEALAND

Arthur Harrop sent it on with a parcel of vegetables to Angus, who was camping at Lake Kaniere. This letter from Arthur is one of only three communications from him that survive.

The *West Coast Times* recorded that the clever 'young lad' had scored 1707 marks out of a possible 2000, but my father on the cutting from the newspaper has crossed out 2000, and admitted there were a possible 2200 marks available.

Apart from the open-air dormitories which the boys started using in 1917, the Spartan regime at Waitaki also involved an early morning pre-breakfast run followed by a cold shower or an equally naked swim. Some enthusiasts persisted in their swimming right through the Otago winter, even breaking the ice on more than one occasion, but this foolishness, I am glad to say, was not compulsory. 'Swedish drill' during a mid-morning break was, and so was a certain amount of games-playing. Rugby football, cricket, tennis and fives were the staples. My father's crop of war-time certificates (given instead of the usual prizes) eventually included 'First Prize Senior Fives Champ. Doubles' in 1917 and '1ˢᵗ Prize Senior Tennis Champs. Singles' the following year.

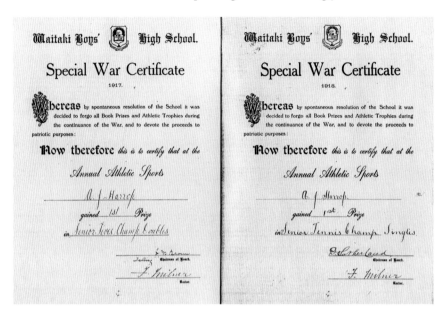

There was an 'Up! Up!' bell at crack of dawn, usually rung by Milner himself. It was said he never used 'Go on!' but always 'Come on!', doing everything with the boys. When they were finally in school after the energetic start to the day, actual classes would be delayed while, every morning, Milner talked about some current topic, about the war news or something he had been reading. 'I have never known anyone who had the power to carry boys along with him as he did', one of his staff recalled. Milner had what we would now call 'charisma'. He was an orator such as few of his pupils would ever hear again. If some of his staff found him dictatorial and over-bearing, the boys, in those war years anyway, tended to be impressed and even – some of them – inspired. My father said that his own love of English literature was something that was 'caught rather than taught'.

But a lot of teaching went on. Frank Milner taught sixth form English himself and a good letter survives written just before Christmas, 1917. 'Dear Harrop', Milner wrote. Then, after a paragraph concerning the school magazine, which my father was editing, the Rector (as he was called) went on to give a reading list. Next term they would be studying Palgrave's *Golden Treasury*, Boswell's *Life of Johnson*, Lamb's *Essays of Elia*, Oliver Wendell Holmes's

Autocrat of the Breakfast Table and George Eliot's *Scenes of Clerical Life* – but also Chaucer, Spenser, Milton, Shelley, Burns, Keats, Shakespeare, Coleridge, Tennyson and Browning. How *English* their reading was! One American, one Scot – and not a New Zealand writer to be had. My father would comment on this later, realising how his literary education had programmed him to thirst for England, Shakespeare's 'precious stone set in a silver sea', the centre of Milner's imagination, though he had still never been there. There would be at least five hours of English a week, probably six, he told my father in 1917. 'I mean to do a lot of oral work and to keep a special Literary Class going of the best men in Forms VI & VA.' There would be regular debates and even something which might now be called Creative Writing. The 'best men' met in the Rector's study. 'Literature and history are to me very vital subjects, capable of giving a boy lifelong mental values. A bit of enthusiasm for literary reading will carry a boy a long way in life.' 'I have the place redeemed altogether from barbarism', Milner once claimed. Here are some of the 'best men' in 1918.

It was my father's reading of English literature at Waitaki (both in school and out of school hours) that gave him 'the greatest mental pleasure' of his schooldays and his love of literature was the legacy he valued most. Like Frank Milner's, Angus Harrop's head was filled with poetry he would quote whenever the chance arose, whether appropriate or not. I can still hear in my head 'The Assyrian came down like the wolf on the fold', 'A thing of beauty is a joy for ever', 'When I have fears that I may cease to be', 'Say not the struggle naught availeth', 'My heart leaps up when I behold' – and a thousand other lines that he would murmur (he was never declamatory) as we did the dishes together or picked blackcurrants for a pie. So it was that I caught that love of poetry with which his headmaster had infected my father.

In the summer holidays of 1916–17 there was a girl called Hilda Valentine who noticed the boy, Angus Harrop, pushing his young disabled brother in a wheelchair round the streets of Hokitika, sometimes stopping so they could both watch a game that was being played. She thought him kind and wondered who he was and where he went to school. She had herself just arrived by coach over the mountains – evidently not in the same coach as Angus – to join her family for the holidays. It was her first visit to the West Coast. She had stayed on as a boarder at Timaru Girls' High School when her father had been transferred to Hokitika earlier in the year as the Education Board's sole Inspector of Schools on the Coast.

Hilda was sixteen and an intense, introspective girl who wrote things in her diary that would have surprised Angus Harrop, whose own diary consisted of the very briefest comments: 'Lantern lecture evening', 'Cricket at nets' or 'Worked all afternoon'. In the previous March, when she was still fifteen, Hilda in her piano lessons was learning to play 'Romance from Tannhäuser' and a Beethoven sonata; but her plan for the future is not a romantic one. She wants to get a scholarship next year and 'then in 1918 to Varsity. Four years to get my M.A., then for teaching till I save £1000 [a huge amount in those days], then for travelling, then back to NZ to do more good in the world.' Boys, men, are not part of her plan. It was impossible to teach (and therefore save) if you were married.

Hilda was typical of her time. Belich tells us that 'girls embraced "evil cram" as eagerly as they rejected noble mass motherhood.' A survey that year found that girls were the highest academic achievers in nineteen co-educational schools out of twenty-two, and already thirty-five per cent of Canterbury graduates were women – a very different situation from that on the other side of the world. Hilda is reading *Middlemarch* and debating 'Which is the greater, Dickens or Thackeray?' How much did you have to have read at fifteen to take part in that

debate? But there was more to life than 'cram'. She learns to ride a motor-cycle – 'nearly', she adds, trying as always to be honest.

The motor-cycle belongs, inevitably, to a boy but he lets her little sister, Lottie, pose in the side-car. 'I like Arthur Lascelles', Hilda writes in her diary. 'I shall see him again on Sunday week.' But boys are a problem.

On 4 September 1916 in her diary Hilda wrote: 'I am trying to think beautiful things and make my mind beautiful, leaving thoughts of love and unhealthy things alone just now. The world is so lovely – the sky and trees and grass, the flowers and the sea. The joy of living is vivid, intense …. I want to be above petty meannesses and thoughts, to be noble, never to be called to act any other part than a simple one. I want the world to be better because I have lived and when I am dying to know I have tried to live so that God could fulfil his purpose in me.' I fear it was God, or at least the ministers of her church, who had made her link love with 'unhealthy things'. But it was also her passionate faith that made her determined to be 'good'. 'I must guard my tongue and actions and show others how happy a place the world is.' The war was far away and her older brothers were in the army; she was evidently not thinking about them.

Hilda liked Hokitika from the beginning. Life was so full in those Christmas holidays that she didn't write anything until 15 January. 'I've neglected you for a whole month and more, diary. Hokitika is a very good place and has some very pleasant people.' She lists the young people she has already met: 'Cyril, Molly, Jimmy, Fitz, Grace, Jim, Isy, Bob, Tommy, Norman, Herbert, Pip, Jules, George MacGregor, George Maunder, Jack, Jessie, Dot, Thirza, Maisie, Teddy, Eileen Coole, Mervyn Smith, Blair, Chrissie and Nessie Tennant, Les

Michel.' What a crowd! But there is no mention of Angus. What fun the crowd had those holidays with dancing and tennis and swimming, and picnics on beaches and in the bush. On 21 January she murmurs to her diary 'Had one of the happiest days of the holidays – and, diary, some new experiences.' She underlines the date on which she had one new experience: '*10 Jan 1917 was the 1st time.*' I suspect she had been kissed. On 1 February, about to go back to school, she writes that Herbert had 'said goodbye properly' last night after the Malfroys' party.

The first mention of my father by this flirting, devout, gregarious teenager, who would somehow one day become my mother, was in the next school holidays. On 15 May 1917 Hilda wrote 'Isy and Tom played Angus and me 5 sets.' I don't know who Tom was, but Isy was Isobel Aitken, her life-long friend, who became Lance McCaskill's wife. 'We won 4 out of 5. Great sets. Angus is nice.' It was fortunate that Angus was not only nice but such a good tennis player. Otherwise I feel it is unlikely that my brother and I would exist. They played a lot of tennis. Hilda attributed 'the breaking of the ice' to a day when they were playing Singles together and, changing ends, she foolishly went under the net and it caught a button on her dress. She had to rely on Angus to disentangle it. Hilda then quarrelled with Herbert, but it was 'good fun' and he was still very much on the scene.

> 24 May 1917 I have just learned the lesson that patience and unselfishness make a holiday ever so much sweeter. Self-forgetfulness is what I must strive after. Then I realised partly from my own experience and partly from reading that it is the noblest and most satisfying way *not* to hold 'free slangy intercourse with boys', but to enjoy oneself while exercising the true girl's gift – sympathy and judicious interest. Arthur Mee's letters are splendid, specially 'To the Girl who loves the Noblest'. I want to love the noblest. I wish some things had not happened, but I have learnt my lesson, I trust.

On 27 May Hilda travelled back to school in Timaru over Arthur's Pass. Isy and Hilda, Cecil, Angus and Jules were all on the coach together. 'Had a decent time. Walked up to help the straining horses.' On her birthday the next month my mother wrote: 'Now I am 17 I must try not to be jealous and selfish and careless. I want to be high-souled and pure-minded. I want to learn to talk less and I want my influence to be felt as good among the girls.' But, oh dear, she feared she was 'lazy and indolent and careless and very egotistical and conceited and miserably self-conscious and I know very little.' She longed to be 'natural and sincere and true'.

Hilda was feeling guilty because, following his first letter, she had met Angus secretly when he came up to Timaru from Waitaki for a football match. When she got the letter she had been slightly surprised and glad. They were both working hard. 'I swotted till 10.30', she wrote in her diary, 'I wonder if I can keep that up? I must do more and talk less.' Told she wrote French with very little 'French style', she determined to read at least a page of French every day. Boys were a distraction. But it was convenient and exciting that she had to take a Third Former to the dentist at just the moment she could meet Angus on the cliff walk at Caroline Bay. 'The view over the sea was delightful', Hilda wrote. Certainly it was not a time or a place for kissing, and anyway she realised that Angus was not that sort of boy.

In January 1919 Hilda wrote 'You have been lost during one of the most eventful years of my life, diary.' She had been transferred rather suddenly in 1918 from school to university 'because a Gammack scholarship was handed on to me.' It is obvious from Angus's 1918 diary, even with those laconic entries, that Hilda had already become the girl for him. 'H. offered G. schol' he wrote on 10 April. (Apparently a first year student had already fallen by the way.) He shares her wish to make a difference in the world – writing carefully at the front in his seventeen-year-old hand – so much neater than the writing I knew:

> Is any home the brighter
> Because you have passed that way?
> Is any heart the lighter
> That you have lived today?

There are only two birthdays in Memoranda at the front, one is his sister's, 29 June, and the other, a day later, is my mother's – though 30 June has no name by it. Frederick, his brother, is remembered, but in code. On Sunday 10 November Angus writes and underlines 'Rem. F's b.18th' and on the 15th in tiny letters with a tick 'Post F's.'

That was the same week as Angus wrote in huge letters PEACE DAY on 12 November. 'Celebrations in town all day. Marched in procession. Bands etc.' And along the side of that week he wrote, 'Influenza raging through N.Z.' Church services were cancelled. The school 'allowed away'. But perhaps it was more dangerous to travel. His last term fizzled out. He had done well: coming top in the exams in every subject except science – even Maths. He collected a certificate as Dux: first prize (Dux of School) for 'General Excellence'.

The cleverest boy in the school looked forward to going to Canterbury University College in 1919 with a splendid testimonial from his headmaster. It outlined his 'distinguished career' at Waitaki, the numerous class prizes, his

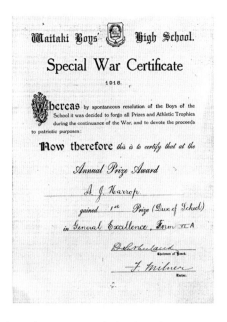

'intellectual leadership', his Somes scholarship for entrance to College House. He was not only 'a conscientious worker' and 'a trenchant speaker at the Debating Society'. He showed 'remarkable facility in French' (in spite of never having heard a native speaker) and shone at cricket, tennis and fives. As editor of the *Waitakian* his articles were 'characterised by literary felicity and vigour'.

On 20 November Arthur Harrop wrote a letter which shows he had abandoned a plan to take a holiday to come down to Waitaki – probably for the Speech Day and Prize-giving that had been cancelled because of the 'flu epidemic: 'I am sorry for your disappointment, son, but many other poor people have much more to sorrow for just now.' He was sad not to be able to thank Mr Milner personally, 'for the care he has taken of you'. The influenza was 'very virulent' on the West Coast. May had caught it, but was now, thankfully, convalescent. 'Fred was pleased with the books' Angus had sent. Arthur told Angus to be guided by Mr Milner about his departure. If it was considered safe to travel he should stay at a good hotel in Christchurch and take every precaution, as influenza was 'now at its height there'. 'Wire from Arthur's Pass,' he said. Arthur told Angus he would 'ask to add my leave to next year's and get a good holiday then, all being well.'

But all would not be well. Within three months Arthur Harrop was dead, but not from influenza. On Thursday 13 February 1919 my grandfather was sitting quietly watching a bowling match in Greymouth at the West Coast tournament; he was a member of the Hokitika Bowling Club's team and the newspaper report said 'had played well on Tuesday and Wednesday'. It went on:

About 4.40 pm, while seated near the pavilion, Mr Harrop suddenly collapsed without any warning. Dr. Usher was present at the time and gave immediate attention, subsequently removing the sufferer to the Grey Hospital by ambulance …. The end came without his recovering consciousness and caused quite a gloom in the community, especially among his club mates who all deeply regret his demise. The deceased, who was a native of Ross and 49 years of age, had been filling a responsible post in the Lands and Survey Department …. A widower he leaves a daughter growing into womanhood and two sons, the elder of whom was going to university in a few days. To the bereaved relatives the deep sympathy of a wide circle of friends will be extended.

There was much more, emphasising Arthur's worthiness. He took 'a prominent part in church matters and was a vestryman of All Saints …. He was honorary secretary of the School Committee.' But that is enough. He had left his three children to fend for themselves. Angus was eighteen and just about to go to Canterbury University College, May was sixteen, and Frederick, the boy in the wheelchair, inarticulate and largely helpless, was now fourteen. What was to become of Angus and May? Worst of all, what was to become of Frederick?

The funeral was on Sunday 16 February. The Valentines, my other grandparents, were there. My two grandfathers were fellow members of the Hokitika Bowling Club. Hilda and Angus had watched them play together in Cass Square. My mother's sister, Nettie, recorded in her diary that 'Mr Harrop had a paralytic stroke' and that the girls 'watched the funeral' after Sunday School. 'Mum, Hilda and I went up to Harrops at Angus's request.' Angus had been round to the Valentines in Stafford Street the night before. 'It is very hard for them', Hilda wrote. She remembered Angus 'sitting beside me on the big settee, unbelieving and desolate'. A note she wrote to him survives. How she must have agonised about what she should write.

Angus Dear,
  I am so sorrowful — but words are so inexpressive. You know that my thoughts are with you and my heart is one big prayer for strength for you.
  Yours very sincerely
  Hilda.

My mother's mother's family: the Jefcoates and the Olivers

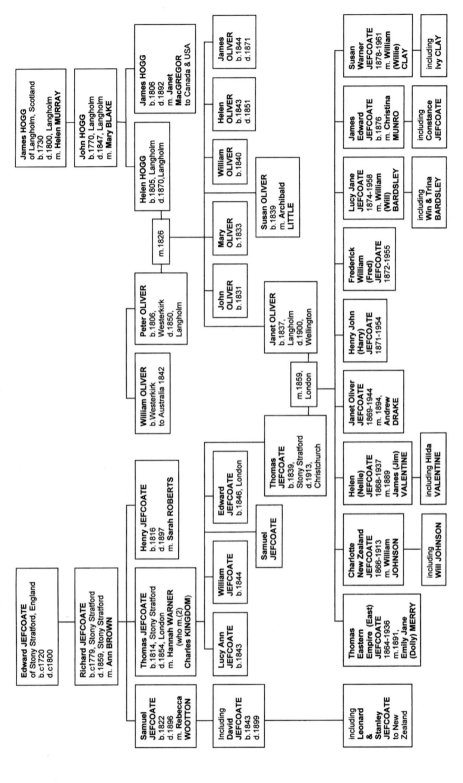

CHAPTER 4

Hoggs, Olivers and Jefcoates

Before I go on with that narrative, I need to leave 1919 and go right back to look at my mother's side of the family. How did Hilda's parents come to be born in New Zealand? When did *their* parents arrive? My mother's mother, Helen (Nellie) Valentine, was born Helen Jefcoate in Christchurch in 1868, the daughter of Janet (née Oliver) and Thomas Jefcoate, who had arrived three years earlier.

I have always been particularly interested in this grandmother's line of descent because I grew up believing that her grandmother, also Helen, was the daughter of James Hogg, the remarkable Scottish peasant poet, author of the *Private memoirs and Confessions of a Justified Sinner*, an extraordinary novel described by Karl Miller (someone to be reckoned with) as 'one of the great works of European Romanticism'.

We have a family copy of the fat first volume of *The Ettrick Shepherd's Tales* and I once wrote on the first page of it in my careful adolescent hand:

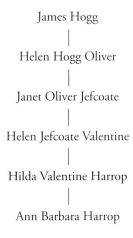

James Hogg
|
Helen Hogg Oliver
|
Janet Oliver Jefcoate
|
Helen Jefcoate Valentine
|
Hilda Valentine Harrop
|
Ann Barbara Harrop

This was long before I was Ann Thwaite. I felt myself lucky to have a poet and a storyteller as my great-great-great-grandfather. It gave me a stab of pleasure when I found 'A Boy's Song' and 'Kilmeny' in Quiller-Couch's *Oxford Book of English Verse* – included even though Hogg was distinctly Scottish – and, later, I felt personally involved when I read Walter Scott's Introduction (written in 1802) to Hogg's letters from his Highland tours, and André Gide's high praise in the introduction to a new edition of the *Confessions* in 1947. Gide was astounded by the book and his admiration increased with every page he read of this subtle and powerful condemnation of religious fanaticism. Karl Miller thinks the *Confessions* a finer novel than any that Scott wrote, more psychologically aware, more compassionate.

The *Tales* we had at home were prefaced with a 'Life of the Author' (initialled J.T.B. and undated), which told as romantic a story as any he had told himself. James Hogg was born in 1770 and it was said that his ancestors 'had held property in the forest of Ettrick as retainers of the Scotts of Harden, the line from which Sir Walter Scott sprang. But both chief and retainer had lost their lands, and the one was practising as a lawyer in Edinburgh, while the other followed the humbler pursuit of shepherd'.

James Hogg's story is one of continued efforts to triumph over adversity, of 'getting on' so impressively that, starting to write as a self-educated boy, he had soon written a song 'sung over all the length and breadth' of Scotland, published a book of poems and eventually found himself dining with Walter Scott, the most famous writer in the land. Hogg drank too much, published a lot and earned very little money. One day William Wordsworth would lament the passing of the 'mighty Minstrel'. In the meantime, they all had mixed feelings about him. After many vicissitudes, the Duke of Buccleuch rescued his situation and 'installed him rent-free in a farm at Attrive', where there now stands his statue overlooking St Mary's Loch.

J.T.B. tells of Hogg's late marriage to Margaret Phillips – in 1820 in his fiftieth year. J.T.B. does not name his children. It was many years before I discovered that James Hogg had officially four daughters – Jessie, Margaret, Harriet and Mary. No Helen. And there was no possibility, it seemed, that Helen Hogg belonged to the next generation, a grand-daughter, as James's only son had no children. There *was* a New Zealand connection. Harriet and her husband, Robert Gilkison, had arrived in Dunedin with their nine children in 1879. I have a letter to my mother from one of their grand-daughters, Norah Parr of Lower Hutt, dated in 1984: 'Sorry about your disappointment; we were always amazed at the number of people *wanting* to be related to J.H. We tried to keep quiet about it.' It was a curious thing to say when, not long before, she had published a delightful book, *James Hogg at Home*.

I remained convinced that there must be some connection. It was unlikely to be a matter of merely 'wanting'. There are three old letters from my Valentine grandfather referring to James Hogg. In one he wrote quite clearly that Helen Hogg 'was a daughter of James Hogg, the famous Scottish poet, who was known as the Ettrick Shepherd.' But my grandmother was dead by the time he was writing; in any case, he said, she was 'not deeply interested in such matters'. Perhaps the reason Norah Parr was inclined to keep quiet on the subject of James Hogg's possible descendants, and the reason my grandmother was also not very keen on the subject, was that they both guessed that Helen Hogg was illegitimate. I decided to try and find out if this were so. I knew there was an alternative chance that she was a daughter of one of James's brothers, but I clung to the hope of a direct descent from the remarkable writer. It's interesting that in 1891 Janet Jefcoate, Helen's daughter, sent to Scotland for a copy of her own birth certificate and, querying why the letter 'L' was after her name, was told that it stood for 'lawful'. Very many births were out of wedlock. My cousin, Helen Davidson, recounting the story of the 'L' put !! by it, as if it was impossible to imagine a birth in our family that was anything but lawful.

I got in contact with Gillian Hughes, who probably knows more about James Hogg than anyone else living. As I write this, she has just co-edited the first volume of his letters, part of a scholarly edition of Hogg's works that already stretches to fifteen volumes, and she is working on a biography. She had quite recently spent some time in Dunedin, where, because of the Gilkison connection, there is a good deal of material of one sort and another. I myself had had the chance to see in the Otago Museum a curious collection of memorabilia deposited by the family. It included Hogg's court dress, in which he thought he had narrowly escaped being knighted by George IV.

Gillian Hughes drew my attention to two daughters of James Hogg born long before his marriage and both acknowledged by him – Kate, born in 1807, and Elizabeth born three years later (not Helen). J.T.B. and Norah Parr had understandably not mentioned either of them. But we know James did not take these results of his 'dizziness' lightly. 'Love is like a dizziness', he wrote more than once, but 'was there ever a young man disgraced by acknowledging a child?' Karl Miller's book *The Electric Shepherd* is good on this no longer embarrassing subject.

I had told Gillian Hughes that Helen Hogg had married Peter Oliver, a tailor, in April 1826; we know for certain that these were my great-grandmother's parents. The name 'Oliver' bound us closer to James Hogg's family. In 1833 Hogg mentioned he had a tailor of that name and, more importantly, his younger brothers, David and Robert, had both married sisters called Oliver. It seemed likely to Gillian Hughes that I was descended from David Hogg, who was known to have had four sons and two daughters, one of whom, Isabel, was born in 1818; the other she had not been able to trace. Working it out from her age on the 1851 census, I realised Helen Hogg must have been born around 1807, before David Hogg married Helen Oliver. Was she *his* daughter?

Checking the Scotlandspeople website, we found there was no Helen born around 1807 to David Hogg – but, to my delight, there was a girl called Helen registered by James Hogg on 27 March 1808, in the right part of Scotland. Gillian Hughes wasn't entirely convinced that it was the right James Hogg and in the end I have come myself to realise that, if there is any connection between my family and the writer's, it must be much more remote than I had been led to believe. In the old Langholm graveyard in Dumfriesshire we found not only a tombstone commemorating my great-great-grandparents, Peter Oliver and Helen Hogg, and their son James, but also an earlier inscription on another grave marking the burial place of what seem likely to be Helen's father, John Hogg, died 21 June 1847 aged seventy-seven, and her grandfather, James Hogg, died 10 February 1800 aged seventy years. So it would seem that I am descended from a James Hogg but *not* from the writer, alas! It is a connection I am understandably reluctant to abandon.

Peter Oliver came from Westerkirk in the upper reaches of the peat-stained

Esk – seven or eight miles above Langholm on the route to Ettrick. Barely inhabited now by the living, there is an impressive and crowded graveyard just over the old bridge at Bentpath. Peter and Helen Oliver lived in Kirkwynd in Langholm, a stone's throw from the old cemetery where we found their graves. Langholm is twenty-five miles or so south of Ettrick and it was here that their daughter, Janet, was born on New Year's Day in 1837, the year that Queen Victoria came to the throne. She was the third surviving among eleven children born to her mother, four of whom had died in infancy and one daughter when she was eight. Susan, two years younger than Janet, was very close to her. By the time of the 1851 census everything had changed.

Peter Oliver, the father of the family, was dead and although John, the eldest son, is described as a tailor, the young man was obviously not in a position to support the whole family as his father had done. Mary, the eldest daughter, now eighteen, was working as a servant at Murray House and Janet, my great-grandmother, at fifteen was apparently employed as a dairymaid in the local inn – no doubt learning some skills which would come in useful when she eventually got to New Zealand.

This energetic, competent girl (I am imagining her from later evidence) must have been eager to see the world beyond the Scottish Borders. She must have heard tales of William Oliver, her father's brother, who had emigrated to Australia in 1842. In his old age he would dispatch a friend, who was in Scotland, to check up on the Olivers.

It is one of these tantalising stories most families seem to have, suggesting how *nearly*, if only things had been slightly different (sometimes a cheating solicitor is part of it), they would have been really rich. In this case, I actually have a copy (made in New Zealand in 1889) of a letter written by Susan Little, my great-grandmother's sister, telling Janet of the arrival of an emissary from Uncle William. He had left when Janet was a child of five and her little brother, his namesake, 'a babe in arms'. Forty-three years later this Australian turned up in Langholm to take a look at the Olivers as possibly worthy heirs. ('Uncle has never been married and is very wealthy. He owns a very large quantity of land in Australia.') And what happened? Janet's older brother, John, by then a man in his fifties, was 'on a spree' and the visitor 'had to go to a public house to see him'. That seems to have been the last they heard of Uncle William's fortune. Helen Hogg Oliver remained the impoverished widow she had been for so many years.

To get back to the 1850s: Janet's father, Peter Oliver, was dead. His brother, William Oliver, was in Australia. Half the Hoggs, her mother's family, had gone to North America. It is not surprising that young Janet was not content to spend her life in quiet, predictable Langholm, however beautiful its situation in Eskdale, however attached she was to her sister, Susan. Gretna Green was a few miles away and it is tempting to think that that had something to do with Janet's thoughts of romance. That was the place, just her side of the Scottish border, where runaway young lovers from England could marry without their parents' consent.

But much more compelling in her imagination was the railway, that amazing modern miracle. Carlisle was not far off and the great London and North Western Railway connected Scotland directly with London. The powerful engines thundered through the countryside, devouring the miles between Glasgow and Euston (stopping in all sorts of unknown places, including Rugby and Wolverton), taking hours for a journey that had previously taken many days.

Some people hated the railways, thinking of the lines – with their associated cuttings, tunnels, bridges, viaducts, stations – as 'odious deformities' and 'dangerous and disfiguring abominations', which wrecked the countryside, stopped cows producing their milk, set hayricks on fire, and put the canal companies and inn-keepers out of business. But most people were entranced. These years when Janet Oliver was growing up were the years of 'railway mania'. Between 1844 and 1847 Parliament authorised the astonishing sum of £250 million to be spent on railway schemes, involving 9500 miles of railroad. People saw the railways as highways to romance and adventure, giving them easy opportunities to see sights they had never seen before and access to different worlds. The railway lines snaked across the country, linking places that had previously seemed impossibly far apart, bringing smooth, swift, relatively cheap travelling to people who, if they had travelled at all (and most had not), had endured uncomfortable, lurching rides and innumerable tedious stopovers.

One of the towns where the coaches had regularly stopped for refreshment and a change of horses was Stony Stratford on the Northamptonshire border, north-west of London, and not to be confused with Shakespeare's Stratford. It had always, from Roman times, been a busy staging post. It was on the Roman road, known as Watling Street, on a direct route from Verulamium (modern St Albans) to Towcester and on to Chester and the North. The High Street of Stony Stratford had for many years had inns and stables to cater for the stage coaches. It is still lined with what we would now call pubs, and houses which were once inns, with their wide archways giving access for the coaches to the stable yards behind. One of these was the Red Lyon and Horseshoe, whose landlord Edward Jefcoate (variously spelt) was another ancestor of mine.

I found Edward's son Richard in the 1851 census. He was described as a farrier and was living alone by then on the Pig Market, a widower of seventy-two. My cousin, Helen Davidson, who did some work on the Jefcoates, told me in a letter about a scatter of respectable Jefcoates – a couple of Henrys, one an M.A., a Northamptonshire vicar, another a mayor. Then she went on to say: 'It seems the devil drink at the Red Lyon and Horseshoe put our Richard, the publican's son, into the workhouse where he died in 1859.' This seems to fit in sadly with the fact that years earlier his two enterprising sons, Thomas and Samuel, had taken their families off to London to work on the railways and better themselves. Their children, Richard's grandchildren, became Londoners, as so many people did around this time.

The turnpike was falling into neglect. Stony Stratford was no longer the bustling town it had been. The railway lines (first of all the London Birmingham, and then the London North Western) by-passed it, transforming the village of Wolverton, just two miles away, into one of the principal railway towns in England, with a huge engineering works and, eventually, schools, a lodging house and a Science and Art Institute, all run by the railway company, LNWR. Richard's sons were moving with the times. Rather than work in nearby

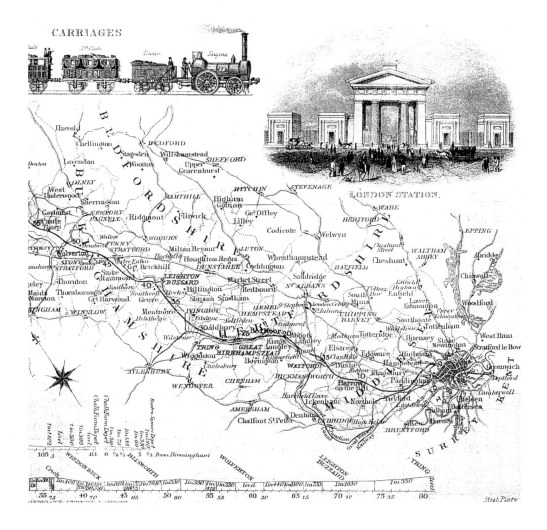

Wolverton, they wanted to be in London at the heart of things. Working for the railway connected you directly with the wonder of the age.

My great-grandfather, Thomas Jefcoate (named for his father), was born in Stony Stratford in 1839, and so were his next siblings, Lucy Ann and William, but by the time Edward was born in 1846, the family was living in the capital, in Charles Place off the Hampstead Road, a very short walk west from Euston Station – still shown as *London* on that early map, as none of the other great terminuses had yet been built.

The area north of the station was in chaos – much of it a vast building site where the new railway lines had cut through the old streets, with little regard for anything in their path. Huge goods yards – tracks and sheds – were being developed in Kentish Town and Camden Town, where hundreds of people had once made their homes. With the shunting yards and coal depots there was noise and movement in every direction. The chaos was caused, of course, by the very phenomenon that had brought the Jefcoates to London. We are used to this sort of thing in England in the twenty-first century, as motorways and Channel Tunnel rail links cut into the heart of London. The Jefcoates from Stony Stratford had never seen anything like it.

Charles Dickens described it in *Dombey and Son* with his usual relish:

> The first shock of a great earthquake had, just at this period, rent the whole neighbourhood to its centre. Traces of its course were visible on every side. Houses were knocked down; streets broken through and stopped; deep pits and trenches dug in the ground; enormous heaps of earth and clay thrown up; buildings that were undermined and shaking propped by great beams of wood. Everywhere were bridges that led nowhere; thoroughfares that were wholly impassable …, fragments of unfinished walls and arches, and piles of scaffolding and wildernesses of bricks …. The railroad … from the very core of all this dire disorder, trailed smoothly away upon its mighty course of civilization and improvement.

The railroad itself was, of course, out of bounds, but the surrounding area, in all that 'dire disorder', was my great-grandfather's playground as a boy. He was six years old when the family moved to London and his father found employment as a 'lampman' at Euston and somewhere to live close by the station in lodgings owned by LNWR. 'Lampman' sounds a lowly and routine job, looking after the lamps. (The next picture comes from Warne's *Railway Alphabet*.)

But in those days, before electricity, 'lampman' was a responsible position. People's lives depended on those lamps. And there were so many people. By 1854 over 10,000 passengers a day were coming regularly into London by train. Commuting had begun.

There was never any doubt that young Thomas would follow his father into employment with the London and North Western Railway. At just the time he joined the company, LNWR was described as wealthier than any other corporation in the world; it employed over 6000 men. Human travel had been totally transformed by the steam engine. The great locomotives, breathing flames and smoke, were a sight to stir men's hearts – and women's too. It was not surprising that for over a hundred years small boys, asked what they wanted to be when they grew up, were inclined to answer 'An engine driver'. Everyone was excited by the railways. As Dickens put it, 'The very houses seemed disposed to pack up and take trips.'

To be employed by a railway company gave prestige and security. Railway workers were in some sense 'servants' of their company, bound by complex rules and regulations, but they were also rewarded with uniforms, housing and reasonable wages. There were stringent tests of health, education and intelligence, and many boys attended night classes to get themselves up to the required level for promotion. High standards of behaviour were also expected. Railwaymen were required to work whenever and wherever they were wanted; there are dreadful stories of mammoth shifts, of men working sometimes for as many as fourteen hours out of the twenty-four.

Thomas's father died when the boy was only fifteen. By that time the family was living a little further north in Craddock Street at the bottom of Haverstock Hill, within the sound of the London and North Western Railway line, Chalk Farm Station and the LNWR depot. Thomas was already working at Euston, perhaps as a messenger, but he was hardly in a position to support his mother and the younger children. How they managed I have no idea; it is a relief to find that Hannah, his mother, eventually married again, a policeman with the rather splendid name of Charles Kingdom. This must have been a factor in freeing Thomas to marry young and in time to take the huge step of leaving for New Zealand.

While he was still in his teens Thomas Jefcoate was promoted to the job of goods guard. This was glory. The men who worked on the long distance trains were a sort of élite, regarding those on the suburban routes, or based at stations, with a friendly contempt. The word 'guard' dates back to coaching days when the protection of passengers (not least from highwaymen) was his principal concern. The railway guard was responsible, equally with the driver, for the safety of his train. He had to see that the carriages were properly coupled, that the lamps were in position, front and rear, check all doors were shut, test the brakes before starting and signal 'All clear' with his green flag. The goods guard had also to make sure of the safe loading of his goods and see that the right stuff was unloaded at the right stop. If the train broke down (as trains did from time to time), it was the guard's job to walk back along the line with his red flag (or red lamp if it was at night) and lay down his detonators about three-quarters of a mile behind his train to alert the following one that the earlier train was still on the line. (Horrendous accidents happened, but not, as far as I know, to any of Thomas Jefcoate's trains.) The guard had to be both physically energetic and literate, keeping a detailed record of each journey, the starting and stopping times at each station, goods carried, any incidents along the way and the names of driver, stoker, fireman, travelling with him. The life of the guard was desirable enough to be celebrated in song.

Now that he was a guard, Thomas Jefcoate found himself provided with housing in a railway terrace in James Street, Rugby, already an important junction in the middle of England. It was inevitable that he would often be unable to get back there at night. It had long been a question in our family: how had Thomas managed to meet Janet Oliver, when he was born in Stony Stratford and she in Langholm, far away beyond the Scottish border? The railway, of course, provided the answer. I imagine Janet had taken a job in Carlisle – moving on from the inn in Langholm where she was working in 1851 – and that it was in the very place where Thomas Jefcoate stayed when his shifts dictated an overnight stay.

However they met, they were both very young and it must have been exciting – a courtship constantly interrupted by Thomas's need to catch his train. They were married on Boxing Day 1859, rather surprisingly in London. This could suggest that Janet's mother, the widowed Helen Hogg Oliver, was not very keen on her daughter rushing (it may have been rushing) into marriage with a mere lad, and an English lad at that, whose family she had never met. There was also the question of denomination. Janet had, unsurprisingly in Scotland,

GASTON MURRAY | ALFRED PLUMPTON

been brought up as a Presbyterian. Thomas, we discover from the marriage certificate, was a Baptist and would remain so, devotedly, all his life, persuading Janet that it was, indeed, the path to salvation.

Although he gives 'full' as his age on that certificate, Thomas was not twenty-one until the following August. Janet was older – twenty-three on New Year's Day 1860, a few days after the wedding. (They would diminish this age difference a little a few years later when they filled in their emigration forms and declared Thomas was twenty-four and Janet twenty-five.)

They were married in the Bloomsbury Baptist Chapel in Bloomsbury Street, which in those days was a continuation of Gower Street beyond Great Russell Street, just south of the British Museum and within easy walking distance of Euston. It was obviously much more convenient than Langholm or Rugby for Thomas's immediate family – but also for his Uncle Samuel and Aunt Rebecca and all the Jefcoate cousins who had made the same journey from Stony Stratford to London and were likewise – most of the men – working on the railway. It is good to see that one of the witnesses at the marriage was Janet's younger sister, Susan Oliver.

I realise, with a start, that Janet and Thomas Jefcoate were married only a short walk away from where that other pair of emigrant great-grandparents, Sarah and James Harrop, were united at St Pancras less than four months later. The Harrops, as we saw in Chapter 2, also took a few years after their marriage to decide to leave England. These Harrops and Jefcoates never met. But the next generation did, and I can't help wondering whether Arthur Harrop and Helen Jefcoate Valentine – who knew each other in Hokitika – ever discovered the fact that their parents, Anglican and Baptist, had been married in the same part of London at almost the same time.

I must now look for the reasons why Janet and Thomas Jefcoate decided to emigrate. I would guess that my great-grandmother had a good deal to do with the decision. How she must have hated the idea of bringing up a family, with Thomas so often away, in a poky house in a railway town, so unlike the Eskdale of her own childhood. It was all very well for Thomas, I can imagine her thinking, rushing up and down England in his fine uniform, with that challenging responsibility, with every day different. Poor Janet was stuck in the small terrace house in smoky Rugby, seeing Thomas briefly when he dashed in between shifts. She was often alone at night, with Thomas in lodgings in Scotland or in his mother's home in north London.

Perhaps Thomas himself was beginning to tire of not being his own master. He had signed up to devote himself exclusively to the service of the company and it was the shareholders who were benefiting from his long hours and hard work. It was sad to be permanently on call, to have to spend so much time away from Janet. Just at this time, in 1862, the *Lancet*, the respected medical journal, was pressing for a limitation in railway workers' hours. Thomas must also have been well aware of what might be called the condition of England. For every sun-lit landscape and pleasant country town he saw from his window, there would be scenes of dismal industrial wastelands, of crowded tenements and dark Satanic mills.

The lithograph opposite, elegant as it is, portrays the railway train 'gliding' (a word that was often used) over the Stockport Viaduct on Thomas's regular route, high above a polluted river, engulfed in the smoke from the chimneys of crowded houses and factories. Was this the world he wanted for his children?

The idea of emigrating to New Zealand seems to have been put into Janet's head by a friend from the Rugby Baptist Chapel, one Charlotte Twigger, who left Rugby for Canterbury in 1863. This useful piece of information comes from a publication celebrating *125 years of Spreydon Baptist Church* – Spreydon being the area of Christchurch, near the Addington Show Grounds, where my grandmother would be born. The writer of this publication gives rather a wrong

impression of Thomas, calling him a 'farm labourer from Rugby'. But it was as a farm labourer (that most welcome of immigrants) that Thomas signed up for the voyage, giving his place of origin as Northamptonshire. Living in London from when he was a small boy, Thomas Jefcoate had certainly never worked on a farm, but he may well have had some experience of rural life in brief holidays with his relatives in Stony Stratford. (The census records are full of remaining Jefcoates.) It is difficult to believe that this keen Baptist actually lied to secure an assisted passage. But it is understandable. There was as little demand for goods guards in New Zealand in the 1860s as there was for 'farm labourers' in Rugby, that busy railway junction.

Janet Jefcoate found herself pregnant early in 1864, over four years after the wedding. Again there may have been early miscarriages or stillbirths. The decision was made to go to the other side of the world. They were offered places on the *Eastern Empire*, an American-built brig, only about two years old, that sailed from Gravesend on Friday, 26 August 1864, with about 300 passengers, nearly all assisted emigrants and nearly all with friends already in the Colony. For the Jefcoates there was the pleasant fact that they were also travelling with friends. The shipping list brackets them together as a party and gives their passage money in one chunk as £105. The party consisted of three young married couples, the Jefcoates, Grace and James Palmer and Mary and Edward Ball, with the Balls' two young children, three-year-old Amy Jane and the baby, Rebecca. It is tantalising to know nothing more about these travelling companions than that Edward Ball was a printer, and from London rather than Rugby.

It is good to know that, though there were many of the same problems – and occasional pleasures – on the *Eastern Empire* as there were on the *Lancashire*

Witch, it was a far less stressful voyage. There was the same seasickness, the same feeling of being caged; there were some rather less violent storms and the same long days becalmed. (Coleridge was quoted again, as the *Eastern Empire* also became 'as idle as a painted ship upon a painted ocean'.) There were the same many months without the chance of walking on dry land. There were also the same delights of albatrosses, of dolphins, of the sky at night and the phosphorescent sea.

The main difference was that there was no infectious disease on board. This voyage is also well recorded in a diary. John Pringle's detailed account can be read in the Canterbury Museum in Christchurch. It must have been a great relief to Janet Jefcoate, my great-grandmother, that the *Eastern Empire* was such a healthy ship. By the time they set sail, she was seven months pregnant. The ship's doctor told John Pringle 'that on no ship that he ever sailed before (and he had made five voyages to New Zealand) had he seen so little sickness.'

A son was born to Janet and Thomas Jefcoate on the forty-ninth day at sea, 17 October 1864, Latitude 03°07'N, Longitude 23°47'W. It was somewhere in the middle of the South Atlantic – perhaps half-way between the two continents of South America and Africa, not far north of the Equator. John Pringle wrote in his diary:

> I have today great pleasure in chronicling the first birth we have had on board, both mother and child are doing remarkably well. A shark was seen today about the ship, which has influenced the lively imaginations of some of the passengers, who associated its appearance with the birth.

The child was called Thomas Eastern Empire Jefcoate, in honour of his sea-borne birthplace; he was always known to my mother as her 'Uncle East'. (I remember hearing about him in my childhood; he died when I was four. How extraordinary to be born in such a place and to carry such a strange name.) Two other babies were born on that voyage, and two small children and one baby died. These same children might well have died even if they had stayed at home; two of them were certainly doing poorly when they came on board. When people lament the continuing terrors and cruelty of the times we are now living in I always think of that great improvement in the developed world, the decline in infant mortality.

John Pringle in his diary tells of times on the *Eastern Empire* when, in 'delightful weather', he not only enjoyed his existence, but felt that the journey came 'little short of a pleasure trip. Habit and hope our best comforters.' I wonder if Janet got to talk with him. He came from her part of Scotland and actually at one point compares a calm sea with St Mary's Loch, where the monument to James Hogg – whom I now admit was unlikely to be Janet's grandfather – had been erected just four years before.

There were other times when John Pringle felt less contented. 'Under the best conditions', he wrote on the sixty-fourth day, 'a voyage is one of the severest tests to try a man. They are lackluster joyless weeks, those spent on the sea. It is a wonder to me how any sane man can be a sailor.'

The sailors on this voyage seemed to be a particularly rebellious lot. Pringle overheard some of them discussing plans for deserting when they reached New Zealand. They had a low opinion of their captain, who was a teetotaller and wanted a temperance ship. When he asked them to scrub the decks after 8 p.m., when the passengers had mostly gone below, they refused to do so, saying that never before had they been asked to work after 8 p.m. The crew were really in control.

On the ninety-ninth day the passengers' monotonous hours were enlivened by a fight. The second mate lost his temper with one of the men and threatened to take his fists to him. When the sailor threw off his oilskin jacket in defiance and faced up to him, the officer attacked him. The two of them were fighting when, as Pringle recorded,

> in the middle of it, the Captain saw them and at once put a stop to it, at the same time summoning the offender aft; the rest of the sailors followed. The Captain was going to put the poor fellow in irons for striking his officer. But his companions would by no means allow it to be done. They coolly told the Captain that if he put him in irons they would leave him to work the ship himself: that in short they would rather be all ironed themselves. Such being the state of affairs the Captain prudently left matters as they were.

There was every reason for the Captain to keep the crew at work – and they, after all, had a pride in the ship too. A full-rigged ship was indeed,

> a noble sight when fairly out in her native element. Her solid, lengthened hull, rising with a graceful curve at her bows and stretching out like the horn of a unicorn, her long jib-bow, her rigging with its framework of ropes and spars and tall towering masts, and then its clothing of canvas, is superb. As a whole it presents a beautiful combination of grace and strength: graceful in its fair and balanced proportions, and strong enough to battle with and baffle the bravest winds and the angriest seas.

Another fight gives cheering evidence of the lack of any racial prejudice among the passengers. One of the sailors had stolen a pair of boots belonging to another, who happened to be black, a native of one of the West Indian islands. In a fight the black sailor managed to inflict a bloody nose on the thief. 'Darkie is a favourite on board', Pringle wrote, 'being a light-hearted, good-natured fellow. But he has shown today that he lacks neither the will nor the power to stand up for himself. His success was rewarded with cheers and congratulations from the onlookers.'

As they neared New Zealand, the spirits of the passengers rose, but by Christmas morning, the 118th day since setting out, there was still no sight of the promised land. John Pringle wrote in his diary: 'Every eye was on the alert and every face bore the impress of expectance; it was two o'clock in the afternoon before a very hazy indistinct appearance of land became visible.' But the wind had dropped and it was 5 January 1865 before they finally arrived, pleased to find the *Eastern Empire* declared 'the cleanest ship ever to berth at Lyttleton.'

The verdict reported by the diary-writer was confirmed in the *Lyttelton Times* of that date, which also praised the ship's Armstrong cooking range, the well-ventilated hospital and the water distilling apparatus. It had been a long voyage, well over four months, but one for which the Jefcoates, with their healthy new baby, were particularly grateful.

Charlotte Twigger, the friend who had come out to Christchurch in 1863 was, I feel sure, there to meet the Jefcoates at Bricks Wharf on the River Avon in Christchurch, where the passengers were brought in a smaller boat. That this Charlotte was important to the Jefcoates is suggested not only by the Spreydon Baptist Church publication I mentioned but by the fact that when Thomas Eastern Empire's sister was born the following year she was given the equally amazing name of Charlotte New Zealand Jefcoate. The name Charlotte went down into the next generation too, so that both my mother and I had Auntie Lotties.

Conditions in these early days were difficult. The Jefcoates lived at first in some sort of 'sod hut' at Spreydon. 'There were no sewers, no water supply, no drains, electricity, gas or transport', we are told. 'From my early days I used to work very hard when we first came to New Zealand', Janet would write to a Hogg cousin in Canada thirty years later. How Thomas was making a living is not quite clear. He was certainly working for the Twiggers, but early on had all sorts of enterprises of his own. He did anything he could find to do, including a milk round (with milk from the Twiggers' farm) which he combined with evangelising to gain support for a new Baptist chapel in the area. One of Thomas's grand-daughters has put on record that 'Grandfather was a fiery Baptist, a born leader, an enthusiastic organiser. He had an authoritative personality, never happier than when managing men and machines.' The goods guard was coming into his own and finding plenty of scope for his energies.

It was a long way from Spreydon to the nearest Baptist church and the new arrivals soon decided that something should be done about it. They worshipped first of all in a sod house belonging to the Twiggers, which had been used as a barn – a one-roomed building, with a thatched roof and a dirt floor. The story is that Thomas said it would do very well. 'We will clean it out, white-wash the walls and level the floor' – at which one of Twiggers' men asked, 'Who is to be the chief corner-stone seeing they are all sods?' and Thomas replied, 'Jesus Christ, the same yesterday, today and forever.'

The first service was held on 17 September 1865, that is late in the very year of the Jefcoates' arrival. By April 1867 the congregation had built a new chapel with the Jefcoates among the founding members. It was opened, free of debt, on a section given by Joseph Twigger at the corner of what is now Sylvan Street and Lincoln Road.

The Jefcoates were still in the Christchurch area when my grandmother, Helen – always known as Nellie – was born in 1868. I'm not sure how she managed to escape a bizarre pair of middle names. It seems to have been not long after her arrival that Thomas had saved enough to take out a mortgage on a farm at Pareora West, ten miles out of Timaru, later identified by my mother as 'beyond the Salt Water Creek estuary and the Chinese market gardens'. A considerable area of land had been bought by Joseph Twigger on the north bank of the Pareora River when the Otipua sheep station had been sub-divided – and he was happy to sell on to Thomas Jefcoate.

Thomas went south with two horses and a dray carrying all the family possessions, which were nearly swept away when he had to cross the Rangitata River in flood. Janet took her three small children by sea, joining Thomas in Timaru. He called his new acquisition 'Prospect Farm' and built the family a large two-storey house, looking more substantial than it really was, and a huge contrast to the terrace house he had left behind in Rugby. My grandfather, Jim Valentine, who would marry Thomas and Janet's daughter Nellie and knew the house from his courting days, said it was made of 'puddled clay' (more commonly known as cob) though 'its walls looked like stone'. Years later he saw it abandoned and in ruins.

Thomas – even as he established his farm and built his house – wasted no time playing his part in improving things for the community. He was very soon, just as he had been in Christchurch, on a committee to raise money to establish the first Baptist church in the area and became its first secretary. And he was on another committee with the task of establishing a school. Pareora West school opened in 1874 with forty-five children on the roll including four of his own, and with Thomas the Chairman of the School Committee. Five more Jefcoate children would follow in due course. After East, Charlotte, Nellie and Janet came Harry, Fred, Lucy, James and Susan – a child every second year until Janet, their mother, was in her forties. The children's names are in the school records and are also shown as borrowers of books from the Pareora Sunday School Library.

Somehow in these years, if we are to believe his obituaries, Thomas was working as a contractor – or at least organising men and machines involved in the making of the main road to Fairlie and, as time went on, he had the chance to use some of his English experience on a good length of the Mt Somers railway and the Caroline Bay rail cuttings. When we were in Timaru my brother and I posed to have our photograph taken above that Caroline Bay cutting, wondering just when and how our great-grandfather had been involved. The 1870s was the major period for the development of both road-making and the railways in New Zealand. Thomas's later financial problems may have been caused by his having devoted too much time in these years to his work as a contractor, diverting his men from things they should have been doing on the farm. Or perhaps he was spending too much time and money on the church and the school.

Prospect Farm seemed to be prospering. In its heyday it had extensive out-buildings, including a mill driven by a portable steam engine, and a great many sheep that cannot be seen in a faded photograph from the 1880s crowded with, as my cousin Helen put it in a letter, 'three drays, nine horses, one dog, one cow, one milk-maid, four other long-skirted figures and six wearing trousers.' A busy scene, suggesting how proud Thomas was of how far he had come.

I have a poor copy of another photo, taken at Christmas 1888, which shows an impressive gathering of the whole family: two stout, prosperous and contented-looking parents, Janet and Thomas Jefcoate, with their nine children, on the lawn beside their farm house. East was by now twenty-four, but looking much older, with his moustache, his sober suit and watch-chain, and a flower in his button-hole. (Was he now working as an auctioneer as he certainly did later?) My grandmother, Nellie, is on East's left, with her hands on her mother's shoulders. They were always close and my own mother would remember years later being taken up by her mother, Nellie, to put flowers on Janet's grave. In the photo the youngest, Susan, aged ten, sits at her mother's feet, bearing the name of the aunt back in England, the sister Janet had not seen for twenty-four years. Janet looks exactly as she was described: 'of a most hospitable and kindly nature.'

Although my grandmother was only twenty when that photo was taken, she had been working for years in the Pareora West school. A local history, *The Southburn Story*, says that in 1879 the daughter of the Chairman of the School Committee, Helen ('Nellie') Jefcoate, 'a pupil aged 11 years and 6 months' was appointed to the position of pupil-teacher. It is an extraordinarily young age for such an appointment. (In their memoirs Jim Valentine writes 'twelve' and my mother 'fourteen'.) The child was, of course, supposed to be continuing his or her own education after school hours with the help of the headmaster. But Nellie seems to have been unlucky. She is said to 'have often gone ahead with teaching when the headmaster, Mr Binnings, was late in his gig from Timaru, having allegedly been "on the binge" the night before.'

There was obviously a need for a different headmaster. The Education Board was worried about the school and picked out Jim Valentine, a clever young man, nearly twenty-three, who had himself started as a pupil-teacher at Waikouaiti and had been much luckier with his headmaster, Samuel Moore, a Dublin graduate, who realised Jim's exceptional gifts. When he was appointed to the Pareora school he had recently completed his teacher's training with a first class B.A. at Otago University.

The Chief Inspector of Schools for South Canterbury said to him: 'See that you put your best foot foremost and don't disappoint me.' He was told that 'a Mrs Jefcoate, wife of a farmer living at Pareora' would look after him. Jim was to report to the Stone Stables at 3 p.m. on 13 December 1886. My grandfather wrote in his memoirs:

> I took to her at once and we drove away from the Stables in a trap. She had to pick up some bread in Woolcombe Street and while we were waiting for the baker to carry the loaves to the trap, I saw a smiling girl dressed in a print frock with small brown rings all over it as a pattern …. Mrs Jefcoate introduced her to me as 'My daughter, Nellie, Mr Valentine, who is to teach in the school with you.'
>
> Never shall I forget that meeting, and that smile; it won my heart there and then and it gives me the greatest joy to say that after three years of somewhat stormy wooing, she married me. I never varied – she was my only love.
>
> It was harder for her to choose amongst all the men that wanted her. She was spared to me for 47½ years. I thank God for those years of close loving partnership. We were always lovers; we always found complete satisfaction with each other ….

Further on in his story, Jim Valentine reveals the fact that at the time of their meeting outside the baker's shop they were both engaged to other people.

Nellie Jefcoate was engaged to the Reverend James Standring, a Baptist minister of twenty-seven, ten years older than she was. Apparently during a visit to Prospect Farm the minister had fallen violently in love with her. Her father had obviously thought it a good match and had urged on an engagement. 'I soon found out there was little affection on her side', Jim Valentine wrote.

> Though she had resigned her position to prepare for marriage, no one was more delighted than she when early in May 1887, after Standring had quarrelled with her father over some religious question, she was able to give him back his ring. I also was nominally engaged to a woman nearly ten years my senior and I at once became free from this entanglement.

Who *she* was and why Jim had allowed himself to become 'entangled' we will never know. 'For the next two years', he went on, 'I acted as an ardent wooer of the only girl I ever loved. It wasn't till June 1889 that she definitely said she would marry me – and she never looked back.'

My grandparents, my mother's parents, Helen Jefcoate and James Valentine (Nellie and Jim) were married on Boxing Day 1889, the Jefcoates' thirtieth wedding anniversary. Nellie had declared that she would not marry him and stay in Pareora so Jim had been looking around for another post. It was hard moving from his own small country school to teach in a much bigger school in North East Valley, Dunedin. It was not just that the school was large, the classes were huge. Jim records that one year he had 'about 120 pupils in Standard 3'. But he was thankful to gain some 'useful experience of the management and the discipline of a large school'. They happily rented a house on a hillside with a fine orchard and plenty of room for Nellie's horse, Victor, to graze. This was a high-spirited creature, 'a descendant of the famous stallion Betrayer …. My wife used to ride him all over Dunedin. Everyone in North East Valley knew her and her pony.'

It was while Nellie and Jim were in Dunedin that things came to a head at Prospect Farm. For years apparently Thomas Jefcoate had been living on a substantial overdraft; the mortgage had never been paid off. Now the bank forced him to sell the farm and some of his considerable assets. (A local history says that the land he owned or leased had a rateable value of £2,504, a vast sum in those days.) Jim Valentine recorded in a letter that 'He realised enough by the sale of Prospect Farm and another farm to pay off all his debts and make a trip to England.'

This was rather remarkable. In the late nineteenth century overseas return trips were practically unheard of. Most emigrants stayed; those who went back, went back because they hadn't been able to settle. Willingly to face two of those long voyages – still very long, even after sail had given way to steam – was unusual, to say the least. They were away when East married Emily Jane Merry (my mother's 'Aunt Dolly') on 16 June 1891. Travelling round England and Scotland, the Jefcoates must have visited many of their remaining brothers and sisters, nephews and nieces and cousins. One of the next generation, Leonard, son of a cousin David Jefcoate – who had been another railway guard but was by now a 'lodging-house proprietor' – seems to have travelled back with Thomas and Janet. He was later joined by his brother, Stanley, so there are now a number of Jefcoates in New Zealand descended from that line, sharing with us an ancestor, Richard, the Stony Stratford farrier.

On their return to New Zealand, Thomas Jefcoate started afresh, taking out a mortgage on Grange Farm at Kapuka, Oteramika, in Southland. Jim Valentine would say it was over 1000 acres, too big a place to handle financially. Thomas's grand-daughter, Constance Whyte, young James Jefcoate's daughter, says that her father considered he had had a raw deal. He had worked hard and long on Thomas's land throughout his youth. He worried that Thomas, ignoring local advice, had tried to produce grain without fertiliser, which had grown well at Pareora and failed at Oteramika. When in 1900 James asked for a partnership or some land of his own, so that he could marry, Thomas apparently would not help him. He had made his own way in the world and he expected his children to do the same. But the reality was that Thomas was again on the verge of selling up. When he entered James's marriage to Christina Munro in the family Bible, Thomas wrote by his own name 'late of Grange Farm'. He was sixty; a life of hard physical work was taking its toll and nothing had gone right at Oteramika. He spent the next years as an Inspector for the Public Works Department in Otago.

For me 1900 is most important as the year of the birth of my mother, Hilda Mary Florence, on 30 June in Timaru – a fourth child for Jim and Nellie Valentine, a sister for Graham, Jefcoate and Janet. For Thomas, her grandfather, it was most important as the year of his wife's death. She died on 5 October 1900. Thomas wrote in the Bible:

> Janet Jefcoate (Mother), the first to break the family link, after forty years of happy married life, at the home of her daughter, Lucy Bardsley, Pareora Villa, Boston Terrace, Wellington, aged 63. She fell asleep saying 'I see Jesus'.

Her body was taken to Timaru for burial; we saw her grave when we were there. It carries a verse that was printed on Thomas's own memorial card:

We shall sleep but not forever.
There will be a glorious dawn;
When we meet – to part, no, never –
On the Resurrection morn.

Thomas Jefcoate, that devoted Baptist, had complete faith in the Resurrection and in some sort of heavenly reunion. Here is Janet's memorial card:

In Affectionate Remembrance

OF

JANET JEFCOATE

BORN AT

Langholm, Dumfrieshire, Scotland, January 1, 1837

DIED AT

Wellington, North Island, New Zealand, October 5, 1900

Entombed in Timaru Cemetery, South Island, New Zealand.

Only "good-night," beloved—not "farewell!"
A little while and all His saints shall dwell
In hallowed union, indivisible—
Good-night !

Until we meet again before His throne,
Clothed in the spotless robe He gives His own,
Until we know even as we are known—
Good-night !

My mother's father's family: the Valentines and the Maxwells. * indicates a couple entered twice

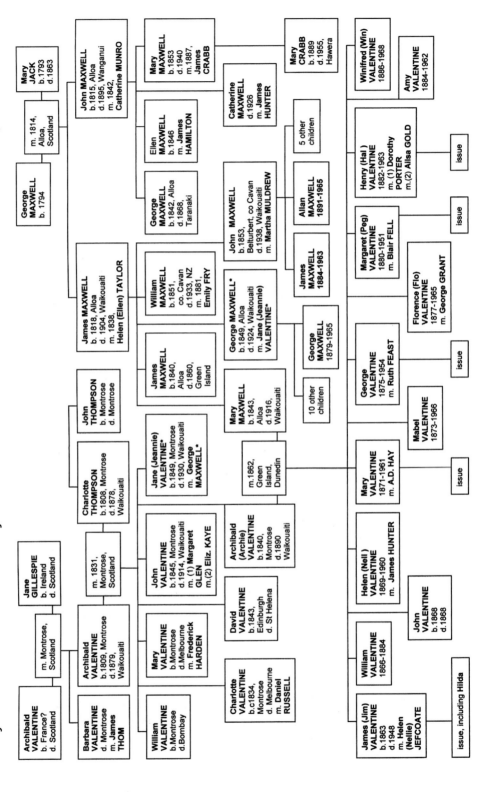

CHAPTER 5

Mainly about the Valentines and the Maxwells

By the time of my mother's birth in 1900, my grandfather, James (Jim) Valentine, was the headmaster of a large primary school, Timaru South, to which he had been appointed around the time this fourth child was conceived. The Valentine family is extremely well documented, as I suggested in my introduction to this book. Between 1937 and 1947 (the year before he died) my grandfather, 'under persuasion' by his children, wrote a long account of his background and his own life. Then in 1968, his much younger sister, my Great-Aunt Win, the last of her generation, also wrote her memoirs, finishing them, as her brother had, only a short time before she died.

One of the problems of writing family history, of making it readable and intelligible, is the repetition of names. It was bad enough with all those Anguses in the first chapter. Now the names are even more confusing. To give an idea of the problems: Jim Valentine's father Archibald (whom I will call Archie to distinguish him from *his* father) married Mary, the daughter of James Maxwell, whose brother, John, also came to New Zealand. Both Maxwell brothers had daughters called Mary and sons called George after their grandparents. There were Johns and Williams on both the Valentine and Maxwell sides and numerous men called James: sons, sons-in-law (Hamilton, Crabb) and grandsons. The women are not so much of a problem apart from the several Marys, who are important, and Jim's sister and wife, both baptised as Helen, though one was known as Nell and the other Nellie. Two of Archie's daughters were Amy and Winifred, named in homage to Sir Walter Scott, and one wishes Guy Mannering and Quentin Durward had inspired some more unusual names for the sons in both the Valentine and Maxwell families. But they generally stuck to the Scottish habit of naming each generation of boys after the previous one.

Another complication is that there were two Valentine/Maxwell marriages. As I said, my great-grandfather, Archie Valentine, married Mary Maxwell. When

Archie's sister, Jeannie, arrived years later in New Zealand with their elderly parents, it was not long before she married Mary's brother, George Maxwell, who was born in 1849, and is not to be confused with his cousin – the other George Maxwell – who was seven years older and is also important in this story. There is obviously a particular need in this chapter for the reader to consult the family tree from time to time.

Jim and Win, the two family historians, give conflicting accounts sometimes of the same incidents, but it is interesting to compare them and realise they are both writing with at least the intention of a scrupulous honesty that is not always found in family memoirs. Both Jim and Win tell sad stories of their paternal Valentine grandparents. Win was too young to remember them, but records an aunt telling her how well she recalled Win's grandfather 'after he had set up a business as a tailor in Waikouaiti, in tailcoat and silk hat (traditional wear for tailors in those days) wobbling down the street and occasionally falling over'.

Jim Valentine does not hesitate to say that both the tailor and his wife 'were the worst of drunkards'. This disgraceful old couple were Archibald and Charlotte Valentine who had come from Montrose on the east coast of Scotland. Win tells another family story that when her father, Archie, had to produce evidence of his date of birth for some reason, he wrote to his mother's brother, John Thompson, back in Montrose, for a copy of his baptismal entry (the only record available at that period), only to discover he had never been baptised. 'One of the many wrongs your parents did you', the uncle wrote. There's another story that the Montrose minister was shocked that these Valentine children never went to church and, discovering Archie had an excellent voice, managed to enlist him in the choir, in return for the promise of music lessons. This happily led to a lifetime of music for him and his own children in New Zealand. Everyone played the piano and both Archie and his son, Jim, would sing with the Waikouaiti Choral Society – in Mozart's *Twelfth Mass* and even the *Messiah*, though Jim admitted 'our choir was not really strong enough for this noble work.'

It is probably true that both Win and Jim emphasised the deficiencies of Archie's parents to give greater credit to their beloved father himself. How amazing it was that he was the man he was, with such parents. My mother, telling the story in her own memoirs, attributes her father's 'excessive horror of the Demon Drink' to these alcoholic grandparents of his, whom she called the skeletons in the family cupboard. It is no wonder that Jim urged his own six children to make a vow of temperance. I see one of my mother's first prize books is *Sunshine from Southern Skies*, by Mrs Harrison Lee of the World's Christian Temperance Union, presented to 'Hilda Valentine in appreciation of her helpfulness in the United Band of Hope, Nov. 30th 1911', the year she was eleven. It included a 'Total Abstainer's Armoury' and much else to encourage the young to be 'patient, persistent and plodding'. Nonconformist Christians tended to see prohibition as crucial at this time for the 'redemption' of New Zealand, but there would never be anything 'plodding' about Hilda Valentine.

Her father, Jim Valentine, had good reason for fearing alcohol. As a boy of fifteen in 1878, if he had not seen her himself, he had certainly heard that his grandmother, Charlotte Valentine, had been found dead at her front door in the Main Road, Waikouaiti, one morning. And he was actually in the same room, trying to sleep on a mattress, when his grandfather died in Jim's own bed the following year, having turned up on the family doorstep in a terrible state. The old tailor had walked from the Old Men's Home in Caversham, south of Dunedin, where he was supposed to be living, none of his adult children wanting to have 'such a terrible old man' in their houses, full of his grandchildren as they were.

Unsurprisingly, the drunken tailor and his wife were not themselves enterprising immigrants; they had arrived ten years after their son, Archie, first came to New Zealand and only when he was already well-established in Waikouaiti, not far north of Dunedin. Archie, my great-grandfather, went to sea as a boy. And so did his older brothers, David and William, who only get a mention here because they were said to have been ships' captains and buried in exotic places: David on St Helena and William in Bombay. Two sisters had gone to Melbourne and set themselves up as tailors and dressmakers in the family tradition. Perhaps they were all wanting to get away, not just from Montrose, but from those unsatisfactory parents, who would later follow some of them to New Zealand.

The Valentines were originally French. The family story has it that they were Huguenots, who left France to escape persecution at the time of the revocation of the Edict of Nantes in 1685. The name 'Valentine' (then pronounced with 'teen' at the end) certainly appeared in a list of Huguenot refugees in Canterbury Cathedral. My grandfather saw it there and my mother subsequently checked it in Huguenot Society records in the library of University College, London. This hardly fits in however with the story Win Valentine, my great-aunt, tells of her great-grandfather (father of the drunken tailor), which has a certain ring of truth.

> My Aunt Jeannie, Father's youngest sister, said she remembered her grandfather very well. He spoke broken English, and she remembered being lifted up to see him as he lay in his coffin. She remembered also her grandmother, of whom she was very afraid, being a big upstanding Irishwoman named Jane Gillespie, who could 'boss a regiment'.

It is impossible for this bossy Irishwoman's husband, the Frenchman with his broken English, to have left his native country as early as 1685, when the flood of Huguenot refugees came to England, for Jeannie was not born until 1849. But I'm sure it is true that a tailor called Valentine had come from France to Edinburgh, and then on to Montrose, but towards the end of the eighteenth century rather than earlier. My Great-Aunt Win visited Montrose in 1923 in time to see the Valentine tailor's and gentleman's outfitters shop at 50 Castle Street. The old shop had gone by the time Jim got there in 1928, and Win regretted that she had not taken a photograph. Jim had to content himself with seeing in the cemetery the grave of their great-aunt Barbara Valentine, 'beloved wife of Captain James Thom', and with walking along the very wharves where his father had played as a child, and where he had first decided to go to sea.

It was not from those wharves at Montrose but from Glasgow that Archie Valentine's ship the *Jura*, 792 tons, sailed for New Zealand on 2 June 1858. He was eighteen years old and one of thirty-two crew on board, together with 375 passengers, of whom over a hundred were children, and another eighteen babies. Again there survives at least one shipboard diary, but readers will already have a good idea, from the *Lancashire Witch* and the *Eastern Empire*, what life could be like on these long voyages.

The *Jura* diary – by a Scottish tenant farmer called John Mathieson – is brief and erratically spelt, just a few pages in an account book. But it gives a more vivid picture of the live animals – and 150 hens – on board ship than any of our other diarists. Though it seems the fresh meat was to be available only for the officers and seven cabin passengers, at least Mathieson got the chance to clip the sheep before they were slaughtered and was given a fleece for his trouble. He records the fact that the *Jura*, like the *Lancashire Witch*, had 'hooping coff' among the children, but fortunately most people thrived 'as well as we did on land.' Four small children died. 'A fue of the children newly weaned dus not thrive so well. They cannot get food so suiteable on the ship for them. The sucking ones dus fine.'

Altogether the *Jura* sailed across the world with remarkably little incident. Most of the talk towards the end of August was how long it would yet take. When they arrived in Port Chalmers, Dunedin's port, on 23 September 1858, they had had 115 days at sea. Mathieson thought: 'A sea voyage is not so wearisome a thing as one would sepose. A week soon slipps away.' In spite of the 'disconvennances and bussel', he suggested, 'there is something grand and noble in it.'

For two young people – a sailor and a passenger – it must have been not in the least wearisome, at least after they discovered each other. From other diaries we know how, in spite of the best efforts of the Captain to segregate crew from passengers, single men from single women, there was always a good deal of mixing. Indeed Mathieson mentions the dancing on the *Jura*, which must have been a pleasure for Mary Maxwell, my great-grandmother. She was just fifteen years old when the *Jura* left Glasgow. Fifty-five years later, when her granddaughter, my mother, was pleading with her father to be allowed to learn to dance, the old woman took Hilda's side. 'Let the bairn learn dancing, Jim!' she said, remembering perhaps the fun they had had when she herself had been my mother's age and had first met Archie Valentine en route from Glasgow to Dunedin.

Mary was travelling with her family. The shipping list gives James Maxwell, his wife, Ellen, and their four children, Mary, George, William and John. In fact there were five, but the eldest son, James, was eighteen and counted as a single man. James and Mary had been born at Alloa near Stirling on the River Forth. But it seems likely that the Maxwells, like the Olivers and Hoggs, had originally come from further south, in the Scottish Borders. Certainly when Jim Valentine as a boy, interested in his mother's family, asked his uncle, Johnny Maxwell, about them, he was told, 'Don't make inquiries about those old folk. More than one of the men was hanged by the English for stealing cattle on the English side of the Liddel that flows into the Solway Firth.' The precision of this reference persuades me that there might be some truth in it, much as one might want there not to be. The Liddel Water is right on the border, joining the Esk, south of Langholm, on its way to the Solway Firth. And the name 'Maxwell' is listed in Carlisle Museum among those of other convicted cattle thieves or 'reivers', as they were known.

My cousin, Helen Davidson, daughter and wife of farmers, wanting me to feel better about this particular inheritance, wrote, 'All farmers tend to be reivers. Don gave a bull reived from Coromandel bush to the new library we all helped to build. Dad rescued chooks and a rooster from a deserted farm-house at Arahiwi-Mamaku – and horses from the bush.' But the lawlessness in the Borders over 350 years was of a very different nature, as the word 'bereaved' reminds us. However, more recent Maxwells had moved further north and become respectable.

The grandfather of the children who travelled to New Zealand on the *Jura* was employed on the Parkhead estate, near Sheriffmuir in Stirlingshire, and had married Mary Jack, lady's maid at the big house. There is some evidence of a good relationship between the lady and her maid, as my Great-Aunt Win remembered seeing Mary Jack's magnificent satin wedding dress, a present from her employer, which on the bride's death many years later was sent out to her granddaughter, Mary Maxwell Valentine, in New Zealand.

In 1849, when Mary Maxwell was six years old, her family moved from Alloa, in Clackmannanshire, Scotland, to county Cavan, somewhere in the middle of Ireland, due west of Dundalk Bay. Here her two younger brothers were born and her father, James Maxwell, was employed for ten years as 'manager of an estate'. So his granddaughter, Win, tells us. That was what she was told and we know in addition only that the youngest boy, John, was born at Belturbert, which suggests his father was employed by the Earl of Lanesborough. In Ireland James Maxwell had certainly saved enough money to buy some land soon after his arrival in New Zealand; he was the only one in our family who was in a position to do that.

John Maxwell, James's brother, left Alloa for New Zealand two years after James had gone across to Ireland. John and his family sailed on the *Agra*, leaving London on 19 November 1851 and eventually arriving in Wellington on 1 March 1852. They travelled up the west coast of the North Island by the beach. In the early years, John Maxwell worked for other people – first at Rangitikei, then at Marangai, and finally at Westmere Lake for Messrs Taylor and Watt. The only son was called George, like his cousin, James's son, for both boys were named for their grandfather, left behind in Scotland. There were three daughters, Ellen, Catherine and Mary – Mary, like her cousin, James's daughter and my great-grandmother, carrying the name of the grandmother left behind in Scotland. So, as I have said, there were two George Maxwells and two Mary Maxwells, all very important in the family story. It is something of a relief that the two Marys didn't marry brothers. James's daughter married Archie Valentine, becoming Mary Valentine. John's daughter married James Crabb, becoming Mary Crabb and the mother of another Mary Crabb, who never married.

In May 1862, John Maxwell had saved enough to buy a farm on the main road between Westmere and Wanganui. He called the farm 'Parkhead', after the Scottish estate where he had worked with his father as a young man. George, his son, had been nine years old when they arrived in New Zealand; now in 1867, aged twenty-five, he was also in a position to buy land. He bought a farm at Manutahi, near Patea, in Taranaki, north west of Wanganui, and it is this farm, known as 'Alva Hill', that makes the story of these North Island Maxwells of central importance to my family. In 1955 my brother David inherited this farm through an extraordinary chance. Asked whose farm it had been, I would have said vaguely 'Oh it belonged to someone called Mary Crabb, a cousin of our grandfather. She had no children and was looking around in the family for someone who deserved some land'; using 'cousin' loosely, that was true. But the connection was really rather remote. If you look at the family tree, you will see that this George Maxwell was Mary Crabb's uncle and a first cousin of our great-grandmother, Mary Maxwell Valentine. The good fortune was that our Great-Aunt Win, Jim Valentine's youngest sister, knew both Mary Crabb and David's situation. She knew that since his days in New Zealand as a boy David had always wanted to farm, that he had worked on another cousin's farm after National Service in the Middlesex Regiment, which included some dangerous months as a platoon commander in the Korean War. Win also knew that he had trained at the Royal Agricultural College in Gloucestershire and had some experience on an English farm. But he had always known on which side of the world he wanted to live.

Win Valentine did not know Mary Crabb well but, she writes in her memoirs, 'I had promised her mother to give her any help I could if she ever needed it.' In 1952 a letter reached Win in Wellington from a Hawera solicitor asking her to come up; Mary Crabb was in hospital, had never made a will and wanted to discuss it with Win. Win was now retired and over the next three years she devoted herself to sorting out Mary Crabb's affairs. There was a great deal of money, not all of it tied up in the farms she had herself inherited: Parkhead and Alva Hill. Mary Crabb was rich, but had, Win wrote, 'been brought up to believe that spending money was a sin'. Win discovered that the family house where she lived in Wilson Street, Hawera, was 'literally falling to pieces; there was not a single room without at least one drip.'

Mary Crabb came out of hospital, moved into a new house, with completely new furniture and fittings, organised by the lawyer. Win came up again and helped Mary sort out the accumulations of many years. Nothing had ever been thrown out or given away. There were, sadly, a dozen baby gowns, which had presumably been Mary's own in the previous century and had been kept (together with three dozen napkins) for the child that she had never had. The house was full of clothes, which had once belonged to Mary's aunt Catherine and to her mother, who had died more than twenty years before, leaving her own wedding dress, worn just that once in 1887, hanging in a cupboard. There were 'pink flannelette chemises, nightdresses and drawers' galore, enough linen to stock a hospital, and letters and newspapers dating back to the 1860s. The Salvation Army, the Red Cross, CORSO and the Boy Scouts all apparently benefited, but much went to the rubbish dump and things were burnt which, as Win said, would have been of great historical interest if only she had had the energy and patience to sort them.

Mary Crabb died three years after the dismantling of the Wilson Street house and, when her will was read, it was found she had followed Win's advice. The Parkhead land near Wanganui went to three elderly sons of Mary Maxwell Valentine's brothers, another George, another James and James's brother, Allan. Alva Hill at Manutahi, to our delight, went to David Harrop, aged twenty-four. The residue of the estate was shared between seventeen other Maxwells and Valentines. Win had tried in vain, as David has since, to track down the descendants of Mary Crabb's aunt Ellen, who had married a James Hamilton in the 1860s and produced numerous children, Mary Crabb's first cousins. David's life would have been rather different if the children of these cousins had cared for Mary Crabb and – closer relatives as they were – had been the ones to sort out her life in the 1950s.

B ut how did it come about that Alva Hill had been inherited by Mary
Crabb? Her uncle, George Maxwell, had bought his land in Manutahi
from a Captain Frederick Ross in 1867. Ross had been allotted the block of
land (purchased originally by the New Zealand Company from the local tribe),
in return for his military service. To say that this was a time of 'unrest' in the
North Island is to underestimate the problems. The words 'rebellion' and
'insurgency' had been in use for years. The situation was very different from
that in the South Island, where there were fewer Maori and relations with them
remained relatively good.

This book is not the place to discuss at length the rights and wrongs of
these Land Wars – or Maori Wars, as they were still called when my father
was writing about them in the 1930s. I leave that to more recent historians, to
James Belich and Michael King. But some background is needed to put this
painful piece of family history in context. The Treaty of Waitangi enshrined the
policy that Maori should never be *forced* to sell even an acre of land, that every
sale should be the result of negotiation and agreement. But trouble, which
began in the mid 1840s, flared in Taranaki in 1855, only three years after the
Maxwells arrived. It may be too simplistic to say, as some did, that the basic
problem was that the settlers wanted more land than the Maori were prepared
to sell and the Maori feared settler expansion that would prevent them living
the life they wanted to live. Trouble flared again in Taranaki in 1868, largely
because of the Government's attempt to confiscate land from the Maori who
had rebelled against it, though there were many Maori, known as *kupapa*, who
realised they would lose more than they would gain by 'driving the Pakeha and
all his works into the sea'.

It is interesting I think to record how my father saw the situation when he
was writing seventy years ago. It can be compared with the evaluation of more
recent historians. In an Introduction, A.J. Harrop explained why he felt there
was a need for his book *England and the Maori Wars* in 1937:

> In this book we are dealing with the darkest period in the chequered story of
> New Zealand and one which still influences the relations of Maori and white
> man. The causes and results of the wars are imperfectly understood today
> and only great episodes of the struggle, such as the Maori defence of Orakau,
> the British disaster at the Gate Pa, and the raids of Te Kooti, have made
> any appreciable mark on what may be called the collective memory of New
> Zealand. We should not forget that a localized struggle about a plot of land
> into which, it may be said, 'some one had blundered', became a widespread war
> of extermination. A British officer who took part in this war wrote: 'You must
> remember we were fighting without gloves, and that it was war to the knife.'
> He was excusing the acts of a Maori leader of friendly natives who summarily

executed more than a hundred captured followers of Te Kooti – and there were many other things done on both sides during the war which could be justified only by some such plea. One of the remarkable things about the struggle is that it was never entirely a war of race against race. Even at the worst periods there were always some tribes who remained faithful to the British cause. It is questionable whether, without them and such leaders as Te Kepa and Ropata, it would ever have been possible to force the followers of the Maori King, of Titokowaru, and of Te Kooti to refrain from aggression – even after ten years. Inter-tribal rivalry had devastated New Zealand with war for centuries, and even the menace of white domination could not produce unity in the ranks of the Maori. That a part of the race could hold superior forces of Imperial and colonial troops at bay for so long a time is a remarkable fact.

By September 1864 nearly 10,000 imperial troops and 12,000 colonial militia and volunteers were involved. By 1868 George Maxwell was one of them, a volunteer with the Wanganui and Kai Iwi Cavalry. Most of the volunteers, like George, were farmers. George had only recently taken over his farm at Manutahi and there was a great deal that needed to be done. His diary for 1868 – which my brother inherited with the farm – is a typical farm diary. It reminded me of the one Philip Henry Gosse, one of my biographical subjects, had kept in Canada thirty years earlier. George is only a little less laconic. Both give the impression of the relentless, repetitive toil farming involves. George was continually cutting: ferns, cocksfoot grass for hay, thistles, firewood, rails for the stockyard. He was pulling up weeds, ploughing, milking the cows, rounding up cattle and horses, clearing ditches, day after day, week after week. Quite often, because he lived alone, he baked a loaf, boiled some beef or patched a pair of pants. The only breaks in the monotony were when, very occasionally, he had a rowdy night with his friends at home, or went over to the Morgans at Brunswick and got drunk, before returning to Manutahi at three o'clock in the morning.

Imagine the attraction of the call to arms. There is no mention, strangely, of any Maori problem in his diary and although George received his arms and accoutrements on 1 February and cleaned them on 2 March, there is no reference to any military training. He was undoubtedly already a good shot and an experienced rider, and he loved the glamour of the cavalry, as they galloped across the countryside. We know that, because at the back of his 1868 diary, George has carefully written out a long anonymous poem called 'The Officers' Requiem', which gives a vision of army life with a strong resemblance to Jane Austen's description of it in *Pride and Prejudice*. We can imagine George Maxwell having his head turned just as readily as Lydia Bennet had hers.

George's diary ends on 8 June 1868, two days before the murder of three men he knew, Cahill, Squires and Clarke, at Normanby, twelve miles north of George's farm. On 29 September 1868 the local newspaper, the *Evening Herald*, reported that 'Maxwell's house near Manutahi was burnt by Maoris at 7 am' that day.

The next we hear of George Maxwell is of his involvement in the notorious incident at Handley's woolshed at Nukumaru on 27 November 1868. The woolshed was in the vicinity of Tauranga Ika, the fortified pa built by Titokowaru, bracketed with Te Kooti in that quotation from my father, and also by Belich, as one of the two great 'prophet-generals' of the time. The woolshed incident is well documented, because an account of it in a history of New Zealand by G.W. Rusden, published in 1883, was the subject of a libel action, *Bryce v. Rusden*, heard at the Royal Courts of Justice in London in 1886. John Bryce won this action and received the extraordinary amount in damages of £5,000 (multiply by at least fifty to get some idea of its current value in NZ$.)

Rusden had written: 'Some women and young children emerged from the pa to hunt pigs. Lieut. Bryce and Sgt. Maxwell of the Kai Iwi Cavalry dashed upon them and cut them down gleefully and with ease.' The libel case involved thirty-two sworn statements taken in New Zealand from both Maori and Pakeha who were present. There were certainly no women involved, but there was a crowd of unarmed adolescent boys. Two of these were killed and several wounded as they rushed out of the woolshed, hearing shots, and found themselves among a body of mounted men, their sabres unsheathed, who lashed about before they realised the nature of the enemy.

From the evidence in Court it appeared that Lieut. Bryce had tried to stop the attack when he realised the situation. But James Handley, the owner of the woolshed, and another witness, George Peake, both named Sgt. Maxwell as one who had wielded his sabre with devastating effect. The Maori version of what happened on this dreadful day, from an interview in 1883 that Uru Te Angina gave to Rusden, appeared for years in a school textbook. George Maxwell never had a chance to give his side of the story. That he was guilty of causing the death of at least one boy seems sadly to be true. It is the word 'gleefully' that was surely a libel. But one cannot libel the dead.

On 28 December 1868 a patrol of the Kai Iwi Cavalry, under the leadership of Sgt. George Maxwell, was deployed to reconnoitre a ridge near the Tauranga Ika pa, just above Handley's woolshed. J.D. Wright, whose father was in the reckless patrol, wrote in his *Reminiscences of Wanganui in the 1860s*: 'We must remember they were local settlers, not highly trained, and all young and keen. They galloped their horses right up to the pa and Sergeant Maxwell was shot and I believe his body stayed on his horse for about a hundred and fifty yards before he fell.'

Another local settler, James Livingston of Hawera, recorded in his diary the news of George Maxwell's death: 'He was a fine young man, killed by the Maoris, while out with his troop at Nukumaru on a reconnoitring expedition.' The local paper had the headlines

CAVALRY ATTACK ON NUKUMARU
SERGEANT MAXWELL KILLED

The reporter commented: 'On Sunday night the Wanganui and Kai Iwi Volunteer Cavalry were ordered out, but the men did not seem to know by whom or for what purpose …. Sergeant Maxwell was shot dead close to the palisade. … We cannot as yet understand how our Cavalry was led to charge a Maori pa; nor can any of the men who were there enlighten us upon the subject.' The reporter's tone was very different from that of another item in the paper, under the headline

IN MEMORIAM

One of the bravest, if not the very bravest of our local Cavalry received his death wound yesterday while heroically leading his men to an attack on Titoko Waru's stronghold at Nukumaru. Mr George Maxwell was one of the first to join the Kai Iwi Cavalry and, although quite a young man, was unanimously elected Sergeant of the troop.

It quoted the official dispatch after the incident on 27 November, with its mention of Maxwell's 'extreme gallantry'.

A few days later George Maxwell was given a funeral with full military honours, a band playing the *Dead March*.

Hundreds of the principal inhabitants of Wanganui and surrounding districts formed the remainder of the procession. The shops, stores and places of business in the town were closed out of respect for the deceased. … Three volleys over the grave closed the mournful proceedings. May we not hope that –

Beyond the stormy battle-field
He reigns and triumphs now,
Sweeping a harp of wondrous song
With glory on his brow.

Twenty kilometres north of Wanganui there is now a town called Maxwell. It was named Maxwelltown in the late 1860s by the landowner Robert Pharazyn 'in memory of Sergeant Major George Maxwell, of the Kai Iwi Cavalry, who was fatally wounded during the Maori Wars in a skirmish with Hauhau warriors near Nukumaru Lake'.

In his will, George left the Manutahi farm to his father, John Maxwell. It was leased to James Crabb in 1887, the year he married George's sister, Mary. On John Maxwell's death in 1895 the farm was left to Mary, now Mary Crabb, and on her death to her daughter, also Mary Crabb, whose search for suitable heirs brought the land to my brother.

Long before his son George's shocking death, there must certainly have been letters from John Maxwell to his brother James in Ireland, making him realise that in New Zealand lay his chance to become his own master.

That it was to Dunedin rather than Wellington that James Maxwell took his family in 1858 is unsurprising. James had gone back from Ireland to Scotland (perhaps he had lost his job at a time when many people did) just when huge – and, as it turned out, final – efforts were being made by the New Zealand Company, in conjunction with the Free Church of Scotland, to recruit emigrants. They were encouraged to buy land from the Company, with part of the purchase price being ploughed back into the colony, paying for roads, bridges, schools, churches and so on. The Otago settlements, unlike those further north, 'had no Maori troubles worth speaking of', as Pember Reeves put it long ago. But the Company had been having problems in recruiting buyers at the sufficient price – £2 an acre – for the land purchased from its Maori owners. It had always hoped for substantial capitalists and some certainly came, but more of the emigrants were men like James Maxwell, who saw the distant country as their one chance to improve their children's lot in life. Sadly, like the Harrops on the other side of the South Island (as we saw in Chapter 2), the Maxwells lost their firstborn son not long after their arrival. James, who had travelled out on the *Jura* as a boy of eighteen, died of pneumonia in his new country just two years later.

We left Mary Maxwell, aged fifteen, and Archie Valentine, three years older, dancing together on the *Jura* in 1858. Mary's father was able to buy land – but rather poor land according to his granddaughter, Win – at Green Island Beach, south of Dunedin. Like the Jefcoates in Christchurch, the Maxwells had neighbours in Green Island whom they had known long before on the other side of the world. The two women, Mrs Ellen Maxwell and Mrs Joanna Cunningham, would walk the eleven miles into Dunedin each week carrying heavy baskets full of butter and eggs they had produced and walking back the eleven miles with stores for the week's meals.

But what of the young sailor, Archie Valentine? His son, Jim's, story and the one my mother told me was that, having fallen in love with Mary Maxwell on the *Jura*, he deserted his ship and lay low while the hunt for him was on. This is almost confirmed by an advertisement that appeared in the *Otago Colonist* in 1858.

£18 REWARD

A REWARD of £3 per Head will be paid by the Undersigned, for the immediate Apprehension and placing in Custody of all or any of the six seamen named as under, who have deserted from the " Jura " ;—

Archibald Ballintine.   Charles McLean.
George Middleton.   Alexander Taylor.
Robert Lamont.   Duram Liston.

J MACANDREW & CO.
Agents for the " Jura "

I say 'almost' because, as you can see, the sailor they were looking for was Archibald *Ballintine*, not Valentine. But the name is very similar and 'Archibald' is unusual enough for this to be my great-grandfather. It fits in with the story Archie himself told Jim. Win has a different story, but she was not yet four when her father died. She wanted to believe a story she says she overheard her widowed mother tell a visitor. She was, she tells us in her memoir, always addicted as a child to listening to grown-up talk:

> Mother told the visitor, Mrs Bates, I think it was, over a cup of tea that Father had returned to Britain on the *Jura* and did two long trips on her …. That two years later he returned to New Zealand on the *Beautiful Star* having taken his First Mate's ticket. But conditions were so horrible because of a brutal captain that the whole crew deserted on arrival in Dunedin.

Certainly a brutal captain is a better excuse than a beautiful girl. There's no doubt anyway that Archie Valentine did desert and that he had to go into hiding. The Otago goldfields were a good place to hide. There were so many strangers and so much coming and going. The Dunstan Rush was at its height and Archie Valentine was in the thick of it. As James Belich has pointed out, 'A wholly unsuccessful miner was a contradiction in terms'. If you didn't find gold, you got out. Living on the goldfields was an expensive business, as everything you needed was being sold at absurdly inflated prices. Both Win and Jim tell the story of Archie's tent being burnt to the ground, Win assuming that he lost his gold with the tent, Jim that he saved it.

They both say that, after various vicissitudes, Archie was able to build a small house in Waikouaiti, thirty miles north of Dunedin, and then marry his sweetheart, Mary Maxwell, the girl he met on the *Jura*. She was now nineteen and he was twenty-two. If it were true, as his children thought, that he was by then established as a contractor, why does the marriage certificate state so clearly that he was still a 'Golddigger'? The details on death certificates are often suspect, for the one person who could give the accurate information is dead. But marriage certificates are different, and it must be true that Archie was still a gold-digger on 30 December 1862 when he married Mary Maxwell in the Church of Green Island.

No.	When Married, and where	Names and Surnames	Age	Rank or Profession	Condition	Name of Officiating Minister (or Registrar)	When Registered
54	on the 30th Decr 1862: in the Church of Green Island	Archibald Valentine Mary Maxwell	22 19	Golddigger	Bachelor Spinster	Rev William Will	30th Decr 1862

1862 — MARRIAGES IN THE DISTRICT OF East Taieri Otago

Archie Valentine built his little house largely with his own hands, the white pine for it pit-sawn in Hawkesbury Bush. He certainly had found enough gold to buy not only the materials for his house but the bullock teams and carts with which he would soon make a good living as a contractor. He had obviously left the goldfields at the right moment and put his gold to good use. Jim tells a story of what his father did with the last little nugget, unearthed when by chance he kicked a tussock after a big flood in the Clutha River. Archie later had it made into a tie-pin, but wore it as rarely as he wore ties. Jim borrowed it one night, unknown to his father, and managed to lose it. It's good to know that Archie 'didn't seem to mind much'. By then his gold-digging days were a distant memory and their trials best forgotten.

My grandfather Jim – James Archibald Valentine – was born in 1863, the first of the twelve children who would be born to Archie and Mary in Waikouaiti – ten of them surviving into adulthood. Long afterwards in a letter, remembering his father, as he always did on the date of his death, Jim regretted the fact that Archie never knew his grandchildren. As he wrote in a letter to Hilda, dated 11 February 1943:

> He had a way with him when dealing with babies. I have known him in a railway carriage take a fractious crying baby from its tired mother's arms – a stranger to him – and in a few minutes the child would be quiet and he could restore it, smiling and happy, to its grateful mother's arms. He was a born

nurse – no one could deal better than he with his children's cuts and bruises. Once I lacerated an ankle horribly on a broken bottle and I can still feel the firm grasp of his skilful fingers as he cleansed the wounds and bound them so that the fearsome bleeding stopped.

Jim, in that wonderfully free outdoor childhood he enjoyed in rural Waikouaiti, was inclined to be accident-prone. His first memory was of escaping from the house just after the birth of his next brother. He was two years and two months old, and all his life could have gone to the very spot where 'a big sorrel-coloured horse was standing', when he teased him with a little stick. All his life he carried the scars of the deep cuts on his brow and chin from the horse's hoof and – worse – from the loss of the sight of an eye three years later. He had one glass eye when I knew him, an object of some interest to my childish stare. I had always thought it was from riding into an eye-level branch and I thought of him whenever my own eyes seemed in danger. Was I told this story to make me think better of my great-grandfather? For it was he, Archie, who had foolishly given in to Jim's five-year-old request for a knife. Jim gives his own version in his memoirs:

> I was in the harvest field on Grandfather Maxwell's farm at Hillhead when the men, including Father, were cutting a field of oats. I asked Father to lend me his knife, so that I could cut with it some toetoe reeds growing up in a gully amidst a heap of stones gathered off the field. While cutting one, I was kneeling on a stone and my knee slipped and my head went suddenly downwards and my right eye was pierced by the sharp point of the knife. I remember holding my hand palm up and seeing in my palm with my other eye a liquid that reflected the colours of the rainbow. That evidently was the aqueous humour of the eyeball for my sight was from that moment irrevocably lost.

By the 1870s there were swarms of Maxwells and Valentines in Waikouaiti, that pleasant settlement between the sea and the hills. The Valentine grandparents, the drunken tailor and his wife, were still alive. The Maxwell grandparents, James and Ellen, had moved up from Green Island and taken a farm called 'Hillhead' at the back of Mt Durden. They would later have a fine farm called 'Woodlands', which remained in the family for over a hundred years. Many of the next generation were farming in the area. Archie's sister, Jeannie, and Mary's brother, George Maxwell, were steadily producing their eleven children, all, like their Valentine cousins, born in Waikouaiti. John Valentine – who had arrived at some stage to join his brother Archie and sister Jean – married Margaret Glen, who contracted TB and passed it on to their children so that later, in the 1880s, there was a succession of sad young Valentine deaths. Then there were

Mary's two younger brothers, William and John Maxwell, though only John produced a family – eight more cousins, born between 1880 and 1897. Some of this younger generation stayed close to Waikouaiti all their lives; others scattered all over New Zealand and indeed the world.

It is remarkable that today, in Waikouaiti Cemetery, there are over fifty graves with some connection with these Valentines and Maxwells. And if you go into the little museum on the main road, having first checked its opening hours, you will find such items of possible interest as a book on *Volcanoes*, John Maxwell's first prize for Geography at Green Island School in 1865 and a splendid undated photograph of the Ladies' Hockey Club, with three of Jim Valentine's sisters, Mabel, Peg and Amy, and their coach, Blair Fell, who would later marry Peg. There are also exercise books full of the numerous minutes of numerous meetings of the Waikouaiti Early Settlers' Association. When they met on 9 April 1920 it was decided that all the arrangements for a coming social gathering should be left in the hands of 'J. Maxwell, Junior', apart from the actual making of the sandwiches for the eighty couples expected.

People had always seemed to be very gregarious in Waikouaiti. My great-aunts would remember the constant baking, the piles of scones and cakes. When years later Win read her older sister's diary for 1888 – the year Nell was nineteen – she commented that there seemed to be hardly a day when they were not visiting or being visited. 'What a vast amount of visiting was done in those days!' It was their main entertainment and often involved not just conversation – gossip – but also games-playing and music-making.

They seemed to be always in and out of each other's houses and yet – on a date it is difficult to determine – there was such a major quarrel between Archie Valentine and his brother-in-law, George Maxwell, that it resulted in a rift between the Valentines and the Maxwells. Closely related as they were, George never spoke to Archie again as long as he lived, nor, because she took her husband's side, did he speak to his own sister, Mary. This seems so sad, indeed tragic, to me that I can hardly bear to record it. Worst of all was a sentence in my grandfather Jim's memoirs: 'The breach was never healed and we children did not visit the grandparents during the remainder of Father's lifetime.'

Jim does not reveal his emotions at this ban though he says in his memoirs how 'sorely' his mother felt the separation between the families. As a young boy Jim had spent a great deal of time with these grandparents. James Maxwell had taught him how to milk a cow by the time he was seven, how to take the honey from his beehives and how to bind the sheaves of cut grain. Jim had used his 'small but select' library, read from the Bible with him on Sunday evenings and watched his weekly shave:

Trained by grandfather, I learned how to build stooks on the grain fields, how to load a dray for 'leading in' the dry sheaves and how to 'crow' on a stack that was building. He had a horse-turned threshing-machine and many a day I have spent in his barn, either bagging the threshed grain, or removing the winnowed chaff, or throwing out the straw. I learned also to drive horses dragging harrows over a ploughed field. Indeed, there were not many farming operations that I did not take part in.

To 'crow' on a stack means to fork sheaves across to the stacker, the man building the stack. Jim often uses words and expressions unfamiliar to me but worth preserving. He was a boy who knew the names of every bird in the bush, taught young 'paroquets' (kakariki) to talk and resented the imported birds, particularly the starlings who ousted the little parrots from their nesting places. Later he was sorry to admit, 'We boys were adept with our shanghais' – their word for their home-made catapults. They plucked and cooked the birds they killed. They fished too in the Waikouaiti River with rods made from 'mako-mako stems 10 to 15 feet long', and hunted rabbits and sprinted and wrestled ('Cumberland' style). They explored the bush which then still grew on the slopes of Mt. Durden and Lamb Hill. There was cricket and boating, in improvised boats, netting crayfish in the creeks and 'boiling them by the hundred in a tin'. At home he had discovered *Chambers's Information for the People*, a couple of volumes a bookseller had given his father in return for a load of firewood. And that led on to the library: 'I think I knew more about those books, their titles and their contents, than anyone else in Waikouaiti.'

All this time his father, Archie Valentine, and his uncle, George Maxwell, had owned a farm together, but Archie was also working as a contractor. He made miles of roads for the old Hawkesbury Road Board. He used teams of bullocks, sometimes three of them, and obtained most of the hard 'bluestone' metal from quarries in Hawkesbury Bush. Jim often went along with his father and watched the men load up the bullock drays and break the stone by the side of the main road. Archie employed dozens of stone-breakers who were paid by the cubic yard. When Jim was around, it pleased him to earn the odd shilling by calculating the cubic measurements of a heap of bluestone. He was always top in arithmetic at school, in English too and grammar. He was on his way – thanks to a good headmaster – to Latin, French and Euclid and to becoming a graduate teacher himself.

Neither Jim nor his sister Win, writing about this period, seemed to know what it was that caused the dreadful rift between Archie and George which led to the separation between the families. Family rows are usually about money, and certainly money must have had something to do with this one. My guess is that Archie's road-building business was thriving to such an extent that he was putting all his time and energy into that and not giving enough of either to the shared farm, though still expecting a share of its profits.

When George protested, I guess Archie withdrew his capital in some sense – perhaps actually sold off his own share of the land – and left George with financial problems, on a farm that was not viable. Certainly Archie had the money available to buy land at Flag Swamp. It was not an encouraging name for a farm and it was always known as 'Stringers', after the manager Archie put in to run it. He was then free to concentrate on his new appointment as Inspector of Roads for the Waikouaiti County, which at that time included Waihemo County. Jim says that Archie was responsible not only for the construction of new roads and the upkeep of existing ones, but even for designing bridges, 'some of which stand to this day, as firm as ever'. Jim was immensely proud of him and heard nothing but good of him from the men he employed and from the County Council that employed him.

Yet it seems to me that he was certainly as obstinate a man as George Maxwell. It was George who refused to have anything to do with his sister's family because of Archie's failure to honour the terms of their partnership. But I think Archie's children's lack of explanation for the cause of the rift between the two families was because, if they had explained it, his descendants would have thought less of Archie. Win tells another story which shows Archie as stubborn and unrelenting, though with some justification. Jim also tells of the break with his church, but does not give any reason for it. Win – very young at the time – heard the story in detail later from her brother, George, and passes it on as having some historical interest, as indeed it has. Win wrote in her family history:

> The province of Otago was settled by the Church of Scotland, which for many years dominated the Provincial Council. One of its rules was that the Sacrament of the Lord's Supper should be celebrated three times a year, and could be partaken of only by church members who had attended the lengthy Fast Day service on the previous Wednesday. No doubt people were supposed to fast and pray all day in preparation for the Service on Sunday, but though the day was observed in great solemnity, right through my primary school days, I never knew of anyone fasting. It was obligatory for all church members to attend church on Fast Day, when all shops and schools were closed, and all work ceased on the farms that they could receive their 'token', which they must bring with them to the Sacrament service the following Sunday, as proof that they had attended the Fast Day service. I remember these tokens – small oval discs, lead I think, with something printed on them. My father's work took him away from home for days at a time, and there came a time when he was unable to be present for the Fast Day service. When he presented himself

at church on the Sunday, without a token, the elders, led by Mr William Mill, ruled that he could not partake. He never entered the church again.

Archie took himself off to the Methodists; what the rest of the family did I don't know, but Mary's loyalty suggests she went with him. In her memoirs, my mother remembered this grandmother as she would have been in church:

> She was quite formidable though tiny, wearing when dressed always a black silk, tight-bodiced, leg o'mutton sleeved dress and an elegant little lace cap on her neat head. To go out she wore a black bonnet of ruched silk or bombazine with ribbons tied under her chin. She was a splendid type of Scotswoman, with a strong character, but a fine sense of humour, very kind and understanding too.

The first daughter, Nell, born in May 1869, was as strong a character as her mother. My favourite story of my Great-Aunt Nell comes from the days when she was a lively child of five, dispatched to Miss Millar's Private School, where it was hoped she would learn to be quiet and obedient. The poor child spent most of her time standing in the corner with her pinafore over her head, a common form of punishment. On one occasion a tell-tale said to Miss Millar: 'Please, Miss, Nell Valentine is putting her tongue out.'

'How do you know?' asked the teacher.

'I can see a wet mark on her pinny,' came the reply. Nell herself would tell this story when, after her father's death, she was running a successful business as a dressmaker and had become, as Win described her with admiration, 'for twenty-six years the main support of the family'. The Flag Swamp farm brought in an income of only £90 a year.

Archie and Mary's twelfth and last child was my Great-Aunt Win herself, born in May 1886, in the year that Jim graduated and went to Pareora as headmaster. It was always a comfort to Win to know that, on the day she was born, Archie stopped the minister's wife in the street to tell her the good news of the birth. 'He was as pleased as if it were the first,' Win was told years later. There was no nonsense about her being yet another girl. The Valentine daughters grew up in a house where the women were expected to use their talents as well as their brothers, and did so in the ways that were open to them in those days.

Jim's younger brothers, George (born 1875) and Hal (born 1882) both became prominent men. George Valentine, leaving school on his father's death, when he was only fifteen, went to work for a dairy company, boarding near Jim and Nellie in North East Valley, Dunedin. By 1912 he was Inspector of Dairy Factories for North Auckland and ended up Director of the Dairy Division of the Department of Agriculture. Hal went into the railways, became a station-master, nearly died in the 1918 'flu epidemic and went on – having studied accountancy in his spare time for years – to be Chief Accountant for New Zealand Railways and President of the New Zealand Society of Accountants. His daughter, my mother's cousin Bili, became Helen Mason, who studied pottery in Japan and whose pots can be seen in the Auckland Museum. One bowl I much admire is here in our house in England, a reminder of a special talent.

As for Jim's sisters, my great-aunts, they were a close band, perhaps particularly united and devoted to their mother because of the rift with her family. Mary and Peg were the only two of the seven sisters to have children. Two others, Nell and Flo, married eventually but late, after their mother's death. Three of them, Mabel, Amy and Win, never married. Nell was the dressmaker and Amy helped her. Mabel and Flo both trained as nurses and ended up as Matrons, Mabel of the Pleasant Valley Sanatorium and Flo of the Wakari Sanatorium at Halfway Bush. Flo was recruited in 1915, went out to Egypt on a troopship and was away for three years – first in Alexandria, treating casualties from Gallipoli, then on the hospital ship *Essikebo* on a run between Salonika and Malta, then in Suez, with men wounded in the Palestine campaign, and finally in England, at a hospital in Walton-on-Thames with casualties from the Western Front.

Dear Great-Aunt Win was the only one of these aunts I really knew. She was a little 'fat dumpling' of a woman, an expression she used herself, recalling that in her early days as a young teacher at Hawea Flat she had boarded with a farm family and feasted daily on their homemade bread and buns. Many years later Win came to our wedding in St Martin-in-the-Fields in London with her great friend, Jean Begg, general secretary of the YWCA in New Zealand. Win even stayed with us in Tokyo. She had trained as a teacher specialising in the education of 'backward' children, those with 'learning difficulties', as we would say now. In the 1920s she studied and worked in London, Winnipeg and at Columbia University in New York. Then, still in America, she worked for a time in a home for delinquent girls, Inwood House, and at Sleighton Farm, the Pennsylvania State Reformatory for Girls, where she was Sub-Matron of the cottage containing the youngest group, already diagnosed as sub-normal. That too was invaluable experience. Back in New Zealand, for twenty years she worked for the Education Department as a special advisor, travelling every year the length of the country from Auckland to the Bluff. Her special concern was to stop children of normal intelligence being branded as sub-normal simply because they were difficult, naughty or could not read. This was in the days before dyslexia was recognised. Teachers in those days, Win said, were not encouraged to look into home circumstances or to use any sort of intelligence testing: 'Some headmasters were interested in the new ideas I was giving them, but few inspectors were.' She had a hard time.

Win had an extraordinary memory. She recorded her first memory of her father without the Victorian prudishness some people would expect:

> My very first must have happened when I was quite a small baby. I lay on the bed, watching Mother dressing on the left, and Father standing at the foot of the bed, wearing shirt, braces, and brown trousers, and using a chamber pot held straight in front of him.

My mother remembered this house – and many others, of course – without any bathroom. She remembered the chamber pots, which someone had to empty, and the trail to the 'horrid outside privy'. There was no such thing as indoor sanitation and my mother would come to consider the introduction of *that* as perhaps the greatest blessing of all the tremendous changes that occurred in her long lifetime.

Win's other memories of her father included his joy when one Sunday morning he was playing the harmonium and singing one of Sankey's hymns, which had just come into fashion. 'Once as I danced around I sang with him "He's the lily of the valley, the bright and morning star", he jumped up in delight and called out to Mother: "She's got the tune; she's got the tune."' Win was three years old. Six years later she had another musical memory worth recording. There was a young blacksmith in Waikouaiti with a splendid baritone voice. 'I verily believe', Win wrote in her memoirs, 'that it was his fine rendering of that remarkable song "The Toilers" that sowed the first seeds of socialism in my nine-year-old breast.'

By this time, Archie Valentine was dead. My great-grandfather died on 6 February 1890, at exactly the same age and from exactly the same cause as my grandfather on the other side, Arthur Harrop. Archie was forty-nine and died of 'apoplexy' – the same sort of paralytic stroke that killed Arthur. Jim attributed his father's death to the rigours of his life as a public works inspector, which obviously had something in common with Arthur's life as a surveyor:

> Years of long hard riding in all weathers, following his trying life as a contractor, helped to undermine his health. The final blow to his weakened body … was when he had to lay off a road to the newly discovered gold reefs at Nenthorn. While on this job he had to live in a tent, at times with snow deep on the ground, and without facilities for drying at nights the wet clothing he had worn by day. Nor could he keep his body warm in bed – it was 'warm on one side and freezing on the other' he used to tell us.

Jim said Archie was 'devoted to our mother and cared for her and sheltered her as long as he lived. On her side she was deeply fond of him and his death "without a word" was a terrible blow to her.' Archie had been ill for some weeks, but had seemed to be getting better when he had the stroke and did not regain consciousness.

Win was not yet four years old, but nearly eighty years later she wrote:

> I have quite clear recollections of his last illness and death. He lay in what afterwards I knew as the sitting-room, perhaps converted into a bedroom for the occasion. On a bookcase in the room was a bowl of beautiful grapes, both black and white. I climbed up on a chair and helped myself to the largest white one. He smiled at me. The night before he died I was sent to sleep at the Mallochs', and howled all night. Next day everyone at home seemed to be crying, so I cried too. My brother, George, in the three-quarter length pants of those days, took me by the hand and said, 'I heard Speckle cackling in the paddock. Let's go and see if she has laid an egg.' The coffin was on trestles in the parlour, where the funeral service was conducted by Mr Christie. The room was full, and many people stood outside. I sat on the knee of Nellie, Jim's wife of six weeks. She was crying, and I looked up at her and asked, 'What are you crying for?' Neither she nor I ever forgot that episode. The coffin was passed through the window to the gate exactly where the hearse stood. The procession moved off past the McDougalls' to the main street …. 'The largest funeral ever seen in Waikouaiti' was the comment.

One of the obituaries declared:

> There was no one more extensively known throughout the County. From the nature of his business he came in contact with most of the settlers …. In his untimely removal the Council loses a servant who discharged his important duties with singular fidelity, impartiality and honesty of purpose – displaying neither fear nor favour, but always activated by a desire to conserve and advance the interests of the County as a whole.

I think there must have been a reconciliation with the Presbyterians if Mr Christie took the funeral service. There was certainly a reconciliation with the Maxwell grandparents after Archie's death. There is a photograph to prove it on the next page.

What would seem to be just a pleasant four-generation photograph becomes instead an indication of a renewed relationship between at least some of the Maxwells and the Valentines, after the birth of the first Maxwell/Valentine grandchild. The photo shows James and Ellen Maxwell, with young Archibald Graham Valentine, my oldest uncle, on his great-grandmother's knee, and the widowed Mary Maxwell Valentine, his grandmother, on the left of her parents and the baby, at the right of the picture. Behind them stand my grandparents,

the baby's parents, Nellie and Jim Valentine. It was taken, I think, in the spring of 1893. You can see that James Maxwell is looking closer to the age of his daughter, Mary, than that of his poor little wife, and that he is still shaving his chin and his upper lip, leaving that odd fringe of beard, just as he had when Jim had watched him as a small boy all those years ago, before the rift between the families.

There was never any reconciliation between George Maxwell himself and his sister Mary Valentine. He obviously felt grievously wronged, and perhaps he was. I naturally try to see Archie's side of the story, not just because he is my great-grandfather, but because his children loved him and admired him so much. What amazes me was that the rift continued after Archie's death. It is difficult to see why George's wife, Jeannie, who was Archie's sister, and the Maxwell grandparents could not have brought about some sort of resolution. But the fact remains that, throughout the entire twenty-six years Mary lived as a widow, George Maxwell never spoke a word to his sister or to any member of Archie's family. How can whatever Archie had done have been bad enough to deserve such unrelenting ostracism?

Win tells the story of what happened when Mary Valentine died in August 1916, only twelve years after her own parents, James and Ellen Maxwell, had died within three weeks of each other. Mary's younger brothers, Johnny and Willie Maxwell, were discussing her funeral arrangements with their nephews, her sons Jim and Hal. Their old friend Mr Cunningham was to be one of the bearers. Six were needed. Young George Valentine was apparently away. The question was: would George Maxwell turn up for his sister's funeral, after all those years of estrangement? When the time came, George Maxwell arrived and silently found his place behind Jim and Hal, taking his share of the weight of Mary Valentine's coffin. The quarrel was over.

My mother's own family: Jim and Nellie Valentine and their descendants

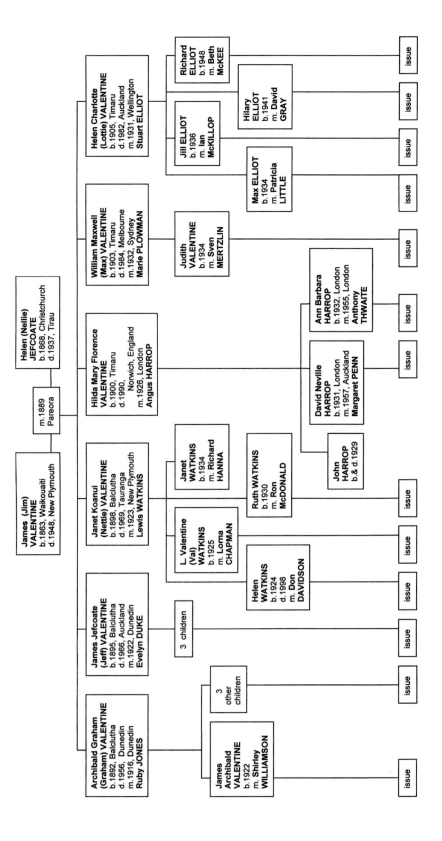

CHAPTER 6

The headmaster's daughter

My grandfather, Jim Valentine, had to come rushing across from the West Coast at the time of his mother's death, but for years he had been teaching much closer at hand. After North East Valley in Dunedin, where he had had that hard time with 120 pupils in Standard Three, he and Nellie had moved to Balclutha, where Jim was to be first assistant in the new District High School; it was in Balclutha that the first three Valentine children were born, my mother's older brothers and sister.

It is difficult to imagine that their father spent a great deal of time at home. Jim Valentine was choir master of the Presbyterian Church, leader of a mixed Bible class and secretary of the Technical Classes Association, which also involved teaching classes at night. He captained the Balclutha cricket team for years and boasted that – in spite of his having only one good eye – he not only took nine wickets in his last match against the Waiwera Club and caught the tenth off someone else's bowling but ended the season as the top scorer. He was a wonder, this grandfather.

It was not surprising that Jim Valentine soon had his own large school. Hilda, my mother, was born in the headmaster's house at Timaru South School on 30 June 1900, less than four months after my father was born in Hokitika, on the other side of the South Island. Her brothers, Graham and Jeff (short for Jefcoate), were seven-and-a-half and nearly five, and her older sister, Janet (known as Nettie) was just twenty-two months her senior. The photo on the next page was taken of Hilda not long after she had learnt to stand with such self-confidence in the winter of 1901.

In her memoirs, my mother called the schoolhouse 'poky', comparing it with other later, larger houses. But it was larger than my father's house in Hokitika and it needed to be. Max (short for Maxwell) was born in 1903 and the sixth child, Charlotte (known as Lottie), two years later. The fourth bedroom, through most of my mother's childhood, was occupied by Jim's sister, Flo, the 'darling' maiden aunt that every family needed and many of them had. This was the Flo who, when she was no longer necessary in her brother's house, trained as a nurse and sailed to Egypt on a troopship. When Max was born, a fifth bedroom – little more than a shed – was tacked on to the house for Graham, the eldest. The girls, Janet (Nettie), Hilda and Charlotte (Lottie), always shared a room; they were good friends as children and would keep in close contact all their lives. Indeed my

mother also exchanged regular letters throughout her life with two of her three brothers. Here are the three sisters in 1905 and 1910. My mother, Hilda, is on the left as you look at it, in the first photo (rather the worse for wear) and on the right in the second.

There are signs that Nellie Valentine, my grandmother, the headmaster's wife, was aspiring to that 'gentility' the historian James Belich is always keen to detect, that 'upward mobility' (to use a more recent term) that played such a large part in the development of New Zealand society. My mother, at the times of her life when she was at home like her mother, followed the maternal pattern: all the

household work should as far as possible be done in the morning. Lunch should be followed by a rest and then, on rising, one put on one's 'better' clothes.

My grandmother even had calling cards and was regularly 'At Home' in her drawing room (second Wednesday in the month) with a wonderful afternoon tea on offer, a silver tea-service and a kettle (but 'that was only electro-plate') simmering over a flame. It is the electro-plated kettle that makes this sound convincing and not a figment of a romantic imagination. My mother also described the 'wafer-thin' sandwiches with their crusts cut off – and eaten by the children in the kitchen when they came in from school. I can remember doing exactly that in north London forty years later.

The children would on occasion be called on to perform. They all played, but my mother was the most serious pianist and indeed, so she says, monopolised the piano from 6.30 to 8 o'clock before breakfast most mornings. In other, less musical, families children were reduced to 'recitations', a word that somehow diminishes the art of saying a chosen poem. Tennyson was a particular favourite: many a New Zealand creek must have been transformed into a brook, and many a warm beach have felt the breaking of a 'cold, grey sea'.

Those afternoons at home, with the house 'spic and span', everything as it should be, made a certain sense. It was good to sit down and gossip. In a busy household with a lot of children there was only a little help. So it was not convenient to encourage the casual visiting known in Pareora and Waikouaiti, though there was inevitably a good deal of that as well. My mother always told me her first memory was of being held up to view the procession celebrating the Coronation of Edward VII in August 1902, not long after her second birthday. A photograph of the procession lined up in Stafford Street, Timaru, shows clearly two huge banners, one reading 'BRITANNIA RULES THE WAVES', and the other, with rather charming informality, 'GOOD OLD ENGLAND'. Home-thoughts from abroad, thoughts of the 'Mother' country none of them

had ever visited, were never far away. Education was entirely Anglocentric, a word never used. In the photographs – taken from 1905 to 1981 – that cram the pages of the South School centennial publication, there is not a single Maori face. That was another New Zealand with which they had no contact.

A later headmaster, in 1929, attempting to make up for this, taught the boys haka, the girls how to whirl poi, and had them all singing 'Hoea Ra', and 'Taki nei taru kino' in two parts. Unhappy with some impressive charcoal tattoos on their pupils' pale faces, the teachers then encouraged the children to become brown-skinned with copious applications of a paste of cocoa and water. I am sure the Valentines would have thought this ridiculous.

In her own memoirs my mother decided her first memory was of spilling some medicine the summer following the Coronation celebrations. Hilda was seriously ill, nearly dying from pneumonia, causing huge anxiety to her mother, who was pregnant with Max. It was a relief when her mother was able to write in her diary, 'My girlie's fever gone at last' and that she was 'getting mischievous again'. But, not long after, to be out of the way at Max's birth, little Hilda was packed off to stay at Waikouaiti with her grandmother.

This grandmother was Archie's widow, who was living with her daughters, the dressmakers, Nell and Amy. Hilda's father went to fetch her when the school holidays came round and wrote in his diary how the three-year-old (she had just had her birthday) was 'filled with delight because of my arrival'. 'I remember', he wrote to her in England over thirty years later, 'you would hardly let me out of your sight.' She had 'won all hearts at Waikouaiti', he quoted from his diary. That was perhaps consolation for an uprooting which could have left the tiny child doubtful that she would ever see her parents again.

I want to emphasise Hilda's childhood absences from home, because surely they must have had some relevance, at least subconsciously, to her believing, as she obviously did many years afterwards when David and I were young, that children can get on perfectly well without their parents, that, indeed, they may flourish and learn to be independent away from home. Hilda's greatest joy as a child was to spend weekends with her favourite cousin, Win Bardsley (just six months older), my Great-Aunt Lucy's daughter, in an impressive two-storey

house called Kite-moana on Wai-iti Road above Caroline Bay in Timaru. These photographs were taken at the Bay around 1911. My Great-Uncle William was Secretary of the Timaru Harbour Board and, with only three children, the family was decidedly better off than the Valentines. Hilda would return home reluctantly to the schoolhouse, pining for butter *and* jam on her bread, for running hot water (installed eventually in 1911), and for a dressing gown and a 'fur muff and tippet', just like Win's.

Hilda shared her cousin's interest in fashion, an interest my mother had all her life and which I did not inherit. As a child, a second daughter, my mother lived largely in hand-me-downs: a sewing woman came twice a year to make their clothes. One year my grandmother had the foolish idea that it would be attractive to have her daughters arrayed in matching dresses – with the sad result that Hilda wore her own, then Nettie's, while little Lottie was in one of the matching dresses for three years on end. My grandmother, Nellie, didn't sew, but she did embroider and knit. She always had some 'fancy work' at hand. Nellie knitted warm underwear and socks. My mother drew attention to the fact (which I hadn't realised, but it fits in with the photographs) that cardigans and jumpers weren't worn in those days.

'Living in luxury', my mother recalled in her memoirs, 'made me very difficult to live with when I returned home and I remember Mother threatening never to let me stay with Win again if I couldn't behave on my return.' Win Bardsley eventually married and disappeared to America, but her younger sister, Trina, married Hugh Speight of the Dunedin brewers. Their daughter, Deirdre, would be born on the same day I was. I always think of this family when I see the ubiquitous Speight's advertisements, though their brewery has long been taken over.

There was another Timaru girl cousin of my mother's age: Ivy Clay, my Great-Aunt Susan's daughter. Here the three cousins are together holding their certificates. It must have been early 1913, I think, when they had just had the results of the Junior National Scholarships, after the easier Proficiency tests which all the children took.

Six years after Hilda's stay in Waikouaiti at the time of her brother Max's birth, the nine-year-old spent an even longer period much further away. Her mother took Hilda (and young Lottie) on a visit to her sister Charlotte Johnson in Waihi in the North Island, just south of the Coromandel Peninsula, and, returning home to Timaru with her youngest daughter, left Hilda there for six months. Charlotte was the first of the family to be born in New Zealand, the one who carried the country in the middle of her name. By 1909, when my mother stayed with her, she had been married for many years to William Johnson, who was apparently chief engineer of one of the main gold mines in Waihi, at a time when they were highly productive. Their older son, Will, had been a familiar visitor in Timaru when he was training in Otago to be a doctor and it was too far to go home to Waihi for the holidays. He would complete his F.R.C.S. in Edinburgh and practise as a consultant in Auckland for many years. But the other grown-up cousins, and indeed the uncle and aunt, must have all been almost strangers to the child. In her memoirs she says how surprisingly little she remembers about this long visit. A photograph taken in the garden of the School House at this time shows Will Johnson (back row left) next to my grandfather with my mother's three brothers and little Lottie, who moved. My grandmother is next to her father, Thomas Jefcoate.

There was one main reason for Hilda's months in Waihi. This was her relationship with her oldest brother, Graham. It was a household, in the School House in Timaru, where boys and girls were treated with surprising equality for the time. Jim Valentine, the headmaster himself, was totally involved with such things as the weekly hair-washing and bathing of the children – a lengthy process which entailed heating water in the wash-house copper and carrying it indoors in buckets to fill the hip bath. My mother mentions quite casually that it was always Max's job to make the custard to go with the fruit pies after the roast meat at Sunday dinner. The boys took their turn at many household tasks, such as feeding the hens, making jam from their own fruit and cleaning the knives in the knife-cleaning machine, a modern piece of equipment they all admired in those days before stainless steel. A ban on Graham and Hilda doing the washing-up together (because of the inevitable spat) suggests how much the brothers and sisters were expected to share jobs.

Graham's behaviour was a source of worry to his parents. He was the oldest, the headmaster's son, and expected to set a good example, not only to his siblings, but to other children in the school. This he could not do. One of his mates, writing in the Timaru South School centennial publication, said that Graham Valentine was 'usually in the thick of any escapades', confirming that the boy 'got a pretty hard time as his father was very strict with him'.

Jim Valentine was very strict with all of them. Hilda remembered all her life the injustice of receiving two cuts on her hand with the leather strap when she was sent to the headmaster with some other small children for failing to get enough sums right. The other children were hit only once. The Valentine children were expected to be better and do better than everyone else. It was fortunate for Jim Valentine that they were all particularly bright. In spite of his attempts to stack the odds against them in order to avoid any suggestion of favouritism, the list of 'Dux Medallists' in the centennial booklet includes all four of the Valentine children who finished their primary education in Timaru: 1905 Archibald Graham, 1907 James Jefcoate, 1910 Janet Koanui, 1912 Hilda Mary.

Corporal punishment was part of life in those days, at home as well as at school. My grandmother, Nellie, used to tell her children of an occasion in Pareora when all nine of the Jefcoate young – the older ones certainly nearly grown up – had come back late from a party, in one of those wonderfully accommodating horse-drawn drays, half an hour later than the promised time. Their father, Thomas Jefcoate, the one-time goods guard, was waiting for his children in the dim light at the door of the farm-house and told them to get into line with the oldest, East, first. Charlotte, the oldest girl, pushed her next sister, Nellie, in front of her, muttering 'You go first', the reason being that she thought Nellie her father's favourite, and it likely that the third in line would get a less severe beating than the rest of the culprits. My mother, telling this story a century later, was amazed her mother and her aunts and uncles had submitted to this treatment. But in fact she had been used to it herself.

In the headmaster's house, there was a horse whip – only used on the boys – along the coat rack in the hall and a leather strap, fringed at both ends, hanging by the kitchen mantelpiece, above the Shacklock Orion stove ('how we had to polish that!' my mother recorded in her memoirs). 'The strap was frequently resorted to, *as in many other households*, when we were naughty children.' My mother's emphasis was obviously meant to suggest that her father and mother were not particularly sadistic and only using the normal methods of discipline of the time. In fact, they were – all their lives – extremely loving and thoughtful parents. That the violence they felt bound to use in bringing up their children was ineffective is obvious as the children – particularly Graham – were serial offenders.

Hilda herself was fiery and irrepressible. In school she was always in trouble for talking too much. Fortunately in the Infants' Room at Timaru South the punishment was not the strap, but rather to stand in the corner with one's back to the class, sometimes even with the humiliation of the dunce's 'high three-cornered hat', rather than the pinny that had covered her Aunt Nell's head long before. 'I must not talk too much' became a theme in my mother's adolescent diary. And it was not only the quantity but the quality of the talking that was in question. I can hear her now quoting Shakespeare to remind me of Cordelia's voice, 'gentle and low, an excellent thing in woman'.

The name 'Hilda' means 'battle-maid', and she was often told how appropriate it was, as she flung herself into conflict with her brother. Graham, seven years older, delighted to enrage her, teasing her until she lost her temper and flew at him, or left the room in floods of tears. Graham left Nettie alone, as she refused to be maddened by him, and little Lottie was too small to be worth worrying.

Graham's teasing of my mother was relentless. There was one wet day when he 'made' Hilda turn a somersault from the top bunk in the boys' bedroom onto the floor – presumably intending her to land on her feet. But of course she didn't. She hit her nose on the side of the bottom bunk on her way down and it bled copiously. She thought it 'resourceful' of him to hold her head over the handy chamber-pot to stop the blood staining the rug on the floor.

Then there was a more serious incident during one of the family's summer camping expeditions. They would all spend five or six weeks of the long Christmas holidays every year by the Opihi River, with a distant view of Mt Cook. They loaded a hired dray, pulled by two horses, with the tents, clothes, blankets, boxes of provisions and crockery, books and games for wet days, and even their bicycles and a large table. Jim Valentine cycled to the campsite, arriving before his family. Nellie sat beside the driver and the six children sat on the long seats on both sides of the dray.

There were three tents: one for the boys, one for the girls – and one for the parents, with a large fly-sheet attached, to give cover for eating and board games at the table if it rained. Usually they ate in the shade 'of the great silver poplar tree at the end of the willow lane leading to our camping place'. The river was not far away – and there was an 'old farm where we collected our milk every morning.' It was all of twelve miles from Timaru, but to the child it was a vast distance into another world.

The first thing when they arrived was to find a good deep bathing pool, for floods had always changed the course of the wide river. They did many of the things their parents had done as children growing up in the country, at Pareora and Waikouaiti. They climbed trees and fished – fish was their staple diet – and they learnt to milk the cows at the Cartwrights' farm. It was all hand-milking, of course, in those days, and not as easy as it looked, as they each discovered in their turn. Their father taught them to swim in the river, cold and 'milky' with melted snow from the Alps. Their mother taught them the art of cooking on a camp fire – boys as well as girls. There were compulsory sessions of embroidery (girls only) sitting on hay bales in the sunshine.

It was 1909 when the alarming incident took place, when Graham's teasing could so easily have had a fatal consequence.

> Graham got me onto an old horse, lent by the Cartwrights, that we hadn't ridden much. He was teasing me as usual and shouted, 'See how fast you can ride and stay on!' He gave the horse such a terrific lash on its thigh, with a thin willow whip he was carrying, that she jumped the gate and bolted down the long lane like a mad creature, with me holding the reins as firmly as I could. The horse galloped so fast I thought I'd fall off and be killed. She careered down the side road, towards the main road leading to the station. I hung on for my life, but I couldn't control her. It seemed miles before I somehow pulled her up and turned her round and made her walk back. We met Graham half way along the road. He had come rushing after me, as scared as I was of what might happen, but mercifully there were no cars on the road in those days. The farmer told us the horse had been a race-horse once; a good thing it was old! Father's punishment was a thrashing for Graham with a painful switch, similar to the one he'd used on the horse.

This terrifying incident remained so vivid in my mother's mind that in her memoirs (written over nearly twenty years), she described it four times, each time in slightly different terms.

But there was another incident concerning Graham which she did not write down. It was strange and a little frightening at the time, but more so when she thought about it years later. It was something my mother told me about when, in her old age, there was a great deal in the media about the 'abuse' of children. She told me that she herself had, all her life, a memory of being pushed to the floor by Graham in their father's workshop and being 'touched inappropriately' (she chose her words with care) by her brother.

I think she rushed inside to her mother, complaining bitterly at Graham's roughness, and her distress precipitated the visit to her aunt's family in Waihi. There is a photograph of Hilda, smiling but clinging to her mother's arm, on the steps of the Johnsons' house. It is too poor to reproduce. Nellie and little Lottie returned to Timaru, leaving the young 'spitfire' (she used the word herself) safe from Graham's teasing.

When she returned, it was after Graham had finally run away from home at sixteen and got a job on a sheep station, Preston's, in the McKenzie country, that wonderful wild area in the west of Canterbury, in the foothills of the Southern Alps. My mother loved that area, and spent a memorable holiday, most of it on horseback, on a sheep station near the source of the Waitaki River, with a school friend, Evelyn Fraser. By then she was seventeen and had long since regained her nerve. She had often ridden when staying with her mother's great friend, Helen Stewart, at Kingsdown, south of Timaru.

Hilda was staying with the Stewarts when, coming in from riding, she felt wet blood between her legs for the first time. Her periods had started. Surely, with an older sister sharing her room, she must have been, in some sense, prepared. But, she wrote in her memoirs, she was grateful to Mrs Stewart, 'lovely to look at and a most enlightened Victorian', who explained things properly and encouraged the girl to have a bath, 'as often as I could'. Her mother believed bathing while menstruating was harmful and she was far too 'modest' (Hilda herself put the word in inverted commas) to give her children any sex education. There is a telling sentence just after that statement: 'Incredible and sad, as I never really caught up until many years later' – a sentence which suggests endless embarrassment and ignorance. A dozen years later Hilda would write to Angus asking him whether he had read Marie Stopes, whose writings had by then told her a good deal that she wanted to know before starting married life. In old age, she was sufficiently uninhibited to talk about the secrecy and feelings of shame and 'unhealthiness' that surrounded sex in her youth – and to do so on tape for one of my daughters who was making a radio programme about changing sexual attitudes.

In February 1913 at the same time as Angus Harrop first travelled over the Southern Alps to Waitaki, Hilda Valentine started at Timaru Girls' High School 'with relief'.

At times it had been hard, those years as the headmaster's daughter. In that same year, as it happened, Jim Valentine resigned from the South School. It had grown enormously in the fourteen years he had been headmaster. By 1912 there were 432 children, and a new building and many extra teachers had improved conditions considerably. When he took on the school, one class had held seventy-five pupils squashed into a room eighteen feet by eighteen feet, and my grandfather would later recall the winter smell of small children 'stitched into woollen vests and petticoats', and his battles with ignorant mothers.

Nearly a hundred years ago, Jim Valentine had initiated all sorts of school activities we might think of as more recent aspects of education: school gardens tended by keen pupils, tree-planting, day trips (Max would recall a long expedition by special train to visit the battle cruiser HMS *New Zealand* at Lyttelton) and lots of music, which the headmaster himself took throughout the school. The song for the Timaru South School Centennial in 1981, over thirty years after his death, included these lines:

> She's had some famous Headmasters; you've heard of J.A.V.,
> The learned Mr Valentine. He got the O.B.E.

My grandfather continued on a path that would lead in 1946 to that O.B.E. In 1913 he accepted an appointment as Secretary and Inspector to the South Canterbury Education Board. As early as 1906, he had been President of the New Zealand Educational Institute and had always been involved in the national scene, travelling the length of the country to attend educational conferences. To list all my grandfather's appointments and achievements would be tedious. At this point, it seems sufficient to say that my grandmother had the fond belief that the family would remain in Timaru for years and designed her own ideal home, brick-built in Craighead Street, Highfield. Here, for less than three years, my mother slept on a sunny verandah with 'my grey cat to keep my feet warm'. Here they celebrated Jim and Nellie's silver wedding with a family photograph. Nettie is on the left as you look at it, then Max behind his mother, Jeff, Graham, with Lottie in front of them and Hilda on the right, resting her hand on her father's shoulder. It was 1914.

It was soon a smaller family at home. Hilda's brothers, Jeff (who had to abandon temporarily his medical studies at Otago) and the reprobate Graham both enlisted for the coming war. 'Our hearts were filled with fear', their father wrote in his memoirs. Graham would redeem himself by being wounded at Gallipoli and becoming part of the legend which immediately haunted the imagination of the whole country, as it still does more than ninety years later. Thousands take part each year in a pilgrimage to Anzac Cove. Those dormitories at Waitaki Boys' High School (Anzac Cove, Lone Pine, Quinn's Post, Chunuk Bair and Sari Bair) I wrote of in Chapter 3 were a small part of a continuous collective mourning. Altogether, out of a total of 8450 New Zealanders who took part in the ghastly campaign, 2721 were killed and 4752 wounded, calculated by Michael King as 'a staggering eighty-eight per cent casualty rate'.

Lieut. Graham Valentine, of the Otago Infantry Battalion, was badly wounded in May 1915, when he was sleeping in the sun, outside his dug-out. It seems a Turkish bullet went through one thigh and the other knee. He was invalided home in a hospital ship, disappointed not to have seen Europe. He was on crutches for some time and spent the rest of the war in the Base Records Office in Wellington. Graham never saw Europe. In one of only two surviving letters to his sister Hilda, he wrote, just after my engagement to Anthony Thwaite in 1954: 'If I came to England, which I have no intention of doing, I don't know how I would get on with a Poet – I see he is only a poet, so maybe it would be OK, but, like auditors, even poets are apt to reproduce their kind: there should be a law against it: however David will help the family to average out.' A teaser to the last.

The Valentine family had only a short time to enjoy their new house in Timaru; in 1916 my mother's father was transferred to Hokitika, where he would soon find himself playing bowls with Arthur Harrop, my father's father. Jim Valentine had been appointed as the sole Inspector of Schools for the Education Board on the West Coast. His memoirs are packed with stories from those years: 1916 to 1920. In the beginning he had been reluctant to accept the posting to Hokitika, which he understandably saw as the back of beyond. He actually used the expression 'beyond the Nile', which seems curiously inappropriate, but also says that he saw the West Coast as 'a forgotten land' – still largely without proper roads or bridges, where the little household schools would rarely have more than half a dozen pupils. Jim Valentine came to love Westland and to see those years as the most exciting and challenging of his life.

Jim's previous knowledge of the area dated from an extraordinarily demanding bicycle tour he and two friends had made in the summer holidays of 1904. How they got to Nelson I don't know – perhaps by sea – but they had cycled from there south to Hokitika and over Arthur's Pass to catch the train at Springfield and return to Timaru. It would have been a mammoth undertaking on a good bike – but Jim's tyre burst irreparably when they were miles from anywhere, and he finished the ride limping along on the rim at seven or eight miles per hour.

Horses were more reliable and most of the West Coast stories have Jim riding the length and breadth of his territory: along 250 miles of coast from Punakaiki (actually in Nelson province), north of Barrytown, to Bruce Bay and Okuru, south of Haast. My grandfather does not give many details of the tiny schools he inspected or the standard of education in these remote places before the days of the Correspondence School. He does say he thought these 'uncertificated' teachers were 'wonderfully successful, so far as their powers allowed' . Generally his policy was to praise wherever possible, condemn as lightly as he could, and 'to spend hours showing better methods'. But he writes much more of the difficulties and excitements of his travelling and of the glories of the landscape. I will quote one particularly purple passage:

> Every year, as I rode back from Bruce Bay, I saw one view unequalled anywhere else on the road. Usually when I came to Cook's River, evening was approaching and for seven miles I rode up the river-bed to the kindly folk in the Williams' house at Weheka. One such approach I shall never forget. It was on Sunday evening, March 3, 1918. I had ridden from Bruce Bay that day, and it was late afternoon as I rode up the wide expanse of riverbed. To the west a glorious sun was sinking over a silver sea – that same sea which Tasman had sailed over in 1642. To my right the silver ribbons of the branches of Cook's River stretched glittering from the Fox Glacier to the ocean. Ahead of me, miles away, the massive peaks, snow-clad and glacier-scored, lifted their white heads into a gorgeously coloured sky – purples and pinks and mauves, ever-changing wisps of vapour, rainbow-coloured – above the varied greenery of the age-old forest, the scarlet band of the flowering rata, well up on the mountain slopes (Tasman and Sefton in the distance). There they all were, one of nature's grandest pictures in our lovely New Zealand home. Some day that area will be a tourist resort, but no tourist in motor-car or aeroplane will ever see those glories as I did, riding quietly and alone on my trusty pony.

We did that journey, years ago, with Jim Valentine's memoirs open on my knee. The distant landscapes, in their magnificence, are unchanged. But we, in the car, drove swiftly over innumerable bridges and had to work hard to imagine the excitement of fording those rivers. Well-contoured roads have replaced the bridle tracks, which were so narrow that if a rider 'met a mob of bullocks just mustered by Jack Cron' there was nothing for it but to take the horse up a side creek where the bullocks could not see him, 'for they were wild and untamed: no rider dared face them.'

Jack Cron imported into the Okuru region well-bred bulls and heifers, whose offspring were eventually driven overland to Ross, where they could now be sent by rail to Otira and then driven over Arthur's Pass; the rail tunnel was still not completed. (What happened, one can't help wondering, if one of Cobb's horse-drawn coaches ran into a wild mob of bullocks on that narrow ledge high above the Otira River?)

Jack Cron is part of another story my grandfather told of his adventures of those years on the West Coast. The Haast River was too high to ford. My grandfather was travelling with the mailman. They reached the river just as the sun was setting and needed somehow to attract Jack Cron's attention on the other side. It was a long time before, at last, the mailman's cracking of his stock whip was answered with a rifle shot from Cron's homestead. They waited until Cron rowed his boat over the raging current, as best he could. He landed far downstream where they fastened the mailman's pony somehow to the boat to drag it up the river to a small beach where it could be loaded and where they could embark. They piled all their gear, including the mailbags, their saddles and swags and themselves into the boat and encouraged the horses to swim over.

Sometimes there was no boat available. On the Karangarua River a man called Andrew Scott acted as a government pilot when the river was in flood. He had a fine horse himself, seventeen hands high, and looked at Jim Valentine's mount with some doubt. 'I had no fear', my grandfather wrote, 'for I knew that my horse, small as he was, was used to crossing raging torrents'. Away Scott went in front, and told Jim to be close behind, keeping his horse's head at the leading horse's rump, not deviating by even a yard from the track he was following. After a worrying encounter with a submerged ridge, Jim got over, drenched to the waist. It was a warm day and his clothes dried on him as he continued on his journey.

There was also some magnificent coastal scenery on the road north to Barrytown. We went there on our recent tour, because a photograph of it was in the album my other grandfather gave to my father the year he was seven, more than ten years before Jim Valentine's story of the Runanga murder. (Runanga, it may be remembered, was designed and laid out by this other grandfather, Arthur Harrop, in 1907.) Jim's story is of a mine pay-clerk being waylaid just outside Runanga, shot and killed and robbed of the £3,000 that was meant for the miners' fortnight's work. The day after this murder, Jim set out on his regular Inspection trip north from Hokitika, with Bedford Moodie, his Agriculture Instructor on the Coast:

> We were well-mounted, and we found constables posted at every strategic point along the road. One of these constables proved almost bellicose that day and ordered us peremptorily to halt while he questioned us. I told him it was easy to see he was a stranger in the district, as no other constable would have halted me, known as I was to every constable on the Coast. He demanded to know where we were going and our business. His manner rather nettled me and I'm afraid I answered him curtly, when I told him we would be found in the hotel at Barrytown that night. He replied, 'Well, I hope your story is true. I'll be there tonight and I'll make a point of looking for you.' Sure enough he arrived about 9 pm. The landlady had given me my usual room, the best in the hotel – the only good room in it, I think. But when the officious constable arrived, he commandeered the good room and Bedford and I had to move to the common sleeping room, one with several beds in it …. The murderer was later apprehended in Christchurch and after trial was hanged.

Today the All Nations Hotel at Barrytown boasts that it was established in the 1870s. A pleasant, friendly place where we were given a free cup of tea in the middle of the afternoon, it has a large notice: WE CAN'T SERVE DRUNKS. LET'S ALL TAKE IT EASY. It warns of a $10,000 fine and offers beds for $1 a night for parties of six *locals*, encouraging them to SLEEP NOT DRIVE.

Jim Valentine's move to the West Coast meant that it was necessary for Hilda to become a boarder in Croomlea, North Street, the Timaru Girls' High School hostel, just five minutes' walk from the school. On 27 July 1916, just after her sixteenth birthday, she wrote in her diary: 'I think I shall like it, though I shall miss the family extremely.' Nettie, her older sister, had already matriculated, but had decided she did not want to go to university, 'though she had a very good brain and should have gone'. 'School is lovely', Hilda wrote a little later. 'And so is Miss Watson.' At Croomlea relationships were without guilt. Hilda had grown up believing that relationships between men and women were bound to be 'unhealthy', unless the two people concerned were set on a path towards engagement and marriage; but friendship with her own sex was totally innocent. Hilda had *no* idea that there could be any latent sexuality in such devotion, just as I myself had no idea when I started my own boarding school life at Marsden in Wellington twenty-six years later. (But I was only nine and she was sixteen.)

Love for girls and women teachers could cause pain, but absolutely no guilt. Hilda wrote openly in her diary about her feelings for Win Watson, a young tennis-playing Otago graduate on the staff. On 16 September 1916: 'I am glad to be back at school. Everyone is so alright. Miss Watson is just so … I wish *she* would love me.' Sadly, three weeks later, Hilda writes: 'Today is Miss Watson's birthday. She just likes me tolerably, if that.' Hilda, all the same, was good at female friendship, making a number of women friends, both at high school and later at university, that she would keep all her life, maintaining close relationships by letter over many years from the other side of the world. 'It is a blessing' she wrote of one such friend. 'Hetty is the most understanding person. She has such infinite patience and endless sympathy.'

I have already quoted from Hilda's diary in Chapter 3. There is a great deal more that reminds me of her perpetual need to be *good*. She said she wanted to be 'humble, helpful and holy'. (In school, perhaps more interestingly, they were encouraging the girls to have 'grace, grit and gumption.') But it was not enough to be good. Hilda had to try to be the *best* at everything. In the Sixth Form at Timaru Girls' High she missed watching the Boys' High School sports because of a heavy cold, but vowed that she would take part in their own sports, cold or no cold, 'for I must be champion'. It is a relief to read two days later that Hilda 'won several events' and ended up 'equal champion with Lulu Carlton'.

Everyone was playing tennis. This photograph of the public courts at Caroline Bay was taken in 1914. Hilda's tennis was impressive long before she met that other keen tennis-player, my father. I still have a pretty blue plant pot she won in 1913 in a doubles match against Oamaru Girls' High when she was only thirteen and a nervous last-minute partner for Timaru's 'illustrious' Head Girl, Eva Day. Hilda tried to do *everything* in the best possible way and hoped she would not go far wrong if she learnt continually from both her Bible and the world around her. But it was not always easy to reconcile the two.

There survive two long letters of 1917, dated 30 September and 11 November, from her 'loving father', Jim Valentine, writing from Hokitika to Timaru when she was seventeen:

> I sympathise much with you in your feelings and your dislikes. It's just old Scotch blood in you that's coming out, and your attitude of mind towards certain happenings during church services is the very same as I had at your age. It's not in your blood to enjoy display of religious feeling or fervour …. But beware lest any form of spiritual pride causes you to fall. For all you know that may be an insidious form of temptation laid before you by Satan to tempt you from your first faith.

And a little later:

> I quite appreciate all your difficulties and understand them too. For I see in your life just mine over again. In my early days of action for Christ, I was very shy and diffident and retiring. I hated to speak of my religious experiences publicly. I greatly disliked taking part in testimony meetings. But as opportunity offered, I seized suitable occasions. I spoke always and only when I had something to say. I never spoke merely because it was expected of me. And I gradually overcame my diffidence, my distaste for public and

open confession. Indeed, I found it a means of grace, and of confirmation in my faith and beliefs, and of fixing my thought and clarifying my spiritual vision. Never forget that Satan is a real enemy of your soul and he will, in most plausible and specious fashion, try to persuade you to hold your tongue where Christ would have you *witness*, and to stay away from meetings where your presence would make conditions better for someone else – and for yourself. It is hard to give you advice as to how you shall recognise these insidious attacks, but, never fear, Christ's power can overcome 'all the wiles of the wicked one' and can keep your conscience so clear that you will always know how to act. 'Trust all, nor be afraid.'

Nothing would ever overcome my mother's distaste for 'dramatic appeals to men and women to decide there and then' that they had accepted Christ as their saviour and His way as the way to salvation. In her memoirs she said she had been brought up as a Presbyterian, but it is obvious from these letters that the services that alienated her were in the Baptist church. Hilda was a natural Anglican – but there was no way she could become one at this stage. Jim Valentine wrote:

> Anglican services may be majestic and grand, but I have noticed that they are to many in the Church like the prayers I hear in the Catholic schools, only a matter of repetition and gabble. I have no sympathy whatever with the arrogant claims of the majority of the Anglican clergy and people. They claim to be the *only* true Church and they deny Heaven to any outside their 'Communion'.

My grandfather was particularly incensed to hear that on some of the troopships 'the Anglican chaplains have denied the right of any other chaplain to conduct services on board'. Jim Valentine encouraged his daughter to read daily from her Bible (as she would do all her life). 'But don't try to solve all your difficulties in a day. Christ purposely hides our way at times in order that we may turn to Him, and just *follow*.'

Angus Harrop was an Anglican, but that was, of course, not a particular problem in 1917. More of a problem for Hilda was to discover that many of her friends, who never went to any church, seemed to be just as 'good' as those who did. It was at a point that she was 'feeling beastly dissatisfied' with herself, as she wrote in her diary. She felt she should be doing more for other people, and not worrying about dividing the population of Hokitika into sheep and goats:

> Is not the world's creed to a large extent the same as the Christian's as far as concrete ideals concerning life? Do not worldly people want to be straight

and true and clean and brave and pleasant to those around? Can't worldly men be 'worthwhile' too? Wherein lies the difference? Is it only that the Christian recognises all these virtues in Jesus Christ and so takes him as his example, knowing that if he tries to be and do what Christ would have him do, then Christ will welcome him Home at last? If that is so, the Christian is so only because he has thought more deeply. Even though both are striving after almost the same thing, the Christian *must* be the better because he takes God into account and has God's help – yet the difference is not always noticeable.

That Hilda was reading George Eliot at the time may have had something to do with this paragraph. She quotes 'the reiterated choice of good and evil that gradually determines character'. George Eliot was well known to be agnostic. Many of my mother's closest friends throughout her life were not Christians, devout as she remained herself. At eighteen she was already convinced that it was only with God's help that she could become the sort of woman she wanted to be: 'gracious, kind, large-hearted, generous-natured (to give much because I have so much), sincere, unself-conscious, serene (i.e. unmoved by petty trials), sympathetic, charitable, wide in views, sunny-tempered, sweet, loyal, true, noble, unassuming.'

I suggested in Chapter 3 that by 1918, when she started at university, my mother had already become the one girl in my father's life. As the events of 1919 unfolded (the death of Angus's father, and the subsequent desperate need to find some solution to the problem of poor disabled Frederick), all my mother's determination to be kind, sympathetic, serene, sweet and noble must have at times made Angus think she felt about him as he felt about her. But that was far from the case. There is one curious passage in Hilda's diary in the week after Angus's father's death. She wrote: 'Angus came tonight. I'm seeing too much of him. – Sat, Sun, Mon, Tues, Wed. It does not do –' And then she added, surprisingly, 'Absence makes the heart –' breaking off before she put into words the suggestion that she perhaps wanted to bind Angus even closer by withholding her presence. Or could it have been her own heart she wrote of? She certainly had no intention of being tied down. There were so many attractive men around (both 'worldly' and Christian). Her diary is full of them. And she still intended to keep the vow she had made at fifteen – to teach, for years if necessary, in order to save enough to achieve her ambition to travel, to see England and Scotland and France, whose language she had spent so many years learning.

J ust once it seems did Jim Valentine take any of his children with him on his
Westland Inspection trips. In the winter of 1919 Hilda records that she and
her older sister Nettie (aged nineteen and twenty) travelled with their father,
the two girls in a 'one-horse gig'. The high point of this trip was a walk on the
Franz Josef Glacier: 'We actually got on to the glacier with its crevasses and its
deep blue ice caves.'

In Hilda's diary this is a rare moment of simple record. She continued a
rigorous process of self-examination. She had left Timaru Girls' High School with
a glowing testimonial from her Principal, Barbara Watt, but the teacher's praise
seemed to have little to do with her own self-assessment. Miss Watt had written:

> Miss Valentine has been our Head Prefect and the leading girl in the school,
> both in scholarship and in athletics .... She has been either 1st or 2nd in
> the Tennis team, equal first in swimming, and a strong member of the First
> Basketball team.
>
> Her character throughout the course has been thoroughly satisfactory: I
> consider her one of the best prefects that I have ever had in the school. She has
> a very strong sense of duty and so much force of character as to give her a very
> great influence over her fellows; and this influence has always been thrown on
> the side of right.
>
> Miss Valentine is also a very gifted girl as regards music: she both sings and
> plays well. I consider that she will be a valuable acquisition to the staff of any
> school, and expect in the future to hear of her as a very successful teacher.

And what was this paragon writing in her private diary? This must have
been a bad day:

> Still impulsive – living for the moment and not thinking of after-effects.
> Always wanting things I can't have – wouldn't be good for me if I could.

Still talk too much – say silly things and regret them afterwards. A forward, moody child, with no self control – show everything I feel. Jealous little cat – impatient and unkind – bad-tempered and show it.

Hilda also sets out, on more than one occasion in her early years at university, her wary thoughts on how one should behave in the company of men:

> I must not act on impulse – I must think of what I'm saying.
> I must not be keen on anything proposed by men.
> I must not be very friendly – that is, I must be quiescent and stationary and let them move all the way towards me – if they want to, they will, and if they don't, then I mustn't want them to.
> I mustn't let them know my views on matters without their seeking them: make them curious!
> Keep self-control perfect.
> Don't respond at once to overtures.
> Keep conversation strictly impersonal.
> Don't let men ask questions – change the subject.
> Don't tell them what you're thinking even tho' you want to.
> Don't think of what you want – self-gratification is often at the expense of the other's interest.
> Don't let them be sure of you – keep them guessing.
> Don't take them into your confidence.
> Don't discuss other people. Don't even mention other girls or men.
> Don't discuss rules of conduct.
> Confine yourself to general topics – work, sport, books, music.
> If you do get excited, don't show it.

What strange conversations Hilda must have had as she whirled round the dance floor with Mr Luke ('lovely'), Mr Gray, Mr Park, Mr Petrie and a dozen others. She had good fun at one supper with Mr Jackson, and coming home with Mr Learmont, 'and I've seen him about ten times today and I wish I hadn't. He asked me to go canoeing on Sunday – I was sad that I had to say No!' Did she really keep in mind her own self-imposed rules? In 1987, in her extreme old age, Hilda noted in this diary: 'It seems impossible that sixty-eight years ago it was the custom for us to call college boys of our own age "Mr"!!'

There are very few – rather tantalising – mentions of Angus in the diaries. On 20 February 1919: 'Angus came.' This was just after his father's death. 'He's going to make a confession to me in the ages to come.' They were both still only eighteen. There were years of university ahead of them. But surely Angus had already determined that he would one day marry Hilda. Was this the confession that could only be made in the 'ages to come'? Or was it, far more seriously, a suggestion that he did not think he should ever have children, thinking of the dire situation of Frederick, his younger brother?

Angus must often have been thinking about Frederick in 1919, in the months after their father's death. His sister May was old enough to start at the Teachers' Training College in Christchurch, where she would soon meet and eventually marry Geoffrey Cuthbert, a fellow student with Angus and Hilda. Pretty and bright, she was not, at this stage, a problem. She was able to live at Bishopscourt, a hostel for women students. This photo that she took at a tea-party there includes Angus on the left and Geoff Cuthbert on the right at the back.

But what was to happen to fourteen-year-old Frederick? We now know that in August, 1919, a place was found for the boy at a Special School in Otekaike, near Oamaru. He was there only a few months when the manager of this school, one Thomas Archey, applied to the Magistrates for an order for Frederick Harrop's 'reception and detention' in the Mental Hospital at Seacliff. Archey describes himself as the 'legal guardian' of the boy, who had just had his fifteenth birthday at the time of the application. There are no names on his file card in the space for Relatives. On one page of the records there is the fact that both mother and father were dead and that neither brother nor sister (then aged nineteen and seventeen) 'were in a position to contribute to the maintenance of the said person'. In fact, a large proportion of the money left by my grandfather – much larger than the share left to Angus and May – had been put in trust for Frederick's maintenance. Was it in exchange for the legal right to use this money that Archey had agreed to take on Frederick at the Special School?

Only four months later, Archey applied to have the boy removed, giving as the reason the fact that he was ineducable. Frederick 'suffers from Friedreich's ataxia which has developed since the age of puberty .... Facial contortions horrible when attempting to speak .... His articulation is very defective and speech difficult to understand. Mental ability nil.' This was certainly the assumption throughout Frederick's time at Seacliff. The medical records over the thirty-two years he lived in the hospital contain many different medical terms: they speak of 'choreoform movements', of 'cerebral cortical irritation', of 'spastic paraplegia', of 'athetosis'.

All these terms could be consistent with cerebral palsy, and now one knows that, although it is often combined with mental disability, it is not always so. I read recently in a newspaper obituary of the astonishing case of Michael Devenney (1959–2004). He was diagnosed with cerebral palsy at the age of two; specialists suggested he would never be able to walk or talk and that he would be completely ineducable. Throughout his life, most people could not understand his speech except 'through a third-party facilitator' – yet he took a Ph.D. at Clare College, Cambridge, and became a government advisor on disability.

This is the hardest thing of all to think about, that somewhere locked inside Frederick's crippled, dysfunctional body, there could have been a normally functioning mind. Close relatives now have access to the relevant records. I read through the fat pile of reports with tears streaming down my face. What did Frederick do all day for thirty years? He was too crippled to take part in the normal therapy of the hospital – the farm work, the gardening, the domestic tasks. On admission, one of the doctors wrote 'This boy's constant movement, and the very imperfect articulation, probably make him appear worse than he is. He salutes when "Good morning" is said to him.' (Fifteen years later another doctor wrote 'Like his kind, he is somewhat brighter than he appears to be.') Early on, the boy's one clear sentence recorded is the sad, inevitable, heart-wrenching 'I want to go home.' But there was no home to go to.

Janet Frame, in the hospital herself when Frederick was still alive, wrote those same five words in a letter to the psychologist, John Money. Because of Janet Frame, we know far more about Seacliff than we can really bear to know. It was a turreted, castellated Gothic castle, standing high above the sea, with over a thousand patients and a farm of over a thousand acres.

Dr Truby King, more famous now for his hugely influential theories about infant feeding, was the Medical Superintendent at Seacliff when my uncle was admitted. His daughter Mary's biography writes of the rhododendron dells, the woodlands of native trees, the rose gardens and orchards. There were pottery classes and weekly dances but none of these were any use to Frederick. Janet Frame described the 'rather shocking conditions and meals', the nurses' uniforms, 'pink like the cherry blossom', with their 'deep pockets full of keys' and all those damaged people living as animals do, with no past, no future, no personal clothes, no possessions, no privacy, no literature, nothing.

It is painful to read the notes made by the observing doctors over the long years Frederick was confined, with no evidence in all those years of any family contact. The doctors are sometimes brutal in their brevity: 'This imbecile is of absolutely no use.' Others are more impressed: 'He tries to make himself useful as far as his limitations permit.' Very late on, the year before his death in 1951, one doctor wrote: 'Freddie is a cheerful, pleasant athetotic imbecile …. His conduct is good but he is deteriorating slowly.' It is slightly reassuring to read 'Usually cheerful and contented', and, over and over again, 'eats and sleeps well'.

At the beginning of this book I called Frederick and Eva, those two siblings of my father, 'the disappeared'. They did disappear entirely as far as we were concerned. I imagine Arthur Harrop as fiercely protective of his younger son; the father's death was a disaster for everyone. As I write, I will try to forget about Frederick, as my father tried to forget him over the long years ahead. I am grateful that I did not know about Frederick and Eva as I was growing up; I think my father was right to spare us this knowledge and that my mother was right not to tell me the little she knew until Anthony and I had our own four healthy children and David and Margaret their three.

But I know, psychiatrists and psychotherapists tell us, that the suppression of painful knowledge can be harmful. 'What cannot be talked about cannot be put to rest', as the psychologist Bruno Bettelheim once said. Frederick's abandonment, his secret, unmentioned life, may have had something to do not only with May's and Angus's anger, but with the devastating strokes, to which they had inherited a tendency, that destroyed both their lives in middle age. I think of the Japanese Nobel prize-winning novelist, Kenzaburo Oe, who cherished and constantly acknowledged his damaged son – and attributed his own strength, both as a writer and a human being, to what could have been his tragedy. Behind every happiness in my father's later life in England – and there were many reasons to be happy – there was his knowledge of his brother's plight, of the boy, the man, living out his days in a mental hospital on the other side of the world.

CHAPTER 7

Choosing partners

If I say that my parents knew each other when they were both still at school, that they both went to Canterbury University College (C.U.C.), won the mixed doubles tennis cup together there and took their M.A.s with honours in 1922, it suggests that their relationship was plain sailing and their eventual marriage inevitable. But this was far from the case.

In one of the few early letters that survives, written in 1919 in the winter following his father's death, Angus accepted Hilda's rebukes and her decision that they should no longer write to each other. This followed quite soon after her diary entry in which she said she knew she was seeing too much of him and feared they were becoming too closely involved. He had now joined her at Canterbury University College, where she (though three months younger) had already had a wonderful first year, balancing rather precariously the claims of her conscience and of her heart, twirling round a number of different dance floors with a succession of delightful young men, including that *lovely* Mr Luke and the *interesting* Erle Schroder. (I can sympathise. In 1953 the Principal of my Oxford college said, 'Ah, Miss Harrop, the charms of one's first summer term are apt to go to one's head.') Miss Valentine in 1918 had ignored the grind of Anglo-Saxon grammar, thinking to get by on her wits to translate that difficult language into the modern variety. She failed that paper and that was why, though she started earlier, she ended up taking her degrees, B.A. and M.A., at the same time as my father, who never failed anything.

In 1919 Hilda could see that this devoted and possibly importunate boy might cramp her style. For her nineteenth birthday that winter, when Hilda was away from Hokitika on the expedition to the Franz Josef with her father, Angus sent her the postcard featured on the next page. On the back, after wishing her many happy returns, he wrote: 'The message on the other side is to be taken quite literally.'

However powerful Angus's feelings were, at this point their eventual marriage seemed unlikely, to say the least. What did seem inevitable was that they would both eventually teach. Angus had not yet thought of the alluring idea of being an unconventional journalist. Hilda was always *trying* to be conventional, to behave in an acceptable, appropriate fashion. She never actually uses the word 'ladylike', but it hovers over all her self-admonitions. 'I must use pure English', she wrote in her diary, 'abjure slang such as killing, decent, ripping …. I must resist temptation to frivolity and pleasure-seeking …. I must not make eyes. I must not do unconventional things.'

Angus wrote to Hilda, who had apparently chided him for his attitudes, his behaviour, his youthful folly.

> Well, concerning your letter, don't you think there is an excuse for people of nineteen not being quite grown up? I really believe that I prefer not to be quite staid and respectable till I am a teacher, anyway. Then I suppose I shall be conventional enough to recognise the foolishness of having been young once ….
>
> I am sorry that I will not be able to benefit by our correspondence, but I quite recognise that there are things beside which that pales into insignificance.
>
> Left quite on my own, as I am now, I have every opportunity to acquire that state of 'grown-up'ness that you recommend – henceforth the wicked past I renounce for ever and look forward to the perfectly commonplace and humdrum career of the conventional man – that character so greatly admirable and so little likeable. I prefer not to keep my own individuality as I am afraid it would make my life a misery by having to be constantly told to keep quiet and not to be eccentric.
>
> I envy your ability to combine a humouring of convention with a preservation of your own individuality, but it's beyond me. When you think of the crowds of utterly conventional people it makes you shudder – and here am I doomed to swell the number!

You will be quite convinced by now that I am mad or even annoyed or both, but really I *am* largely serious …. I am serious now to the extent of hoping that convention won't be allowed to kill your friendship

For yours very sincerely, Angus

'Left quite on my own as I am' – how could these words of the orphaned boy not touch her heart? But it was as well they did not. They would be friends, not lovers. They both had a lot of growing up to do, and Connon Hall and College House in Christchurch were just sufficiently far apart to allow them to get on with that.

Looking back in 1925, Hilda wrote to Angus:

You have felt more or less the same towards me since we were at school, haven't you? … Ever since 1917 you have played an important part in my life, sometimes more and sometimes less. 1918 and 1920 were specially 'plus' years, 1919, 1921 and the early part of 1922 rather 'minus' years, weren't they, tho' the undercurrent was always there and since 1922 it has grown steadily stronger. And yet it was in 1919 that I remember someone telling me that I would marry you one day and, tho' I firmly refused to entertain the idea, far underneath there was a feeling that perhaps in spite of myself I would.

Hilda Valentine had begun her university career with a part in a rather impressive achievement. On arrival in Christchurch in 1918, with that unexpected Gammack Scholarship, she had spent a miserable week at the YWCA and then moved to a friend's aunt's house when she found the YW hopeless for studying. Thinking of the years ahead, she and two other young women students made a bold request for an interview with the university's Board of Governors. The girls succeeded in convincing the governors that an old house on the corner of Park Terrace and Chester Street West, which the university had bought the previous year, should be for women rather than men. The new hall was named after the first woman to graduate from the University of New Zealand, Helen Connon. It appears, indeed, that she was the first woman to graduate with honours in any university in the British Empire – an interesting distinction. She had been the Principal of Christchurch Girls' High School before her marriage in 1887 to Professor John Macmillan Brown. By 1918 Helen Connon Brown was dead and Professor Brown Vice-Chancellor of the University.

The photograph on the next page of the first six students who lived there hung in Connon Hall for many years. They were, from left to right, Eva Rowe, Hilda Valentine, Grace Aitken, Rosa Innes, Myrtle Bell and Muriel Innes. Connon Hall provided a home (if only a shared room) for Hilda during her entire

time at C.U.C., while her father, Jim Valentine, was moved by the Education Department from Hokitika, briefly to Christchurch and then, in August 1920, to Taranaki as Senior Inspector of Schools. He and my grandmother bought a house in St Aubyn Street, New Plymouth, where he lived for the rest of his life. The house itself, which I remember well from the 1940s, still exists, moved from its original site (when the present Southern Cross Hospital was built) to Motunui, a rural location outside the city. Here is the house, dominated by hats, on a very special occasion, the wedding of my aunt Nettie to Lewis

Watkins, a handsome young farmer she had met while staying with a friend. It was 8 May 1923 and the two bridesmaids in those particularly large hats are Hilda (on the bride's left) and her sister, Lottie. Jim, my grandfather, can just be seen at one side of Lottie's hat and Nellie, my grandmother, at the other.

Hilda went to New Plymouth first in the Christmas holidays of 1920–1. 'Not as good as the Coast', she wrote in her diary, missing Hokitika and the crowd of friends. Later there would be crowds of friends in New Plymouth and she would climb the mountain and look back with nostalgia on sunny days reading in Pukekura Park, a few minutes' walk from the house where my brother and his wife now live, high above the sea.

Angus found Hokitika unbearable, he said, after Hilda had moved away. During his time at C.U.C., for over four years College House in Rolleston Avenue, Christchurch, became his home. Established as a residential college for male students, and soon to expand, there were only fifteen men when Angus moved in, just enough for a rugby team. My father is at the left of the front row as you look at the photo.

The Principal of College House, John Russell Wilford, Professor of Divinity and Canon of Christchurch Cathedral, had been born in Norfolk in England, not far from where I live now. He was an excellent man, humorous and gentle, with an equally excellent wife. Wilford's autobiography, *Southern Cross and Evening Star*, tells first of his early years at Waikari, where the vicarage scullery became knee-deep in water every time it rained heavily and enterprising rats skimmed the cream off the milk pans with their tails.

College House was different. It was exactly what Angus needed, beginning at the university so soon after his father's funeral. Looking back years later, he saw his time there as 'blissfully happy: days in the sun, dashes from the tennis courts in Hagley Park into the House for a shower and into College for a four o'clock lecture, playing "rotten cricket" in a yard with an expansive – and expensive – boundary of windows on two sides.' Angus's photo album is full of pictures of young men, solemn in team photos or larking around with motor bikes and guitars and, for Carnival, outlandishly dressed, suggesting a crowd of suppressed transvestites. Here Angus himself (back left) is in the university tennis four which won the Canterbury Lawn Tennis Association's A Grade Competition, 1921–2, with the proud boast, Played 6; Won 6.

My father wrote a footnote to Canon Wilford's book which ended 'He brought to Christchurch something of the college spirit of Cambridge.' Wilford had graduated from Christ's College, Cambridge, where he had taken the Greek Testament Prize. There were other Cambridge influences. Angus read History, English and French in his first year, Economics and Philosophy with History in his second, and his Economics teacher was Jack Condliffe, who, after the war had been N.Z.E.F. scholar and Gresham Research Student at Gonville and Caius College, Cambridge, before taking up a Chair at C.U.C. in 1920, when he was still only twenty-nine. It became inevitable that my father would dream of Cambridge and it was Jack Condliffe's suggestion that he should aim for Caius.

Until I first saw C.U.C., I imagined that Cambridge, when my father finally got there in 1923, would have been profoundly different from anything he had seen before. But the old buildings in Christchurch bear a strong resemblance to those of an English university.

Now that Canterbury University has moved out to Ilam, the buildings my parents knew are known collectively as 'the Arts Centre' (Te Pokapi Toi O Otautahi). The splendid campus along Worcester Street (which runs down to Cathedral Square) contains cloisters and quadrangles and a Great Hall, which continue to delight the eye, but they share the site with Annie's Wine Bar, a weekend Food Fair and market, the Southern Ballet Theatre's headquarters and a number of other cafés, galleries and theatres.

Canon Wilford and Jack Condliffe (as I knew them) were two among a group of outstanding men at C.U.C. in the 1920s. Of them all, James Hight (then Dr, later Sir and Rector of the University), the New Zealand-born Professor of History, was the greatest influence on both my parents. They loved him and would have been happy to know his name is so well commemorated at the University today. As Leicester Webb wrote in the *Listener* on Hight's retirement in 1948: 'Information can be taught, a task our universities do well. And knowledge can be fitfully communicated. But wisdom? How are men taught to be wise? Only by example.' Dr Hight was wise, but he was also extremely well organised. His cyclostyled annotated reading sheets, 'monuments to energy and erudition', were both daunting and inspiring.

I have in front of me three History papers my father faced for his B.A. in 1921. There were two on European History since 1500 and one on 'Outlines of the Development of the Colonial Empire of Great Britain'. The range of questions was extremely wide. As New Zealand's history would eventually become my father's special subject, it is interesting to see what he chose to write about at the age of twenty-one.

'To be successful a colony must answer some economic end'. Illustrate this principle from the history of British colonisation.

How far did a) the Quebec Act of 1774 b) the Constitutional Act of 1791, provide a satisfactory solution of the problems of Canadian administration at those dates?

Discuss the effects of the abolition of slavery upon the development of the West India Islands.

Sketch the history of the relations between English and Dutch in South Africa.

What influences have been exerted upon Australian history by a) convictism, b) gold-discovery?

Give some account of Gibbon Wakefield and his connection with the colonisation of New Zealand.

It was a relief to my father when he heard he had won the Senior Scholarship in History, for money was always a problem for him. Dr Hight had prepared his students excellently. He sent them out into the world with certain standards of scholarship – of accuracy, of application – which served my father well, both as a historian and as a journalist. I have over the years of my own biographical research often heard in my head Hight's comforting assertion of the value of negative evidence.

There were two other admired teachers, of whom my parents spoke from time to time: Arnold Wall and James Shelley. Both were Englishmen; both had been to Cambridge. Wall was Professor of English; his dry humour, unaccompanied by any vestige of a smile, was immensely appealing. James Shelley, then Professor of Education, eventually left the university to become Director of Broadcasting for New Zealand. My father credited him with the growth of interest in drama throughout the country.

It was to Professor Shelley my father went ('as a deputation of one') to ask for the formation of a Canterbury College Drama Society. The programme of the first production in 1921 bears witness to A.J. Harrop's brief appearance as Robert Carne ('a solemn prig with no digestion') in *The Two Mr Wetherbys* by St John Hankin, 'the theme of whose plays is in the main the criticism of social convention and hypocrisy.' As secretary of the new society, my father, I suspect, wrote the programme notes. It was a theme after his own heart.

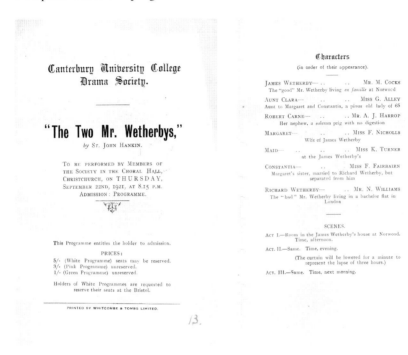

Canterbury University College
Drama Society.

"The Two Mr. Wetherbys,"
by St. John Hankin.

To be performed by Members of the Society in the Choral Hall, Christchurch, on THURSDAY, September 22nd, 1921, at 8.15 p.m.
Admission : Programme.

This Programme entitles the holder to admission.
PRICES :
5/- (White Programme) seats may be reserved.
3/- (Pink Programme) unreserved.
1/- (Green Programme) unreserved.

Holders of White Programmes are requested to reserve their seats at the Bristol.

PRINTED BY WHITCOMBE & TOMBS LIMITED.

Characters
(in order of their appearance).

JAMES WETHERBY— .. .. MR. M. COCKS
The "good" Mr. Wetherby living *en famille* at Norwood.

AUNT CLARA— .. .. MISS G. ALLEY
Aunt to Margaret and Constantia, a pious old lady of 65

ROBERT CARNE— .. .. MR. A. J. HARROP
Her nephew, a solemn prig with no digestion

MARGARET— .. .. MISS F. NICHOLLS
Wife of James Wetherby

MAID— .. .. .. MISS K. TURNER
at the James Wetherby's

CONSTANTIA— .. .. MISS F. FAIRBAIRN
Margaret's sister, married to Richard Wetherby, but separated from him

RICHARD WETHERBY— .. MR. N. WILLIAMS
The "bad" Mr. Wetherby living in a bachelor flat in London

SCENES.
ACT I.—Room in the James Wetherby's house at Norwood. Time, afternoon.
ACT II.—Same. Time, evening.
(The curtain will be lowered for a minute to represent the lapse of three hours.)
ACT III.—Same. Time, next morning.

/3.

Hilda Valentine meanwhile was herself making a series of public appearances as a singer. For three years in Christchurch she trained with Millicent Jennings and in her memoirs considered these 'private singing lessons' had 'enriched my whole life'. Miss Jennings herself had 'trained abroad and was an artist to her fingertips'. On Sunday evenings there were concerts in the Town Hall for returned soldiers. She dressed her pupils in beautiful long satin gowns and draped them with glittering necklaces. My mother particularly remembered singing, in a trio, Frank Bridge's 'Drop, drop slow tears'.

This was the glamorous romantic life that was at the edge of my mother's dreams – far removed from the reality to which her singing lessons led: some temporary singing teaching at Christchurch Girls' High (which helped to pay for the lessons) and the responsibility for teaching music at New Plymouth Girls' High School. Playing the piano remained more important than singing. I always thought she took her L.R.A.M. – Licentiate of the Royal Academy of

Music – but she doesn't mention it in her memoirs. She often used to play for us to sing together when I was a girl – all the old folk songs: 'Annie Laurie', 'The minstrel boy to the wars has gone', 'Barbara Allen', 'Molly Malone' and so on. I still remember the words and the pathos in them. There seemed to be a lot of lone maidens in those songs, including the one who early one morning, just as the sun was rising, was heard singing in the valley below. But it was the minstrel boy who brought tears to my eyes as I stood at the piano.

I also remember my mother's stories of long before I was born – of trying to play the piano and teach singing at the same time. It was impossible to see what the New Plymouth girls at the back of the class were up to. Her friend Nance Tizzard, who taught science in an adjoining laboratory, could see through the window and made Hilda realise she needed to find a girl to play the piano, so she herself could conduct and keep an eye on what was going on.

At C.U.C. in 1921 and 1922 Hilda saw very little of Angus except in lecture rooms or on the tennis courts. She was entranced by a man called George Lockwood, an athletic 'Blue'. For her twenty-first birthday in June 1921, George sent Hilda a big box of violets and her diary is full of references to him. I have a copy of the Oxford edition of the *Ingoldsby Legends* which George gave to Hilda for Christmas 1922 and in which he inscribed a verse of his own, beginning:

> Long have I sought for subtle compliment
> And turned my Christmas wish a thousand ways ….

In a notebook at that time Hilda wrote a summary of Clifford Bax's *Square Pegs*, 'a rhymed fantasy for two girls'. It cannot be entirely a coincidence that in her summary the character called Hilda 'longs for a romantic, chivalrous lover', whereas the other girl wants 'a strong, silent man'.

Angus was sometimes inarticulate, if not silent, and strong enough for a working and playing schedule that would have floored many men. There is a note surviving from him in which he says how much he wishes he could 'conquer that feeling which ties my tongue'. There is another note where he says 'I don't think it was not knowing how or nervousness which restrained me. I told myself we had elected to follow a certain path ….' They were to be *friends*, that was all. It certainly seems that this studious young man (with his self-confessed faults of 'temper and selfishness') was not exactly what Hilda wanted. At the end of 1921 she was writing in her diary how 'understanding' George Lockwood was. 'May I be more worthy and may this happiness be a lasting one.' Angus could not dance. Hilda loved dancing and George was an excellent dancer.

If the highlight of the university year was the Easter Tournament (held successively in Dunedin, Christchurch, Wellington and Auckland), the highlight of the Tournament could seem to be, not the matches, nor the debates, but the ball. In the *Canterbury College Review*, the year the Tournament was in Christchurch, A.J. Harrop wrote as follows:

> I thought at first it was rather –
> Well, going a little farther
> Than the truth, to say that all
> Come merely for the Easter Ball.
> But the more I think it out
> The less I am inclined to doubt ….
> Who has not music in his soul
> May well be crossed from Fortune's roll,
> And he who these days doesn't dance
> (To give, he says, his soul a chance)
> Must learn with us to play and frolic.
> All pleasure is not alcoholic!

To 'give his soul a chance', he says, Angus did not dance. How easy it was if one danced, so he could imagine (so *she* knew), to be overwhelmed by the *physical* charms of one's partner. My mother, in her memoirs, admitted how important the dancing was. For one thing it allowed, indeed encouraged, a degree of physical intimacy, of permissible sexual excitement, that tennis certainly didn't. Angus and Hilda might win the university mixed doubles together, playing if not exactly frolicking. But it was George Lockwood who danced.

It is fortunate for my very existence that George was a Roman Catholic and an only child. His devout mother was so nervous of his marrying a Protestant that she did not invite Hilda to their home. But George persevered for years, sending to New Plymouth two volumes of Charles Lamb's *Letters* (and an 'idiotic' letter of his own) for my mother's twenty-fourth birthday. He was by then working as a solicitor in Christchurch. Hilda had gone to see him in his office before she left to take up her teaching post and said they should not remain in touch. In England later on, a mutual friend told her 'it had taken George a very long time to get over my departure and he didn't marry for about eight years'.

In Christchurch Angus began to give up the idea of teaching and focus on the possibility of a career as a writer. He had always written easily and quickly, had edited the school magazine at Waitaki, and had taken over from Erle Schroder the College House magazine in 1919 at the end of his first year. One of Angus's earliest pieces in *The House*, when he was still only nineteen, was titled 'Thoughts on the Present Discontent' and is highly political. 'As we learn more about the social conditions of New Zealand today', the boy wrote, 'we cease to wonder at the discontent abroad in the land.' He described the miserable conditions in a mining village and the lot of a soldier's widow living with her two children in a single room in Wellington. Was this the Peace they were still supposed to be celebrating? Angus was already anticipating a Labour Government, though it would be sixteen years before the discontent and the Depression led to the first socialist victory under Michael Joseph Savage, whom Belich would describe as 'the most loved Prime Minister in New Zealand history'.

Angus became the first Canterbury student to take the new Diploma in Journalism in 1921, the same year that both he and Hilda took their first degrees. This is one of the three relevant bits of paper:

There was always a long delay between the taking of examinations and the results, for all the papers were assessed on the other side of the world, extraordinary as that may now seem. My mother in her memoirs said that this was 'so New Zealand standards were recognised in England'. It certainly had something to do with the fact that most of the heads of department were English in those days when Canterbury, Victoria (Wellington) and Auckland were all constituent colleges of the University of New Zealand, and only Otago in Dunedin was a university in its own right.

In 1921 what interested Angus was honing his skill as a writer while earning some useful money. In November he applied for a job at the Christchurch *Press* in the same splendid honeycomb-windowed building, just off Cathedral Square, that still houses the newspaper today. In his memoirs, he described what happened like this:

> My entry into journalism was achieved with little difficulty or formality, the only obstacle I can recollect being the inability of M.C. Keane, editor of the *Press*, to find a place for me to sit for the interview. His room was full of papers and of books, waiting to be reviewed or merely read; it was a mystery to me where and how he managed to write …. His room was no reflection of the quality of his mind. His style was clear and concise and owed something perhaps to the fact that he had taken a First in Mathematics. His satirical and witty commentaries on men and affairs were among the best that have ever been done in New Zealand …. It was a proud moment when I found myself a member of his staff.

The university term was just over when Angus started work as a *Press* reporter on 23 November 1921. His laconic diary entries indicate a hectic schedule, with the usual flower shows and cricket matches, but also a great deal of time in the courts: Magistrates', Supreme, Divorce, with conciliation commissioners and arbitration courts for variety. He also soon found himself promoted to the role of film critic, reporting on the Monday night change of programme at the cinema. The advertisers had to be pleased. 'So many inches of advertising meant so many inches of first night "criticism".' When the show ended at 11 p.m., Angus would have a hasty interview with the conductor of the orchestra – for these were the silent films, of course, with the necessary live music. (It was still half a dozen years before the first talkies.) Then he would rush back to the office and turn out before midnight a column on what he had seen, impressing Alec Burns, the chief sub-editor, with his regular efficiency.

My father, writing later when he had had a good deal of contact as a reporter in London with film stars and directors (he had even received a leather visiting card from Tom Mix), pondered an interesting question nearly seventy years before the films of *The Lord of the Rings*. 'Why', he asked, 'do the great American film magnates never take a few principals to New Zealand and use that magnificent background for one of their super-films?'

At the *Press* they were all pleased with young Angus Harrop. The editor had always been keen on the idea of graduate reporters, but didn't often have the chance to employ them. Angus's new job was exactly right for him. Not only was the experience invaluable and the money a great help (enabling him to save something toward his longed-for time in Cambridge) but the editor built him up as a coming man, a name to be looked out for. Keane referred to him in editorials, helped with the publicity for his first book, and encouraged him when, in 1923, he set off for England, to write copiously for the *Press* about anything and everything he found interesting.

Somehow in 1922 Angus managed not only to work for the paper but to represent C.U.C. at tennis, finish the research for his M.A. thesis, and finally to take his M.A. with first class honours. A list in the *Press* shows that only eight students had achieved first class honours in the History M.A. in the preceding ten years. When in 1923 the results were announced there were just two History Firsts in the Dominion, both at C.U.C. In the April 1922 Tournament – in Auckland that year – Angus played tennis for C.U.C., and reported the games for the *Press*, which resulted in a telegram of congratulation from the paper ('YOU ARE HANDLING TOURNAMENT LIKE A SEASONED VETERAN') and praise from the Lawn Tennis Association in Wellington.

For *her* M.A., taken alongside the second of two teacher-training years, Hilda switched from English and French and joined Angus as a historian, working with Dr Hight. Angus's thesis, which became his first book (already quoted in Chapter 1 of this book) was on 'The History of Westland'; Hilda's was on 'Relations between White Men and Maoris up to 1839'. I have the theses in front of me as I write, substantial, imposing volumes. Full of illustrations and relevant maps, they are black-bound with gold lettering. Hilda's was typed by her sister, Nettie, not long before her wedding.

In her bibliography my mother lists an impressive amount of primary material, including logs of voyages by Tasman, Cook and Julien Crozet and documents of the Church Missionary Society, but her introduction makes a modest enough claim to 'disperse the chaff and garner the grain' from a lot of 'old books'. In her conclusions she sums up the period after 1840 like this:

> During the next twenty years the bitterest enmity was to exist in the Colony, an enmity born partly of the harsh and unjust treatment which it has been shown the natives had to endure in the period we have dealt with, and augmented by the folly of white men during the next decades. The end of our period, however, marks the beginning of the proper solution of the problem. Great Britain at last assumes her responsibility, and the relations between white men and Maoris now receive the attention which their importance demands.

It was Professor Hight who suggested the subject of Angus's thesis. As early as 3 December 1919 (at the end of my father's first year at C.U.C.), Hight wrote to him:

If you decide to take up History as your M.A. subject, I would suggest an Historical Account of Westland as a suitable subject for research …. Try and get the newspaper people interested and persuade them to allow you the use of their files. Find out where the Proceedings and other official papers of the Westland Provincial Council are kept in Hokitika, if they do remain there ….

It was all good advice, and the thesis owed a good deal to the files of the *West Coast Times* and the archives of the province. When it was published by Whitcombe and Tombs as *The Romance of Westland*, with the sub-title 'The Story of New Zealand's Golden Coast', the book had the sort of coverage of which every young writer dreams. Many column inches in newspapers all over New Zealand drew attention to the book. The *Otago Daily Times* said 'He writes clearly, capably and carefully and every page bears evidence of ungrudging labour cheerfully undertaken.' The *Taranaki Herald* praised the writer's application of 'a trained mind and first-hand knowledge'. Only the *Lyttelton Times* sounded a sour note. Though the book was 'undoubtedly interesting', the reviewer found the young writer 'had not realised the splendour of the opportunity offered by this material …. Bald, colourless language is our besetting sin when we try to recover the story of our past.' It lacked the *romance* promised in the title. Romance, as he knew only too well, was not my father's forte.

Hilda Valentine left C.U.C. with glowing testimonials. Though she had continued to criticise herself unstintingly in her diary (regretting her own impulsiveness, her arrogance, her continued tendency to talk too much), everyone wrote highly of her. The Matron at Connon Hall said Hilda was 'absolutely reliable, conscientious, courteous and obliging. Hers is a very strong character, which, combined with tact, has made her invaluable on committees. Her influence has always been for good.' She had not only represented Canterbury at tennis, but had also captained the Basketball Club for two years. Professor Hight praised her 'very clear and easy style of writing' and Professor Wall declared she had a 'special aptitude for literary work'. The Principal of the Training College even praised her ability to control a class. She was all set for a useful teaching career – and was duly appointed as an assistant mistress at New Plymouth Girls' High School, beginning in February 1923.

Professor Condliffe, in his testimonial, wrote of Hilda Valentine as someone who had become 'a valued friend' – that was a friendship that lasted all their lives. Jack Condliffe also mentioned Hilda's skill as a speaker at the Dialectic Society and the fact that one year she had won the Women's Speaking Competition.

Only one speech survives – one Hilda made at a women's meeting of the university Christian Union, which shows she had apparently overcome the reluctance she had expressed to her father at the age of seventeen to speak out about her own faith. 'I am not asking you,' she said, 'to become sober, serious-faced, sad seekers after truth. But I am asking you seriously to consider whether you are doing your best to make your life a thing worthy of its Giver, a thing that is of use in the world.' Religion had everything to do with making the world a better place. Belich writes of a 'slow-burning sense of trauma in the New Zealand of the 1920s' and quotes a 'nervousness' that society was in 'grave danger of decline and collapse'. Hilda spoke to her fellow women students of 'a crisis in the affairs of the world', of the possibility of 'a tremendous social upheaval, a revolution' and of the 'great evil of profiteering' and exploitation. For all her singing and dancing and her involvement in the games people played, Hilda was obviously as aware as Angus was of what Belich called 'trouble in Paradise'.

They said goodbye to each other in May 1923 when Hilda was in Christchurch. The photograph below of the 1922 graduates, just awarded their degrees, was taken on 12 May and contains them both among thirty-four men and sixteen women. As you look at it, Angus is seventh from the left in the back row and Hilda fourth from the left in the second row.

Hilda and Angus would not meet again until August 1926. From their later letters it is clear that Angus had seriously considered making a proposal of marriage to Hilda on that last evening they had together. As it was, it seems he did not even touch her. He had loved her steadily already for nearly six years and she, as she would later admit, had been feeling closer to him all through their final year, sitting with him in History lectures, going to those Monday night films he reviewed for the *Press*, getting to know him better. He did not propose, though 'self-control is a virtue I find hard to practise' he told her later.

He would wait, encouraging her to think of following him to England without ties or obligations. He would rely on the power of his pen, on his own language (bald and colourless though it might be), to win her.

After they said goodbye, Angus wrote to Hilda in New Plymouth: 'I met a former foreign editor of the London *Daily Mail* the other day (on a tour of the world) and he is taking me under his wing in Fleet Street in the long vac.' It looked as if he would be able to support himself during that vacation without drawing on his savings. The 'former foreign editor' was travelling with young A.G.A. Harmsworth, the nephew of a formidable uncle, Lord Northcliffe, the one time Alfred Harmsworth, owner of the *Mail*, the *Times* and much else, who had died the previous year after a world tour of his own. Harmsworth may have remembered his uncle saying as he set off: 'I want to understand the riddle of the Pacific …. I want to know this great Empire of ours.' Northcliffe had been known to bewail the lack of 'Empire knowledge' among London journalists ('Who will report the Imperial Conference?').

In Christchurch young Geoffrey Harmsworth naturally called in at the *Press*. Alexander Burns, the chief sub-editor, was also – for thirty years – New Zealand correspondent of the *Daily Mail*. Burns introduced Harmsworth to the bright young reporter who planned to be in England soon. They talked and played tennis together. In Australia Harmsworth read in the *Press* of Angus's First and the award to him of a travelling scholarship – a return ticket to England and £100 (perhaps NZ$8,000 in current money.) Harmsworth wrote from the Carlton Hotel in Sydney to congratulate Harrop and looked forward to seeing him in England. It had been a lucky meeting for my father, whatever one thinks of that popular, disreputable newspaper, the *Daily Mail*. To Angus in New Zealand it meant Fleet Street, the Mecca for all young journalists, 'the hub of the universe', and he could hardly wait to get there. Cambridge and Fleet Street! What a potent combination it was for the boy from Hokitika.

In New Plymouth Hilda Valentine spent three and a half years teaching at the Girls' High School. It made a great difference to her that her family was a short distance away in St Aubyn Street. Hilda was very close to her mother.

Nellie – this grandmother of mine – was the sort of mother who wrote 'Hurrah!' in her diary whenever one of her adult children visited. She was one of those women who feel rather lost without a large household to cater for. She took up croquet and became a champion, but it was always her family who occupied her mind. Yet she was good about letting them go. I have a copy of the letter she wrote to Australia to welcome Marie Plowman, engaged to Max, the last of the family to marry. Nellie said she had perfect trust in her children's judgment in choosing a partner for life. 'We love our children dearly and have done the best we could while we had them with us and now can only pray they lead honourable and upright lives doing all the good they can for those around.'

Hilda was often in St Aubyn Street, especially when her sister Nettie came home for five weeks with her new baby daughter, Helen, described by her delighted father as 'soft as velvet'. When the baby's grandfather, Jim Valentine, retired as Taranaki Schools Inspector (with lots of presents and praise), and was sent to the Cook Islands to report to the Education Board, Hilda, seeing them off, wrote 'It is wonderful to have such parents.'

In term time Hilda lived at Strandon, the High School boarding house for out-of-town girls. In school she was expected to teach English, History, Music and French. She was very popular. She would write in her diary of her room filled with flowers from the girls: roses, violets, freesias. Some of her pupils stayed in touch with her all their lives, grateful for her 'good grounding in French', for instance, though she had still never heard a French person speak.

But there were inevitably some dreadful days when the children were out of hand and they giggled not only in Prayers. There was a great deal going on. They were always rehearsing or practising something: part-songs, games, gavottes, a stage version of *The Rose and the Ring*. Hilda veered between being exhausted, disgruntled, and 'much in love with teaching'. It gave her pleasure that she moved from Grade D, at which trained graduates began, to Grade C in the shortest time then known, but, typically, added in her memoirs: 'Such things don't really matter, but when one is old it does give one satisfaction to set against all the things one is *not* proud of in one's long life.' In her diary at the time she recorded one important lesson she had learned: 'If people think well of you, you strive to be worthy of their regard.'

Angus Harrop's last big job for the *Press* came with the great South Island floods of May 1923.

> Rail and telegraph communication was cut off and reporters were sent north and west to find out what was happening. As I knew the Midland line to the West Coast well, I was sent in that direction. I shall never forget my feelings when, after trudging along the track in pouring rain after the train stopped, I came upon the Midland Line suspended over a chasm for which the epithet yawning was not only right but irresistible. Here was a story and my first big scoop, if I could cover it properly and get back to the train before this solitary link with Christchurch left on its return journey. My luck was in that day, for I fell in with the District Engineer, learned how the line would be diverted, nearly but not quite missed the train through talking to a ganger before the

welcome fire in his hut, and wrote the story on the train on the way back to the office …. One phrase from the story sticks in my memory. 'Only a photograph' I wrote 'could do justice to the scene.' Incredible as it may seem, the possibility of a photograph sullying the staid columns of the *Press* was then quite out of the question. Although the *Weekly Press* appeared with pages of illustrations, the daily preserved the tradition of the London *Times* with no pictures.

Before finally leaving the *Press*, Angus prepared the material for a highly illustrated twenty-eight page supplement 'Linking of East and West', which was published on 4 August 1923. (By then Angus himself was travelling through the Panama Canal.)

This was the day of the opening of the long-awaited Otira Tunnel through the Southern Alps – at that time the longest tunnel in the British Empire. Much of the material for the supplement came from his work for his thesis, but he managed to make one of the very first journeys through the tunnel, long before it was officially open, riding in a truck with Evan Parry, engineer of the English Electric Company. Of course Angus thought of the numerous journeys he had made in a Cobb's coach behind sweating horses, of 'days that would not come again'.

In July Angus travelled to Wellington where he would board the *Remuera*, his ship for England. He had packed this photo of Hilda, the gold propelling pencil and the 'pair of military brushes' presented to him by his colleagues on the *Press*.

He had his photograph taken with the Godbers, his mother's sister's family. And there was the chance to say goodbye to his sister, May, and some of his friends. The laconic diary is full of names as well as 'Get passport', duly ticked, 'Send money to England' and so on. On 13 July he wrote 'Saw Massey'. Among his papers there were a number of letters of introduction for this 'distinguished' graduate, including one from J. Macmillan Brown, by now Chancellor of the University of New Zealand, which ended with the expectation of his professors that A.J. Harrop would 'do them honour in the universities of the homeland'. There was also a letter from William Massey, the Prime Minister, addressed to whom it might concern, saying that he would 'personally appreciate any assistance' given to A.J. Harrop in carrying out his studies.

Eighteen years later Hilda would hear from Aunt Louisa Godber the sad story of a stressful day, the sort of thing that rarely gets recorded. In a letter, she told Angus:

> Aunt L. told me about the day before you sailed from Wellington. You had had a very strenuous time beforehand (as always!) and were tired out. May and Geoff had just arrived and when you all went to tea at Kirks you had to wait and May said to L. – 'Don't let him make a fuss.'

My father always wanted everything to be perfect, especially anything he had arranged himself. I can imagine the situation so well. There he was, leaving for England the next day, wondering (even though he had that return ticket) whether he would ever come back, whether he would ever see his family – or Hilda – again, wondering whether he had made the right decisions – abandoning Fred, leaving May, though she *seemed* to be all right, attached as she was to Geoff Cuthbert. The emotion in the crowded tea-room must have been considerable. To be kept waiting for their tea when time was running out, when he could not find the words to fill the waiting – it was intolerable.

Angus had very mixed feelings about leaving. He wrote to Hilda, 'I try to console myself by thinking how I will appreciate it when I come back .... What do they know of New Zealand who only New Zealand know?' It would be eleven years before his return. For her birthday, just before he left, Angus sent Hilda a copy of *A Miscellany of Poetry 1920–1922*, edited by William Kean Seymour. It included a poem by Alan Porter called 'A Desperate Lover', with the lines

> She mocks me, varies,
> Now kind, now cold,
> Pieced of contraries.

Angus did not draw attention to the lines. Inside the book there is a piece of *Press* paper on which he wrote: 'To Miss Hilda Valentine, On having attained the age of 23 years, A birthday gift and a goodbye message From hers devotedly, Angus J. Harrop.'

Angus travelled on the *Remuera* with the only other student in a similar position. D.H. Black, Senior Scholar in Mathematics as Angus was in History, would also never use the return half of his ticket. Black was an athlete – 440 yards inter-university champion earlier in 1923. (Over seventy years later his grandson, Roger, running for England, was Olympic silver medallist over the same distance.) Don Black was on his way to Emmanuel College,

Cambridge, to work under the great New Zealander Ernest Rutherford at the Cavendish Laboratory, and would have a glittering career as a government scientist, much involved with the development of radar during World War II. The two young men had scarcely known each other in Christchurch at C.U.C., but the travelling coincidence turned them into life-long friends. They accepted their Ph.D.s together at the Cambridge Congregation on 23 April 1926.

Dr D.H. Black became my Uncle Don and his wife my Auntie Maida, making up for the absence of blood relatives in England. They and their three children were immensely important to David and me when we were growing up. In our Norfolk garden we have silver birch trees (now taller than the house), which came as tiny saplings from the Blacks' Ascot woodland where nearly forty years after that Degree Day my father's ashes were scattered beneath the trees.

Because the *Press* encouraged Angus to send back regular dispatches, I know far more than I suspect my readers will want to know about everything that happened to him on the voyage, and many things that didn't. His fluent pen on the *Remuera* celebrated Richard Hakluyt (pioneer of the Pacific, sixteenth-century navigator), Pitcairn and Easter Islands (including, of course, the mutiny on the *Bounty*), the excitement of visiting Panama City on the day on which President Harding's death was announced, the history of the Panama Canal, and so on. There was even a long piece on 'Killing Time, the Ocean Traveller's problem', with a great deal about deck games, including some funny stuff about the dangerous art of riding a pogo stick on a tilting deck. It was crossing the Equator, the arrival in the northern hemisphere, which shows the real regret – whatever lay ahead – at leaving New Zealand. Angus had left 'the hemisphere of opportunity – where there is room for every man to live a full and satisfying existence, if he is prepared to work hard.' He was now in that northern hemisphere 'which has witnessed the major number of the epic struggles mankind has waged since the beginning of time'. Would his luck hold out if he continued to work hard?

Angus arrived in London on 18 August 1923. The *Press* duly published his account of the day of his arrival in those days when people arrived fresh and energetic off a ship rather than weary and jet-lagged off a plane: 'MY FIRST DAY AT LORD'S. A NEW ZEALANDER'S IMPRESSIONS.'

He had got through Customs in Southampton by 11.15 that morning, bought a paper to read on the train and check what was going on, and was on his way to Lord's Cricket Ground within half an hour of arriving at Waterloo and dropping off his luggage at a hotel in Southampton Row. He wrote: 'The New Zealander loves the old game, though he plays Rugby better.' Hobbs and Hendren were due to play and perhaps he would 'see Chapman hit out hard and bold (as Keats might have said) in the style which delighted us at the Lancaster Park ground in Christchurch'. The match was England versus the Rest; it had rained and an impatient crowd was kept waiting for hours while the turf dried out. The game did not start until 6 o'clock. My father, for once, was not impatient, enjoying his first experience of England. He went back to his hotel 'feeling I had made a record for Lord's for that day at least – I was the only one in the crowd who thought he had had his money's worth.' That night, not wanting to waste a moment, he saw the Ben Travers farce *Tons of Money* at the Aldwych Theatre. 'Excellent', he wrote in his diary. In the next week he was at the Adelphi for a J.M. Barrie play, at Daly's for *The Merry Widow*, and at Queen's Hall for a Henry Wood concert after dinner with Geoffrey Harmsworth.

Angus wrote to Hilda: 'Words are weak to describe it all and I cannot even make the attempt. You MUST come to London while you can enjoy every minute. Don't save it up as a treat for your old age. This is *the* life.' He suggested she should read the Christchurch *Press* if she wanted to know what he was up to and ended his letter with a cool 'Best wishes from Angus'. Other early letters from England to New Zealand were longer but equally impersonal and unemotional. He was making no demands on her at all, cleverly allowing Hilda to feel completely free. This would have exactly the effect he wanted.

It was not an easy correspondence – constantly trying to catch the mails on particular ships. Letters often arrived in batches (piled up via Panama or San Francisco). It could take nearly three months to get an answer to a simple question. Hilda was feeling acutely the absence of that devotion she had known was there for so many years. She was now the one who would need to make the first move towards a renewed intimacy. By April 1924, loving his letters, missing him, finding herself thinking about him more and more, nearly a year after they had said goodbye in Christchurch, Hilda made that move. Writing frankly, as they had agreed to do, she could at last write to Angus:

> I do want you so.
> You have all my love,
>   Hilda

Angus was not slow to respond. He thought that at last she had 'seen the light'. He said how much now he would love 'building castles in the air. I look forward to the time when you will be in England, and, after the first inevitable awkwardness (for we have advanced rather far by correspondence!) we enter into joy.' He said he had not asked her to marry him on their last evening in New Zealand because he thought she hadn't made up her mind 'whom you liked best'. He 'lacked the courage to put it to the test'. He had feared it might have meant the end of all his dreams. He had hardly believed he would ever see written in her writing 'You have all my love'. But, now that he could begin to believe that it was true, 'I want you fiercely. Love is a wonderful thing and a terrible one when we are so far apart. I know from your letters that you suffer just as I do. But the suffering will only make the ultimate joy greater by contrast, when at last we can say in each other's arms what we have now to write:

> *You* have all *my* love,
>   Angus

On his first Sunday in England Angus had explored London, starting his tour with his first look at Carmelite House, the home of the *Daily Mail*. He must have been worried that his fortuitous meeting with Harmsworth in Christchurch might lead to nothing, for he wrote in the *Press* of a Fleet Street in which

> Some papers are turning away men they have had for twenty years. For the Dominion journalist, entry into Fleet Street is at present almost impossible. The London papers require specialists and men steeped in the English atmosphere

.... The primal law has never had better illustration than in Fleet Street; for only the fittest survive. Many are called, but few are chosen; and these few run the risk of returning again to the outer darkness. What then must be the charm of a street to which ascent is so difficult and from which descent can be rapid? The true journalist loves to venture ....

Angus was not yet a true journalist. Perhaps he never would be, for he spent most of his life straddling the irreconcilable worlds of Fleet Street and Academe. In 1923 his aim was set at a Cambridge doctorate. He said he had 'sunk all his capital', that small inheritance from his father, 'in getting a reasonably good education'. 'With optimism born of ignorance', he once wrote, 'I imagined I would make political science my subject and I had tentatively selected Thomas Hobbes, author of *Leviathan*, published in 1651', but at Cambridge he was directed back into the path to which Dr Hight had first introduced him. He agreed to work on the relations between England and New Zealand 'from the time of Tasman to the Taranaki War', giving 'for the first time the story of the rise, decline and fall of the New Zealand Company and accounts of the French and German projects for the colonization of New Zealand.' The thesis – written almost entirely from original sources – was eventually published in London in 1926, with an introduction by Lord Jellicoe, who had been in command of the British fleet at the Battle of Jutland in 1916 and had just retired as Governor-General of New Zealand.

Angus became a postgraduate member of Gonville and Caius College, Cambridge, in the autumn of 1923. His supervisor was E.A. Benians, later Master of St John's College. At that time he was helping to plan the *Cambridge History of the British Empire*. He asked Angus one day who he thought would be the best person to edit the New Zealand volume, eventually published in 1933.

The young man declared James Hight was the only possible choice. 'I don't suppose the views of a very junior research student did influence the editorship of the New Zealand section, but it pleases me to think that they did.'

Dr Hight certainly got the job and in due course invited Angus himself to contribute two of its chapters: Chapter V on 'The Companies and British Sovereignty, 1825–1850', and Chapter X on 'New Zealand and the Empire, 1852–1921'. His fellow contributors included J. Macmillan Brown, J.B. Condliffe and, of course, Hight himself.

Angus loved Cambridge. He retained a deep loyalty to it throughout his life, though he showed only the mildest displeasure when, thirty years later, I myself turned down Newnham College, Cambridge, in favour of St Hilda's College, Oxford – one of those lightning decisions, like only a few we make, that changed my entire life. Cambridge – and indeed Oxford – in the 1920s was much more socially mixed than is generally supposed. 'Nearly half the undergraduates', my father discovered, 'were assisted by scholarships' and the postgraduates were from equally various backgrounds. Angus grumbled about the cost of everything and the petty regulations and the dons who took so seriously the 'mimic battles and oratorical contests in the Senate House'. There was a case for 'better ventilation and more baths', but the impression he would carry away was not the 'intolerance of its regulations, but the tolerance of its general outlook', the easy access to good talk, and memories, inevitably, of crocuses and daffodils on the Backs in spring and the glories of King's College Chapel and the famous old gates at Caius of Humility, Virtue and Honour.

Most of my father's close friends at Cambridge were New Zealanders, fellow members of the Heitiki Club, which met alternatively in Oxford and Cambridge. He was very busy, with a lot of journalism on top of his academic work and all the letters he was writing to Hilda. He played tennis for Caius, he belonged to the historical societies, took out a life membership of the Union and worked on a rather conservative magazine *The New Cambridge*, which happened to advertise for editorial assistance at just the right moment.

Gonville & Caius Coll. Lawn Tennis Club.
1st VI.

Dear Sir,

 Will you play for the above Club

v. *A Queen's Club VI*

on *Caius*   *Ground*

on *Sat.*   *next, at* *2·15*

If unable to play please let me know **at once.**

C, Gonville Court.   W. E. TUCKER,
         Hon. Sec.

90.4.24

A. J. Harrop.

"The New Cambridge."

Caius College,
Cambridge.

A. J. HARROP.

'No experience necessary' the notice said, and the editor must have been impressed by all the experience Angus already had. The All Blacks' tour of 1924–5 then gave him the chance not only to continue to write for the Christchurch *Press* (which drew special attention to his 'brilliant little studies of successive games'), but also to write for the London *Observer* and the *Daily Mail*. At one point in the *Observer*, as 'a New Zealand correspondent', Angus was emphasising the amateur nature of the national game. The players received 'not a single penny from the tour'. He also praised the Maori aptitude for the game which 'has given them the opportunity of showing those qualities of courage and chivalry which all European observers used to remark on in describing Maori warfare in New Zealand'.

But it was a controversial tour. Some of the British papers, depressed by the endless defeats, called the New Zealanders 'ugly' players, 'unnecessarily violent', 'bare-faced obstructionists' and unscrupulous 'slingers of fists'. Angus would have none of that. He reported on nearly every match, in spite of the demands of the Cambridge term, and made his second visit to France in the Christmas break. A grim postcard of the ruins of a church at Ypres bears his annotation: 'All Blacks at Ypres, Jan. 8, 1925.'

Angus was first in Paris in June 1924, in his first long vacation, 'studying the French records, newspapers and magazines of the time when the agitation to force the French Government to colonise New Zealand was at its height'. He worked there again a year later. His excellent French (particularly remarked on at Waitaki) had proved its value.

There was a point when my father wondered if it would make sense to give up the idea of a Ph.D. and concentrate on earning his living as a journalist. But that seemed like a sort of failure and he persevered. His developing friendship with Harmsworth must have helped him to get the summer job promised so lightly in Christchurch the year before. On 14 July 1924 Angus wrote to Hilda:

I went to the *Daily Mail* office for a preliminary interview at 12.30 today. Was discussing the business with the News Editor when the phone rang with word of a nursing-home on fire in Kent. Three minutes later I was downstairs waiting for a *Mail* car and a photographer and en route to my first Fleet

Street assignment. Marvellous but true. A pleasant twenty mile motor ride on a perfect day – quite a good story to gather – and a pleasant ride home. So now I enter the ranks of the employed.

Angus would defend Lord Northcliffe (who had died in 1922) against his detractors because of his insistence on reasonable salaries and working conditions, and he maintained Northcliffe could not be blamed for the 'cheap sensationalism' that disfigured the paper after my father's own time there. It was the *Daily Express* my father could never stand. He was naturally an omnivorous newspaper reader; the papers I remember we had delivered were the *Times*, the *News Chronicle* and the *Daily Herald*.

Angus was rather dazzled by England, but never less than clear-sighted. He returned from a magical Christmas in a country house in Dorset (thanks to Lady Frances Ryder, who organised hospitality for overseas students) to find London brilliant under a deep fall of snow, but he also recorded the rapid decline of the white stuff into 'rivers of black mud'. He loved the fact that the *Times* was 'I·N·D·E·X·E·D', as he put it, which would save him weeks of work. He loved the theatres and music halls, the parks and libraries and cathedrals. He longed for Hilda to share them with him.

In their letters, while not telling anyone else it seems of their hope to marry eventually, Hilda and Angus worked out their ideas of how they might live together. They both agreed that 'human love could never be really perfect' but they were optimistic. At one point Hilda said she did not want Angus 'to change in anything'. 'I'm glad you are exactly as you are.' But later he wrote that she was right, that he did 'take things too seriously. My excuse is, of course, the wretched money problem …. In England, taxed to an extent unbelievable in lucky New Zealand, getting married is a serious business.' This was just when he was deciding to go down from Cambridge in the summer of 1925 and to finish his research and writing for his thesis in London, where most of his material was. 'It is because I want to be able to make you happy I worry so much.'

Angus's sister, May, had now married Geoff Cuthbert in Gisborne. Geoff had a job to go to in Manchester and they were travelling across the world. 'I have written to them at Sydney and Colombo and I am keen to hear of their experiences', Angus wrote to Hilda. In these years he was always closely in touch with May.

Everyone was getting married, but Hilda – who had scorned the idea of marrying in her fifteen-year-old plans – was still having doubts. She was reading *Jude the Obscure*, which didn't help. She wrote to Angus that she was 'scared – dreadfully – that I shall fail to satisfy you for always. Nearly every man I know seems to require someone other than his wife to entertain him at some time or another – much more so than the other way round – they seem unable to help themselves.' Even lovely Jack Condliffe 'had made an utter fool of himself over Noëline Bruce, for a time' though Jack and Olive 'are really devoted to each other'.

> I seem to have been hearing of a lot of marriage tangles lately, and the upshot of it all is that I keep wondering, not as I once would have, whether you would satisfy me – strangely enough that never occurs to me at all now – but whether you won't find me insufficient at times. I think once a woman has definitely made up her mind she takes a delight in following out the course she has undertaken, but man does seem to be a polygamous animal. The thought will keep obtruding on my mind that you are different, but I wonder if I am thinking so because I want to.

And who was 'Frank' who obtruded into her letters at this point? Hilda wrote to Angus when 'Frank' telephoned Strandon, the girls' boarding house in New Plymouth.

> I told him he could walk with me, not that I wanted to see him much, but at least he was a change from eternal femininity and he amused me …. I'm quite willing to be friends so long as I control the business and of course I do, absolutely – he wanted to kiss me tonight and he said he didn't see why I shouldn't as it would be only a pally sort of kiss, but I said No quite decidedly and told him I didn't want to which is undoubtedly true. There isn't the vaguest shadow of desire now – rather distaste …. Frank remarked on my general air of happiness tonight – tho' of course he couldn't realise quite why.

Hilda and Angus were keeping their plans a secret 'in case it didn't work out', she would say to me years later. It was after all a long time since they had set eyes on each other. There was no question – they both recognised it entirely – that it was his going away to the other side of the world that had at last brought them so closely together – a nice paradox. 'It will be dreadful if we don't *like* each other when I arrive', Hilda said in one letter. There was always that possibility. But in letter after letter they had thrashed out their ideas on how to make their marriage work.

Late in 1925 Angus wrote: 'It's only seven or eight months now before we know our destiny …. We must take our life together as one long adventure in happiness and I think we should get plenty of fun in planning to make both ends meet without fore-going any of the real pleasures of life – travel, reading, theatres and music.' He was working on his dancing, had had a number of lessons, and when reporting for the *Mail* on a show in the Empress Rooms at the Regent Palace Hotel found himself dancing with 'the world's tango champion!' The exclamation mark was his, but fortunately 'it was *not* a tango' and he got on 'reasonably well'.

In New Plymouth Hilda was saving every penny she could. She would not marry, she said, until she could afford to buy her own piano. Nellie was suggesting to her daughter that the way to be happy in marriage was for the wife 'to do whatever her husband wants her to do'. Hilda reported this.

Angus wrote:

> You ask me how I like the idea of being an autocrat. But, of course, if a man really loves a woman he should be able – most times at least – to want her to do just the thing she would like to do herself. I expect that I shall fail rather badly in achieving this but I shall at least try.

In another letter Angus referred to a comment Hilda had made on her sister Nettie's small children (a boy, Lewis Valentine, known as Val, had quickly followed the first baby, Helen.) Observing carefully, when she stayed at the Watkins farm, Hilda decided that the bad days were more or less balanced by the good ones. Angus and Hilda would read Marie Stopes' *Married Love* and know about birth control. (Interestingly, just at this time Ettie Rout's *Safe Marriage* was banned in New Zealand.) But there seemed no question now that eventually they would want children themselves. Angus wrote:

> I am glad that you have always taken a thoroughly normal view of the physical side of marriage and of having children. It is an important aspect of marriage, though not the only or even perhaps the most important matter. To my mind the physical side gets unnatural emphasis from the careful way in which most people – and even those about to marry – refrain from saying anything about it …. Strange that the most natural phenomenon in the world – without which there would be no world – should be thus tacitly obscured or ignored.

Angus had every reason in the summer of 1926 to feel optimistic about the future. In April he had paid with joy the considerable cost of being properly clothed and was delighted that his sister, May, could be in Cambridge to see him get his Ph.D. Almost at the same moment the confirmation came from Methuen, one of the best London publishers, not only that they would publish his thesis as *England and New Zealand*, but that they were also interested in further books. Now employed full time at the *Daily Mail*, he had, albeit with mixed feelings, worked through the General Strike – feeling sympathy for the miners, but thinking that what was at stake in Carmelite House was the freedom of the press. He had been promoted and, while still doing a good deal of reporting and interviewing, was based in the leader writers' room where the

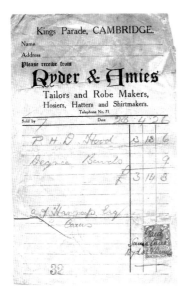

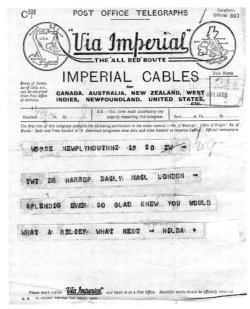

contentious article 'For King and Country' – which condemned the General Strike – was actually written, though not by him.

Hilda cabled from New Plymouth when she heard the good news, but her 1926 diary suggests she still wanted to feel free. On holiday in Tauranga early that year, there are lots of mentions of 'Ron', sailing back in the yacht *Kingfish* in the moonlight, dancing and playing bridge. Ron is 'really entertaining'; there was a walk with him and a 'ripping picnic in the Buick', which made me feel again how very nearly I might not have existed. But her tickets were booked. She was to cross from Wellington on the *Marama* to join the *Beltana* in Australia. She had now given up the idea that she would teach on her arrival for it was not possible both to marry and teach. (No married women were employed in teaching until another war made it necessary.) There would be plenty for her to do, Angus suggested. 'Work often divides married people. But I think mine will draw us even closer together.' Hilda had already done some research for him in New Plymouth, checking old newspaper files. Now there would be not only research, but typing, proof-reading and so on. But he assured her, 'You will always come before my work or anything else.'

'Our dear girlie left us for England', my grandmother wrote in her diary on 26 May 1926. The family knew the real situation. Hilda's doctor brother, Jeff, sent her £5 (something like $300), which she could regard as a wedding present, 'if you do decide to become Mrs Harrop'. Loaded with other presents, including a travel rug (with in one corner 'H.M.V.' – her maiden initials),

Hilda left New Plymouth still maintaining at the High School the fiction that she was off on a long holiday. She was keeping Angus out of the picture. They liked the idea of avoiding gossip. It was one of the things my father loved about London, that nobody knew who you were; you could do whatever you felt like doing without the sort of talk that inevitably went on in Hokitika, Timaru, Christchurch and New Plymouth. He was longing for her arrival. 'I am so wearied with waiting', he wrote.

Hilda travelled slowly to England via Australia (with long stops for loading cargo) and the Cape of Good Hope. Her shipboard diary, partly filled in by her friend Vida someone-or-other ('an enfant terrible' according to my mother), is full of flirtatious adventures on the *Beltana*.

Wearing no engagement ring, Hilda was naturally an attraction for the young officers and wireless operators, married and unmarried ('How indeed can one tell?'). Their names litter the diary. Two or three of them even crop up in London after her arrival, including the darling, charming Fourth Officer: 'I love the way we behave disgracefully and then when people pass try to look so quiet and good', she wrote. It was a way of killing time. She had abandoned long ago all those resolutions about how to behave with men. Angus had once written:

> I like to think of you imagining what we shall do when we meet – I do it so often myself. I expect I shall be casual. I know I shall be excited. There will certainly be a railway journey and a taxi with a boarding place of some description as a necessary anti-climax. Please think over what you would like to do on your first night in London. We shall do it.

By 1926 'the boarding place' was somewhere Angus knew very well and Hilda would appreciate it too. The address was 5 Gordon Street, Bloomsbury, just behind University College, with an excellent landlady, Miss Leete, who had become a firm friend and would be an honoured guest at the wedding. When Angus had told her he wanted a room for a friend arriving from New Zealand, she had assumed it would be a man, and was pleased and surprised when it was Hilda. Fellow residents in Gordon Street included three delightful young New Zealand women, the Todd sisters, Moyra and Kath, and Helen Bakewell, known as Tui. None of them ever married; all of them became important to our family. Both Kath and Tui would be doctors; I assume they were still studying at this point. Moyra was a singer and became my mother's closest friend. She was sending 'heaps of love to yourself and Angus John' when skiing in Austria the winter after they first met.

Hilda reached Tilbury on Saturday 7 August and Angus was there to greet her complete with bowler hat, striped brown suit and walking stick – the man about town. Hilda had teased him in one of her letters that he should own a bowler hat and he had obviously gone out and bought one. Whether his appearance pleased her she does not say. She does say how good Angus was to her, how thoughtful he was – so that she found a selection of books, chocolates and writing paper waiting for her in her room at Miss Leete's. That first night they saw Fred Astaire dancing in *Lady Be Good* at Daly's Theatre in Leicester Square.

The next day was 'wonderful' and Hilda declared 'I love London'. She always would. They fooled around on Angus's typewriter and this evidence survives. It was still easier to write rather than to talk. The words 'In fact this is a red letter day' were typed, of course, with the red half of the typewriter ribbon.

```
                                                    5 Gordon street
                                                    London W.C.I.

   Dear Hilda, .

           After waiting so long for your arrival,it now seems almos
   too good to be true that you are really here at last. In fact this
   is a red letter day.



   Dear Angus,

           London is a perfectly beautiful place and  I am content



   £WERTYUIOP        "/@£_&'()¼
   `^', é
```

The Todd sisters had a car and, while Angus was working at the *Daily Mail* that Sunday afternoon, they drove Hilda out to Kew Gardens. Everything was delightful, heavenly, enjoyable, decent and ripping. (She had forgotten her determination to abjure slang.) Best of all – great news – on 16 August, just over a week after her arrival in England, Angus and Hilda found a flat at 4 King William Street (now William IV Street), off Trafalgar Square, opposite the old Charing Cross Hospital. 'Very central', as she said.

Then it was time to look at churches. There had apparently been no question, from the moment of their reunion, that they would marry. They considered St Clement Dane's and the Savoy Chapel, but decided on St Martin-in-the-Fields, the parish church for the new flat. They cabled their wedding date – 20 September – to New Zealand. My grandparents found the cable waiting when they returned from the Cook Islands on 30 August. 'Bless her!' my grandmother wrote in her diary. They were soon making plans for their own trip across the world. Hilda's first letter from London didn't reach New Plymouth until 14 September.

By then, splashing their carefully saved money, Hilda and Angus had had lunch at Frascati's, dined at the Ivy, seen *Hassan, The Plough and the Stars* and *St Joan*, heard Moseiwitsch and Harriet Cohen play, and visited Ely and Cambridge – where they walked to Grantchester 'over the path Rupert Brooke trod many times'. They played a lot of tennis in Lincoln's Inn Fields. The sun shone.

On 8 September Hilda started living in the flat. 'The place is filthy but lovely', she thought. 'We sit on our Chesterfield and gloat.' There was a lot to do. By the 18th the new piano had been moved in and things were more or less straight. Angus's sister, May, arrived from Manchester with her husband, Geoff Cuthbert. It would be 'hateful' saying goodbye to them the following year. Geoff took this photo of May, Angus and Hilda in their hats.

After this, May and Angus would never again live in the same country. Marie Stewart came to the wedding from the Midlands. She was a new friend whose sister, Rena, had taught with Hilda in New Plymouth. One day Marie would be my godmother, along with Jean Struthers, who, as Jean Cunningham, had been at C.U.C. with my parents.

Hilda wrote a card to her sister Nettie on September 20. It was nine years and four months since Hilda and Angus had first played tennis together in Hokitika.

> Here I am running round on my wedding morn in my pajamas and blazer. Marie and May won't let me do one thing …. Perfectly ripping they are and tho' of course I can't help missing Mother and you and Lottie, I am very very happy and serene. A. is very nervous and won't be happy till it is all over …. My Victorian posy of pink roses should be here from Bond Street any minute – It is a lovely day. And nice big Geoff will be a great comfort to me as he takes me down the church. I feel you are thinking of me. Heaps of love,

Hilda

PART TWO

Together, Apart, Together

CHAPTER 8

Remembering, not forgetting, New Zealand

Five years after my parents' wedding, Eric McCormick was one of many young New Zealanders who called on the 'small office' in Gower Street, Bloomsbury, of the agent of the University of New Zealand, A.J. Harrop. McCormick would long afterwards be described by Michael King as New Zealand's 'leading cultural historian' and by Belich as 'the brilliant critic'. After his death in 1995, Auckland University Press published a collection of his autobiographical writings, *An Absurd Ambition*, which includes this passage about my father.

> A post-graduate scholar himself, he had gained a Cambridge doctorate, but had stayed on in London to eke out a living in this part-time job, which he combined with the editing of a weekly paper, the *New Zealand News,* and the writing of books based on documents in the Public Record Office. He belonged to an era when the borders between journalism and scholarship were ill-defined, and even then the High Priests of History dismissed his compilations with scorn. I have often found them useful, and for the man I feel nothing but gratitude. He suggested I should try Cambridge, advised me to apply in person, and gave me a letter of introduction to an official of the Registry who was also a Fellow of a college.

I have quoted this passage at rather more length than it deserves because it is – apart from his obituaries – the only summing up of my father's career that I have ever read and it startled me by its affectionate inaccuracy. 'Eking out a living': how was it that Angus Harrop gave this impression of finding it difficult to make ends meet? How was it that McCormick – librarian of the Hocken at Dunedin, 'Assistant Dominion Archivist', as he was – thought that Harrop's 'compilations' were dismissed with scorn? I think this conclusion was based solely on G.H. Scholefield's review in the *Listener* of *New Zealand After Five Wars*. Published in England in 1947, with a striking epigraph from Allen

Curnow's poem 'Landfall in Unknown Seas' ('the stain of blood that writes an island story'), it was my father's last book and Scholefield, the historian (High Priest or not) certainly suggested in his review just how uncomfortable the mixture of scholarship and journalism could be. No one at the time (and I have all the numerous reviews, neatly pasted up by my mother) scorned his historical research in the four important early books, based as they were so closely on primary sources that had not previously been studied.

It is surely significant, when assessing A.J. Harrop's status as a historian, to draw attention to the fact that not only was he invited to contribute to the *Cambridge History of the British Empire* but also in 1950 to write the additional chapters to the new edition of Pember Reeves's masterpiece, *The Long White Cloud*, which drew the comment from Lord Bledisloe, one-time Governor-General of New Zealand, 'I am so very glad that you, with your exceptionally gifted pen, have brought it up to date.'

I can see that, when writing about my father, I am in danger of the very fault of which he was accused in his only biography: *The Amazing Career of Edward Gibbon Wakefield* (1928). It is easy, as I know very well, for a biographer to become defensive and over-sympathetic; there is a natural desire to see the best in someone about whom one cares enough to write a book. (How much more to see the best in one's own father.) A.J. Harrop felt that Wakefield's role as one of the founders of New Zealand had been inadequately recognised. It is interesting to see that, seventy years later, Belich, while still giving plenty of space to Wakefield (unlike Michael King), thinks of him as part of 'the old Pakeha myth of origin', a 'deified ancestor', with feet of clay. My father's long-ago objection was that there was always far too much emphasis on the feet of clay and not enough on Wakefield's undoubted achievements. Part of the appeal to my father was certainly Wakefield's unconventionality. He defended strongly Carlyle's description of Wakefield as a 'democrat in all fibres of him'. Drawing particular attention to Wakefield's 1831 essay on 'the Bold Peasantry of England', my father wrote, 'He was always on the side of the poor and a critic of the idle rich.'

A.J. Harrop's biography did, as he had hoped, draw a huge amount of attention to Wakefield and his brainchild, the New Zealand Company. 'His memory', the *Auckland Star* agreed in a review, 'had been shockingly neglected.' There were over fifty reviews, with plenty of praise, from the London *Times* 'Book of the Day' and a large spread in the *New York Times Book Review* to long assessments in all the leading papers in New Zealand, where A.H. Reed bound their own edition of the Allen and Unwin sheets from London. There was inevitably a lot of space given to Wakefield's extraordinary abduction of the heiress Ellen Turner and his consequent time in Newgate gaol. But the newspapers recognised the real debt New Zealand owes to Wakefield: 'His services to the cause of responsible government, his insistence on a good type of settler and on a balance between the sexes, and his resolute opposition to convict colonization.' My father thought that there would have been a strong chance that, without Wakefield, New Zealand might have become a French colony. All the time Angus had spent in the archives in Paris and London made him convinced that that had been a real possibility. Without Wakefield, 'the Dominion's history would have been vastly different', as one of the reviews put it. A.J. Harrop would be disappointed that, though Lord Bledisloe paid for an annual wreath for Wakefield's grave in Wellington and there are a score of streets with his name throughout the country, it is probably true that 'Wakefield' means very little to most twenty-first-century New Zealanders.

My father's strong pro-Wakefield stance was, I think, partly due to his close contact with Wakefield's very elderly nieces, Alice Freeman and her cousin Fanny Torlesse, and his great-grand-daughter, Irma O'Connor. Irma was herself writing a book which appeared in 1928 as *Edward Gibbon Wakefield: The Man Himself*; she appears over and over again in my mother's diary of this period, but later returned to Auckland and became woman's editor of the *New Zealand Herald*. It seems particularly remarkable in the circumstances that the family made available to my father all the valuable private papers in their possession, including letters that had not been seen by Richard Garnett, Wakefield's only previous biographer, thirty years before. Angus visited both Mrs Freeman and Miss Torlesse before Hilda's arrival and persuaded the former to add to her vivid recollections of her uncle during those last years in Wellington I referred to in Chapter 2. It moves me to think that my father knew so well someone who knew so well Edward Gibbon Wakefield, who died in 1862. Alice Freeman recorded: 'I was the only pleasure left to him at the end of his disappointed life.'

There was a further memorable five-day visit to Mrs Freeman in the summer of 1929, the year after the book was published. She lived in Malvern and this was the place where Wakefield and John Robert Godley had walked together in 1847, discussing 'a very pleasant colonizing project'. My mother was a little awed and embarrassed by her visit; she had not been before. Many years later she told me that it was at Malvern she had her first experience of a chauffeur and a butler, and of having her suitcase unpacked for her by a lady's maid, who was distressed, laying out her black evening dress for her, to find that Madam had forgotten to pack her black lingerie. Hilda thought she had blushed and failed to admit that she did not possess any such underwear. That was what she told me and indeed wrote down in her old age on the back of a photograph of Alice Freeman's daughter. The interesting part of this story is that it can remind us of the unreliability of memory. Hilda's 1929 diary reveals that on 17 July, several weeks before the visit to Malvern, on the same day she bought the 'beautiful black dress', she bought 'black crepe de chine undies' to go with it. What we remember can be as important as what actually happened.

Mary Freeman, Alice's daughter, became a close friend of ours over the years ahead, a frequent visitor and donor of wonderful presents when David and I were children. I think she had no other children in her life. One present remains. It is a measure of the affection the family felt for my father that I have on my desk as I write a copy of Priscilla Wakefield's sympathetic *Reflections on the Present Condition of the Female Sex* (1817), with the ownership signature of her grand-daughter, Edward Gibbon Wakefield's sister Catherine, Fanny Torlesse's mother.

Though Eric McCormick's summing up, with which I began this chapter, is not at all the way I would see my father's career, I can agree that it may be true that no one takes seriously as a historian someone who edits a 'weekly paper'. (Incidentally the *New Zealand News*, of which I will write more very soon, was for a long time a fortnightly, though it indeed survived to the twenty-first century first as a weekly and today in electronic form.) Nor is it a good idea if you aim to be recorded in the *Dictionary of New Zealand Biography* to live most of your life in London, however bound up with your native country that life continued to be. One of A.J. Harrop's obituaries would say: 'If his abilities were not immediately apparent it was due to his sense of modesty, almost akin to shyness', an odd attribute for a journalist. There was indeed a strong strain of modesty and self-deprecation in my father; there was never anything thrusting or ambitious in his demeanour. If he did not have the glittering career predicted for him as a young man, it was because glittering was not his style. The explosive impatience his sister muttered about at tea-time in Kirks in 1923 was visible throughout his life only to his family. Every now and again Hilda mentions it in her letters to her mother, while continually saying how happy she is. She assured her mother, several months after the wedding: 'We have not yet had our first quarrel – arguments, of course, but nothing more.' The impatience in these early years would be with circumstances, not with her. When the *Daily Mail* news desk phoned the flat with an urgent story for him on his day off, when he was just about to shop with Hilda in Soho or play tennis with her – and hoping to play bridge with friends that evening – she had to calm him down and usually could. Whatever he had said in his letters, work had to come first.

But there was no doubt Angus had turned out to be a delightful husband, ('such a darling'), reading poetry to her while she dried her hair by the fire, and bringing frequent presents, such as *Winnie-the-Pooh* on publication day in October 1926. (It would be five years before there was a child to share it with them.) When she felt rotten, 'A. looked after me beautifully.' Even his dancing was improving. Hilda gave him foxtrot records as part of her Christmas present – and a gramophone to play them on. (Moyra Todd gave them Schubert's unfinished symphony newly recorded for His Master's Voice – '3 big records, both sides'.) Hilda wrote to New Plymouth about her happiness and 'joy in living'. She felt just 'tremendously thankful'. Angus had even become domesticated, though in his letters across the world he had claimed not to be. Hilda now often wrote in her diary: 'A. and I did a good big wash.' 'A. and I made blackberry and apple jam.' Even, occasionally, when she had been out with one of her friends and he got back first: 'A. had supper all ready for us.' Those irregular newspaper hours did have some compensations.

Those who knew Angus and what he wrote certainly appreciated his abilities and his unusual capacity for unrelenting hard work. It was impressive the way he worked. He was an easy, compulsive writer. In these first years of his marriage, he was holding down a full-time job at the *Daily Mail* which had such odd shifts (often 2 p.m. to 11 p.m.) that he had enough time to complete his biography *The Amazing Career of Edward Gibbon Wakefield* (much of the research he had done while working on his thesis), send innumerable articles to the *Press* in Christchurch and other New Zealand papers, and in late 1927 start his new project *The New Zealand News*.

Before that, Angus had every opportunity to return permanently to New Zealand. James Hight, their beloved History professor, spent a good deal of time in King William Street in 1927 when he was on a sabbatical exchange. He used to leave his violin (my mother called it his fiddle) on top of Hilda's piano and call in for some music with her whenever he had an hour or two to spare in London. When he came to lunch, he helped Hilda with the dishes. Dr Hight had written to them on the news of their marriage to say how sure he was that when he arrived in England he would find them 'a very jolly sight for weary eyes'. And he and many others did. On his way back to New Zealand, Dr Hight wrote from Washington, D.C. to ask Angus 'how he would view the prospect of accepting a post at Canterbury College leading to a Professorship?' A little later, Angus also had a cable from the *Press* in Christchurch suggesting he might return to take up a job. Acceptance would undoubtedly have led eventually to the Editorship of that paper, which continued for years to publish everything he cared to send.

But life in London was too good to give up. Hilda relished everything: exhibitions, lectures, plays, opera, concerts, and the place itself, the grand buildings and ancient alleyways she saw every day. She could even put up with the 'filthy London dirt' and the thick fogs in those days before the Clean Air

Act. She certainly supported Angus in his decision not to return. Far from 'eking out a living' as McCormick had described, Angus's chosen path meant that they were able to enjoy, as a result of their hard work, all the things he had said to Hilda made life worth living: books, music, theatre and above all the chance to travel, not only in Europe, but also on a number of occasions to the other side of the world. They could always afford, even in these early days, to eat well, to have help in the house, to wear good clothes and to buy their Christmas presents at Liberty's.

That convenient flat off Trafalgar Square was often full of visitors eating delicious home-made food. (It was so rare for Hilda to have lunch on her own that she commented on it once in her diary.) She always wanted to be a perfect housewife (at a time when the word was not derogatory) like her grandmother and mother before her, though their circumstances were so entirely different. There were many bright New Zealanders in London in these years, looking for wider fields, 'more fertile soil in which to flourish', as Michael King put it. Some stayed only a year or two, others settled down as permanent expatriates, still waiting eagerly for every ship with New Zealand mail on board. ('Fifteen lovely letters!' my mother would exclaim in her diary.)

Hundreds of New Zealanders found their way to King William Street and later to my parents' successive houses in North London. They would include lots of impoverished postgraduate students grateful for a good meal, such as John Beaglehole, later to be Professor of Commonwealth History at Victoria, and Clarence Beeby, on his way to becoming New Zealand's Director of Education and later Ambassador to France. Many of the names mean nothing to me, but the Milners were there several times in 1929 (Hilda thought Angus's old headmaster charmingly modest), and there were lots of Todds, coming and going, including Charles the founder of the dynasty, flourishing on motor cars and later oil.

At a time when, in King's words, 'women's domestic reputations could be made or lost according to how well they scrubbed their front doorsteps', my mother's life in London was unusually unconventional. At the flat, of course, she did not even have a doorstep. She wrote to New Plymouth: 'These topsy-turvy hours don't suit my ordered conventional mind one bit, after my years of living to bells, but I expect it is good for me really.' If she still saw herself as conventional and still heard the high school bells in her ears, she was becoming more flexible and undoubtedly 'modern'.

Hilda was getting a good deal of journalism published herself. Alan Mulgan, literary editor at the *Auckland Star*, who had just written a best-seller called *Home* about his own experiences in England, welcomed Hilda's articles and encouraged Angus to send more on the cricket tour that was going on. When

Roger Blunt was playing for New Zealand (or for Canterbury) it was a particular delight; they had been at College House together. Like Angus, Hilda found it easy to write about anything in her daily experiences. The walks she loved to take round London made a good series: A WALK IN THE CITY, A WALK IN MAYFAIR and so on. When she went to hear Alfred Noyes or Humbert Wolfe read their poetry or Bernard Shaw and G.K. Chesterton debating 'Do we agree with Socialism?' at the P.E.N. Club, she would write about it all for the New Zealand papers.

My father had paid for their honeymoon on the Riviera – their first visit to France together – not only with a series of articles for the *Press*, but with a pamphlet, *Nice, the Sunshine Centre* for George Lunn, the travel firm that had arranged their tour.

That was the joy of being a journalist. The obituary writer in the London *Times* said of A.J. Harrop that 'while university life would have seemed to be his forte, the attraction of journalism intervened'. It was more fun than the historian's slog (so familiar to me as a biographer) of sitting day after day in the Public Record Office in London or the Bibliothèque Nationale in Paris, copying out documents and reports and then trying to make sense of the story they told.

For the journalist every day was different, and sometimes Hilda was able to go with her husband. In 1927 the *Daily Mail* sent Angus for two weeks to Yorkshire to report on preparations for the total solar eclipse that summer, mistakenly believing, he said, that as he had a doctorate he must know something about astronomy. They stayed in a hotel in Settle while the Astronomer Royal appears to have camped in a wet field at Giggleswick. The *Daily Mail* had arranged for an exclusive account from him. 'He dictated this to me in his tent a few minutes after we had the good fortune to see the most thrilling of all sights', Angus wrote. The clouds had parted just when it seemed certain they would see nothing. They talked about it all their lives.

As a staff reporter of course Angus had to write to order, but this included interviewing lots of interesting people. One day it was the head of the C.I.D., 'miles from home with a party shooting partridges', who told Angus: 'My job is to catch Bolshevists.' Another day it was Dean Inge of St Paul's, after the notorious occasion when an elderly clergyman – denounced by Inge as 'a brawler' – led a protest at the heresy of the Bishop of Birmingham. Angus also interviewed every New Zealand Prime Minister who visited London, starting with Gordon Coates, and such diverse characters as an Australian race-horse trainer, Gracie Fields on the subject of the Sunday openings of theatres, Toscanini's manager just before a concert at the Albert Hall, Marconi on the future possibility of 'wireless communication with Mars' (at a time when there still wasn't any with New Zealand), and R.C. Sherriff whose brilliant play *Journey's End* had shaken even Frank Milner into temporary pacifism. It was impossible to imagine what lay ahead. My father interviewed Baron Hayashi, the retiring Japanese Ambassador, who said 'Britain is naturally anxious to protect her interests in the Pacific, but the Singapore base does not seem to be a solution of the problem. I think the scheme will be a waste of millions of pounds.'

It is interesting to read this journalism, knowing what came later. The scrapbooks of cuttings have many stories that are curious. Few if any will now remember there was a serious proposal to roof over a stretch of the Thames to form a central London aerodrome. Everyone at this time was excited by flying. Angus quoted Sir Alan Cobham, who had set up records flying to India and the Cape, saying that a time would come when 'aeroplanes will be more common than cars'. I myself remember, on a visit to Hendon Aerodrome as a small girl, being told exactly that and imagining a sky constantly criss-crossed by buzzing planes. However clogged the roads, one must be glad that that prediction, unlike Baron Hayashi's, turned out to be false.

Another headline of my father's has a different resonance. PILFERING – THE SPORT OF THE AGE. In the story my father wrote that 'the habit of pilfering has become so general that it is no longer looked upon as theft. "Scrounging" is as rife in civilian life as it was in the Army during the war.' Pints of milk were lifted from doorsteps, spoons and overcoats from restaurants, vegetables from allotments and washing from clothes lines. Daily 'helps' helped themselves to anything they thought they could get away with. I include this typical piece of popular journalism as a reminder that these were the Depression years, that life for a great many people was not as rosy as it was for my parents. There was every chance that the people stealing vegetables from allotments were actually hungry. This at a time when my father, on a lavish Press trip to Wales, enjoyed a first-class ticket and a 'wonderful nine course dinner'.

In one article for the *Press* on how to get on in Fleet Street, Angus wrote 'I think I would rather be, say, part proprietor of a small country newspaper in New Zealand than work in the editorial department of a London daily. In London you are one small unit in a complex organisation in which nobody, not even the editor, is indispensable.' How brilliant it would be to be his own boss, to be proprietor with Hilda of a small newspaper of their own – but in London, for that was where they wanted to be.

Angus was always extremely loyal to New Zealand. He never talked about his country as housing 'a Philistine community', as the poet Rex Fairburn did. He would never have described New Zealanders as 'mentally and spiritually … one of the backward peoples of the earth', as the novelist Jane Mander did in 1932. But he preferred to live in London. He had the idea for the *New Zealand News* one day as he walked down the Strand to Fleet Street in 1927 in the summer after his marriage. He had been in New Zealand House, then at 415 The Strand. He was closely in touch with the High Commissioners and their office all his life. On this occasion he had overheard, not for the first time, some visitors bitterly complaining how little news there was of New Zealand in the English papers. It was 1931 before it was possible to telephone New Zealand – and even then it would be hugely expensive. With letters coming by ship and taking so long to arrive and few people having our family habit of clipping the newspapers, New Zealanders in England could feel totally out of touch with what was going on in their own country. Angus and Hilda decided they could, by themselves, run such a necessary paper, if they got sufficient support from the New Zealand Government and from advertisers. And they did. Hilda was particularly taken with the idea of something she could do with Angus and largely from home. 'Girls didn't work after marriage in those days', she wrote long afterwards in her memoirs, 'And I wanted to work.'

There was no doubt at all that when they were in New Zealand, like most of the literary young of their generation, my parents had dreamed of 'Sussex downs and quaint old England's quaint old towns' (to quote Denis Glover's 1936 'Home thoughts'), but, now they were living in England, they came more and more to be thinking constantly of New Zealand. When he arrived, my father had been thrilled by his ability to get published not only in the huge-circulation *Daily Mail*, but also in the more prestigious, long-established *Spectator* and *Observer*. From now on – until things changed in 1941 – what thrilled him was that he had the chance to be largely his own master, freelance, self-employed, writing his books and publishing their own little paper. What kept them in England, in fact, was the same sort of thing that had driven a previous generation, such men as Thomas Jefcoate, Hilda's grandfather, and Angus Campbell, one of his own, to cross to the other side of the world.

Of course it was far too soon to give up a regular salary. Angus stayed at the *Daily Mail* until August 1928 when it would not agree to his working shorter hours. He then moved to the *Sunday Dispatch* – another large circulation paper – where he was able to work just three twelve-hour days a fortnight, which fitted in with everything else he had to do. Describing the *New Zealand News* once in a radio talk, Angus listed his materials: cables and newspaper clippings from his correspondents in New Zealand, lists of callers at New Zealand House in London, 'personal paragraphs' and reports of things of New Zealand interest going on in England. As the only New Zealand paper in London, he said, it needed to reflect all shades of opinion and did not take a party political line. The paper also encouraged New Zealanders in England and Europe 'to act as missionaries in popularising the products of the Dominion and its attractions.' It celebrated its seventy-fifth birthday in 2002 in other hands, looking quite different, but with its aims and coverage still the same. I was glad to see that the front page of the special birthday issue had a photo of my father alongside such 'Kiwi legends' as Kiri Te Kanawa, Edmund Hillary and Lord Rutherford. The paper has seen some limp years, most notably when I myself suddenly had to edit it when my father had a severe stroke in 1960 on his way to New Zealand by ship and my mother had to rush to his bedside in an Australian hospital. It flourished for many years, keeping thousands of readers in touch with New Zealand until, in 2007, it was transformed into a daily electronic edition and the glossy monthly magazine *New Zealand Inspired.*

Although the paper did have paid staff from time to time, it was always basically a family business, with the result that my parents could rarely go away together for more than a week or two. The *New Zealand News* could seem a nuisance when we were children. From this time on my mother's diaries become less interesting; she had less time or taste for introspection. 'Did N.Z.N.' is a frequent entry. Most of her writing energy went into her work and into the dozens of letters she wrote every month.

The support of New Zealand House was vital to the new enterprise. Bert Drew, the Publicity Officer, had been a friend of my father's from when Angus first came to London. He had been at the wedding. He came to lunch at the flat on 14 October 1927 and 'we talked *paper.* The book-keeping will be the worst', my mother wrote in her diary. The idea at the beginning was to post the first issue 'to all New Zealanders in Europe whose addresses are on record at New Zealand House', and encourage them to subscribe. It made a great difference when my father approached advertisers (such as the N.Z. Shipping Co, and the

Trans-Pacific Passenger Agency in Cockspur Street) that he could write that the High Commissioner 'is in sympathy and a government advertisement has been promised.'

In the seventy-fifth birthday issue the New Zealand Government's £260 a year – a considerable sum in those days, which must have given my parents a real feeling of security – is described as a 'grant'. I always understood it was seen as a payment for regular advertising and publicity. A full-page advertisement in each of the twenty-four issues a year cost £200 with a good reduction for those who 'come in with the first numbers'. More of the big companies involved with New Zealand took permanent space.

The printers chosen, Bonner & Co. Ltd., established in 1884 as the Chancery Lane Press, were then in Cursitor Street. When they moved to 92 Fleet Street, my father was delighted. They became owners of a Fleet Street paper. The first issue appeared on 29 November 1927. 'THE DAY' Hilda wrote, 'The excitement came with the first 500 copies at 12.15. Irma came to lunch and then we had a very busy time till 7.' They went out to dinner and worked again when they got home. A surviving carbon of a letter to the printer from my father included: 'I shall ask you to band, address and post 1,000 copies; we shall do the balance ourselves.' Were they really addressing and wrapping 500 copies on their dining table? It seems so.

In New Zealand the paper had some unsolicited publicity from D'Arcy Cresswell, the poet. My parents had met him at a P.E.N. Club meeting in London and saw a good deal of him when he was in London, though their hospitality can hardly have compared with that of Lady Ottoline Morrell in Bloomsbury, where he was more likely to meet Siegfried Sassoon and W.B. Yeats than fellow New Zealanders. I was six years old when I was taken to tea with D'Arcy Cresswell in St John's Wood. He was the first poet I met and his name has always had a magical ring for me. I was told how, after being wounded in the war, he sold his poems for sixpence each from door to door and had published his story in *The Poet's Progress* in 1930. The story, I think now, was rather better than the poems. Faber and Faber took on that book and it was because of D'Arcy Cresswell that I first heard the name of the publisher who would one day be my own.

Cresswell was an enthusiastic supporter of the *New Zealand News*. I found a cutting, presumably from the *Press*, when he was back in his 'wild savage wonderful land' early in 1932:

Mr D'Arcy Cresswell, the New Zealand poet, interviewed on his return to Christchurch this week, spoke very highly of the success at Home of Dr A.J. Harrop. Dr Harrop, he said, had managed to keep in circulation an excellent little paper devoted entirely to New Zealand affairs. This was a tremendous feat, considering how few New Zealanders there were in Europe, and he thought that no New Zealand man in England, once he had read the *New Zealand News* would ever be without it, assuming that he wanted to remember, and not to forget, his own country.

What I did not hear as a child was the more extraordinary story I think my parents did not know, of young Cresswell's unsavoury involvement in the case of Charles Ewing Mackay, the bi-sexual lawyer who was Mayor of Wanganui. A group of his political opponents commissioned Cresswell, visiting the town in 1920, to act as an *agent provocateur*. Mackay fell into the trap. When Cresswell, as instructed, told Mackay he had to resign as Mayor or he would report the matter to the police – at that time when homosexuality was illegal – Mackay, in a panic, drew a gun and shot and wounded Cresswell. Mackay was tried for attempted murder and sentenced to fifteen years hard labour. Eventually, after his early release just at the time when my parents first met the poet, Mackay was himself shot dead when covering as a journalist a clash in Berlin.

Hilda had written in 1927 to her parents: 'If only you were near I'd have nothing left to wish for.' On 18 January 1928 Nellie and Jim Valentine duly set off from New Plymouth after a number of 'great send-offs' from the 'croquet ladies', 'church folk' and their dear son, Max, who was still at home. They crossed to Sydney to join the *Bendigo*. By the time they left Australia, they had received thirty-one letters from New Zealand. At first my grandmother was not impressed by 'the usual life at sea'. 'Not much good for me', she wrote in her diary, 'Too lonely' – an interesting comment on a ship crammed with people she did not know. By the end of the slow journey she could write, 'Goodbye to the dear old Bendigo after nearly nine weeks.'

The Valentines were in England and Europe, coming and going, until the end of November. 'All was lovely in Hil's dear wee home', Nellie wrote in her diary when they arrived. 'Angus is so kind. Had flowers and chocs in my room to welcome me. Very comfy and happy.' Hilda loved showing her parents the London she already knew so well. On Sundays they went together to the Bloomsbury Baptist Chapel, where Nellie's parents, Janet and Thomas Jefcoate, the railway guard, had been married in 1860, though Hilda had now been confirmed into the Church of England and usually went to St Martin's.

My grandparents, on this one and only visit to England, enjoyed all the usual sights: Changing the Guard, the Tower, Kew Gardens and Richmond, the Zoo, Lord's, and those special treats so many visiting New Zealanders experience – Trooping the Colour and a garden party at Buckingham Palace ('gorgeous time'), when Hilda surprisingly wore a dress they had bought for Lottie for 49/6. Nellie and Jim went everywhere: Bath, Bristol, Bournemouth, Oxford, Windsor Castle and further afield to ancestral territory in Scotland and a Cook's Tour to Belgium, France and Italy. But they were always pleased to get back to London.

When Hilda, unexpectedly, in her new unconventional mode, went off for five days' holiday in Moyra Todd's car, Nellie was understandably bereft. 'So quiet and horrid without Hilda', she wrote in her diary. Jim was busy helping Angus with the *New Zealand News*, pasting up and proof-reading, making himself useful as he had always done. Moyra obviously thought Hilda needed a break. She had written in her diary, 'I felt depressed.'

That was surely because she and Angus had just made the momentous decision to buy a house, a family home – to leave that convenient little flat off Trafalgar Square and move into the conventional suburbs, where children would have a garden to play in. But she was still not pregnant and it was a strange time to be taking on a mortgage, with Angus cutting down on his hours in Fleet Street to give him more time for the *New Zealand News*.

They bought 43 Highfield Avenue, Golders Green, N.W.11, on impulse. They had gone to see another house and on the way back to Brent, the tube station (eleven stops to Charing Cross), they saw a FOR SALE on number 43 and 'went in – and bought it!' It was not a smart address. Evelyn Waugh, when

he lived with his parents in Golders Green, is said to have substituted Hampstead on his writing paper, even though it meant his letters took a day longer to reach him. (I can see these niceties mean little in New Zealand, but I have to admit that I like the fact that my birth certificate gives Hampstead, not Golders Green, as my place of birth.)

As you can see, 43 Highfield Avenue looks an insignificant three-bedroom semi, but it actually had four and Hilda and Angus made it sound grander by turning the dining room into a library, lining it with bookshelves and having room there for their two desks, side by side. The breakfast room, off the kitchen, made

an adequate dining room. Upstairs, the smallest bedroom was immediately the 'nursery', though there was still no child.

They moved in on 25 June 1928. Jim Valentine, a far more practical man than his son-in-law, was soon doing all sorts of jobs. Nellie loved the garden where she could knit or darn socks while Angus worked at his typewriter. Behind the house, there were green fields that would soon be built on. Hilda thought they were in 'a lovely neighbourhood', within walking distance of Hampstead Heath and with lots of tennis courts nearby. They would watch babies in Golders Hill Park and go to church in Temple Fortune, or walk as far as Jack Straw's Castle, names I would find marvellous as a child.

On her parents' last night in England, Hilda wrote in her diary: 'Mother taught me to crochet edges for Ann Barbara's shawl.' It was 29 November 1928. It gave me a shock, reading my mother's diaries for the first time recently, to see my own name four years before I was born. So my mother, to her joy, had conceived just over two years after her wedding and – she apparently felt sure of the fact – was looking forward to a daughter. It seemed some sort of compliment to her particularly close relationship that year with her always beloved mother. 'I'm sure *you* have no Victorian ideas left,' Hilda said to her at one point, regretting the 'narrowness' of her dear aunt, Lucy Bardsley.

Moyra Todd spent a lot of time staying at Highfield Avenue at this period. Her sister, Kath, now a qualified child psychiatrist, had gone off for work experience at John Hopkins Hospital in the States. Moyra's car was very useful; in those days when so few had cars parking it was never a problem. 'It was lovely having Moyra with us during the happy months of preparation', Hilda wrote. The first months of 1929 were inevitably dominated by getting ready for the coming child. But they were also getting used to the new suburban life. Angus was playing a lot of tennis with Moyra; they were all becoming gardeners. Hilda took a more minor role in the rigorous annual spring cleaning than she would otherwise have done. She was lucky that 'Mrs B.', her excellent help in King William Street, was prepared to travel out to Highfield Avenue. Hilda combined working hard on the *New Zealand News* with a varied social life. Moyra was inclined to spoil her: lunch at the Ivy, tea at the Ritz. There was lots of music. When Hilda came home from a day in the country with Marie Stewart she had a carriage to herself, put her feet up and read French aloud.

But the lectures she now attended regularly were at Cromwell House on Highgate Hill, the headquarters of the Plunket Society in London. She learnt how to put baby to bed, heard about 'the normal baby', and listened to advice on bathing, dressing, diet (after weaning from the breast) and a good deal else. She became devoted to the ideas of Truby King. Having a baby also involved a lot of shopping and sewing. She bought the large things: cot, bath, pram. Lovely presents started arriving in the post, including 'a parcel of beautiful things for Ann Barbara' from the grandparents, posted at a port on their way back to New Zealand. Hilda apparently did not consider that she might have a boy. She made a great many clothes herself, 'wee coats' and frocks and nightgowns, and also bibs, flannelette sheets and a cot cover with crocheted sides. A carpenter came and put up bars at the nursery window, making it safe for an adventurous toddler.

On the 28 April Hilda wrote in her diary. 'A tragedy: the curtain blew over my scent spray and the scent removed all the polish on one corner of my dressing table.' This followed rather soon after frozen pipes and an evening when she had arrived home alone to find the house had been burgled. There was 'an unholy mess', but not a great deal had been taken. Even so, after the incident with the scent spray, she wrote 'Life is hard!' How hard it was actually going to be I think she had never imagined. Before the end of May she had packed 'Ann Barbara's suitcase' to take into the nursing home.

On 1 June Hilda wrote 'Waiting is tedious'. The baby was due any day. The doctor was perfectly satisfied, told her to exercise and be patient. Hilda and Angus walked a good deal; they watched children playing in the park. On 7 June she saw her doctor; she was trying to be patient. She read Katherine Mansfield's letters aloud to Angus and played the piano. On 10 June the doctor rang and said she should go into the Nursing Home in the morning. Her mother had written in her diary: 'Hilda's address in June 1929, D.V., Caerthillian Maternity Home, 87 Fordwych Road, NW2.' It is the address on my birth certificate, the birth certificate of Ann Barbara Harrop; but I wasn't born until October 1932.

On 11 June 1929 Hilda wrote: 'We came here by taxi and I have been given 3 doses of quinine and an enema and a boiling bath – and still nothing has happened. It *is* annoying.' She was not really worried. Days went by and then on 14 June: 'Dr J. came at 5 – couldn't hear my baby's heart. He was born about 8.30 p.m. A. came to me at 12.30.' That is all. In those days fathers were discouraged from being anywhere near the birth. I imagine Angus, tired and worried, having heard nothing, being woken at midnight by a phone call with the dreadful news.

There is very little more in Hilda's diary as the days pass, apart from Moyra and Kath calling with flowers, Angus bringing grapes and strawberries. 'He is wonderful', she wrote. Joyfully anticipatory letters arrived from New Zealand on 19 June and that was 'very upsetting'. Presents for the new baby kept arriving. Her parents cabled when they heard the news. 'Everyone is so good to me', Hilda wrote, 'But it is so hot and my thirst is raging.' As was customary in those days, they kept her in bed for weeks; it was twelve days before she sat up briefly in a chair. Getting up after so long in bed, she was so tired that 'I felt I never want to get up again.' The boy and the name they had given him is not mentioned again in her diary. The only reference to the whole sad business was a brief sentence on 11 July: 'I packed away baby clothes.' She had given her doctor the address of her doctor brother, Jeff Valentine, in New Zealand, presumably so he could tell her family, far away as they were, exactly what had gone wrong. The letter does not survive.

Many years later my mother and I sometimes talked about this older brother of mine and thought about his absence in our lives. She never told me that, in the months of waiting, it was a daughter that she had imagined. In her memoirs she wrote:

> My first baby, John, was stillborn – so longed for – and in those days I wasn't even allowed to see him and my poor Angus had to take the little white box to the nearest cemetery in West Hampstead in a taxi by himself. It seems unbelievable now. The baby was late and the doctor gave me quinine to hurry things up and that proved fatal …. The worst thing was that I was kept in the two-bed room, even though the other occupant had her own new baby. Incredibly lacking in understanding.

I grew up knowing about John. I knew nothing, as I've said, about my father's brother, Frederick, or his sister Eva, who died as a baby. Now I think of my father holding the coffin of his firstborn on his knee in the taxi, thinking about his siblings and wondering whether he would ever have healthy children of his own. I tried to find out from West Hampstead cemetery what would have happened when my father arrived; would there have been any short service of committal? Would there have been a marked grave? No one knew. I discovered that quinine indeed had 'a stimulant effect on the pregnant uterus', but it is now defined as a 'protoplasmic poison'. Its possible toxic effects were obviously unknown in 1929.

One curious result of thinking carefully about this tragedy – and there is no doubt that it *was* a tragedy which stayed with my parents all their lives – is to realise that if John had survived, I would not be the person I am, writing this. My modern parents, readers of Marie Stopes, were into family planning and would certainly not have planned three children under four. The birthdays were like this: John, June 1929, David, February 1931, Ann Barbara, October 1932. Until I read my mother's diaries and saw my name late in 1928, I had even thought that if John had lived, they might have been content with their two boys.

Before David's happy birth and my own, there are some things I should record. In the summer of 1930 Hilda Harrop was one of New Zealand's four representatives at the Quinquennial Conference of the International Council of Women, held in the Hofburg, the Imperial Palace of Vienna, a grand affair with thirty-four countries represented by 600 women. The Christchurch *Press* carried the sub-heading 'NEWS FROM MRS HARROP'. As usual on these occasions, the talk between sessions, the contacts out of the conference hall, the evening entertainments (in this case delightful visits to opera and Austrian homes), meant more than the formal business, the lectures and committees.

'Another wonderful day!' Hilda wrote to 'dearest Angus John'. She was having German lessons in every spare moment from a friend of the Todds. She was reading *All Quiet on the Western Front* and had already read *Goodbye to All That*, but the war seemed very long ago and the atmosphere was optimistic and idealistic, though it was tiring to cope with 'the squash and the bustle and the Babel of tongues'. Teaching at New Plymouth Girls' High had hardly prepared her for the 'torrents of French'. The basic proposition and subject for debate seventy-five years ago sounds very familiar: 'Women have shown they can do what men can do. Now the question is "Do we want to do it?"' Certainly, all the delegates agreed, the public is demanding from the women's pages of the newspapers something more than fashion and recipes.

Angus wrote to say 'Enjoy yourself!' but told her that, without her eye on the proofs, a few misprints had appeared in *N.Z.N.* He also told her there was 'a new bundle of Columbia records'. He now had a record column in the *Sunday Dispatch* to add to everything else. His long hours on duty there on three days a fortnight were something of a problem, but he needed to do whatever was wanted as he hoped to take unpaid leave very soon for a visit to New Zealand and return to the *Dispatch* afterwards. It was at this point, in December 1930, that he received an unexpected letter from the Registrar of the University of New Zealand to see if he were interested in succeeding J.W. Joynt, M.A., who was hoping to retire as the University's Representative in England. Joynt, a distinguished former headmaster of Nelson College and lecturer at Victoria, had been in the job in London for twenty years. Angus *was* interested and agreed to take it on, provided that it was understood it was for him a part-time job, with secretarial assistance in that small office at 88 Gower Street that Eric McCormick remembered. Angus wrote to Wellington: 'I have other commitments, including historical research, which I wish to fulfil.' The major commitment was, of course, to their young newspaper, the *New Zealand News*. Other newspaper work could be abandoned but not that.

The new job also brought my father the prestigious position of representing New Zealand on the Executive Committee of the Universities Bureau of the British Empire. Angus did this university work for a dozen years and indeed continued to represent Canterbury University (as it would become) in London until 1950. The job involved the supervision of the preparation and printing of exam papers and sending them out to New Zealand, the receipt of the students' scripts and their dispatch to the different external examiners, and innumerable selection committees, with experts in the particular field, for posts in the Dominion. Angus once said that Lord Rutherford, retaining a keen interest in his own country, was always willing to help where posts in Physics were concerned. One of his maxims was 'Make sure not only of the man, but his wife'. She had to be someone who could adapt to life 12,000 miles away. It must have been rather intimidating for those candidates who had a Nobel Laureate on their selection board. The selectors always had confidential reports from heads of departments who knew the applicants. Angus considered Rutherford 'one of the quickest readers between the lines of these reports.'

The plan had been to go to New Zealand late in 1931, returning in May 1932. Angus had already sounded out Alice Evans, the London correspondent of the New Zealand Press Association, a stalwart friend who had often made up a four for bridge in the King William Street flat. She agreed to edit the *New Zealand News* in their absence. With the new appointment the plan was postponed until February 1934, by which time David was three and I was seventeen months. Philip Sykes, then a postgraduate student, took over the university work while we were away.

Lord Rutherford comes into another story from these years. In November 1932, not long after my birth, my father resigned from the *Sunday Dispatch* to concentrate entirely on New Zealand affairs: the University, their little newspaper, and the books he wanted to write. One of the first things he did was to organise a six-course dinner and reunion at Frascati's Restaurant in London

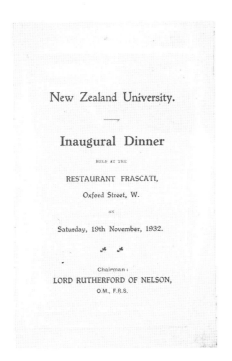

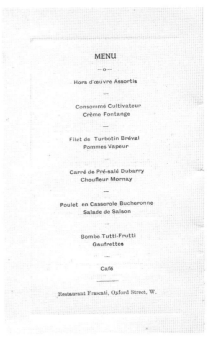

for nearly a hundred graduates of the University of New Zealand, at which Lord Rutherford took the chair. My father read a telegram of greeting from Professor Macmillan Brown, the Chancellor of the University. (It is interesting that, of the assembled graduates, thirty were doctors from the medical school at Otago.) My mother had to leave early to feed me. Talking to Lord Rutherford before she left, she was asked what prep school David was destined for. Hilda said they had not yet thought about it. Rutherford then said, 'You should send him to Southwell, my brother-in-law's school in Hamilton. Mrs Sergel is my sister and it's a very good school.' Hilda said lightly it seemed rather far away as they lived in London; but that was exactly where David went in 1941, for reasons the date may suggest.

The Harrop family, now complete, left England for New Zealand in February 1934. We travelled on the *Akaroa*, a splendid Shaw Savill luxury liner, which was making its maiden voyage after a complete transformation just the year before. It had two swimming pools, the indoor one floodlit in various colour schemes. There was a gymnasium, a children's nursery (with a Red Indian tent, rocking horses and so on) and there were parquet floors for dancing. Every cabin had fresh air direct from the side of the ship, natural light from a port-hole, and many of them private bathrooms.

No doubt my father had negotiated a special fare in return for advertising and editorial publicity in his paper. The regular round-trip fare was £112 and many of the passengers were tourists, using the *Akaroa* as a cruise ship rather than as a mere means of getting to New Zealand.

Tourism was the new growth industry in the 1930s. There was a need for 'an authoritative guide to those Antipodean shores', now that some people were 'fortunate enough to travel half-way across the world to take a holiday.' 'The cost of the journey from Europe is easily offset by the low price of travel and accommodation where the English pound is worth 24 shillings.' Allen and Unwin, one of London's leading publishers, certainly saw the market for such a book, good for armchair reading in England too and useful for New Zealanders themselves, as more and more of them would soon surely have the means to explore their own country. This leaflet (below) was part of a publicity campaign for the book.

A.J. Harrop left England with a contract for *Touring in New Zealand* in his luggage. When it was published the following year (he had finished it before he got back), it was widely praised on both sides of the world. The only criticism (this from the *Otago Daily Times*) was that Dr Harrop rarely writes 'in a personal vein; one wishes he had more often.' But more than one reviewer noticed his infectious enthusiasm. It was fine publicity for the Dominion, said the *Dominion* newspaper in Wellington and several writers in New Zealand suggested that the Government should make sure the book had a wide distribution abroad. A Gisborne paper, reviewing the book, would report that the author on his brief visit to Poverty Bay had made 'a host of friends'.

The ideal book for the traveller, fully descriptive and illustrated from excellent photographs.

TOURING IN NEW ZEALAND

by A. J. HARROP

Ph.D. (Cambridge), M.A. (N.Z.)
Author of "England and New Zealand," etc.

In fact, my parents already had a host of friends throughout New Zealand and their return after so many years away (eleven for my father, eight for my mother) caused quite a stir.

There were lots of pictures in the papers and a flurry of invitations to my father to speak all over the country. Wherever he went, my father was asked questions – about everything from the fall in the price of butter in London to the issue of freedom of speech – and his most casual comments were reported in the papers. If I had been old enough to think about such things, I might have thought he was a celebrity. As he toured the country gathering material for his travel book, he spoke to the New Plymouth Rotary Club, the Palmerston North Citizens' Lunch Club and many more. He gave talks on the radio on such things as 'journalism in London' and the prospects for the All Blacks on their next tour. He was a guest of honour at a lunch given by the Waitaki Old Boys and at the inaugural meeting of the P.E.N. Club in Wellington. Most importantly, Dr Hight invited his old pupil to give the chief address on the occasion of the conferment of degrees at Canterbury University College on 10 May 1934. They stood together in the cloisters for the photo on the next page.

'You are free to choose your own subject,' Dr. Hight had said. It was not a bland speech. Dr Harrop suggested that the university colleges of New Zealand were failing in one of the two main functions of a university. They were giving

an extremely good education to their undergraduate students, whose results continued to impress their examiners in England. But the colleges were not providing adequately for postgraduate research, either in the Arts or the Sciences. This was why so many of the best graduates were lost to the country. The professors and lecturers 'have little or no time for doing, or even adequately supervising, research'. 'It is hardly too much to say that the mental vigour of a nation is attested by the standard of its universities' and the University of New Zealand was seriously underfunded by the Government. Angus always thought that original research was the 'best preventative of intellectual stagnation'. The large classes and numerous weekly lectures faced by the staff would 'appal a Professor in England'. Not only was New Zealand sending most of its best graduates overseas (many of them not to return), but it was becoming difficult to recruit new staff in England when the first question he was asked by potential applicants was 'What facilities are given for research?' Here of course my father spoke from his experience as Representative of the University of New Zealand in England. But he also drew attention to the drastic salary cuts in New Zealand in these Depression years and concluded with some remarks about the unemployment situation: 'The tragedy is that we are training men for leadership and giving them no chance to lead.' It was hardly an inspirational address and the new graduates must have sat there glumly wondering what lay ahead for them. Whether this speech had any effect on government policy I have no idea; it was certainly widely reported. A leader in the *Dominion* referred to a point Dr Harrop had made about the need for quality rather than quantity in the

universities, a point made in England years later in the oft-repeated phrase of
Kingsley Amis: 'More means worse.'

At different times the newspapers suggested A.J. Harrop was in New
Zealand primarily to confer with the University of New Zealand 'on a variety
of questions', to gather data for a book on England and the Maori Wars (a
sequel to his *England and New Zealand*), to explore the country thoroughly
for a travel book and to acquaint himself with everything that had changed
since he had left in 1923. For my mother, the most important reason for this
1934 visit was the family reunion. Here she is on arrival in Wellington with
her sisters, Nettie and Lottie, and her parents. My mother is the daughter next
to Jim Valentine.

She was glad for us to have the chance to meet grandparents, aunts, uncles,
cousins, for the first time in our short lives. We children travelled a good deal,
and so did my mother, both with us and without – though none of us for nearly
as much as the 8000 miles my father claimed for himself in the Preface to
Touring in New Zealand, quite apart from the 25,000-mile round trip by ship.

David and I spent a lot of time getting used to the attentions of strangers. My
mother retained a memory of looking up from her deck-chair on the *Akaroa* to
see two men, who had been playing table tennis, lifting me (seventeen months
old) on to the table for the fun of seeing me totter along it, determinedly climb
over the net (an enormous obstacle) and proceed in triumph to the other end.
In New Zealand we were often left with friends or relatives (strangers to us) and
the care of a temporary nurse from nearby Karitane, while our parents gadded
about.

My father wrote in a letter of one brilliant day at Hanmer Springs, when he
was staying at the Lodge, described in his book as 'one of the finest hotels in

New Zealand'. It started with a swim in the hot springs at 7.15, continued with eighteen holes of golf in the morning, three hard sets of tennis in the afternoon (admittedly doubles), a walk with Dr Hight, then 'mountaineering by motor to the Look-out' and after dinner 'a few rubbers of contract', finishing with a short run round the moonlit town at 10.30 p.m. I rather hope the 'run' was in the motor, not on foot, after such a day. 'It is possible, but only just', he wrote in *Touring in New Zealand* 'to drive a car up to the Look-out, and those who wish to add one more thrill to their journey might well make the attempt.' So the tourist in New Zealand was being offered thrills already, in those days so long before bungy jumping.

We were all together when I had my second birthday in Gisborne, staying with my father's sister and her family, not yet in Australia. We met our small cousin, Cynthia, the one who, years later, quoted that Larkin poem: 'They may not mean to but they do.' David and I were usually happy enough as long as we were together. My first demand in the morning was always 'Boy!' It was the name I gave my brother. My own name would cause some problems. My mother – all her life – resolutely used both my names. I was always 'Ann Barbara' to her. The double name had, I think, more to do with Christopher Robin than with Princess Margaret Rose (as she was then known). Children and many other people, unsurprisingly, were more inclined to call me 'Annie B.' or simply 'Ann'.

In 1934 we had a good fortnight on our uncle and aunt's farm in the Waikato, which we would later come to know so well. But most of our time was spent in New Plymouth with our grandparents.

On 5 November, the day before we sailed out of Napier on the *Tamaroa*, Jim Valentine, my grandfather, wrote a letter to 'dear Hilda and Angus'. Jim was himself now a J.P., a member of the Victoria College Council and of the Senate of the University of New Zealand. He had just been appointed Chairman of the Taranaki Education Board. In the *Taranaki Daily News* he was quoted as saying that there was 'a state of crisis' in the schools, the result of the declining birth-rate, caused mainly by the economic depression. 'From 26 for every thousand in 1913 it had dropped to 17.' Jim had taken a great interest in his son-in-law's views on education and immigration – both of which were so desperately needed they both thought. But in his farewell letter to the ship, it was of his grandchildren Jim wrote:

> Ever since you left the words of Psalm 107 have been passing through my thoughts. 'He maketh the storm a calm so that the waves thereof are still ....
> So he bringeth them unto their desired haven ....' The house has seemed very empty and very quiet since Saturday morning, I don't think I ever in my life

felt parting more sorely than I did on leaving you. Ever since, I have been putting away things handled by the children and the one thought has been 'Never again will their little hands touch this'.

Jim Valentine could hardly have guessed that David and I would still be young children when he saw us again. It would only be six years before we were back in the safety of New Zealand.

CHAPTER 9

A strenuous pair

There was a pile of nearly forty letters and telegrams waiting for us on the *Tamaroa*, together with flowers and books and cakes. Leaving New Zealand was not taken lightly in 1934. Among the letters was one from my mother's sister, Lottie. 'I hope, oh I do hope', she wrote, 'the happy moments of your visit have outweighed the annoying ones.' This suggests that there had been, inevitably, some strains and stresses for the London family in adjusting to the very different lives of their friends and relations. My parents had, I think, been most relaxed during their time with Kath and Moyra Todd, who were then living in Auckland. Moyra was David's godmother and the friendship with her, begun in the Bloomsbury boarding house, had become the deepest and most important in Hilda's life. This photo of Hilda with Kath and Moyra was taken on a picnic near Auckland.

The Todds were soon to return to England to live in South Square in Hampstead Garden Suburb, only fifteen minutes away from the Harrop home in Highfield Avenue. The Todd sisters knew that different London life and so indeed did my grandparents in New Plymouth, from their happy visit in 1928. For my mother's sisters, Net and Lottie, however, it remained mysterious, glamorous certainly, but a little threatening, suggesting values and experiences far removed from their own.

Looking back on our eight months in New Zealand, Lottie wrote: 'It has been much more natural to think of you and your doings controlled by the same hours. When I'm feeding and tucking up Max [her baby son carried the name of his uncle] – you're not just meditating on arising to begin the day we've finished with. Of course, to you it's a brand-new day, but I always have a sneaky little second-hand feel about it.'

Late in 1934 – not long before Christmas – we were back to those second-hand days, days indeed that were long over by the time their descriptions reached New Zealand, for there was still no regular airmail between the two countries. It was often three months before a reply came to a question asked on the other side of the world. Now we were once more on our own, almost out of the reach of the family, that 'dear octopus, from whose tentacles we never quite escape' and never really want to, as the playwright Dodie Smith once put it. If Hilda's life was very different from that of her sisters – the one on the Waikato farm, the other in Auckland – she remained always in touch with them and shared the things they had in common, above all, the problems of raising 'good' children and running the sort of spotless home their mother had encouraged them to want. But the warm, loving letters always carried the awareness of the great gulf between their lives and hers.

We returned to Highfield Avenue to a community far removed from the anonymity of the flat in central London. In the suburbs everyone knew what was going on. Close neighbours, the Reynoldses two doors along, had become close friends. (As friends they had the added advantage of having access to a tennis court belonging to Eileen Reynolds' parents, the Ravens of Red Roofs, not far away.) Eileen reported that there had been four student tenants at No. 43 in our absence, not just Philip Sykes, later an eminent industrial chemist, who had been running the university office in my father's absence. The young men had left sheets and towels hanging on the clothes line in the garden, day after foggy day, instead of sending them to the laundry as everyone did in the winter, if they could possibly afford to do so. The linen was never quite the same again and a French polisher had to spend an entire morning working on the dining room table. But Eileen had had fires on and flowers arranged for our return, and a casserole in the oven. Everyone thought, in theory, that it was good to be home.

David and I had, however, been thoroughly spoiled on the ship and indeed for much of the time in New Zealand, enjoying endless admiration and affection. 'People take far too much notice of them', my mother wrote. Life at home for us was very dull in comparison. Remembering Virginia Woolf's opinion of 'infantile anecdotage', I quote, a little reluctantly, from the record my mother was keeping of my every remark. I was two years and two months old and my words were not music in my mother's ears:

> Yesterday morning when I asked A.B. if she would have her milk she said 'Ann don't want no blinkin' milk!' She *screamed* today because Nannie brought her in from her pram instead of Mummy or Daddy. 'Ann want Ann's Daddy', and 'Please may have Ann's Daddy?' was the pathetic cry most of the day.

In many of the photographs taken in New Zealand I am in my father's arms; and I had obviously been used to having both my parents around a good deal on the ship, even though my father had been working on *Touring in New Zealand*. The Karitane nurse, Norma Welch, whom we had brought back to England with us, was no substitute. The family was rarely now to be as calm and composed as we look in this photograph, taken in Wellington.

My mother had been interested in maladjusted children long before David and I had had any chance to become maladjusted. She had attended numerous lectures in London before her children arrived and read countless books on 'mothercraft' or indeed 'parenting' – the more general term she favoured, considering (in her modern way) that fathers played an important role. She was, of course, intelligent enough to realise that after losing her first child, her tendency would be to be over-protective, to worry about us too much. And worry she certainly did. We suffered not from neglect or abuse (as is the common lot of writers of childhood memoirs), but rather from a sporadic surfeit of attention and from abiding anxiety.

In New Plymouth in 1934, when we were so small that she had still not had much chance to put into practice any of the things she had learned, Hilda herself gave a talk at the YWCA on 'the principles of modern child guidance'. The *Taranaki Herald* reported her saying that 'The child, who would be described as difficult, maladjusted, nervous, neurotic or unmanageable, was often of quite superior intelligence and was capable of developing into a good citizen, if given the proper guidance. How may the child be guided over the many pitfalls? Very often,' my mother declared, 'the parent is the worst person to guide him.' She spoke of the child guidance clinics being established in England, but so far New Zealand, she said, 'had not done much in this direction.' It was something she knew about from her aunt, Win Valentine, whose special subject it was.

Hilda spoke of the importance of nursery schools. Children were not clay to be shaped according to the will of the adult in charge, but more like plants, containing in themselves all the possibilities of growth; the adult is like a gardener, who must give the plant suitable soil and nourishment and prune it carefully so that it develops into the finest possible specimen. As adults, as parents and teachers, she said, we must develop in ourselves the right attitudes. She concluded, as if she already feared she was inadequate for the task that lay ahead, 'So much easier said than done.'

It was much easier (if not quite so interesting) to go to parenting classes, to listen to lectures on 'Child Motivation', 'Temperament, Disposition and Character' and 'Fears and Jealousies', than to rear two vociferous, strong-minded infants. My father always wanted everything to be perfect. He had looked forward so much to what he had described in 1925 as a 'long adventure in happiness', but sometimes it must have seemed that far from adding to their happiness, their longed-for children were disturbing it.

My mother, as I have said, was eager to be good at everything; indeed she always aimed to be the best – the best dancer, the best tennis player, the best student.

> Good, better, best.
> Never let it rest
> Till the good is better
> And the better best.

Now she tried too hard to be the perfect mother. We knew she was often dissatisfied with *herself*, rather than with us. There is a story of her exclaiming, when struggling to put pleats into a dress she was making, 'Oh, I'm no good.' To which, I said, consolingly, aged three-and-a-half, 'You are *quite* a good mother.'

We were both bright, there was no question about that, but we were difficult. In the record my mother kept, she would often write of one or other or us both: David (or Ann Barbara) 'is going through a difficult stage'. But when were we not? As small babies we had been remarkably co-operative and perhaps gave a false impression of what was to come.

As a modern mother in the 1930s, my mother naturally subscribed to the theories of Truby King, still renowned in New Zealand as the founder of the Plunket Society, 'for the promotion of the health of women and children'. He was the champion of 'Breast is best', of learning from animal rearing, the 'scientifically proven', most effective feeding of babies, which had cut the infant mortality rate at a time when bottle-feeding had become widely popular, both in England and New Zealand.

Truby King has already appeared in this book as the Medical Superintendent of Seacliff, near Dunedin, the mental hospital where my uncle Frederick was confined. *The Little One's Log Book*, the book in which my brother's first days were recorded, was by Eva Erleigh, a keen disciple of Truby King. It was first published in 1927, with this new edition in 1930, the year before David was born. It has delightful illustrations by E.H. Shepard, more famous, of course, for his illustrations for A.A. Milne, of whom more later. The book was largely to be filled in by the child's mother, but the text followed the Truby King line that no baby should ever be fed at night ('that is between 10 p.m. and 6 a.m.'), that absolute regularity in feeding was important during the day, that he (or indeed she) could be trained from the very first week to have regular bowel movements, and that, amazingly, 'no napkins should be necessary when he is one year old'. The small baby was to spend most of the daylight hours, winter and summer, outdoors, with the hood of the perambulator down except in very bad weather. Fresh air and solitude were essential for a good baby. This was the proper beginning for the desirable life of self-reliance and independence.

The older child should of course eat only wholemeal bread, with wholemeal flour for its cakes and puddings, and there should be a plentiful supply of fresh fruit daily. 'Margarine should never be allowed to replace butter.' 'Rising is advisable as soon as the child wakes in the morning, however early this may be, as this establishes a good habit, and often prevents many bad ones.' The 'bad ones' included thumb-sucking and, worse, masturbation. Indeed Eva Erleigh suggested children ideally should be 'taught to sleep with their hands under their pillows.'

As babies, David and I apparently both did all the right things, wherever our hands were. The Truby King regime suited us. Hilda was even able to record of David at ten months, 'Dr Myers says he eats his crust most intelligently.' My own baby record is in a large rose-pink notebook, now faded and indeed water-stained after its two journeys round the world. It begins with a great deal of information no reader of this book could possibly want to know. Indeed, I hardly want to know myself all those carefully recorded facts about my infant months – the weight gains every week, the weaning, the first steps and the gradual appearance of all my teeth, each one duly dated.

Later it becomes more interesting and, such was our interaction, it inevitably became a record of us both, brother and sister. The first indication of any real problem, I think, was on the *Tamaroa* coming home from New Zealand in 1934. We had already been known to bite each other. That was bad enough, but it was far more serious when we took to biting other children. Their mothers took strong exception and Hilda felt ashamed. Where had she gone wrong? And why was it that her small daughter was particularly given to storms – to screaming and fussing? This sort of behaviour was forgivable at fourteen months, when it was first commented on. I always wanted what David had and to do whatever he did and screamed lustily when I couldn't have it or do it. A year later, however, the wretched child was still getting into these 'furious tempers whenever she can't have everything she wants and stamps her wee feet up and down tempestuously and screams'. It was behaviour that continued from time to time, year after year.

One of my earliest memories is of one Sunday morning in my nursery in Highfield Avenue when I was already four. I kicked up a most terrible fuss because I wanted to wear my old brown shoes to church and my mother wanted me to put on some new white buckskin ones the Todds had given me. Hilda called it 'a shocking scene'. Most of my rages at this time were to do with clothes; I was constantly pitting my own will against my mother's. All these years later, with no one to oppose, I have adopted for most occasions a uniform of black trousers and black shirts or jerseys so that I don't have to think about clothes, one of my mother's favourite concerns.

Hilda read in her books that 'full-scale temper tantrums in toddlers ought not to arise'. Yet here I was, beyond the toddler stage, and still capable of horrendous sound and fury. Ordinary naughtiness Hilda could cope with. 'The imps were being impish', she wrote in her diary, or, more seriously, 'the children were little devils' – a word not lightly used by someone with Baptists in the background. She could understand our experiments – mixing face powder with her best scent, or rolling a pumpkin down the stairs.

What she could not tolerate, because they reflected so badly on her parenting skills, were tantrums, rudeness and, above all, violence. That rhyme about the 'little girl, who had a little curl right in the middle of her forehead', was often applied to me, though my baby curls had gone. 'When she was good, she was very, very good. And when she was bad she was horrid.'

Reading recently about my childhood in my mother's neat, legible handwriting, I would often feel I was reading about some other person, someone far removed from the consciousness I have of myself. My mother wrote mainly of her children's cleverness and reprehensible behaviour. The photographs, more familiar to me, record a different childhood. We are nearly always together, David and I, having happy times. There are smiling shots of us on holiday at Middleton-on-Sea and Walton-on-the-Naze and in a camping coach (Southern Railways) near Exmouth. We can be seen walking hand-in-hand through a buttercup meadow in Devon. We were kings of the castle at the seaside. At home we were at the top of the tree in our garden, paddling in our little paddling pool, climbing our climbing frame. David posed with a chimp in the Pets' Corner at the Zoo, while I stood solemnly by a sheep. I would have preferred the chimpanzee, but did not say so. I knew when I got home I would be asked, like Jane in the A.A. Milne poem on the next page.

Have you been a good girl?
Have you been a good girl?
Well, what did they think that I went there to do?
And why should I want to be bad at the Zoo?
And should I be likely to say if I had?

This was childhood as it was meant to be. And as, indeed, it often was. There are of course no photographs of smart answers and outrageous fusses. The important thing was that life was never boring. Philip Larkin, that favourite poet whom I have already quoted in relation to parents, once described his own childhood as 'a forgotten boredom'. Much of mine I have forgotten. But I know it was never boring. It gave me an appetite for life I have always sustained. I can truly say that I don't know what it is to be bored. I have been frustrated, furious and hurt, but never bored. There have always been books for the times when nothing is happening.

There were books from the very beginning. One of the earliest anecdotes (which suggests the sort of thing that must have irritated my brother) concerns the reading aloud to us, when I was only two and a half and David four, of the terrible story of Polyphemus from *Stories from the Odyssey*. I have the book in front of me as I write. It carries my mother's almost adult signature: Hilda M.F. Valentine. Was it suitable reading for infants? I find it interesting that my mother thought so. I had forgotten Heath Robinson's nasty illustration of Odysseus exulting over the defeated Polyphemus, but I had certainly never forgotten the story of the one-eyed giant dashing out the brains of Odysseus's men, or the hero's clever plan to make the giant drunk and blind, so that he could evacuate the survivors clinging to the undersides of his giant sheep.

At the time we were fascinated by the names. At breakfast the day following that horrific bedtime story we were both chanting 'Poseidon, Poseidon', so our mother asked us 'Who is Poseidon?' and I was the one who came up with the answer: 'He's the daddy'. 'Whose Daddy?', our mother persisted, and, yes, I had taken it in (along with the gore and violence – 'the blood gushed out and the eye frizzled and hissed'). I correctly answered 'the daddy of the big giant'. It was indeed Poseidon, the god of the sea, who was Polyphemus' father and who pursued Odysseus 'for ten long, weary years'.

This story reminds me of one I tell at the beginning of my biography of A.A. Milne when he was exactly the same age – two and a half – and enraged his older brothers by answering a question before they did. Like A.A. Milne, with his 'Cat!', I heard my Poseidon story more times than I wanted to hear it, but it certainly started me off knowing it was a good thing to listen carefully and come up with the right answers. As Milne put it: 'In Papa's house, it was natural to be interested; it was easy to be clever.' I can't remember a time when I couldn't read, but this doesn't mean I was a particularly early reader. There is only one mention of my reading ability in my mother's record. She wrote that I could read 'anything' when I was six, which is hardly precocious.

Stories from the Odyssey were seriously violent stuff. But there was plenty of more everyday bad behaviour in our other books, which may well have reinforced my own. I was interested to find that of the books listed as received for the Christmas when I was five, most of them are still in my house and all of them are still alive in my mind, unlike the other presents: the dolls, the trumpet, the tea-set from Dr Hight, the Mickey Mouse nailbrush or even the 'shop' from Daddy and Mother, of which I have no recollection whatsoever, though surely it must have been worth remembering. The books included *Angus Lost* by Marjorie Flack, a picture book about a Scottish terrier, remarkably like the Todds' dog, Jock, and *Squirrel goes Skating* by Alison Uttley, both of which I loved, though they might have seemed rather juvenile fare for someone who had been listening to *Stories from the Odyssey* nearly three years earlier. I enjoyed sticking our book-plates in them: the illustration seemed to be of us.

There was more substantial stuff in *Alice in Wonderland* (though our edition had the Margaret Tempest coloured illustrations, not Tenniel) and *Famous Animal Tales*, 'pictured anew' by Ernest Aris, where we met not only the Ugly Duckling and the three Billy Goats Gruff but the alarming story of Brer Fox, Brer Rabbit and the Tar Baby. The rhythms here have stayed with me: 'The Tar-baby said nothing, and Brer Fox, he lay low.' Foxes were bad role models, of course. But so also, surely, were the Mad Hatter ('eh, stupid?'), the Cook who threw all those pans at the Duchess and the baby, and the Queen of Hearts, who was a great one for screaming.

The behaviour was far better in our favourite bed-time listening. This was a serial story our father told us in which we ourselves were major characters. It was based loosely on our 1934 travels to New Zealand and back and was a story – as my father said – 'that went straight ahead and told what actually happened to people', though the 'people' included a party-giving duck and three seagulls,

Billy, Bobby and Sally. The duck was originally called Jemima Puddleduck, but was transformed into Wilhelmina Webfoot ('Willa' for short) when my father met a refugee called Frederick Ost and hoped to publish the story with his illustrations. The question of Beatrix Potter's copyright was then involved.

Round the World with Willa Webfoot was not, in fact, published until after the war, by which time the David and Ann Barbara who had featured in the original stories had grown a good deal. I retain some affection for the book, particularly for the wilder flights of my father's imagination, but there is too much geography in it, and there was no chance at all that David and Ann Barbara would share the fate of Christopher Robin.

The reporters and photographers arrived and wanted Willa to say something for publication.

I have already mentioned the fact that my father bought *Winnie-the-Pooh* for my mother the day it was published in 1926, very soon after their marriage. We had all four of the Milne books from our earliest days, and again it was the rhythm of both the stories and the verses that made them lodge in the child's mind for a lifetime. I wonder now, thinking about it from this long perspective, whether the memorability of Milne's poem 'Rice Pudding' had something to do with the fact that fussing seemed natural behaviour to me. There's that repeated Shepard drawing of the furious Mary Jane, so angry that she kicks her shoe in the air:

> What is the matter with Mary Jane?
> She's crying with all her might and main ….
> I've promised her sweets and a ride in the train,
> And I've begged her to stop for a bit and explain ….

But when I screamed and fussed and cried with all my might and main, there were certainly no sweets or rides in the train, but rather solitary confinement in the bathroom for at least five minutes until I calmed down and said I was sorry. I was locked in, of course, for at three, the first time this punishment was tried, I announced I would just come out again. I was also good at slamming doors, having early on perhaps got the idea from Hilaire Belloc's Rebecca. His *Cautionary Tales* were certainly congenial reading:

> A trick that everyone abhors
> In little girls is slamming doors.

There were times when Hilda was in despair. Who could blame her for going down to the end of the town, as she frequently did, without consulting us? Our grandmother wrote consolingly and a little complacently from New Plymouth:

> We all do think our training has been useless at times, but one just has to keep on keeping on and evidently ours turned out not so badly …. But the same thing has to be told and drilled over and over again …. We need great wisdom certainly and there's only One who can give it. He will if we *ask* and expect.

Nellie Valentine sent sunlit photos, such as those overleaf, and wrote of happy family reunions: Elliots, Watkinses, Valentines, with sometimes as many as 'ten bairns'. Hilda would have liked to have had a look at those bairns, to check that they weren't so much *better* than us, for she feared that they were. I think my mother's fault was that she took our upbringing rather too seriously, read too many manuals, analysed our behaviour and talked about it with us in a way that exacerbated it.

Hilda was still wanting to be as 'high-souled and pure-minded' as she had wanted to be at seventeen. Her Christian faith was fundamental to her life. In those far-off days at Timaru Girls' High School she had wanted her influence

to be felt as good among her fellow-pupils. How much more so was it with us, her susceptible children. My mother was continually being pulled in different directions – between her instinct, which told her life was made for pleasure, and the way she had been brought up, which had ensured that she was constantly aware of the need for unselfishness, sacrifice and, of course, the nurture of the next generation, the passing-on of a life of prayer and service. We were taught to pray as soon as we could kneel, in gratitude, and to help us to be better children.

Thank you for the birds that sing.
Thank you God for every thing.

We were told that 'when we are cross or angry God cannot make us hear him', and we were encouraged to tell God at night what naughty or unfortunate things had happened during the day. We were also taught, very early on, to realise how lucky and privileged we were. Fifty years later when she was writing her memoirs for the family, Hilda would comment on her 'privileged life' and David would use the phrase for her title.

My mother knew how lucky she was to have the life she had. It would be totally inaccurate to suggest that Hilda Harrop was a tennis-playing, hat-buying, party-giving young journalist – though she certainly was that – who found her children irksome. We were at the centre of her life, but she hated to be tied and, anyway, hadn't Truby King suggested the parent was not always the best carer, that children often flourished best when taught to be independent of their mother? Hilda had not, of course, read John Bowlby, whose views about the prime importance of the constant maternal presence were not published until 1952.

In 1935, when I was not yet three, Hilda (having made careful plans for the *New Zealand News*) took off for a fortnight in Geneva, where Jack Condliffe, their old Economics Professor at Canterbury, was now on the Secretariat of the League of Nations, and my father was spending a month as an official New Zealand 'observer' of the sixteenth Session. He was sending to the *Dominion* in Wellington articles which also appeared in other papers throughout the country. Hilda left us with Norma Welch, our Karitane nanny, and would write to her sister: 'I am bringing them up to stand on their own feet.' It would eventually prove a useful training for what lay ahead.

One postcard survives, signed 'Love, Norma', written on a picnic 'In the Park'. 'The infants', she wrote 'are still being models …. I went upstairs this afternoon when they were supposed to be resting and found the Tamaroa in full sail for N.Z. on A.B.'s bed.' That was hardly 'model' behaviour, but certainly the sort of thing that any trained nanny could take in her stride. It was a 'topping' day and we had tomato sandwiches 'from our own garden' (undoubtedly with wholemeal bread) and a sponge cake of Norma's own making. Norma was obviously a treasure.

If only she could have stayed throughout the years ahead. My mother wrote in her 1936 diary a list of the things to remember when considering an employee. Facing Norma's return to New Zealand, my parents had decided to embark on a very 'modern' solution to the child-care problem by employing young foreign women, who were keen to see London and learn English and would live as part of the family while giving the mother the freedom to work and enjoy life without the children's constant presence. (It was a solution I would adopt myself thirty years later.)

Hilda wrote down that she required the girls to be 'Quick and thorough. Methodical. Cheerful. Healthy.' They should be prepared to play with the children and do some ironing and cooking. In return they would have plenty of free time, their own bedroom with a radio, 'meals with us' and the very unusual benefit of a refrigerator.

My mother spent a great deal of time and energy in these years finding people to fill this role, above all to look after us. (She nearly always had, in addition, someone to clean the house.) She had written in her diary in 1928, before she had any children and soon after her parents had gone back to New Zealand, that she found it delightful 'to have no one else to think about'; there were just the two of them, Hilda and Angus. Most people know that feeling of relief when visitors, however beloved, *go* and one can resume one's own casual, selfish patterns of living. The trouble with children, as we find out, is that they usually don't go, not for many, many years.

My mother always wanted to have someone else on hand to share that gruelling, unremitting care that children involve. There were so many delightful things to do, so many lovely invitations, so many places to enjoy, so many new people to meet and entertain. In one particular week I counted up that my parents had thirty-four New Zealand visitors, not all on the same day. At one point – she had been writing about the 1936 Congress of Universities of the British Empire in Cambridge, where at a dinner she had sat next to the Master of Caius – my grandfather, Jim Valentine, wrote from New Plymouth: 'I felt quite proud to think that you were meeting such interesting – even illustrious – folk and that you felt quite at home with them.' In that same letter her father was able to tell her that as a member of the University Senate he had seen a report on Angus's work, recommending an increase in his salary to '£400 in English currency' and praising him lavishly as 'capable and enthusiastic' and 'always giving the university work precedence over his own private work. He would be hard to replace should he determine to devote himself to literary work.'

The university work brought many interesting contacts as well as the routine business, and so did the *New Zealand News*. There were plenty of references to 'work' in my mother's diary, but also dozens of desirable distractions. The days of long introspective diary entries were over and it is tantalising to read the merest naming of most events, Ascot and Wimbledon, the Chelsea Flower Show and theatres and concerts and dinners galore, including one for the New Zealand air ace, Jean Batten – soon to break a record with a five-day flight from

Australia. At least my mother did comment on her: 'as charming and modest as ever'. But there is no way of knowing what Hilda thought of Eliot's *Murder in the Cathedral* or of Gielgud as Romeo, Evelyn Waugh speaking at a Book Fair or Shaw and Wells at a P.E.N. dinner, with J.B. Priestley in the Chair.

For the most part adult and childish pleasures were totally separate, though we sometimes watched our parents play tennis or squash and they took a keen interest in our own first tennis lessons. In the summer of 1937, David, aged six, was taken by his father to Lord's for his first cricket match. And that same year, visiting the Hampstead Squash and Fives Club, where our parents regularly played, we shared our first sight of a television screen. I can remember it well, the wonder of it, in a warm dark room – but not what was actually there on the small screen in one of the first telecasts from Alexandra Palace – a service soon to be disrupted (when only a very few people had a set) by the war.

In the four years between our return from New Zealand and the end of 1938, we were in the care of nine different young women, most of them German, all with their different methods, attitudes and expectations. Mostly, I suspect, they found us too much, and left rather earlier than they had intended. I have clear memories of only one of these women: Randi Petterson, a Norwegian, with whom we always stayed in touch. (As an adolescent, after the war, I visited her in Oslo.) The others blur together, so that I hardly know how to write about them. Some even go unnamed (except as Fräulein) in my mother's diaries and letters and in that pink notebook in which she continued to write from time to time.

One Fräulein who is named – Anne-Marie Jacobs from Kiel – stayed a little longer than most. We had German lessons with her every morning after breakfast. My parents had obviously realised how easily small children can pick up a second language and they were keen to give us the chance to learn. To me now it seems strange that we learnt German in 1936, the year of the Axis pacts between Germany and Italy, and between Germany and Japan, the year when Hitler recognised Franco's provisional government in Spain. It was also the year when Hitler is said to have refused to shake hands with Jesse Owens, the black star of the Berlin Olympic Games. And, closer to home, it was the year of the 'battle of Cable Street', when 100,000 clashed with Mosley's Fascists in London's East End, and a Jewish tailor and his son were thrown through a plate glass window by the 'blackshirts'.

It was the year when Edward VIII abdicated and most people (if not he) were realising the true horror of Nazism. Some of our closest friends were Jewish – among them the family of the distinguished New Zealand physician, Dr Bernard Myers, and a number of refugees from Hitler. How could we, in 1936, learn the language of *Mein Kampf*? I am reminded that it was also 'the international language of liberal Jewry', and the language of my parents' favourite composers: Beethoven, Mozart, Haydn and Schubert.

My parents knew French already. Indeed my mother had taught it at New Plymouth Girls' High School and my father had spent long hours reading it in the Paris archives. And they had always been interested in German, the other great European language. My father had recommended my mother study German on the ship coming to England in 1926 and she had certainly had German lessons in Vienna in 1931. Now in 1936 my father went on a walking tour in the Rhineland (not more than twenty-five miles in a day) to see for himself what was going on, to witness 'something of the fanaticism of Hitler's followers', as well as *Tannhäuser* and footpaths by 'rushing torrents' that reminded him of the West Coast tracks he had walked as a boy.

Soon after his return, it was my fourth birthday party and – it pains me to admit – David and I entertained our visitors with 'a German dialogue'. There was a party of twenty – adults and children – and no suggestion that we forgot our words or realised how inappropriate it was. What the long-suffering audience made of it I have no idea.

David took a particular dislike to poor Fräulein Jacobs. My mother recorded in the rose-pink notebook that he annoyed her 'by using most ungallant language. "Dirty beast" is a favourite expression we find very trying. I tell her to ignore him, but it is difficult.' It was this sort of thing and what our mother mourned as a complete lack of social graces, plus a nasty incident when I was punched in the local library, that made my mother take up Kath Todd's suggestion that David should have some sessions with her. Close friend of the family as she was, she was also a child psychiatrist and it was natural she should want to improve the situation. On 30 March 1937 David, aged six, started having an hour with her once a week, and loved it. In May my grandfather wrote: 'I'm glad that Kath has summed up David's attitude …. No need to worry.' But worry my parents did.

1937 was an emotional year for my mother. We were in church on Sunday 20 June when a cable came to the house. The resident Fräulein opened the cable (the delivery boy had asked if there were an answer) and read:

MOTHER DIED IN SLEEP SATURDAY MORNING AT NETTIES
FUNERAL TIRAU MONDAY LOVE LOTTIE

The girl rushed into our good neighbour, Eileen Reynolds, and Eileen rushed over to St Barnabas, Temple Fortune. It was a terrible shock. Nellie Valentine was only sixty-nine and her recent letters, which would have given some warning, had not yet reached England.

My gregarious, busy, croquet-champion grandmother, whom I was too young to remember, had had some pains in her chest, but had found it extremely difficult to take things more easily. Nellie herself said it had caused quite a sensation among her friends, for the energetic Mrs Valentine was never ill. Before she left home to see a specialist in Auckland, her nephew Will Johnson, she wrote, 'I have all I want and the very best husband in the world – I hate to leave him', little thinking it was a final farewell. Her last letter to Jim from the Tirau farm, where she was supposed to be resting, began 'My Best of Men' and told him that 'Dear old Net had the house spotless and a lovely afternoon tea waiting.'

'I'm being good and resting so I'll soon be quite fit again', she had written in May, telling her daughter of the celebrations of Coronation Day in New Plymouth, with ninety entries for the wood-chopping contest in Pukekura Park and a match at Rugby Park. In the morning Jim Valentine had been invited to speak at Fitzroy School 'and as we had actually seen the Crown Jewels he could make it interesting'. In fact, my grandfather could make anything interesting, but Nellie regretted there were 'no buns or sweets or medals for the children'. She had been rather thrilled on 14 May when 'she actually saw Mrs Harrop's name' in the list of those who were present in Westminster Abbey.

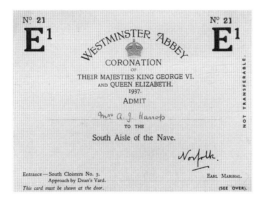

At the Tirau farm in May, Nettie had also been thinking of Hilda in the Abbey. 'It must have been wonderful to be there and to hear all that beautiful music.' She and Lewis had stayed up late and listened in on the wireless. Hilda's letter about her day to 'Dear Everybody' was much copied when it arrived by air via Australia. In fact, making yet another copy – this meant painstakingly writing it out by hand – was one of the last things her mother did on the day before she died.

Hilda typed three long packed pages, which began:

Before the rush of this busy life blurs the impressions of the most wonderful day of my life, I must try to tell you something about it. I was one of the six New Zealanders resident in London to be invited to Westminster Abbey for the Coronation – A. was asked if he would like an invitation, but he preferred to see it from a stand in the Mall.

In her memoirs, Hilda says Angus did not want to *dress up* and that large Mr Forsyth, the Representative in London of the New Zealand Meat Board, sitting next to her, had to wear 'court dress with tight knee breeches and a little sword in a scabbard. He kept apologising to me for his "tooth pick" as he called it, which he found very hard to manage and which dug into my side.' She was sitting in a marvellous position in the nave, so close to the aisle that she could have touched the processions as they went past. She was moved by the sight of the dark head of the Queen, about to be crowned with her King, the only bare head among all the tiaras and feathers of the other women.

At the end of her letter she wrote 'We have been especially busy with A's book on the Maori Wars, which is *nearly* finished.' Angus had decided that the *New Zealand News* (from the printer's address at 92 Fleet Street) should publish this book in England, in association with Whitcombe and Tombs in Australia and New Zealand, in a carefully costed and priced limited edition of 1000 copies. *England and the Maori Wars* came out at the end of 1937, with 500 subscribers already, handsomely produced with a striking and colourful jacket by the young New Zealand artist F.H. Coventry, who (only ten years later) would illustrate my own first published story. My father's book was dedicated 'To MJ Savage, the Minister of of Native Affairs and to the future of the Maori race'.

There is a nice tribute to my mother in the Acknowledgements, just as there had been in the Wakefield biography: 'Where original documents of a very controversial period are being studied for the first time, the task of sifting the material in order to include the essential and to eliminate the irrelevant, however interesting it may be, is a heavy one. For much help in this and the many other tasks connected with the production of this volume I am deeply grateful to my wife.' They had been working on this project (for which the copying of the primary sources must have itself been a monumental task) during the whole of their marriage; it was a sequel to *England and New Zealand*, which had come out over ten years earlier.

James Hight, their favourite historian, acknowledged his copy in a January 1938 letter and referred to his own involvement in the ongoing saga of land claims:

Now I have been exceedingly busy these last few days, having a meeting of delegates from all the Runangas of the Ngaitahu people … in connection with the 90 year old Land claim regarding the Ngaitahu Block reserves. I took the opportunity of mentioning your book to the meeting. I hope this Govt. will definitely settle the claim. The book is undoubtedly your masterpiece so far and a work that should attract the most notice, dealing with such a large amount of new material.

James Cowan reviewed it in the *Auckland Star* as 'masterly', 'a most necessary book', and wrote to say it was 'a splendid piece of work and useful continually for reference.' Cowan's letter makes one realise how recent this history was, for he himself as a youth had heard Te Kooti's own side of the story and had retained a great admiration for him as a soldier and strategist. Arthur Berriedale

Keith, Professor of History at the University of Edinburgh, where my father was an external examiner, wrote to him that it would be 'the authoritative history of the period.' The University of New Zealand conferred a Doctorate of Literature (Litt.D.) on my father in recognition of this book.

I mention these things a little boastfully and could quote from a hundred more reviews: 'highly important', Christchurch *Press*; 'accurate and clear', Wellington *Dominion*; 'a first class piece of historical writing', *Birmingham Post*; 'a piece of true historical scholarship', the *Spectator*; etc. etc. But more interesting, I think, to the general reader, seventy years later, is a whole page written under the title 'BOOKS IN GENERAL' by David Garnett, then literary editor of the *New Statesman* but now so much better known for his Bloomsbury connections, his marriage to Virginia Woolf's niece Angelica, and so on. He was the grandson of Edward Garnett, who had written the first biography of Edward Gibbon Wakefield. David Garnett declared in the *Statesman* on Christmas Day in 1937 that 'I am going to give myself a Christmas present of a more recent biography of him called *The Amazing Career of Edward Gibbon Wakefield* by Dr A.J. Harrop, since I have just read his *England and the Maori Wars*, which is an extraordinarily interesting book in which Wakefield just appears.' Garnett acknowledged that the new book was based largely on official memoranda, Colonial dispatches and the like, but he found it riveting and the page he wrote about it was the sort of review a writer dreams of. There were very soon no copies to be had of that clever limited edition – much as it would seem to me to be, as Cowan called it, a work for reference rather than for reading.

A.J. Harrop was now undoubtedly established as, and often called, one of New Zealand's leading historians, something I had not quite realised myself until I looked carefully into the reception of his books. It was therefore not surprising that my father was now approached to write the volume on New Zealand in Jarrolds' widely advertised *MY COUNTRY* series, which had already covered England, Scotland, Ireland and Wales and for which the publishers claimed they had obtained the services of authors 'who are widely known and distinguished men of letters'. My father and his predecessors, Edward Shanks, A.G. Macdonell, Lord Dunsany and Rhys Davies are now all faded names. Only Dunsany gets into Margaret Drabble's *Oxford Companion to English Literature*.

My New Zealand came out in July 1939 and the last section, difficult to write as it must have been, was full of references to what was currently going on, quoting from the Christchurch *Press* some harsh criticism of Neville Chamberlain's foreign policy and of the lack of consultation with New Zealand at the time of Munich. Angus wrote from personal experience of both the League of Nations and of the Imperial Conference in 1937, when the New Zealand Prime Minister had strongly criticised the attitude of the British Government to the League of Nations.

My New Zealand was seen as a contribution to the celebration of the hundred years since the Treaty of Waitangi, a centennial that was to be sadly overshadowed by the outbreak of war. One section of the book shows how far my father himself had come in the fifteen years since he had first arrived in England, excited by everything he saw. In 1939 he wrote:

> We are still captivated by the beauty of England's countryside, enthralled by her pageantry, impressed by her astonishing achievements in so many spheres. But it would be idle to deny that our gaze is now straying beyond the West End and the lanes of Devonshire.

Angus now wrote of poverty and unemployment, of the extremes of wealth which shocked him in England. He praised New Zealand's radical heritage and its comparative freedom from class distinction, and in particular the current Labour Government, the Savage ministry, which had pledged to ensure a high minimum standard of living for the whole community. 'We have set our faces against the aggregation of wealth in private hands and we have made equality of opportunity an actual rather than a theoretical basis of our society.' But, he wrote, 'we have been so busy with the struggle to provide in a single century the material amenities of civilisation that we have neglected those finer flowers of the mind …. We have taken our ideas and most of our ideals from other lands.' He criticised 'the inadequacy of the efforts made to preserve and encourage the Maori language, customs and traditions.' He went on to lament the smallness of New Zealand's population, then not much more than one and a half million, and ended the book with a strong case for the admission in large numbers of Czech refugees from Hitler.

> We need more people to justify our claim to monopolise one of the fairest places on the earth. Our High Commissioner has boldly championed the cause of those whose liberties have been destroyed by the Nazi machine.

The Czechs had been sacrificed in what was now obviously a vain attempt to avoid a war. In these years the New Zealand High Commissioner in London, Bill Jordan, with Savage's full support, often had cause to criticise British foreign policy. Angus was always closely in touch with the High Commission and was able in the *New Zealand News* to publicise New Zealand's distinctive position, though there was never any doubt that *when* (there now seemed to be no 'if') it came to war, New Zealand would again stand by the United Kingdom.

On 20 September 1938 a young woman, Hella Müller, arrived from Teplitz in Czechoslovakia to help in our home. But far from being a refugee, she turned out to be a Sudeten German and a vehement Nazi. So little did she understand the political situation and England's attitude to Hitler that when my mother suggested she should return home, she said, 'But England will fight *with* Germany this time' – against the Bolsheviks. My mother went on to write of the way the news, the adult talk, the digging of trenches and so on, was making David extremely anxious.

'On the night of Hitler's Nuremberg speech', my mother wrote, 'he kept waking up and calling out "Has Hitler finished his speech yet? Is there going to be a war?" The trouble is that he reads everything he can find and takes far too much interest in what is going on.' He was seven years old and had been passionate about newspapers for years. At four, David had regularly cut out the cartoon strips: Teddy Tail in the *Daily Mail* and the Arkubs in the *News Chronicle*. When our parents were going to Geneva in 1935 the first thing he had asked was 'What will I do for newspapers?' (Told to pray for his parents' safe return from Geneva, David had asked, 'What will God do to you if I don't ask him?')

In the summer of 1937, when the future had not yet grown so dark, my mother had visited New Zealand friends in Woodside Park, a London suburb further north, on the edge of open country. Some of the green fields she saw were about to be swallowed up by the development of the New Woodside Park Estate. A few houses were already being built, more were on the drawing board. Hilda went into the Estate Office to look at the plans and realised there was a chance for them to have a say in the building of their own ideal home. She dreamed of a house considerably larger than 43 Highfield Avenue, with a spacious entrance hall and a large study as well as four bedrooms and the wash-house she thought essential. There would be a garage too, though there was as yet no car. The plot she considered was a quarter of an acre, running down to common land on the banks of the Dollis Brook, but with easy access to excellent shopping in Finchley High Road between the Swan and Pyramids and Tally Ho!, names that I happily added to Temple Fortune in my private word-store. Four days after my mother had first seen the site, we all went out together. 'A. liked it as much as I do', Hilda wrote in her diary. 'The children had a lovely picnic – made a hay-stack.'

Woodside Park was two stops from the High Barnet terminus of the Northern Line and easily reached from the offices of the University of New Zealand in Gower Street and of the *New Zealand News* in Fleet Street. But it provided us children with the chance of some approach to country life, with the brook just beyond our back fence and, only a short walk away, the village of Totteridge –

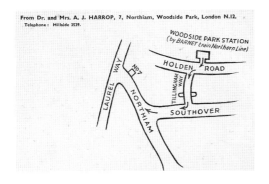

From Dr. and Mrs. A. J. HARROP, 7, Northiam, Woodside Park, London N.12.
Telephone : Hillside 3539.

complete with cricket ground, ponds and picturesque old houses. There was even – up Laurel Way – an extensive farm belonging to the A1 and Dollis Dairies, supplying North London with its daily milk. My parents would send out this postcard to help visitors find their way to the house.

Now my mother had the opportunity to put some of her ideas into practice, with lots of consultation with the estate architect. As early as 1934 Hilda had listed at the back of her diary all sorts of possibilities in a new house, such as 'copper pipes all concealed', 'chromium fittings', 'clothes chute from bathroom', 'windows that can be cleaned both sides from inside', 'telephone alcove', 'hot air central heating', 'ironing board cupboard like a grandfather clock', 'outside hatch for milkman', as well as the more obvious 'built-in bookshelves' and 'hatch between dining room and kitchen'.

We four, the Norwegian Randi Petterson who was with us, and our tortoises, Oswald and Colonel Blimp, moved into 7 Northiam in April 1938. This photo was taken at 43 Highfield Avenue not long before we moved. Had we been told not to smile? Four days after the move there was a service of blessing, including prayers for all who worked there, all who visited and for the children of the house.

Train up a child in the way he should go
and when he is old he will not depart
from it.

Blessed are the pure in heart
For they shall see God.

He shall gather the lambs in his arms
and carry them in his bosom.

O Lord, protect thy little ones on earth,
in sleeping or waking, from every
danger of body and soul.

The name of the road was something of a problem. Potential deliverers of goods – and a great deal was delivered in those days – would pause, wanting to write down 'street' or 'gardens' or *something*, but it was just that: Northiam, after a village in Sussex we never visited. My mother didn't achieve everything in her list of modern conveniences; we had solid fuel central heating, not 'hot air', but that was unusual enough in 1938. There was also a water-softening system, with a weekly ritual of testing and salt-filling, and the wash-house contained the most up-to-date washing machine, though (with no drier available) the electric mangle was a constant threat to the small fingers longing to help feed the sheets through its rubber jaws.

In the kitchen was our huge gas refrigerator, acquired in 1935. I also remember very clearly one thing that was surely an anachronism: a panel with numbers which jumped to indicate in which distant room a bell had been rung. Useful when one was in bed with whooping cough, perhaps, but this was not a household where servants answered bells, however much my mother might at times have wished that to have been the case. Did she and Angus, working on the *New Zealand News* in their study, desks side by side, ring a bell to summon a cup of tea? I don't think so.

David and I had both attended an endearing pre-prep school at 15 The Drive, Golders Green, just round the corner from Highfield Avenue. It was run by the Misses Mabel and Violet Druce, two large, comfortable ladies, and their friend Miss Fallowfield. I had long wanted to sneak in with David and was overjoyed when I was at last allowed to go on two afternoons a week, only to find myself making raffia mats, an occupation not much to my taste. I remember the purple raffia and the cut out circles, cardboard with holes in the middle, through which one had laboriously to thread the stuff. Much more impressive was an orange piece of cloth David was weaving to make into a prize-winning purse for our mother's Christmas present, complete with zip. I was full of admiration for that purse and was always far less good than David with my hands. He was already a fine gardener, with rows of little carrots and excellent spinach, and, amazingly, when we were moving, he was considered old enough to sort out the coal shed.

There must have been some conventional education at our first school, as well as the handcrafts, for when we started at Holmewood School in Woodside Park, not long before my sixth birthday, I was dismayed that it didn't feel like 'real school'. There was a lot of playing around. I wanted to get on with more serious things. My strongest memory of Holmewood (on the Finchley side of the railway line) is of being accused by my teacher of being a 'chatterbox', an accusation my mother had constantly suffered thirty years before. I can see the classroom now and remember just where I was sitting, but I think it was only inside my head that I shouted 'I am NOT a box.' Years later I turned this memory into a picture book story with a despairing teacher introducing into the playground a large wooden box in which she hoped her pupils might learn 'it is better to be silent'. (They did not, of course.) I chattered and flourished.

But David did not flourish at Holmewood. In fact, at this point he was not flourishing at all. There seemed to be some 'deep-seated trouble', my mother was told by the school. He needed to take life more easily and not get so worked up. Bruno Oertel can't have helped. Bruno was the five-year-old grandson of John Rankine Brown, Professor of Classics at Victoria College, Wellington, and on the Senate of the University of New Zealand. My grandfather, Jim Valentine, had also been on the Senate and the two men must have had conversations about their grandchildren on the other side of the world in those dangerous years. At any rate Bruno, son of a New Zealand mother and a German father, came to us from Krefeld to learn English, which strangely his mother had never used with him. He came in the summer of 1938, presumably with the idea of preparing him for life in distant New Zealand.

Bruno was only a few months younger than I was but apparently much less able to do things. My father called him 'Mr Noah', a joke that must have been lost on the poor child himself, because he always said 'No!' when asked to do something – or if he had had enough to eat. I found him babyish. 'Kein pusch mehr' he would say, when I wanted him to go higher on my swing – a splendid wooden structure the house-builders had made for me at the end of the garden. (Pride would have a fall one day when I jumped from the seat at the top of its swing and – though I had done it many times without accident – managed to break my wrist.) My mother wrote that Bruno was 'a dear wee boy who settled down very happily' and I want to believe her. It is sad that my main memory of him was of an unfortunate incident when we were having a bath together and I leapt out, furious with him for having introduced a horrible thing 'like a brown submarine', as Roy Fuller called it in his poem 'Horrible Things'. My mother was too embarrassed to write about it in the pink notebook, but the image has stayed with me all my life.

As usual, in the three months Bruno was with us we regularly visited the Todds in South Square. Here we are sitting with Moyra in the sunshine – Bruno in lederhosen – in the very month when Neville Chamberlain flew back from Munich with his foolish promise of 'peace in our time'. A few days later the Germans marched into Czechoslovakia.

One of the ideas behind the move to Woodside Park had been to give us more outlets for our energy, more space to let off steam, less chance to get under our worried parents' feet. There was an empty section next door and a stream to play in, as well as the delights of a larger garden. When our neighbours from Highfield Avenue, the Reynolds boys, came over to visit us we could play in the stream, as shown opposite, and even (with parental supervision I suppose) boil a kettle on a camp fire.

The boys' father, known as Uncle Lofty, had been to Canada on business and brought us all back coloured overalls, which we delighted to wear. I was very much 'one of the boys' and when I was in a skirt rarely to be seen without a grazed knee. One is clearly visible in the original of the wigwam photo. That horrid distinction between girls being made of 'sugar and spice and all things nice' and boys of 'slugs and snails and puppy dog tails' was completely irrelevant. David and I were equals in both sweetness and wildness, though I never went so far as to bang a visiting curate on the leg with a plank, as David did. It was also important in our story that at *school* I was a model pupil (with neat writing and top marks) and he was not.

We were mostly loyal to each other and united against the adult world, but it began to seem obvious to those very adults, analysing and worrying about us (as David continued to have his weekly sessions with Kath Todd in South Square), that we were spending more time together than was good for us. David had never settled at Holmewood School, where too much attention was paid to his deficiencies. His left-handed writing and poor spelling would suggest dyslexia (a word not yet coined), if it were not for the excellence of his reading, the best in his class. He was tested at the Tavistock Clinic, his IQ an impressive 146, and described by a new psychiatrist, Dr Lucas, as 'brilliant', 'with a most original mind'. His parents were warned to handle him carefully and not to 'crush' him with too much 'orthodox learning'.

The curate's leg was probably the final straw that made Hilda and Angus accept the Todds' suggestion that David should live with them for a while and see Dr Lucas regularly. He was with them for most of five months, leaving us on 8 November 1938, the very day that Bruno also left. Hella Müller, the ignorant Nazi, went back to Germany and my mother wrote in the pink notebook: 'The house is so peaceful with only A. and Ann Barbara, who is very good and very little trouble' – the first time in my six years that she had ever written any such thing.

David went back to school with the dear old Misses Druce, who understood him so well; he had lunch there every day and tea three times a week as well. The South Square household (well run by servants, including Brett the butler) was apparently little disturbed by the addition of a seven-year-old boy, who flourished in the calm atmosphere. I remember the calm of South Square. Even Jock, the Scottish terrier, seemed to bark less than other dogs. David kept closely in touch with us, phoning every two or three days, and we often exchanged visits. In February he was home for a week or two over his birthday while Moyra and Kath skied at Zermatt. My mother wrote in the pink notebook that Moyra was 'firm', that she called David 'a splendid lad', and that he was 'as happy as the day is long'. All the same it was an unnatural situation, and towards the end he was counting the days until he finally came home. When I was ill in March 1939 (influenza and earache again) David and Moyra sent me this card:

There was an inevitable reaction from both of us when David came back. Hilda had to devise a 'Pleasant Home Competition' to see who could get least angry. (Was *she* angry or only us?) I seem to have been the more angry – perhaps envying David his long 'holiday' in South Square and finding it difficult to resume sharing our parents' attention. But it was now the summer of 1939 and there was more to worry about than childish bad behaviour.

We were on holiday at Portreath on the north coast of Cornwall that August. It was good to get away from London; everyone was getting away from London. In fact, on 1 September there was a long-planned mass evacuation of schoolchildren. Nearly one and a half million children left the cities for the comparative safety of the countryside. It was thought air-raids would begin immediately after war was declared – and few thought that, after Austria and Czechoslovakia and the advance into Poland, Hitler would take any notice of the ultimatum.

In my mind there has always been a clear division between those last carefree days before the war and the dark anxious days that followed. Before the war we played on sunlit sand and picnicked on Cornish pasties, which came still warm on the bus from Redruth. We explored caves, sailed our boats in rock pools, poked our fingers in the sea anemones and jumped over the waves that rushed up the beach. Then we heard, over the air, the tired old voice of the Prime Minister, Neville Chamberlain: 'This country is now at war with Germany.' It was that day, 3 September, 1939, that Winston Churchill said:

> Outside the storms of war may blow and the lands may be lashed with the fury of its gales, but in our own hearts this Sunday morning there is peace …. Our consciences are at rest …. This is not a question of fighting for Danzig or fighting for Poland. We are fighting to save the whole world from the pestilence of Nazi tyranny.

In Cornwall we were put to the task of filling sand-bags and waited, wondering what would happen. (I am the girl on the left with a ribbon in my hair in the photo below.) One day we took a bus across to the south coast, passing the time, and somehow stumbled into a 'restricted coastal zone'. A nervous young soldier barked at us 'Halt! Who goes there?' I can see the path now, high above the sea, and his raised rifle, and hear that accusing voice.

In reality, talk of war, the fear of war and preparations for war, had been going on for years. My father, then working two nights a week on the News Desk at the *Daily Telegraph* (having, it seems, some time to spare with his two recent books out of the way), was in a good position to know rather more than most what was going on. He had been in Danzig in 1937 and was taking a particular interest in the fate of the Poles. We had ourselves been sheltered from much of the fear, but we were already equipped with gas-masks (no one who had one could ever forget the rubbery claustrophobia of the testing) and identity discs (my registration number CGBL53/4 etched on my mind forever). We became used to new concepts, such as A.R.P. (Air Raid Precautions) and First Aid. Angus was an A.R.P. warden, just too old and much too short-sighted to be called up. Hilda, having forgotten the skills she had used as a young volunteer in Hokitika in the 1918 'flu epidemic, took a lengthy training with the Red Cross and spent many hours in the First Aid Post in Totteridge, waiting for something to happen.

We were all waiting for something to happen. David started in October 1939 at his new 'progressive' prep. school, Burgess Hill, which had somehow mysteriously become a boarding school in the safer countryside, a delightful place where he called his teachers by their given names, had his own garden and learnt to ride on a pony called Peggy. The idea was that teachers were nurturing and tolerant, the children co-operative rather than competitive. I returned to Holmewood when it eventually re-opened and remember the scary wail of the siren as we practised our air-raid drill, filing down to the shelters.

Barrage balloons hung over London. We stuck sticky strips of paper across our windows so that they did not 'shatter in the blast' (what did *that* mean, I wondered). At night, across those windows, we drew thick blackout curtains so no glimmer of our lights would show to the sky above. Sometimes, when I should have been asleep in my dark room, I drew back the curtains and watched the searchlights scanning the sky. In Fleet Street the blackout was so intense that my father took to waving a white handkerchief to avoid bumping into people. And still the bombers did not come.

But the news on the radio got worse. Denmark was invaded, then Norway in April 1940 (we thought of Randi). In May, Holland and Luxemburg and Belgium were overrun. There were terrible stories of what was happening in the occupied countries. The retreat from Dunkirk began at the end of May. That month – as Churchill took over as Prime Minister – the word 'invasion' was mentioned in the House of Commons for the first time. A question was asked: 'Has the Government not prepared any plans to combat the invasion of this country?' After the fall of France in June the Joint Chiefs of Staff told the Government that 'We must regard the threat of invasion as imminent.' Leaflets were distributed with orders about what to do 'if this island is invaded'. It made scary reading.

My mother spent a couple of days just at this time staying in Hampshire with Eileen Reynolds, who had taken her sons there for safety. It is obvious that Hilda was leaving the final impossibly hard decision to Angus. 'If you want us to go', she wrote, 'you'll make inquiries about ships.' Certainly New Zealand seemed the natural place for us to be. Angus had wanted to give Hilda the chance to see her father again. The war had seemed to make such a holiday impossible; now he decided she should take us out of harm's way and return (if it were safe to do so) as soon as we were settled. 'It's a great chance to see everybody and miss the winter', he wrote encouragingly to Hilda in Hampshire.

On 19 June the British Government accepted the plan to evacuate large numbers of children overseas to America and the Dominions. In two weeks over 200,000 applications were received, and all over the country other children

Issued by the Ministry of Information on behalf of the War Office and the Ministry of Home Security

STAY WHERE YOU ARE

IF this island is invaded by sea or air everyone who is not under orders must stay where he or she is. This is not simply advice : it is an order from the Government, and you must obey it just as soldiers obey their orders. Your order is "Stay Put", but remember that this does not apply until invasion comes.

Why must I stay put?

Because in France, Holland and Belgium, the Germans were helped by the people who took flight before them. Great crowds of refugees blocked all roads. The soldiers who could have defended them could not get at the enemy. The enemy used the refugees as a human shield. These refugees were got out on to the roads by rumour and false orders. Do not be caught out in this way. Do not take any notice of any story telling what the enemy has done or where he is. Do not take orders except from the Military, the Police, the Home Guard (L.D.V.) and the A.R.P. authorities or wardens.

What will happen to me if I don't stay put?

If you do not stay put you will stand a very good chance of being killed. The enemy may machine-gun you from the air in order to increase panic, or you may run into enemy forces which have landed behind you. An official German message was captured in Belgium which ran :

"Watch for civilian refugees on the roads. Harass them as much as possible."

Our soldiers will be hurrying to drive back the invader and will not be able to stop and help you. On the contrary, they will were overhearing the sort of anxious conversations we heard. My mother said that she and Angus sat up all night trying to make the painful decision. It was invasion rather than bombs my parents feared for us. It was not just safety but freedom they wanted us to have.

We were not part of the Government scheme. With his contacts at Shaw Savill (regular advertisers in the *New Zealand News*), my father was able to book us passages on the *Ceramic*, leaving Liverpool on 17 July. On 1 July the Channel Islands were invaded. Among the residents who were to suffer the German occupation was old Canon Wilford, my father's mentor at College House in Christchurch. The next day the *Arandora Star*, packed with children (as well as German and Italian civilians en route to internment in Canada), was torpedoed in the Atlantic with the loss of 682 lives. On 10 July the Luftwaffe attacked a British convoy in the English Channel. Was it not more dangerous to go rather than to stay? The debate went on.

I knew nothing of such things. At seven I didn't even have much idea of time. I was told we were to go to New Zealand for the 'duration'. I didn't know what it meant, but it sounded exciting and positive, not unendurable. I thought I would soon be back. I had no idea how far we were going and how long it would take us to get there.

There were farewell parties; we had lunch at the Strand Palace Grill and Daddy took us to see Shirley Temple in Walt Disney's version of Maeterlinck's *Blue Bird* – which seemed the most beautiful thing I had ever seen – while Hilda went to see *Rebecca* with Moyra Todd. We were pleased to hear we could take our bicycles with us; mine was just six weeks old, a 'fairy cycle', blue and shiny. We could not take the tortoises.

Friends came to see us off at Euston Station, the London terminus, and brought books and barley sugar. My father came to Liverpool with us. There was a great deal of waiting around in the train on the outskirts of the port. Troop movements, we were told. My father got increasingly irritable. At last we were in the Docks area. My mother wrote: 'The first man we saw was Captain Lishman, who said he could get Angus a pass for the ship.' I was not surprised. My father always knew someone. In fact I had the idea that he knew everyone in New Zealand. We left our parents dealing with Customs, Emigration, the Censor, or whatever all the bureaucracy was. David and I went off 'very happily' with someone from the ship. I have no recollection of saying goodbye to my father. Did I weep and storm and tell him to come with us? I don't think so. My mother's account in the pink notebook is totally without emotion, apart from that one phrase 'very happily'. David and I stood on deck with our mother at the railing of the *Ceramic*, high above the quay, and watched Angus walk down the gangway and out of our lives. It would be nearly five years before we saw him again.

CHAPTER 10

Out of harm's way

'Whatever happens it is best for a child's life to go on as normally as possible', my Aunt Nettie, Hilda's sister, had written to their father, Jim Valentine. But there would be very little that was normal about our lives, David's and mine, for the five years to come. They were interesting, yes, even thrilling at times, but not normal, if 'normal' for a child means a regular pattern of school and one's own home, with both parents readily available.

I was too young really to remember the 1934 ships, the *Akaroa* and the *Tamaroa*, however many times we had played at going to sea in North London. So the *Ceramic*, when we boarded on 17 July 1940, was an extraordinary place to me: the neat cabin, the long corridors and scrubbed decks, the saltwater baths, the strange warm smell from the engine room and the fresh breezy scent of the sea. The words were interesting too: windows were portholes and staircases companionways. Strangest of all was the look of the sea itself – when we were out of sight of land. It surrounded us in a circle, stretching as far as our eyes could see and suggesting that the world was certainly round but also flat.

At the beginning of our voyage, when the sea might hide the dreaded U-boats and there could easily be other enemy ships just beyond the horizon, we carried

our life-belts wherever we went or at least had them close at hand. But as we ploughed south the rules were relaxed. We knew our Boat Drill, what the siren sound would mean and where our own muster station was. Angus, in London, 'tried not to think too much of the ship and its course.' He began 'to breathe more freely' when a week or two had passed and we seemed to be beyond the most perilous waters.

Soon after we left, Angus had given Alice Evans, the New Zealand Press Association representative in London, a letter 'hoping she will carry on the paper', the *New Zealand News*, 'should anything happen to me.' Life was becoming dangerous. An aged friend in Henley had written admiring Hilda's departure for our sakes: 'My courage would never rise high enough to take me outside the Old Land while Tumult and Destruction rage.' The long-awaited Blitz on London began with the first terrible raids on 7 September. My father's letters, which we eventually read in Australia, were full of his experiences, recounted in a deliberately unsensational tone. In the *Daily Telegraph* night newsroom he was in the thick of things, 'answering three telephones at once', sending out reporters and sometimes himself attending the regular press conferences at the Ministry of Information. 'It is hectic work,' he told Hilda, 'but one cannot do much else than work these days and at least one has all the news, censored and uncensored.' He knew what was going on, though he could not always write about it. The journalists worked in the shelter when an air-raid warning sounded. The huge noise of anti-aircraft fire could not reach them in what was actually a basement library store-room, fortified not with sand-bags but with the thick-bound volumes of the *Telegraph* and the *Times*. Angus could even joke in a cable (not an easy feat):

> NEWS DESK TELEGRAPH
> WELL PROTECTED
> BLAST EXCEPT VERBAL

On 26 September 1940 Angus wrote to Hilda at 3 a.m. in a quiet moment at the *Telegraph*. The destruction of the New Zealand University office in Bloomsbury would eventually mean the end of the overseas examination system:

> Things have been pretty hot in London this week …. I was rung up the other morning to be told that 88 Gower Street was a casualty. The office is in a terrible mess, but there had been no fire. It was at 5.30 in the morning so no one was there. I took away the files and all the most important things. [RECORDS SALVAGED he cabled New Zealand.] We had a few incendiaries on the *Telegraph* roof last night, but they were quickly put out. There were some big fires round us, but I still have to experience any real apprehension

of danger. I was on the roof the other night (complete with tin hat), but I shall not take any unnecessary risks …. One can get used to anything and it is something to be helping in getting a paper out to spite Hitler. But it is very clear that we did the best thing in getting the children away with you.

Not long after we left, Hitler had seemed to postpone his invasion plans, concentrating on his attempts to destroy the R.A.F. (which already had many New Zealanders flying with it), to blockade the ports and reduce London to rubble. Between September 1940 and the following spring 40,000 civilians were killed in the Blitz in cities all over England and many thousands more were injured and made homeless. It was not until June 1941, when Hitler turned his attention to the eastern front, that the prospect of imminent invasion finally receded.

That casual mention in Angus's letter of being 'on the *Telegraph* roof' is amplified in this extract from a talk he gave on Australian radio about his Fleet Street experiences. He spoke of Hitler's sustained attempt to break London's spirit in that period before Russia and America entered the fight.

> For some weeks one of my nightly jobs was to climb on the roof as the warning sirens went and, under the sketchy protection of a tin hat, watch the search-lights picking up the German raiders as they came in to the attack on the city. When the 'immediate danger' warning sounded I retreated to the basement newsroom and wrote a guarded paragraph about the strength and direction of the raid. As the attacks grew heavier and more regular – at one period there were raids on fifty-seven consecutive nights – the paper contented itself with the official description of the raids.

Forays on the roof were then restricted to a fire-watching rota. My father wrote how lucky he was to be working at nights and therefore able to get some sleep during the quieter days. He was regularly driven home by a colleague as dawn broke and the 'All Clear' sounded, varying the route as streets were blocked by debris and by salvage teams at work on the stricken buildings.

Later, when Alice Evans gave up and retired to Wales for the duration, my father rented her flat in Clifford's Inn, just off Fleet Street, and went out to Woodside Park only for his one free day a week. He wrote lightly to us of the situation there. The destruction of a large Victorian house in Holden Road, on the far side of the Dollis Brook, had rather spoiled his view and Kerry, our neighbours' dog, 'got a bit of a shock the other day when he was standing on their garden wall, thinking of nothing very much, and the blast from a time-bomb explosion blew him off it'. A bomb had fallen ten yards beyond our fence. The fence was down, but the house stood, apparently unaffected.

By this time, Angus was no longer alone in 7 Northiam. Mrs Moore, an Irish woman who had cleaned the house for us, had been delighted to accept the offer to move in as housekeeper with her family – her husband and two children, Ivy aged four and the baby, John. Angus, always particularly fond of children, good and bad, became devoted to these two substitutes.

I didn't see that photo of the interlopers with my father until after the war, but I certainly remember stabs of jealousy when Angus, thinking to entertain me, wrote of what Ivy was up to or how he could usually stop John crying with a familiar game of 'Peep-Bo'. Why were *they* allowed to stay in England while we weren't? Why were they in *our* home? Did my Daddy tell them Willa Webfoot stories at bedtime? I didn't really want to know.

My father had written that he was living 'from day to day like everyone else', and I spent my time living in the present too, as children usually do. It was useless to regret the vanished past and impossible to imagine what the future might bring. As a friend of mine once put it:

Children exist in a continuous present and make no presumptions about the future. They know already that the world is a startling and unreliable place, where anything is apparently possible and in which you are required to conform to mysterious codes imposed by the adult world. Every child picks its way through a complex minefield of requirements, learning self-preservation as it goes.

There is a good deal of evidence that at seven I was, if sometimes labelled 'spoilt' and 'difficult' and 'different', already remarkably tough and well-equipped to negotiate the minefields. But there were dreams, nightmares indeed, in the narrow bunk bed on the *Ceramic*. I remember dreaming, not of my father, but of our two tortoises, Oswald and Colonel Blimp, who have made only a marginal appearance in this story but who had been a significant part of my pre-war life. I dreamt more than once of the two small creatures floating away on their tortoise shells, on their lovely shiny backs, upside down and helpless in the Dollis Brook, the stream that ran across the common land at the bottom of our garden. It is vivid in my mind to this day, that dream on the *Ceramic*.

Vivid, too, is the memory of bending the stiff menu cards, discarded in the dining saloon after every meal and collected by me to make into books for my stories, using the blank white backs of the cards for my writing. None of these stories survive, but this is hardly to be regretted, as I am sure they were as dull and straightforward as my letters at the time. It was always reality that concerned me, not fantasy, and I had not yet found any way to make reality interesting beyond the interest of the facts themselves.

I could watch the sea endlessly, wondering at the long wake of curdling foam astern and the luminous furrows at the prow. When it was dark, we looked at the sky. We went up on the deck with Mr Pharazyn, who had volunteered to teach the crowd of children astronomy. Young Mr Pharazyn on astronomy – this was amazing for a child who had previously been taught no subject more extraordinary than reading, writing and arithmetic, and those by women who seemed to me elderly, though perhaps they were not. Our textbook on the deck of the *Ceramic* was the sky at night. The whole sky was cupped above us, glittering with stars. We were told we were looking into time as well as space, that the light from distant galaxies had taken millions of years to reach us. How astonishing were these glimpses of the wonderful as the sky changed as the ship moved into the Southern Hemisphere.

One night we could not study the stars. Clouds had blotted out every one. It was the darkest night I had ever seen and the *Ceramic* moved across the sea as if it were not there. At 2 a.m. on Sunday 11 August 1940, when we were in the South Atlantic 600 miles off the Cape of Good Hope, there was a huge crash and long shudder, followed by six frightening hoots of the ship's siren, the alarm signal. In the blackout, our liner, crammed with mothers and children on their way to safety in Australia and New Zealand, had been struck by a freighter, the *Testbank*, slightly off its course. At the time we thought there had been a torpedo. It was because of the possibility of enemy attack that we had practised our Boat Drill. A collision was unimaginable, with so few ships and so much sea.

It was only much later that I realised it was a miracle that the *Ceramic* had stayed afloat. Apparently, if the collision had been a fraction later, with the point of impact ten feet nearer the middle of the ship, many of the crew would have been crushed as they slept and there would have been little chance to close the water-tight doors, which saved the ship from sinking immediately. Hilda wrote to Angus: 'Seven seconds later and we should have been in eternity.' Two days afterwards I wrote to my father a long excited description, which included the fact that there was – we had seen it ourselves – a huge hole.

Nine-year-old David had behaved in an exemplary fashion, calm and efficient under stress – out of his bunk in a flash, making sure we had warm clothes, our lifebelts, our 'skedaddle' bags. What I didn't tell my father was that I myself, at the last moment, faced with climbing over the side of the ship into a frail lifeboat, suspended from ropes on davits, far above the choppy sea, had panicked and refused to get in. I was seven years old and the Captain himself picked me up like a baby from where I lay on the deck and put me safely into the lifeboat, where I tried to pretend that no such scene had occurred, but wept quietly because, in the confusion of my undignified departure, my Peter Rabbit, in his velveteen trousers, had somehow got left behind on the deck.

We were heading for a Royal Navy cruiser, H.M.S. *Cumberland*, which had answered our S.O.S., when a P&O liner came into sight and, as we came to the top of a wave, we saw flashing semaphore signals, which apparently told us to wait for the liner. After two hours or so on the choppy sea, feeling more and more seasick, we were able to climb up a gangway into the palatial calm of the *Viceroy of India* and an eventual reunion with my lost rabbit, which did a lot to make me feel there was some justice in this chaotic world.

We had seven weeks in Cape Town, waiting for a ship to be available for us to continue our journey. The *Ceramic*, badly damaged as she was, did manage to limp into port so that our baggage, including our bicycles, survived and eventually reached New Zealand. The *Ceramic* itself – one of the last of the great four-masters – was repaired, only to be sunk in December 1942, torpedoed in the North Atlantic with the loss of 656 lives.

Shaw Savill, the shipping company, put us up, with some of our fellow passengers, in the Marine Hotel, Sea Point, within sight of the beach, a much

Dear Daddy.   Aug 13ᵗʰ, 1940

at 2 o'clock on Sunday morning
Mummy and David were awakened
by a terrible crash and clang,
Mummy woke me and soon after
that the steward came in to say
get every thing ready and
then come upstairs, for another
ship had banged in to us,
we were up all night
waiting. In the morning we
went to see the damage.
there was a broken life-boat,
and broken railing, four port
holes smashed, and a huge hole
in the front of the ship which
some one said you could drive
a london bus in, soon we
received orders that we would
have to leave, the ship as soon
as possable. other ships were
comeing in sight. In the
morning we had packed as
much as we were aloud to
take. we had orders to get
in the boats in a few minutes
we were sailing the sea in
about an hour we were on
the ship that came to rescue us.
We think we will be reach-
ing land soon.

more salubrious place then than it is now. I learnt to swim in the large rock pools, full of treasures I would recognise sixty years later when I was working on the Victorian naturalist, Philip Henry Gosse. It was the South African winter, moving into spring as week after week went by. It was as warm as our summer in Cornwall the year before.

Angus heard the news of the collision in the *Telegraph* newsroom and cabled. Hilda replied: 'SAFE WELL HAPPY COMFORTABLE DELAYED LOVE'. Angus added commas and sent it on by post to his sister, May, now living with her family in Melbourne and expecting to welcome us in August. 'What an adventure for the children', Angus wrote to her, 'It was something rather worse than this that we envisaged when we could not face them going alone.' Evidently they had considered and rejected the government scheme, with official escorts dealing with crowds of parentless and often unruly children. 'As it is', my father continued, 'they will now be able to add Cape Town to their repertoire. In future they will have to make up stories for me instead of my doing it for them.' Our adventures had suddenly become more dramatic than any Willa Webfoot had faced, intrepid traveller though that duck was.

We would indeed have stories to tell all our lives. My own children would have their own dramas, including evacuation from a burning Benghazi in the middle of the night during the Six Day War in 1967. But I would always be able to silence their protests about being left for a few hours with some sort of child-minder by reminding them that I had to put up with not seeing either of my parents for *years*.

One memory of Cape Town I have often recalled is of walking down a tiled passage in the hotel – perhaps on our very first day – and greeting with a cheerful 'Good morning' the black woman who was on her knees scrubbing the floor. What I remember is her blank black face as she looked up at me, puzzled and silent, as if she had never ever before been greeted by a hotel guest.

Life in South Africa was pleasant enough for the *Ceramic*'s children, with the beach and good walks along the coast and drives into the flowery foothills in the hotel manager's van. We eventually, to our mothers' relief, spent some weeks at school, and I remember my delight in discovering that the word 'spoek' was Afrikaans for 'ghost'. But the uncertainty and the lack of communication (except by expensive cables) with their husbands was having an extremely bad effect on the women.

By the time of my eighth birthday on 4 October 1940 we were on our way again, pausing to load coal in Durban. We celebrated with rides in rickshaws pulled by Zulus in full ceremonial rig. I have forgotten other birthdays in a long life, but not that one.

The *Themistocles*, a filthy and superannuated passenger ship, arrived to rescue us only when the *Dominion Monarch*, about to set out for us, had been commandeered as a troopship. Conditions on the old *Themistocles* were not good and tempers easily became frayed. Hilda wrote to Angus, 'Now we are slowly steaming farther away from you – still with no letters. It seems an eternity.' He would write to her: 'I shouldn't worry too much if the children are difficult. In these times it would be a wonder if they were not.'

Difficult we certainly were on the slow voyage across the Indian Ocean to Australia. Boat Drill made us nervous, reminding us of the night of the collision. My mother wrote to Moyra Todd:

> This interminable voyage drags on its weary way. Everyone is ready to fly at everyone else – cumulative effect of jaundiced livers, too little exercise, too many children about, close stagnant air in the cabins, continual dim lighting within the ship, small progress against the terrific gales, chilliness, hard beds, little sleep. In spite of it all we know we are a lot better off than you in England.

I don't think my mother really believed that last sentence. Certainly the fear of death was always present – at least for the adults who followed the news. Already she was thinking they had made the wrong decision. U-boats were everywhere and we were still in South Africa when it was reported (though I knew nothing about it myself until much later) that the *City of Benares* had been struck by a torpedo in the Atlantic. The ship carried a hundred children travelling under the official Government evacuation scheme. When their lifeboats were lowered as the ship started to sink, blocks jammed, ropes twisted or broke, and children were tipped screaming into the wild, dark sea. It was exactly what I had myself most feared. Seventy-seven children drowned that night, including one whole family of five; the scheme was abandoned.

My mother went on with that letter to Moyra:

> How I long to get settled again. I miss you most frightfully, especially today. David was playing a game of Battleships in the lounge and Ann B. came up and annoyed him – he hasn't been very well for the last three days – and he hit her. Mrs Kelly, sitting near, hit him and, you can imagine, the fat was in the fire. He tried to hit back – fortunately I had heard Ann B. cry and dashed in – or I hate to think what might have happened. I got him outside and eventually calmed him down. He agreed he had been naughty, but said Mrs K. had no right to hit him …. *She* said she was sorry to upset me, but if he smacked a girl in front of her she would *always* smack him …. Several people around said they were glad she had done it as they had been dying to smack him for weeks. She thought my methods all wrong – doctors [i.e. psychiatrists] knew nothing about children. David needs a good thrashing every time he is rude etc etc …. Now I feel I daren't let D. out of my sight for long – and yet he *is* better. I wish I could go back nine years and retain the knowledge I have now, I'm sure we should all be much happier.

Hilda's friend, Mrs Campbell, had difficult children too (her Deirdre was our greatest ally), but said she'd

> much rather have good, well-behaved children even tho' dull, rather than high-spirited, difficult ones. I haven't quite got to that stage yet. But I long for Kath's breezy commonsense and your unshaken affection, albeit with your wholesome astringent shaking up of me. I find I'm still very intolerant. I find it hard to be agreeable to some of the women on this ship who have sailors in their cabins at night. I suppose there are always scandals on a ship, but this seems worse than usual. The only other passengers are about thirty sailors and soldiers – Australian soldiers returning invalided, and sailors who have been doing a gunnery course in England. I feel continually 'prickly'.

We got to Australia finally, to visit, as planned, my father's sister May in Melbourne and my mother's brother Max in Sydney. There was a pile of letters from Angus waiting for Hilda in Melbourne.

At this point Angus was able to use an airmail 'Clipper' service (in the previous century, clippers like the *Cutty Sark* were very fast sailing ships, though now the term referred to an airplane), routed surprisingly through Lisbon, Durban and India to Australia. Too many ships with mail on board were going to the bottom of the sea, but most of the planes got through. It was expensive, but Angus wrote, 'This is the sort of extravagance I feel entitled to when I am doing three jobs at once', with no chance to get to the theatre. He told Hilda that he thought 'Perhaps the most impressive thing of the whole show is the way human nature has adapted itself to the maddest, most unnatural form of existence we could have conceived a few years back.' He was himself amazingly adaptable and indeed could say at one point that he was 'enjoying being in the best story since newspapers began'. He would report on seeing the City of London in flames – the cathedral ringed with fires, 'its dome and cross standing out in a lurid light, apparently doomed to destruction.' Next morning, Angus 'walked up and saw how narrowly St Paul's had escaped and St Bride's still burning'.

Using the tube in the evening was a strange experience, with the platforms crowded with people taking shelter and trying to sleep. Angus was on the committee of the New Zealand Forces' Club in Charing Cross Road and his greatest pleasure was in supplying the Club with flowers from his garden. He would carry great armfuls of them in from Woodside Park on the tube after his day off, burdened as if he were a florist, and delight to hear the comments and see the smiles the flowers brought to people's tired faces. He told Hilda how good it was to see their own sweet-peas (they were his favourite flower) in the newsreel of Mrs Churchill officially opening the Club. There were vegetables too. DIG FOR VICTORY, the posters encouraged, and Angus could boast, in the second winter of the war, that they had not had to buy a single vegetable and had given quantities away. He wrote to Hilda of one effect of the war: communities which were once collections of isolated houses were now all united, 'many people who used to be merely selfish are now thoughtful of others', discovering that 'kindness is the quality that makes life worth living'.

The *New Zealand News*, edited in intervals from his work at the *Telegraph* ('in his sleep' he once said to Hilda, wishing she were there to help him), had become more or less an official New Zealand Government publication. Two thousand copies of each issue were dispatched free every fortnight all over the place, wherever New Zealanders were serving. The extra cost was covered by the National Patriotic Fund. Angus was in close contact with the New Zealand military authorities and able to comply with 'a sudden request to bring out the next issue of the paper a week early owing to certain movements.'

Together with news from the other side of the world, the news of home the men wanted most, the paper carried many stories of heroic New Zealanders. When Angus organised what was mainly a Waitaki reunion lunch at the Savoy, a guest of honour was young James Allan Ward, who had won the V.C. with Bomber Command, putting out a fire on the wing of his plane. They went to a film together after the meal and Angus was saddened by his death (at twenty-two) over Hamburg a few months later. He was saddened too by a survivor, Pilot Officer Ellingham, who had actually sat his law exams in Woodside Park the year before and was now hideously injured. 'Most of his plane was scraped off the trees.' Angus visited him regularly at a hospital in St Albans and wished the boy had been at East Grinstead, where a brilliant New Zealander, Archie McIndoe, was performing miracles of plastic surgery.

In the *New Zealand News* office Angus fortunately now had the help of a young woman, Clare McKenzie, whom he had met when they were both volunteers at the New Zealand Forces' Club. Hilda might also have been a little jealous of the fact that she was taking over much of what had been Hilda's own work. When they at last met in April 1942, Hilda would describe the usurper in her diary as 'flippant and bright and keen on her job'. Hilda might have been a little jealous too of a mysterious colleague, 'Miss Howells', who made a frequent appearance in Angus's letters and needed 'cheering up' because her fiancé was in the Far East. But Hilda and Angus obviously trusted each other completely and they had no reason not to. Hilda worried that Angus's letters were so 'impersonal'. He said he was always conscious of the censor reading his typed letters. But he brought himself to say in his own (almost illegible) hand how

> I often lie awake for hours, when if you were here I should be soothed and asleep in a very short time. When you do come back I feel we shall be even happier than we were before because we will know what it means to be without each other – and since the Blitz it takes a lot to worry me …. It is only to one who has shared so much that I can really talk …. There are many dangers still ahead, but I feel we will survive them and see the beginnings of the new world that must emerge from the war. Whatever happens you know that you have all my love.

Of course the long separation was grim, but they both kept remembering that 'millions are worse off'. Moyra Todd, also aware of that fact, yet wrote of feeling 'real intense physical fear' when lurking in the shelter, hearing the ghastly noise: the bombs dropping, the zooming of the planes overhead. The Todd sisters left South Square after four bombs fell close by and 'our cellar walls actually swayed'.

Moyra assured Hilda that Mrs Moore, the housekeeper at 7 Northiam, was 'a very fine person (as you know) and most anxious to look after Angus well.

He has worried more about your and the children's safety than about bombs.' In fact, two ships were sunk off the Australian coast just at this time, prompting Angus to cable Hilda that she should travel overland from Melbourne to Sydney. But we did not. In Australia the war seemed very far away. Hilda described a sumptuous Melbourne tea provided at a bridge party (admittedly with a collection for the Red Cross). It included 'tipsy' cakes, cream cakes, strawberry sponges and six different kinds of sandwich. She was very homesick, staying with her sister-in-law's family and talking a lot about Angus. Fortunately May was 'much nicer' and a 'much easier person to live with' than she had been in 1934. The traumatic motherless childhood she had shared with my father and their poor damaged brother was, I think, not mentioned and May was giving a good impression of having won through her own angers and depressions with the help of some sort of therapy or counselling. But I have her daughters' sad evidence that the apparent victory was only temporary.

At this point, Cynthia was ten and Gillian five, the latter then 'a dear little chubby girl', whom I next enjoyed meeting sixty-four years later on my first return visit to a totally unrecognisable Melbourne. In 1940 I went to school with my cousins – protesting at first ('Why didn't David have to go?' Well, it was a *girls'* school). I enjoyed it when I got there; I was always really a natural schoolgirl, loving as I did pens and ink, desks and books.

Cynthia was inclined to be jealous of the fact that her mother found her nephew delightful; David responded by being exactly that. (Perhaps May had always wanted a son; perhaps not. The therapy she had had was when she was pregnant with Gillian. It is easy to imagine that Frederick had been in her mind.) David was 'ingenious', wearing his overalls and getting as dirty as he liked. He made 'a house under a table round by the garage and "wired it" and carpeted it and made it most elaborate.' A home from home, in fact. He was always making things, impressing all his practical relatives, whereas I seemed to be mainly playing with dolls and writing long letters to my father, trying out different endings, such as 'With love from your darling daughter'.

When we were on the *Largs Bay*, I told him that, leaving Melbourne and 'about to move out to sea, David and I threw streamers over the side and Uncle Geoff caught them, which was very clever, don't you think so?' I can remember that, and the sad moment when the coloured streamers snapped and we waved goodbye to the little group on the wharf, including an aunt I would never see again. Not that May had had much time for me. My mother's letters reveal that she thought me 'rude', a dreadful word much used in my childhood. I was not, I feel, 'offensively or deliberately discourteous' or indeed 'coarse and inelegant' or even 'rough' – to give some of the dictionary definitions. But I was always eager to interrupt adult conversations, to join in. I was always demanding, it seems, more than my fair share of attention. 'Don't interrupt' was a very familiar injunction and yet I still do it, sixty-five years later. Indeed we all do it in our family, eager to get words in edgeways in the hubbub of conversation.

Writing about my 'rudeness' to Angus, Hilda admitted that on the *Largs Bay* she hardly saw me. I had found some friends and could play happily for hours. I was becoming, it seems to me now, remarkably self-confident for an eight-year-old. We were allocated two cabins, rather far apart. Hilda would, of course, have liked to have one to herself and for us children to have the other. But David insisted on sharing one with her – and I apparently didn't mind being far away in the other. I was 'tough' – the word would begin to be used of me, and it was better than 'rude'.

'I love Sydney', Hilda wrote to Angus. But who could not? I loved it too when I stayed there again not long ago with David's son Christopher, who, like his great-uncle Max, has married an Australian. In 1940 Max was the younger brother Hilda had not seen since 1926. Max Valentine had left New Plymouth in 1929, intending to see Australia on a working holiday and go on to England. But he got caught up in the slump; with so many people in financial trouble, accountants were apparently in great demand. He settled down, became 'nicer than ever' and married Marie Plowman, who was not only 'the most generous, sweet-tempered, thoughtful soul' (with one 'interesting' small daughter, our cousin Judy), but had the added advantage for us of a brother with the best yacht in Sydney Harbour and a 'marvellous Packard' with a chauffeur.

Hilda allowed herself not to worry about the fact that Australia seemed to be unable to take the war seriously. We had a wonderful twelve days, swimming off a selection of glorious beaches, sailing on the harbour (with the *Queen Mary*, at anchor, towering high above us), visiting the koalas in Taronga Park. Dale

Trendall, a New Zealander my parents had entertained a good deal in England, had recently been appointed to the Chair of Greek at the university and he gave a lunch for Hilda there, reminding her of all the things she loved – and making me think that perhaps she wished Angus had opted for an entirely academic life.

When it was time to leave, the sailing of our new ship, the *Aorangi*, kept being postponed. We were not told the reason for the delay. It turned out we had to wait to be escorted by H.M.S. *Achilles* across the Tasman. German raiders were in the area and the passenger liner *Rangitane* had just been sunk, after having landed a large group of government evacuees in New Zealand. In that disaster six people, returning to England, were killed and many more survived to be taken prisoner and then marooned on an island called Emirau off Papua New Guinea. On the *Aorangi* David and I spent most of our time in the gym – or in the lifts. We never seemed to tire of pressing buttons and zooming up and down between the decks, tolerated by the 'bell hops' whose job we had taken over. It must have been a huge relief to Hilda, if not to us, when we finally disembarked in Auckland on 3 December, four and a half months after leaving England.

Hilda had thought a great deal about getting to New Zealand, to the desired end of that long journey. But it had never really been decided what we were going to do when we got there. She had happily imagined a little more travelling (visiting all the friends and relations she had not seen for so long) and then six months or so in New Plymouth, housekeeping for her father, until we were sufficiently settled and she could return to Angus in London. Certainly our grandfather had expected us. He had written: 'I work in the garden preparing the family's food supplies for the summer and next winter. It's a long time since I had to provide for the needs of more than two.' But Hilda's siblings had vetoed this plan. Jim Valentine at seventy-eight was far too old to have children in the house for any length of time, and his sister, our Great-Aunt Mabel, though she would be happy to have a holiday with her sisters in Waikouaiti, had no intention of being ousted from her comfortable role as her brother Jim's housekeeper.

Jim Valentine and Hilda's older sister, Nettie Watkins, came up to Auckland to greet our arrival in the *Aorangi*. We stayed with the other sister, Lottie Elliot, and her family in Disraeli Street, Mount Eden. Graham, the teasing brother, was still in the South Island, and the doctor brother, Jeff, wrote a letter from a military camp in Te Aroha, welcoming her back to her 'native heath'. His words were a little disconcerting.

I am exceedingly glad that you and your bairns have arrived safely and I hope that your stay among us will be happy and contented. We may have contrary opinions about how things should be done, but we shall no doubt find a happy solution after you have got the hang of things out here.

Hilda wrote to Angus: 'After so much journeying, I'm almost afraid we won't know how to settle down quietly. I foresee a difficult time ahead and the sooner school begins the better for the children.' But it was early December, the summer holidays were just beginning. Whatever schools we were to go to would not open again for many weeks. It was decided that Aunt Nettie would take us down to the Tirau farm in the Waikato almost immediately, while Hilda stayed on with Lottie before joining us for Christmas. Lottie was the most 'well-balanced' of her siblings; Hilda was always at ease with her.

David's future was soon satisfactorily decided. He was to go as a boarder to Southwell in Hamilton, the very prep. school for boys Lord Rutherford had recommended when David was not much more than a baby. Southwell turned out to be ideal for him. It had the encouraging atmosphere he needed. He soon made one friend and reported himself 'on talking terms with all the rest of the school'. When Angus in London read David's detailed description of the school day (dictated to Hilda in the holidays) he thought it 'rather regimented'. But it suited David most of the time; he knew where he was. Hilda thought the headmaster, H.G. Sergel (Rutherford's brother-in-law) was 'a pet', always one of her highest terms of praise and endearment. (David was often 'a pet' himself in the year ahead; I don't think I ever was.) Mr Sergel would write long letters over the years, full of comment on 'our mutual friend'.

Before she left New Zealand Hilda was to see David, confident from his role as the compère in *1066 and All That* (chosen, he thought, largely for his English accent), go on to be the announcer at the Southwell School Sports Day in 1941. Standing on bricks to be tall enough for the microphone, he would say, with no paper to read from, such things as 'Will all boys running in the 220 yards handicap under-12 now get ready.' His school report described him as 'one of the keenest boys in his class', his general behaviour and progress 'excellent'.

David made a good early impression at the farm too. Before the year 1941 was out, Hilda would be able to write of that previously difficult, unpredictable boy: 'He is an engaging child and everyone loves him.' At first David's relationship with Val was not so easy. Val was the only boy cousin, with three sisters: Helen, seventeen, Ruth, ten, and Janet, six. Val was fifteen that December and boarding at New Plymouth Boys' High School, where David's own sons and grandson would go many years later.

On our arrival Val had teased David (reminding Hilda of her brother

Graham's teasing when she was David's age long ago in Timaru). He teased him about his English ways, thinking to toughen him up ready for Southwell. Hilda had to speak strongly to Val about it, which did not endear her to her sister. The gulf between their lives, their ways of doing things, was almost immediately apparent, however much affection remained and however many shared memories. Nettie was extremely kind but (like Hilda herself) she wanted to rule the roost. 'Domineering' was the word my mother used. There was no way the two of them could have lived in the same house, even for a few months.

Moyra, recalling her own previous return to New Zealand, wrote from England with some good advice:

> Don't let New Zealand upset you. I hope you're not getting too much of your relatives, or letting yourself feel worried by possible criticism. For all families criticize. What now about your idea of returning in the English spring? I don't think I would. I'm sure you've had enough of sea travelling for many a long day. Anyway there are too many raiders about at present. Don't pine too much for this end of the world …. A job of work is the only thing that matters these days.

Moyra Todd was now quartermaster of a Red Cross Convalescent Hospital at Elton Park near Peterborough. Hilda longed to do something for the war effort, but 'What am I going to do with Ann Barbara?' she wrote to Angus. She thought I was really too young – at eight – to go to boarding school. 'I shouldn't worry about A.B.', my father replied, 'I think she would settle down anywhere.' Hilda was glad and rather amused at the way my uncle, Lewis Watkins, suggested she should leave me with them on the farm. 'Lewis was charming when he said they would consider it a privilege if I would let them keep Ann B., as they would feel they were doing that much directly to help Britain.' As a farmer, of course, Lewis was also producing as much food as possible, a vital part of any 'war effort'.

So what was Hilda to do now? When the school terms began she would no longer be tied but free as she had always liked to be. But she was feeling guilty about being in the relative comfort and safety of New Zealand. The jobs she wanted to do were on the other side of the world. 'If only the Navy can settle the worst of these dreadful submarines', she wrote to Angus. 'I'm not needed here.' But first, in January 1941, we were to have a holiday in New Plymouth with our grandfather, where Hilda could relax, with Aunt Mabel away. It was almost like having a home of our own. She could run the house in her own way and we could eat all the foods we liked. Interestingly she listed omelettes and pancakes and tomato sandwiches, though I was not yet a vegetarian. We all enjoyed Jim Valentine's company. He had followed our progress across the world with intense concern. She had found three letters from him waiting for her in Melbourne and he had transformed her letter about the collision into a news story for the *Taranaki Herald*, so that all her old New Plymouth friends and pupils were aware of what had happened and were anxious to see us. 'Scores of people have been asking about her', our grandfather wrote to Angus before we got there.

Hilda wrote to Angus from New Plymouth, forgetting the joys of Sydney: 'We're all happier than we have been since we left London – Daddy is such a serene person. His energy is amazing, and he goes his own way calmly and leaves us to go ours. The children have been so much easier to handle – indeed I have really enjoyed them for the first time for months.' This was largely because we were responding to the fact that our grandfather thought us both 'grand youngsters', just as he had in 1934. On the five ships and with our other relatives in Australia and New Zealand, Hilda had always been anxious about what we would get up to next and about other people's opinions. Now she was trying to be 'placid and amused' by us.

Jim Valentine wrote happily to Angus after we left – David to go to Southwell, I myself to return to the farm:

> They had a good time here, especially David, who had the free use of my tools and tins full of nails. He used them too – the place is littered still with his products – battleships, yachts, aeroplanes. He has some inventive genius.

That Christmas – in fact on Christmas Day itself – Ruth Watkins, aged ten, had also written to her Uncle Angus:

> It is lovely to have Auntie and David and Ann here. We have lovely games. Ann has learnt to do lots of things on the horizontal bars that Daddy put here. I am writing with the pencil Janet gave me. Ann gave me a rubber. David always feeds the hens. David and Ann can get up to the calves and very proud of it they are ….

So the London children were getting used to country ways. I can remember how large and strange the calves seemed at first (the cows, of course, really were), and how we eventually plucked up courage to feed them – and felt their rough tongues on our milky fingers.

Numbers of my childish letters survive but they give little idea of my life at the farm when my mother wasn't there. When Hilda arrived from Wellington to take us on holiday in 1941 (in May to Mount Maunganui, in August to

Rotorua), she did not record the fact that Ruth was, as the months went by, not always sure it was 'lovely' having me around. She was a natural leader and we sometimes clashed. She was used to her little biddable sister, Janet, and was not keen when I challenged her ideas. In the pink notebook Hilda, ignoring the problems, wrote: 'They play beautifully together in the whare, on the bars and everywhere. They make up poems and do Sunday School lessons by correspondence.' I remember the *Outlook* Knots and Puzzles; one of the surviving corrected sheets carried the text, with my own neat colouring in:

BE SURE YOUR SIN WILL FIND YOU OUT

There was certainly no disguising my sins – my tendency to 'skite' (to show off), to interrupt, to argue and to question anyone else's decisions. Like my mother, I always thought I knew best. I had never been a good little girl and it was difficult to start being one now, however hard (if sporadically) I tried.

When I started in Standard Two at Tirau Primary School early in 1941, my father wrote: 'Ann Barbara must have put up a world record by going to school in four different countries in not much more than six months. A good lesson in geography.' I liked my year at Tirau and didn't even mind going to the school fancy dress party as a bag of Reckitt's Blue – that indispensable aid in those days for every housewife keen on the whiteness of her washing. Adopting the Pollyanna tone I would often use to cheer my parents, I wrote: 'Ruth went as a water lily and Janet as a cape gooseberry. I went as a bag of blue and I think we all looked nice.' Unfortunately, Jimmy Best, my partner in the Grand March, did not go as anything.

For my birthday that year I longed for – and was given – a large teddy bear, like the ones my cousins had. At nine I was a little old for teddy bears, but I wanted him 'to hug when I am lonely in bed'. I was becoming stereotyped as a tough, stormy child, but I have him still, this bear, and his lack of fur testifies to how much hugging went on in those wartime years. As the news from London worsened, my Aunt Nettie worried that she might have to break bad news to me. My father's death no longer seemed a remote possibility, but she continued to believe it was best to protect children as much as one could from what was going on in the world. Even so, David and I never forgot for one moment why we had left our father and our home 12,000 miles away. There is a tiny note from me 'For Daddy', which asks the question which was often in our minds: 'Please write and tell me what it is like hearing bombs droping. Do they make a big noise? Have there been any bombs nearer than the bottom of the garden?' And my father duly answered with the help of a lot of SSs and ZZs on his typewriter.

Hilda's letters to Angus in 1941 are full of depressed reactions to the news from the other side of the world. Most depressing of all was the evacuation from Crete that May, 'the Gallipoli of its era'. She set herself a task, which must at times have made her unpopular, of waking up New Zealand women to the fact that the country was at war. In 1941 it seemed to her that unless their own men were actually in camp or already overseas, many women lived their lives exactly as before, ignoring the government injunctions to conserve petrol, save paper, wear clothes longer and make do with New Zealand-made products. She got tired of hearing people grumble about government restrictions and, understandably, about such things as an eagerly-awaited imported carpet going to the bottom of the sea – while they had apparently no understanding of the huge issues at stake. In England, Angus was seeing the war as a struggle for the democracies to exist at all – not simply as a war about abstract ideas.

Travelling round New Zealand, catching up with friends and relations all over the country, Hilda gave a great many talks (five in a week at one point), telling of her experiences in England, her Red Cross training, and the mood of the people when she left. She spoke to all sorts of organisations: University women, Red Cross groups, W.V.S. meetings and so on. In Timaru she recognised women who came up after her talk – though she hadn't seen them since she left school in 1917. 'I always feel a bit of a fraud', she wrote to Angus, 'because I left before the bombing began, but the collision makes up for that a bit. I'm trying to make them think – but it's almost hopeless.' Dear Aunt Louisa Godber exemplified a total lack of understanding of the situation in London, encouraging her nephew to 'run hard if you hear an enemy plane'.

Throughout 1941 Angus had been telling Hilda to wait to leave until the seas were less dangerous. But she was reluctant to wait. 'I have been dreadfully homesick', she told Moyra. Angus had written saying the fact that they were apart 'at a time like this, when we could be of so much help to each other, makes me nearly weep …. I simply do not let myself think too often of how much I should like to have you back.' But he remained glad she had taken us, glad we were getting to know New Zealand, which before the war was 'the one thing I wanted them to do and didn't quite see how it could be managed.'

Hilda hated the idea of the journey, 'but I can't stay living in the lap of luxury here when I have a job to do in London and the chicks don't need me. They are as happy and as busy as they can be. They are at an age when they are – and should be – fully absorbed in school and play.' She was convinced of that. 'What am I doing so far away from Angus and the life I love?' Hilda asked Moyra. 'I'm coming back because I'm not needed here.'

But there was then no chance of a passage to England and she *was* needed. With the help of glowing references from Dr Hight and her old Head in New Plymouth, Hilda took a job at the Correspondence School run by the Department of Education in Wellington and a small flat in Hill Street, near the Parliament Buildings. She had masses of friends in Wellington and was out to dinner constantly. Her sister, Nettie, had encouraged her to take a job while she was waiting for a ship. Angus had said there was no need for her to work, but added: 'There is no doubt you are constitutionally incapable of vegetating.' This was true of them both on opposite sides of the world. 'I think I would be better at it than you', Angus wrote, 'But on present indications I am unlikely to get the chance.'

It was during this time that Hilda saw a good deal of the pianist, Dorothy Davies, whom they had entertained when she was studying in Europe. After a period at the Sydney Conservatorium and time involved in the foundation of the New Zealand Broadcasting Service, Dorothy had had two years at the Royal College of Music in London (where she gained the highest marks of her year) and had afterwards worked with the great Artur Schnabel in Italy. Dorothy's

music was the most important thing in her life. In this photo she is at the piano with the other members of her trio: Marie Vanderwart (cello) and Erika Schorss (violin).

But there were many other things Hilda found sympathetic. Dorothy Davies was also passionately interested in language, in literature, in history and art – all the things my parents themselves valued. Moreover, at forty, she had recently married Reuel Lochore, who had been a friend of my father's at Waitaki. Reuel had taken a doctorate at the University of Bonn and, like his new wife, also had a relaxed cosmopolitan culture that my mother found deeply attractive.

Hilda had already decided that I should go to boarding school when she left. 'For parents who make the number of mistakes we have made I feel sure a good boarding school is essential.' Now Dorothy and Reuel Lochore living in Wellington, unlikely to have children themselves, and extremely interested in us, suggested they should be my guardians. It was settled – Angus liked the idea a lot. But it was also made clear that if anything happened to our parents, the Todd sisters had agreed that they would bring us up.

Meanwhile I was still living on the farm and going to Tirau School with my cousins when Hilda was asked to come and help. Her sister Nettie was in a critical condition in the Mater Misericordia Hospital in Auckland. On 7 October, trying to shut her door properly as they drove along, in those days before seat-belts, Nettie had fallen from the car, moving at 45 m.p.h. There were internal injuries, her jaw was broken in four places and one knee cap was smashed. 'Net's accident is tragic. It's a miracle she wasn't killed.' It did indeed seem possible she would die; her recovery was very slow.

When she had first seen her three Watkins nieces on our arrival in New

Zealand, Hilda had been delighted with them. Helen at seventeen was a very capable girl, level-headed and calm, Ruth was 'a darling', and little Janet was 'very sweet and so pretty' with her big brown eyes and fair hair, 'but spoilt, of course'. ('She seems to live principally on bread, butter and Marmite, milk and ice-cream.') They were all 'very intelligent' and 'so musical'. Now Hilda began to see them differently.

Angus had been writing to Hilda: 'We are entitled to some real life. It is only ersatz at present.' There was no question of Hilda leaving New Zealand if Nettie's family needed her. But did they need her? It soon became apparent that Helen and Ruth, anguished, thinking constantly of their poor absent mother, resented their aunt's presence. Helen certainly felt she could have managed to run the house herself. Ruth could not bear the way Hilda did things differently from their mother. Neither of them, understandably, could accept their aunt's concern with their vowels. Fortunately Janet remained 'a dear wee soul and we have lots of fun'. She was too young to realise fully her mother's situation.

The darker side of life at the farm emerges clearly from the long disturbing letters my mother wrote to Angus and Moyra from October to December 1941, a time she describes in her memoirs as the worst period of her life. The general atmosphere, with the awful reports from the Auckland hospital, deteriorated daily. Hilda worked hard, determined to give her sister when – if – she returned nothing to complain of. With Helen's help, she spring-cleaned the house, she said, as it had never been cleaned before. She cooked excellent meals. She was always a very good cook and her brother-in-law, Lewis, admitted that she fed them well, making the most of the farm produce, even using twenty eggs in one day's baking. She washed vast quantities of clothes and lengthened seventeen dresses – 'only one of them A.B.'s'.

Hilda had too much time to think as she did all this tedious work, the never-ending round including ironing and mending. She was sad that neither Helen nor Ruth took any interest in the travels of their aunt or her stories of London. 'If I mention anything they make me feel I'm boasting.' She wrote to Angus:

> I'm only now realising how thoroughly Net and Jeff disapprove of me and my ideas and the life I lead in London(!) – the way I've brought up my children and so on. It comes out gradually in talk with Helen. In my innocence I thought they liked to see me smart – instead they *hate* it. And I find they are incredibly narrow in their views. I really didn't think such people existed today – yet, because of family loyalty, they still think they love me …. The more I see of other people's ways of life the more I like our own. I love you more and more. Don't get used to doing without me.

Hilda went to bed early, to get away from Lewis and write her long letters without interruption. Lewis was 'a dear in many ways, a kind, upright soul'. But they had nothing in common apart from the strange fact that he had married her sister. She expected she annoyed him as much as he annoyed her. He was irritating mainly because he was not Angus. She particularly loathed darning another man's socks.

'The more I see of other husbands the more I realise what a wonderfully thoughtful generous soul Angus is and, most of all, how interesting', she wrote to Moyra, who had no husband, interesting or dull. At the farm there were some good times. Lewis encouraged Hilda to learn to drive – a useful skill in the country. ('I can back out of the garage now', she wrote.) But petrol was in short supply. Then there was the piano. Helen sang beautifully and admitted, when Hilda played Schubert and Handel for her, 'No one in Tirau can play these accompaniments'.

And then there was me. I wrote to my father: 'I like having Mummy here very much indeed and I am trying to be a good girl.' I might have *tried*, but Helen was 'disgusted' that I behaved so badly when my mother was about. Apparently my Aunt Nettie kept me in much better order – though my mother said 'A.B. talks and talks and is awed by no one.' My mother was on the defensive: 'I'd rather have her so lively and such a spitfire than the sulkiness and head-hanging of these children when things don't please them.' She assured my father that, even if I was boisterous and argumentative, I was 'full of vitality and very responsive'. And I could be calm. I would read aloud to my mother while she mended.

Helen thought I was (at nine that October) unappreciative of all that was being done for me. Fortunately – until I read these letters recently – I had no idea that my cousin had so disapproved of my childish self. I held a happy memory of a few years later when she praised my packing skills. I became expert at packing suitcases if not at a great deal else. 'How little understanding they have of the child', my mother lamented.

I told my mother I missed my father more when she was at the farm, which she thought understandable. She read me one of his letters where he wrote about 'pottering' in the garden. I said, 'Oh, "pottering", that's a word Daddy always likes and I haven't heard it for a long time.' Hilda was somewhat comforted by the fact that my Tirau teacher described me as 'quick as lightning'. Maybe I would turn out all right in the end.

Hilda wrote to Moyra: 'I feel I have failed badly with these children .... I feel my character is deteriorating.' She felt an 'utter failure', both as an aunt and as a mother. The dreadful news of Pearl Harbor, that Japan had now entered the war and that New Zealand itself might be threatened, came while Hilda was at the farm. But she was still determined to get back to England somehow. 'I don't see that the children would miss much if my ship goes down. They really have no need of me. My beloved husband is another matter – but even he has got used to being without me. This isn't hysterical – I really feel it's worth taking the risk to get back to England and away from this life of relatives, with whom I have so lost touch that I can't get back.'

Nettie Watkins returned to the farm from hospital on 17 December 1941, ten days after Pearl Harbor and ten weeks after her accident. She was without teeth and very crippled, but glad to be home and to be able to run her own household. Val was back from New Plymouth and David from Southwell. We left soon afterwards for a holiday, first in hotels in Taupo and Napier and for a happy Christmas with friends who taught at a Maori school in Wairoa, the Grieves. Hilda found her own serenity (always a quality she much valued) and self-confidence returning. What she called 'a general air of disapproval' at the farm had not seemed to worry me. Indeed, most of the time, 'A.B. and Jan and Ruth played wonderful games'. Even so, I knew my cousins preferred David – part of that was, of course, his novelty value. He was a boy and, like Val their brother, mostly away at school. There was also the fact that they resented any attention my kind Uncle Lewis gave me, thinking to make up for the fact that I was, at least temporarily, fatherless.

The idea that I was aware that I was not much liked comes, not from any memory, but from my mother's recording in a letter ten-year-old Helen Grieve's casual comment one day: 'Oh, I do like Ann Barbara.' I apparently replied, 'Well, that makes a change for me.' I look rather happy in this photo with the Grieve sisters. David was actually a little jealous; it was so unusual now for *me* to be the popular one. His aggressive past was long forgotten and he

was glowing that Christmas from doing well at school – top of his class in Agriculture, Geography, Essay and Poetry, second in Scripture and Reading. Only Maths and handwriting remained a problem.

Throughout 1941 there had been a great deal of discussion about how Hilda should get back to England. Angus had been keen for her to try to get to San Francisco in an American ship, see the Condliffes there, cross the continent by train and join a convoy in Halifax. After Pearl Harbor this was impossible. It would have to be the old Panama route with long dangerous journeys across both the Pacific and the Atlantic. But she still wanted to take the risk.

> If I am unlucky it will be wretched for you; you must promise me you'd try to build your life afresh without grieving too much. But I think God means that I should be able to put into practice all the hard lessons I've learned since I left.

Angus had seen a good deal of the New Zealand Prime Minister, Peter Fraser, when he had been in London for discussions in June 1941, liked him a lot and was sure that, if Hilda required any help, 'the P.M. would do his best for you'.

This was 1941. By 1942 everything was different, with Pearl Harbor and the fall of Singapore. New Zealand's casualty lists lengthened. Malcolm Mason, then husband of Hilda's potter cousin, Helen (known as Bili), was missing in Libya, and my cousin, young Jim Valentine (Graham's son), had been taken prisoner in Malaya. Hilda had seen them both in Wellington not long before they left New Zealand. The stories of both these prisoners of war would capture my imagination. Malcolm would write about his remarkable escape in Italy in his book *The Way Out*. Jim buried some jewellery he had bought for Shirley his fiancée, which after the war was recovered and restored to her. Here were the seeds of my own children's novel *The Camelthorn Papers*, though poems were buried, not jewellery, and I set the story in Libya not Malaya. Years later, Jim became Chancellor of the University of Otago, one hundred years after his namesake grandfather took his B.A. at the same university. Years after that we called on him in Dunedin, saw my book on his shelf and amazingly, sixty-two years after it was buried, Shirley showed me her gold and opal pendant and chain. Jim has the family face, a strong resemblance to our grandfather and great-uncle Hal (whom I once confused) and to his cousin Val Watkins.

As the time finally came early in 1942 for our mother to leave, David became more and more worried about her departure. With Japan in the war, the Pacific had, of course, become even more dangerous. 'Don't let Mummy go to England' he wrote to his father. Hilda wrote to Angus:

He said he hated me to go. I'm perfect! I said 'Oh, no I'm much too impatient', but he said 'only when we deserve it!' I do dread leaving him. He is always kissing me these days. I told him he must write his thoughts to me when we can't talk – 'But I couldn't,' he said 'the censor would see them.' Ann B. is much tougher than he – she should be the boy.

'I hate leaving the children', Hilda wrote to Moyra, feeling very differently from how she had felt at the farm. 'Now the time draws near I wonder why I decided to come back, tho' once I see my husband I'll know.' Angus had cabled 'THE SOONER THE BETTER'. To him she wrote 'I feel I should be with you and life will have real meaning again.' On holiday with our grandfather in New Plymouth in January 1942, she added,

> Every night poor David says how short the time is getting. 'I couldn't bear it if anything happened to you.' He thinks he might never see me any more. I'm very matter of fact and optimistic to him, but inwardly I feel the same. But dispassionately I know it is good for the children to be at boarding school and have such marvellous holidays in this lovely country. They are both self-reliant and independent.

At not quite eleven, David (for all his sensitivity and worrying) was prepared to go back to school in Hamilton by a roundabout route, as the Stratford railway line was blocked by floods. It meant going by railcar to Marton and changing on to the Main Trunk Limited express at 11 p.m., finding his seat alone in the dark. 'He insists he'll be all right.' When I was being particularly wilful, David asked 'If we were in England would you send Ann Barbara to Dr Lucas?' And of course Hilda said she certainly would. David worried about me, feeling the responsibility of being left with such a sister. 'She is such a show-off and if I tell her not to, she pinches me!' That was certainly the sort of behaviour that would not do at boarding school. Hilda agreed I also had other faults. 'She *is* a little boss – and yet she is so sweet in lots of ways.' David's swimming togs had blown off the line and disappeared and I insisted on spending all my savings on buying him new ones as an early birthday present. We were swimming every day in the salt water pool at Kawaroa and passed our 'fifty-yard' certificates.

To Moyra, David's godmother, Hilda was enthusiastic about what an interesting child he was. She knew I suspected he was her favourite. 'Ann B. is interesting too, but not so lovable. Boarding school will be very good for her.'

My mother put a great deal of effort into finding the right school for me. She had thought of Waikato Diocesan initially, where my cousin Helen had been, then – after the Lochores' enthusiasm, wanting me to be nearer Wellington – she looked at several, including Nga Tawa and Chilton St James. Hilda finally settled on the Samuel Marsden Collegiate School for Girls – Marsden – in Wellington itself. Marsden had a lot going for it. It was an Anglican school. The headmistress, Gladys Mayhew (an elegant slim grey figure), was English and so were a number of the staff. The buildings and grounds in Karori were excellent and so was its academic record. Moreover it boasted that Katherine Mansfield had been a pupil in the original school in Fitzherbert Terrace. Hilda was assured that, on her return to England, the school would take special care of me and keep her in touch with my development.

Hilda's already mixed feelings about leaving us in New Zealand had obviously been intensified by the news of the war in the Pacific. Our grandfather was digging a slit trench in his New Plymouth garden. Japanese submarines were reported in Auckland Harbour. 'Japan is making such rapid progress', Hilda wrote in January 1942 as she stitched nametapes on my new green Marsden clothes and packed her own trunk with things NOT WANTED ON THE VOYAGE.

I started at Marsden on 4 February 1942 and do not remember the day. 'Ann B. perfectly happy', Hilda wrote in her now laconic diary, and I have to take her word for it. She had finally secured a passage on the *Akaroa* (familiar from our 1934 voyage), which was first taking a crowd of airmen to Halifax for training in Canada. Its departure kept being delayed. Singapore fell on 15 February. It was becoming more and more obvious it was an insane time to leave. As a child I had no idea that this was so but Hilda certainly knew of the danger of what she was doing.

We had two more Saturdays together, going across the harbour on the first to the Godbers' new holiday house 'at the Bay'. It may be remembered from Chapter 3 that the Godbers were my great-aunt and uncle who owned the confectioners' and patisserie in the Artcraft Cinema building opposite Parliament. Angus called it 'the family gold-mine'. Many years later my Great-Uncle Fred's obituary in the *Dominion* would remind people of the connection with Katherine Mansfield's garden party (those 'beautifully light and feathery cream puffs') and call Godbers' 'the most famous pastry-cooks in Wellington for 101 years.' It reported that Great-Uncle Fred had himself claimed to have been the long-ago delivery boy and to have gone on to become a family friend. I have happy memories of helping in the shop myself, eating delicious things and staying up late when I was with them on a Friday night. The shop did not close until 9.30 p.m., after the last of the cinema-goers had rushed in for ice-creams in the final interval.

The Godbers' holiday house was actually at Eastbourne, but the south-coast-of-England name seems totally inappropriate. I see it as Katherine Mansfield's 'Crescent Bay' with 'bush-covered hills' behind, 'the silvery, fluffy toi-toi', the white dunes, the sandy road, the big gum trees, the wooden houses with their verandahs and the shore of the harbour littered with the sea-weed which I would, over the years, press in a scrapbook, where the delicious glowing algae would eventually become dry and dull.

My mother and I said goodbye to each other on the following Saturday, after lunch at my Great Aunt Win's in Kelburn. Again I have no recollection of what should have seemed a momentous day. There is no comment in my mother's diary beyond the bare fact, but I wrote to my father that I was sad at my mother's 'departing', a suitably solemn word. I had, of course, no idea that, saying goodbye as a small nine-year-old, I would not see my mother again until I was – still small but feeling extremely grown-up – looking forward to my thirteenth birthday.

CHAPTER 11

The last lap

Marsden was security for me in an insecure world. The school became my home. We were homeless, David and I, but we both felt entirely safe at school, if not always entirely happy. I did worry about my parents (less as time went on), but I don't remember any fear myself, in spite of the trenches being dug in the school grounds and the warm air-raid clothes we put out each night on our bedside chairs. In *Te Kura*, the school magazine, someone wrote that 'Never before in her short history has New Zealand stood in such danger.' There were plans to evacuate the school to Masterton if the Japanese ever attacked Wellington. The country, which had seemed the refuge most remote from the sickness of Europe, was now threatened by a different enemy. But eventually the threat receded and the bloomers and coats on our chairs became 'earthquake' clothes. There were earthquakes, but rather minor ones, strange but not alarming.

A letter survives from my form teacher, Barbara Gregorie, written to my mother on my tenth birthday in October 1942: 'Ann Barbara has had a very happy birthday. With her happy nature every moment of living is a joy to her.' In the past I had been defined as irrepressible, rude and argumentative. Now at Marsden I was considered articulate, keen and enthusiastic. I flourished in an atmosphere of approval, as who does not? Mrs Gregorie went on to tell my mother that 'far more than the average child she turns things over in her mind, relates them to what has gone before or finds their parallel in something she has heard, read or even experienced.' Moreover 'she has a great sense of humour and (a great asset) is always ready to laugh at a joke against herself.'

Miss Mayhew, the Head, in her end of term reports, constantly stressed 'what a happy member of the House' I was. She told my mother they liked the fact that I was such a 'live wire' and had 'a strong streak of commonsense'. 'At first we tried to do our best for her to make up for the lack of her home. Now we have a real affection for her. Everyone says she is "a dear little girl".' After so much negative evidence of my character (mostly from my mother, of course) I can't resist including these tributes to my ten-year-old self. A recent history of Marsden, *Marsden's Women and Their World*, describes 'a culture where women are encouraged to be different and to assert their individuality.' I certainly feel that that was so over sixty years ago.

One of my contemporaries, with whom I had a friendship that lasted all her life, was Barbara Haldane, known as Holly. A farmer's daughter from Waipukurau, she married John Yaldwyn, at one time Director of the National Museum in Wellington, before the days of Te Papa. It was Holly, a librarian, who, with David, helped to keep me in touch with New Zealand literature throughout my English years. She sent me such things as Michael King's fat biography of Janet Frame, inscribed '583 pages you haven't had to write'.

When I was first thinking about this book, not long before Holly's too-early death, I quoted Mrs Gregorie's remark about my 'happy nature' in a letter. Her response was characteristically tart. Holly was Head of the House at Marsden in 1949, long after I'd returned to England, but she did not have the same fond memories I had.

I've been thinking about Mrs Gregorie's remark to your mother and indulging in hindsight. Certainly the first thing that came to mind was of course that Mrs G. would be saying everything she could to set your mother's mind at rest. I can imagine Mrs G. thinking that anyone in Britain had enough worries because of the war .... I think of us as being fairly cowed with the risk of punishments always present – order-marks for 'hairs in brush', for goodness sake, and my first error was that I had left a glimpse of white sheet showing beneath my blue counterpane. That was punishable by an order-mark too. I suppose it was good training, but I don't remember ever having time to relax. Don't forget the cold showers to begin each day. How did we stand it all?

My memory of you is of a serious person, very well-behaved, who observed the rules absolutely. We had to stand aside for any adults in the corridors and you used to flatten yourself mercilessly against the walls .... I have this clear picture of you in the brick corridor along past the Shell and IVB classrooms [where we were in 1943 and 1944], doing just that. I think you learned at an early age to keep your head down and out of trouble. I wouldn't agree that yours was a happy nature at that time. I don't think you were particularly unhappy either. If Mrs G. had told your mother that you endured life stoically, and with courage, I would have agreed.

It amuses me, that considered reply from my friend, based it seems on one clear memory, for I have the evidence (and she hadn't) of the order-marks we were both given – to take one example – in the second term of 1943. I was given a total of forty-nine, while Holly herself had only twelve. 'Very well-behaved'? I don't think so. But I know I appreciated the structure even as I broke the rules. We used to sing about wanting our foolish ways to be forgiven, and the joys of 'ordered lives', in a hymn that became a favourite of mine. My evidence for our order-marks comes from the one issue of a magazine Holly, Barbara Whitman and I produced in 1943. They let me take this unique publication home with me and I have it still. This is a typical news item written by Holly and starring the three of us:

CAROLS at HOMEWOOD.

Carols were sung at Homewood on Sunday 5th. December, (day after Pauline's birthday), at 3 p.m. by the combined choirs of the SAMUEL MARSDEN COLLEGIATE SCHOOL for GIRLS, and Queen Margaret's, and Wellington Girls College.

The lack of grub was just certainly, disGUST·ING, ABOM'NIBBLE ATROTIOUS, and APPAULINE

The choir was led by these 3 famous, excellent, superb sopranos. Annie B. Harreep, Babzella Wheetiman and Holeek Haldeen.

B.H.

There were a lot of rules at Marsden. I listed some of them in a letter home and in one to David. No running in the corridors, no whistling inside, no talking after lights out. No this. No that. And of course NO HAIRS IN BRUSH. I once wrote a story called 'Running in the Corridors'. I imagined a girl seeing a future of endless running, as a result of that childhood prohibition: 'down pavements, through department stores, even in the corridors of town halls and in the aisles of cathedrals, in places where otherwise she might well have preferred to walk.' I described the curtained cubicles in which we slept on the Little Balcony: 'Bed, chair, dressing table, wardrobe. That was all. Not even a desk. You did your prep with everyone else in the Prep. Room. Rows of you; heads bent over books, shuffling your feet, itching, spilling ink as you dipped scratchy pens in the two ink-wells allowed to each table.'

I described too what happened when you got a lot of order-marks. On at least one occasion, like the girl in my story, I had to carry my House flag up to the platform in front of the whole school assembled in the Hall – and deposit it ignominiously in a stoneware drainpipe, gleaming like the best toffee, while the House flags of better behaved girls flew from a sloping rack, with the House with the fewest order-marks at the top.

That was a disgrace. I was certainly not well-behaved. 'I try hard to be good, but however hard I try I still get into some bad scrapes', I wrote to England. But I am inclined to think that I *did* have a reasonably 'happy nature', though I don't mind the idea of being stoical and courageous as well. I enjoyed life. I had a lot of good friends and some excellent teachers, including Kathleen Strombom and June Hillary. Miss Strombom took us for English literature and history and although I now consider the books that we read – including *Cranford* and *Ivanhoe* – to have been strange choices for the age we were, my reports show 'a keen interest'. We were taught science by Miss Hillary, whose brother was later to be the famous Sir Edmund. She is best remembered for the tales she told us when we were lucky enough to have her on our table at meal-times.

Very early on I wrote to David: 'I like boarding-school very much and I am very proud of my green Marsden uniform.' There was no need to pretend to David and I obviously meant what I said. A few weeks later, when my mother was still crossing the Atlantic, 'in peril on the sea', I wrote to my father: 'I am very happy at Marsden. It is certainly a lovely school.' And the following year I actually wrote, 'I adore Marsden.' In St Mary's Church, across the road, I loved to sing in the Benedicte: 'Oh all ye Green things upon the earth, praise ye the Lord!'

But how partial a view the surviving evidence provides. Never, in all my thirty years of working as a biographer, have I been so aware of how the writer's picture of the past can be entirely affected by the nature of the evidence. How different it might be if other letters and diaries had survived. How completely different this particular chapter would be if I were relying entirely on memory (my own and other people's) rather than having available many words written at the time. I realise it is easier to recreate a past in which one has not shared.

My parents wrote to us all the time. I have none of the hundreds of letters they wrote while I was at Marsden. They must have been destroyed or mislaid when we left New Zealand in 1945. But I have a thick pile of my own letters to them; those missing were ones they never read. Many ships were sunk; many planes were shot down. But many letters survived the journey. On one occasion, returning to school after an Easter holiday with the Lochores, I wrote to David to tell him I found *ten* letters from England waiting for me. Miss Mayhew described to my mother how I smiled and hugged them to myself and how she encouraged me to talk about them if I wanted to.

My friend Sukie Bogle, whose own English parents were in Fiji, remembered how good our mothers were at writing to us. In fact mine bombarded me with questions, which were sometimes tedious to answer. She was desperate to know – now she was so far away – what was going on in our lives. She had much more idea of David's for he had been at Southwell for a year when she left, whereas I had only just started at Marsden. She wanted not just to know but to influence my diet, my reading, my clothes, my prayers.

From my brief answers I can deduce her questions and can now imagine how much more she must have often wanted to know. Yes, I went to the dentist recently and the drill didn't hurt at all. No, I don't wear a bow in my hair as it is too much bother to tie every morning. Yes, I usually wash my own hair, but sometimes Matron does it and nearly tears it out by the roots. Yes, I still say 'Jesus tender shepherd' every night. What I didn't tell her were the words included in a prayer I found in my own childish hand in a book she had sent:

> Thank you for keeping them safe so far during this war. And hasten the time when wars shall cease and there will be peace in all the world. God bless all the soldiers and sailors and airmen that are fighting for us 'specially those who are sick, wounded or suffering. Help me to be a good girl and please make tomorrow a fine day. Amen.

I did have, I think, a steadfast belief in some sort of mysterious God watching over me and over my parents on the other side of the world. 'What a long face God must have,' I had said as a tiny girl many years before.

There is little other evidence that I was a pious child. Left to myself, not answering questions, I would tell my parents about the results of games and exams and about picnics and expeditions with the other boarders on Johnson's

Hill or in Wilton's Bush, with suitable illustrations. I was, obviously, not very good at drawing but this gives a good idea of what we got up to in days before teachers became scared of Health and Safety regulations.

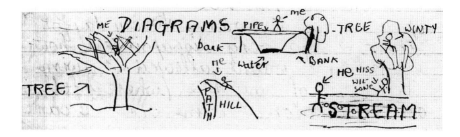

In my letters there is a great deal about food. Sparing my parents, I did not write about the regular school meals with their liver riddled with veins (or were they arteries?) and the slices of grey flabby mutton, which would eventually turn me into a vegetarian, as it became obscene to me to put pieces of dead animals into my mouth. But my mother must have sighed when she read my description of a bread-eating contest ('I myself ate 10 slices') or of an out-Saturday with Winty Agar 'at the Bay', when I listed and drew the delights of several meals, which included more than one 'pink drink', buns, sweets, bananas and ice-cream. ('The one drawback THE SANDFLIES.') The ferry across the harbour, the Cobar, was often at this time crammed with American marines and somehow (I'm not sure how) we would find ourselves enjoying Babe Ruth candy bars and vacuum-packed salted peanuts – unfamiliar and delicious fare.

I would also regale my parents with accounts of my life as a playwright and an actor. In my own plays (and my contemporaries were apparently quite happy to act in them) I tended to take the leading *male* roles. 'I made up the play and I'm the hero, Lord Robert.' Another day I was a German Gestapo officer, with a strong resemblance to Charlie Chaplin, and once 'I started writing a play this morning about a town boy who goes to stay with his cousins in the country.' I wish that one survived, even to disappoint me with its banality.

In Shakespeare's plays my roles were minor. I was merely an elf in *A Midsummer Night's Dream* when Titania and Oberon 'looked spiffing' – I can imagine my mother's reaction to that, remembering how she had tried to abjure slang as a girl. In an extract from *King John* ('the part where Prince Arthur is going to have his eyes put out'), I was an executioner with 'a *real* axe, cord, irons etc'. Like a great many other things that happened in my Marsden letters, this was 'great fun'. There was a band at one point with Margie Laybourn at the piano, Barbie Whitman on the triangle, Sukie Bogle on the tambourine and myself with the cymbals. 'Everybody says we make the most dreadful row, but it's great fun.' We had a club too – the S.S.S.S., the Seventeen Sisters of the Silver Star, which suggests rather a large membership.

But sometimes I could get very solemn. 'Let's hope "the hour of destiny that lies so close at hand" will hurry', I wrote in July 1944, acknowledging the quotation from a prayer Miss Mayhew used nearly every morning. I was by now eleven and that January had told my parents that in New Zealand '1944, the victory year' was on many posters. 'Let's hope the people's suspicions are founded for once.'

Like my mother, I had become a compulsive letter-writer. It was an intense pleasure to make up yet another flowery ending to a long rather factual letter, such as 'Miles of love from your darling daughter.' I rarely wrote about my schoolwork and even more rarely about my feelings. We had a regular letter-writing session once a week, supervised by a teacher, but I often wrote in bed in the summer when I was supposed to be going to sleep. I once recorded that I was writing in a tree, 'in an awkward but comfortable position', and once in a French class with Miss Robins ('awfully crabby'), who discovered what I was up to and destroyed my half-written letter so that I had to begin again.

What is interesting to me now is that in all these years of letters, I can find only a single instance of my actually grumbling or complaining to my parents. Just once I wrote 'I hate walks on wet days.' But even that was more a statement of fact.

Punishments were deserved and just. When we broke the rules (as we so often did) we knew what we were doing and what was likely to happen. As Miss Mayhew put it, 'Ann Barbara has her "ups and downs", but she takes correction in a good spirit.' I think I must have been sensible enough to realise that my parents had enough to worry about without worrying about me. I even told them I loved those cold showers Holly mentioned. 'They sort of wake you up.' I *was* indeed stoical.

Very rarely – and only when I was nine – do the letters suggest that I needed comfort. I wrote extremely warmly about Pattie Luke, my Richmond house-captain. Had she been asked to keep a special eye on me? I rather think so. I told my parents: 'Whenever I get into trouble she always helps me if she can. Pattie is 18 and understands when you feel unhappy.' It was the only time I ever used that word. Pattie and her sister Raema gave me my first *William* book, an inspired choice for a ten-year-old's birthday, and later, with amazing generosity, Pattie gave me a beautiful Marsden doll she had had herself as a child. I still have the green school tunic among my own grandchildren's dolls' clothes.

I had a 'pash' on Pattie Luke. That was the word we used and it may derive from 'passion', but there was certainly nothing sexual in the feelings we had for our chosen heroines. I knew very little about sex though I had once seen the word FUCK scrawled on a sea-front shelter and had been shocked without knowing quite why. I don't think my mother had used the word 'sex' when she had given me a private talk about the facts of life before she left New Zealand. We had walked across a paddock at the farm where I had often seen new-born lambs still attached to their placentas. Before the war in England we had had a book called *How You Began* by Amabel Williams-Ellis, which was about evolution ('over 90 million years or more') as much as about human biology. I knew that babies grew for nine months in their mother's wombs. But the book said nothing about how they got there or how they got out again. My mother had tried to tell me. It had all sounded very odd and I remember worrying (and feeling side-tracked) by the role of my navel, having not really understood, and not wanting my mother to know that I hadn't.

From our beloved seniors we needed maternal kisses, no other kind. As Fay Weldon put it in her memoir, growing up in Christchurch at exactly the same time, 'Like Queen Victoria before us we had not heard of lesbianism and wouldn't have believed it if anyone had tried to tell us.' When I had lunch in Sydney recently with my old friend Winty Agar (now Fysh, of the QANTAS family), she told me a sad story of her later Australian school where she had innocently climbed into the bed of a homesick girl to comfort her with a hug – and had been both dismayed and amazed by a teacher's reaction. How could it be 'wrong' to comfort someone? At Marsden bedtime visits from prefects to small juniors were part of the pattern of life. 'Some people could tuck other people up more at nights', one of us had written in the Personal column of our 1943 magazine. That year I was the smallest and youngest girl in the Upper School and still in need of tucking up. On the facing page is a section of the annual school photo. The front row from left to right: Ann Barbara Harrop, Winty Agar, Margie Laybourn, Barbara Haldane, Gaye Castle, Barbara Whitman. I thought myself extremely plain and indeed I was. Winty and Margie were beautiful, the others interesting. I remember thinking my appearance so nondescript that I wondered anyone could recognise me.

My memories of Marsden are often not reflected in my letters. I never told my parents that I wept. But I remember crying myself to sleep – not in the Little Balcony cubicle but in a dormitory at the corner of the large House where we lived. I remember the position of my bed in the room and the noise of possums beyond the windows, using as a climbing frame the scaffolding erected by painters working on the outside of the House. Reason has suggested to me that this was in February 1942 when I was first at the school and that the men were just coming to the end of work begun in the long Christmas holidays. But if I checked (I have no wish to), I might well discover that the House was not

painted at that time, that my weeping was not, as I used to believe, because
I was alone in a House full of strangers, because my mother had just set out
on a dangerous voyage, because I thought I might never see her again, but
rather because, at some quite different time, my friends had temporarily turned
against me.

I have only a vague recollection of this. Sue Fetherston (once Sukie Bogle)
wrote recently, when asked for her memories of that time, now over sixty years
ago, when we were both young:

> I remember you being 'sent to Coventry' at one point – for some (probably
> imagined) slight. [Or did she mean 'skite'?] You took it with great dignity and
> went about your business and I, I'm ashamed to say, had not the courage to go
> against the herd and seek out my pal. It's weighed on my mind ever since, so
> that serves me right – I hope you don't hold it against me.

I do remember another dire time (again not mentioned in my letters home) when
my dear friend Winty Agar stuck together the pages of my autograph album
with glue, as revenge for something or other. I wailed: 'It had my Grandpa in it
and he might die and I might never have his autograph as long as I live.' When
I told Winty about this in Sydney recently, curious to discover *why* she did it,
she was appalled and had no memory of the incident. But she admitted she
was sometimes jealous of me. She was in as bereft a situation as I was with her
father on active service in the Mediterranean and her New Zealand mother in

Australia. She thought I got much more loving attention from the staff than she did – perhaps because I was *English* and so much smaller. We were good friends all the same and have been all our lives – especially at a time when we both had babies in Tokyo. The incident of the autograph album remains a mystery.

This photo is of the IVB boarders in 1944. I am at the front with Holly on my left, Sukie next to her and Winty with her hand on Sukie's shoulder. The others are (from behind me) Audrey Pease, Dawn Garner, Barbara Whitman, Eve Donald and Peggy Pritchard.

I was very close to David in these years. He had stopped telling me off and I had stopped pinching. Once, when told he could collect me from school any time after nine, he promised to arrive at half a minute past. We exchanged regular letters and I told him things I didn't tell our parents – though the fact that these letters survive means, I think, that he sent them on to them. To my parents in early August 1943, I said simply, 'We've been getting into a good deal of trouble lately and will be glad to begin a new term.' To David I wrote:

> On Monday night Matron caught us out of bed *tons* of times and talking *millions* of times, so she has separated us and I'm sleeping in the Lower School playroom, but as I quite like sleeping in there it's not much of a punishment. We had lots of other punishments too … such as having prep early and going to bed early: no cocoa or barley sugar for a week and missing Saturday dancing. I'm getting a bit sick of school and longing for the holidays 'cos everywhere you go here someone blows you up.
> Gee whiz! I wish the war would stop. Don't you?

In spite of these occasional outbursts, David would report to England after the holidays: 'Ann is getting on well and enjoying herself as usual.' I was, as I have already suggested, a natural schoolgirl, and most of the time I relished the fact that Marsden bore such a strong resemblance to every school story I had ever read. What larks we got up to! One day we found an unlocked door – intended for electricians and such – on the far side of the school hall. We laid our plans. I remember creeping on the bare earth under the floor of the hall. It was a dark mysterious space and we lit candles so we could see. (Where had we got them? How did we have matches?) We crouched on the earth to eat the feast we had brought with us. We told ghost stories, though no one was very good at telling them. I can smell the earth and the candle wax now. This was exciting. I don't think we were caught, though we must have been dirty, and certainly the door was locked when we next returned. What if it had been locked while we were under the hall? We scared ourselves by thinking about that.

We were always planning feasts with tuck acquired from visitors or 'daybugs'. David's letters were full of talk of tuck too. He wrote to Hilda: 'Will you ask Aunt Louisa if she will send me a rich fruit-cake in a tin?' (I like the adjective – not just any old fruit-cake.) Commenting on this to Angus, Hilda wrote 'You'd think he was a greedy boy.' Which he was not.

I told David, but not our parents, of one plan that went wrong – when a cache we had hidden in a locker was discovered and we were forced to take all the delicious food up to St Mary's Orphans' Home – a just punishment indeed. 'We had tons of stuff too: sausage rolls, meat pies, doughnuts, fruit-squares, bananas (about 9 of each thing), mixed cakes and fizzy drinks.' In my accounts book (compulsorily kept) there were multiple entries for 'toothpaste'. Dorothy Lochore charitably suggested I was supplying the whole dormitory. Obviously the money actually went on tuck, though I am sure we were never really hungry. Illicit feasts were simply something schoolgirls had, so we had them too.

My grandfather, Jim Valentine, wrote to my mother just before she left New Zealand, telling her to reassure Angus that none of the family felt that the holiday care of David and Ann would be either a burden or a bother. 'They are worth all that is done for them.' Grandfather would not be able himself to have us to stay in New Plymouth for we would be 'too much' for his house-keeper, our Great-Aunt Mabel, who had no experience of children. But he would take a keen interest in our welfare. He wrote: 'My thoughts will be with you every hour. I know that as you face unknown dangers you will put your hand into the hand of God for He will supply all your needs.'

In fact, Hilda's seven-week voyage on the *Akaroa*, in spite of all the dangers, the depressing war news and the crowd of airmen on board, seems to have been very similar to all those other twentieth-century journeys, with lots of reading, games and intimate talks with strangers. Hilda learnt to drink whisky and won the Deck Golf tournament. She 'felt anything might happen, tho' I'm not nervous, thank God.' After going through the Panama Canal, the *Akaroa* sailed close to the American coast – close enough for her passengers to see people moving, close enough for the life-boats to get to land if they were attacked.

They went ashore in Halifax, waited there to join a convoy and finally reached England safely on 15 April 1942.

There was a joyous reunion. 'I love you so much and will try to prove it', Angus had written just before she had sailed. Hilda was sure she had made the right decision. She was with Angus and she was at home. They were certainly still New Zealanders, but they were also Londoners, and always would be. Her old friends were important too. Everyone seemed to be in remarkably good spirits. 'When so much devastation is all around you, you simply cannot bother about trifles.' 'We have almost passed beyond caring about *buildings* now', Angus had written in May 1941. The office at 92 Fleet Street still stood and Hilda was glad to play her part again on the *New Zealand News*, knowing how much the servicemen relied on it to keep them in touch with home. Her return allowed Angus to concentrate on his new work for an Australian paper and for the University of New Zealand. They had new cards printed.

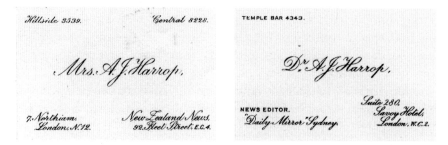

There was other interesting and important voluntary work Hilda could do. In her memoirs she put it like this:

> When I returned from New Zealand Angus had a job arranged for me in the Red Cross Educational Books Section .... I worked two days a week in South Kensington (quite a journey by tube from Woodside Park) despatching examination papers in all classes of subjects, including life-saving and football refereeing, to many prisoner of war camps in Germany and Italy. I also spent two mornings a week searching for wanted text books in Charing Cross Road's second-hand bookshops and in the Red Cross bookshop in Wigmore Street, lent by *The Times*, where parcels of books were received from all over England.

The scheme's headquarters were at the New Bodleian in Oxford and many of the courses that the prisoners were taking were far more academic than my mother suggests. She could use her own judgment about what books might be useful, but there were often specific requests and limitations. She would be asked for 'as many copies of *Pride and Prejudice* as you can find' but for 'no book-keeping or nursing texts published before 1932'. The organiser Ethel Herdman wrote from

Oxford: 'You really are a brick to do all the odd jobs and the skilled labour with such goodwill and efficiency.' One exchange of letters with a Maori prisoner in Stalag VIIIB, Sgt. Harry Taituha, resulted in his becoming a regular *New Zealand News* correspondent from Auckland after the war.

The first Sunday that Hilda was home she gave a tea-party at 7 Northiam. Lady Margaret Stewart came with Eric Baume to enjoy the New Zealand fruit-cake and shortbread she had brought back with her. Lady Margaret Vane-Tempest-Stewart was a daughter of the 7th Marquess of Londonderry and was at this time – and my mother must surely have realised it – deeply involved in an affair with Eric Baume. Eric had been at school with Angus and a year before had head-hunted (to use a phrase not then coined) Angus Harrop to be his News Editor and deputy at a new World Cable Service being set up by the Australian *Truth and Sportsman* group to supply exclusively their new evening paper, the *Sydney Daily Mirror*. Until now all the Australian papers had shared the services of the Australian Associated Press. The plan to set up a London service to give the new paper an edge over its rivals was ambitious and expensive. News had to leave London by 4 a.m. for the next day's evening paper. So it was all evening and night work – but Angus was used to that.

Angus left the *Daily Telegraph* without regret. Hilda, then still in New Zealand, was more apprehensive. She knew the reputation of the associated New Zealand *Truth*, its populism, its sensationalism. Indeed Angus himself had once called it a 'rag'. Was the new paper just another scandalous tabloid?

And what about Eric Baume himself? He might have been at Waitaki with Angus (and agree with him that it was the best school in the world), but his reputation was dubious. 'I feel uneasy', Hilda wrote to Moyra, 'But you know how Angus always thinks the best of people.' Baume was the son of a flamboyant lawyer and Auckland M.P., who had died when he was a child; his mother was the first woman to stand for the New Zealand Parliament.

Eric himself was as flamboyant as his father, noisy, thrusting and undoubtedly glamorous. When Hilda last saw him in Sydney in 1957 she wrote to Angus: 'Eric is – Eric.' By then he was very conscious of his audience of millions (T.V. and radio as well as the papers) and 'all the people who think his word is gospel'. In the end he became, after all his tumultuous years as a hard-drinking philanderer, a devoted Anglican, reconciled with a forgiving wife. In 1941 he inscribed his lively autobiography 'To my life-long friend, Gus Harrop, Litt.D., Ph.D., M.I.R.R.O.R.' This was an adventure they were on together and they remained intensely loyal to each other. Though they were so different, they each admired the other's skills and flair and relished the scoops they were able to make. They cabled the news of the German attack on Russia two days before anyone else believed it.

In 1941 Hilda had been cheered when she heard from Frank Milner, the men's old headmaster: 'I feel that now the British brass hats, Civil Services (especially Heads of Departments) and so on need all that Baume gives them. In spite of the journalistic swashbuckling vein I think he is doing good work. While not a fervent admirer, I can see that Baume is for the Empire and for British-American co-operation and I think that Angus's modesty, taste and scholarship will restore the balance.' Did Milner realise that *both* men were Socialists?

Angus told Hilda not to worry. He told her he had nothing to do with *Truth* and reminded her that Eric was a nephew of their old friend Dr Bernard Myers, which seemed to lend him some sort of respectability.

> I understand him very well. All that happens is that I am paid well for running a service which is in opposition to the monopoly I complained of in *My New Zealand*. What could be more congenial? I would pay entertainment tax for this sort of job – and where else would I be allowed to carry on two other jobs with what should be a full-time one? I can see that Baume is going to leave me almost complete control, except for his own commentary.

Later he would indeed be in charge when Baume went off to be a war correspondent. Later still, in 1944, he would himself hand over to his deputy when he set off for New York on his way to the far side of the world.

'It's about the biggest thing that has yet happened to me,' Angus told Hilda, delighted with his new job. At the beginning Baume had given him the task of recruiting staff and he had easily persuaded a number of good 'grossly underpaid' journalists to leave the *Daily Telegraph*. One of his roles was to authorise the staff's expenses – 'more worrying than the main job of covering the news.' Angus was also supposed to 'cultivate contacts at the office's expense' – a brief that could cover all sorts of interesting encounters.

The new cable service was established, not in half-demolished Fleet Street, but in the 'swish' Savoy Hotel, between the Strand and the Thames. At times the Savoy itself seemed to be the hub of the universe with Churchill giving a lunch there for the new U.S. Ambassador, John G. Winant, and hordes of interesting people coming and going. When the *Sydney Daily Mirror* Cable Service moved in, the hotel was already thronged with journalists, including many Americans, not least because it was said to have as thick a set of walls as anywhere but the Tower of London – which was not available.

'I must admit that carrying on a new service in a luxury hotel in an air-raid has some element of the fantastic', Angus wrote to Hilda on Savoy paper. Gunfire and planes outside; Carroll Gibbons and his orchestra within. In the restaurant at three in the morning, Eric and Angus found themselves discussing Rudolf Hess's arrival in Scotland by parachute with messages from Hitler ('one of the best stories of the war') 'with Quentin Reynolds, Noel Coward, Hector Bolitho and Carroll Gibbons. We all agreed it was like a fairy tale come true, the sort of things novelists conceive and cut out because it is too wildly improbable.' Forbidden by Hilda to swear, Angus adopted 'Hector Bolitho' as a suitably resounding alternative. Bolitho, who had been born in Auckland, was a prolific writer, much read in his time; he presumably did not know how our family took his name in vain.

Brendan Bracken had written from the Ministry of Information: 'The Savoy Hotel has ceased to be just a hotel. It's a Newspaper House and largely responsible for the shortage of whisky in the country.' But it *was* a hotel and Tich's Bar and the restaurants were always available when the journalists needed a break. The management treated the odd fire-bomb as if it had been a tiresome incident involving a waiter burning the crêpes Suzette.

My father only occasionally spent the night in the Savoy. Two nights a week he would manage to get back to 7 Northiam, but on the other days, in the early hours of the morning he would make his way on foot to Clifford's Inn, to Alice Evans's flat, which he continued to rent throughout these years while she remained in Wales. Hilda, that keen Londoner, found the flat a great bonus when she got back and they would spend many nights together there, without seeming to worry that it was a good deal more vulnerable than their house in the suburbs. They liked the fact that they could walk – rather than take the tube – even if it was through streets strewn with rubble and glass. They had to get used to the grime of a burning city.

Hilda recalled in her memoirs that the nearest miss they had at the house was soon after her return when 'one night a cluster of "Molotov cocktails" – fire bombs – fell on the Green Belt by the Dollis Brook, just beyond our garden'. That was what she wrote. She also recorded a more frightening night later in the war:

A 'buzz bomb', no, I think it was a rocket, rushed over Finchley. We heard it
cut out and wondered breathlessly where it would fall. Horrid suspense. The
bang and blast shattered the windows at the front of the house and burst the
lock on the front door. The bomb had buried itself in the hill opposite, on the
edge of Totteridge .... If it had cut out 2 seconds earlier it would have landed
on our house.

The front-door lock had whizzed across the hall, above the Morrison shelter,
and sunk itself in the cupboard door at the other end of the room. Broken glass
was everywhere, on their beds upstairs, on the top of the shelter. Next day the
windows were boarded up until they could be replaced. 'We hugged each other
thankfully.'

This was the sort of thing our parents were relieved that we were missing. It
seems appropriate now to write about those 'marvellous holidays in this lovely
country' that they had been so keen for us to experience. The school holidays
were marvellous and memories of them form a large part of what I think of
as my happy childhood. 'You always forget me in the holidays', Hilda once
complained to us both and on one occasion I apologised for not having written
one of my weekly letters with the excuse: 'I've been too busy enjoying myself.'

I was with Dorothy Davies and Reuel Lochore that holiday and being
with them was always enjoyable. The farm belonged to other children. At the
Lochores' we were the children of the house. Without children themselves
('much as they long for them,' my mother said), they were the most loving,
relaxed and flexible of guardians. If there were more people wanting to sleep in
the house than there were beds, in the early Hataitai days, we went along and
borrowed a mattress from the Alleys. Geoff Alley was Reuel Lochore's cousin
and brother of the more celebrated Rewi, who spent most of his life in China.
Geoff had early enjoyed the fleeting fame of an All Black and went on eventually
to be New Zealand's first National Librarian.

I wrote home from 96 Te Anau Road, high above Wellington harbour:
'Living a few doors away are Judith Alley (10), Ruth (6), Roderick (Rockie) 4
and Patrick 6 weeks.' Patrick hardly counted but, of course, I had 'great fun'
with the rest. Dorothy described 'a good mix-up of bicycles, cats and children
– with Rockie Alley, the lone male, bringing up the rear, making loud, roaring
noises to get himself heard.'

This was soon after Hilda left; David was at Southwell and I was there for
the weekend from Marsden. In the May holidays that year David – who had
turned eleven – was there too and Dorothy recorded an evening when, with
no suggestion of the need for childminders or babysitters, David and I gave a
dinner party:

Reuel and I went out one night to dinner and the children had the three Alleys in and cooked their own. Sausages and mash and baked apples. Did everything, prepared it and all. When we came home all in apple-pie order, children in bed asleep. Pretty good? All helps towards self-dependence.

Reuel and Dorothy were as keen as our parents on self-reliance and self-expression. If we wanted cakes and biscuits to take back to school we made them ourselves. We were always encouraged to make our own decisions and indeed often treated as much older than we were. We rose to their expectations and responded to their wit. A key-word in the household was 'co-operation'. In our last long holiday with them, over Christmas 1944, Dorothy would write (much later, for she was always a reluctant letter writer): 'The children were co-operative to almost a perfect degree and always seemed to know what they wanted to do, which is such a help.'

They were both extremely busy. Dorothy Davies, who kept her maiden name professionally, would be described after her death as 'one of New Zealand's most distinguished pianists, a legend in her own life time'. She was constantly in demand both as a performer (sometimes in her trio, with 'cello and violin) and as a teacher. I remember her in her sandals, with her untidy hair and loose clothes, walking from the tram up the Marsden drive to collect me, when it was much more usual to see mothers – with neat costumes and permed hair – arrive in smart cars.

Reuel Lochore, a brilliant linguist, worked long hours in the Department of Internal Affairs with what Michael King described as the 'highly secretive job of officer in charge of aliens'. This is not the place for me to retell what King called 'the strange story of Reuel Anson Lochore'. King's readable essay first appeared in *Metro* magazine with a highly misleading photograph of Reuel in Germany sitting damagingly near to a swastika banner. The piece is now easily accessible in King's own collection *Tread Softly for you Tread on my Life*. I was devoted to Reuel and consider him extremely lucky to have had a friend to refute so convincingly – and at such length – the posthumous slurs on his character in the autobiography of the Czech refugee, later New Zealand manufacturer, entrepreneur and arts advocate, Fred Turnovsky. Those smears are shocking evidence of how easily reputations can be ruined.

Michael King recorded his own happy memories of staying with the Lochores, of 'hot clear days' 'filled with writing, swimming, conversations and music'. It was for him a taste of 'an artists' community'. It was exactly this that Hilda had wanted us to have and which we had in abundance in many school holidays. Many of their friends were Jewish refugees. The suggestion that Reuel could ever have had fascist sympathies is ludicrous to anyone who knew him as we did. Like Angus, Reuel was a strong supporter of Peter Fraser's Labour Government. He loved Germany – for its music, its literature, its past – but was extremely glad to get out of it in 1935. He hated to see the two great nations trying to destroy each other. That we needed to destroy fascism was obvious. The game he and I played endlessly in the evenings was the old game of 'Battleships', now re-named 'Smash the Nazi Navy'.

Both Dorothy and Reuel were deeply unconventional. What surprised me as the years went by were not the crazy ideas Reuel eventually embraced (sad as it was to hear of them), but the fact that someone like Reuel could hold high diplomatic posts, representing the New Zealand Government successively in Bangkok, Singapore, Kuala Lumpur, Delhi and Jakarta and ending his career as his country's first Ambassador to Germany. Even if everything ended in tears, this was a remarkable career and Reuel was a remarkable man. *Metro's* photograph of him in shorts and coolie hat, winning an over-fifties cross-country walk in front of a delighted Malayan crowd, reminds me of the Reuel I knew.

Dorothy found it 'exhilarating' to have us in the house. 'They are grand kids,' she told Hilda. We responded to each other's energy. Dorothy records that I had decided I was going to be a writer and she was always encouraging. The lesson Dorothy hoped to teach me – and certainly did – was 'to learn to be alone and to enjoy it'. Writers and readers – like pianists – need to spend much of their time alone. Dorothy and Reuel both loved us and cared a great deal about what was going on in our heads. In a letter to Angus, Reuel decided I was good at making the best of whatever circumstances I was in and confirmed Marsden's opinion that I could be happy anywhere, even if he thought my happiness was 'usually quite self-centred'. David, as usual, scored points for being extraordinarily helpful and thoughtful. 'Most of our efforts go into trying to make him a bit more selfish.' David was always eager to please and I did not seem to care whether I did or not. Fortunately, with the Lochores, I usually did.

They knew how important it was for us to feel they could always be depended on and welcomed us whenever we wanted to come. Negotiating with our aunts and great-aunts over Easters and out-Saturdays was often complicated. There were four great-aunts in Wellington, two from each side. They must have felt they had a duty to invite us out from time to time. Our aunts, Hilda's sisters, Nettie and Lottie, shared the major school holidays with the Lochores each year. Hilda had given Dorothy a list of all the relations and Dorothy wrote that she wished it had been annotated: 'not so favourite' and so on.

The Lochores owned a section at Porirua and had great plans to build a house on it one day. We used to go there – the ten miles by train – in the Hataitai days, work and play on the section, and return to Wellington with, in our rucksacks,

eels we had caught for Stripey the cat. Then they sold 96 Te Anau Road and bought two houses, one in Eastwood Lane, Porirua, and the other – which they converted into a studio and a flat to let out – in Tinakori Road, Wellington, not far from the Godbers and on the tram route down from Marsden.

There were two grand pianos, one in the studio, one at Porirua. Dorothy practised for hours every day. Michael King lists 'Beethoven sonatas, Bach, Rachmaninov, Schubert'; I would now add Mozart and Debussy. As a child, I knew only that it was wonderful music and I was lucky to hear it. When later I read D.H. Lawrence's poem 'Piano', I identified with that child 'sitting under the piano, in the boom of the tingling strings'. But often I was listening from my bed in the dusk with my door ajar, the better to hear. Aware of the hours of practising that were needed to be any good, I didn't want Dorothy to teach me, even when my Marsden friend, Margie Laybourn, became a keen and gifted pupil. Dorothy wrote to Hilda: 'Darling Annie has the ears and perception to be a listener and will derive much relaxation from music, which she will always need to seek ….. She and Reuel sing together over the dishes, folk songs mostly.'

Surprisingly (as it now seems), I liked it when Reuel chanted

> Little orphan Annie's
> Come to our house to stay –
> To wash the cups and saucers up
> And put the pans away.

Was it that my parents were fading and that the word 'orphan' seemed affectionate rather than dire? As I've already said, my mother complained that we forgot her in the holidays.

Porirua was then a quiet little township, very different from the commuter suburb, with its own light industry, that it became soon after the war. From our section we could see the tall chimney of the large mental hospital. Porirua was not a place to be mentioned by name at school. Children can be cruel and someone would inevitably have suggested I was spending my holidays in a 'loony bin'. Thinking about that now I feel particularly glad that my father had kept from me the knowledge that my uncle was in Seacliff, that other mental hospital far away in the South Island.

There was good river swimming at Porirua and there was the sea at Titahi Bay. We climbed the hills with picnics, swung on supplejacks and once got lost and had to find our way down by following a stream. Plimmerton was not far away. Margie's family had a house there and we spent a lot of time in the sea. I have memories of riding the waves in a borrowed canoe and no one telling me to 'be careful'. We were outside most days whatever the season of the year. Both the Lochores were keen on compost, on organic vegetables, on the delights of growing things. Reuel wrote to Angus: 'The section is getting more attention now that we are living out here; David will no doubt make a real gardener of me. Still, my main feelings about gardening are Candide's – it's one of the few occupations in which you can be sure you are not ill-using other human beings.' That was the Reuel Lochore I knew. I can see him sucking on his pipe, and his amused eyes. Dorothy and Reuel had the ability – Janet Frame would think impossible in New Zealand – 'to lead the kind of intellectual and moral life they chose'.

That life was very different from the lives our aunts led in Auckland and at the Tirau farm, but we had good holidays wherever we were. The next photo was taken on a damp Auckland day in May 1943 when we were staying with our Aunt Lottie and her family in Mount Eden. We stood up straight and smiled – a little self-consciously – knowing the photo would be sent to England. David was twelve and I was ten. We look, as we were, competent travellers. I can't work out how many times I took the Limited express on the Main Trunk line going overnight up the middle of the North Island. But I remember the names of the stations as we left Wellington – the Maori names sounding, in those days, something like this: Pie-cock, Para param, Why can I? After that I was usually asleep, curled uncomfortably upright. Only once I remember a moonlit glimpse of snow-capped volcanoes with Ruapehu smoking. If we were going to the farm, David met me at Frankton Junction where we changed trains.

At the farm I remember going out with my cousin Val to see if any new lambs had been born and being lifted up on the back of one of the draft horses which had been brought into use again because of the shortage of petrol for the tractors. I remember Val impressing me by cracking his stock-whip in the air and letting me ride on the back of his motorbike, bumping over the paddock. Aunt Nettie had made a good recovery from her dreadful accident. It was as if those sad days in 1941 had never been. Val and Helen seemed nearly grown up.

We four younger cousins – Ann and David HARROP and Janet and Ruth WATKINS – now formed a special holiday club: the Harwats. The 'lovely games' Ruth had mentioned in her long-ago letter to her uncle Angus became Club activities and challenges, which form some of the happiest memories of my childhood. This was the sort of New Zealand experience my father, in particular, had wanted us to have. Ruth, the eldest, was the leader and made up all the rules. She told us:

> Good fun in the hols means that you must know a little more than the average child about outside activities. You must promise, on your honour, that you will do your best to be a true Harwat – that is, just a decent kid, who is friendly to all, smiles under difficulties, who doesn't hold too high an opinion of him/herself and remembers that God gave us this earth and our lives to be happy with.

I perhaps continued to hold rather too high an opinion of myself for Ruth's taste and was not quite the 'decent kid' she would have liked me to be, but I certainly loved the things we got up to. We learnt how to light a good camp fire and how to tie useful knots and we tried to track pukekos, wriggling through the hayfields before the grass was cut. Uncle Lewis had offered us sixpence if we brought back a tail feather, but of course we never got near those elusive birds.

Writing about the Harwat Club later, when she was herself a teacher, Ruth explained to her pupils:

> It was hard for my cousins being so far away from home and we had to think of a lot of interesting things for them to do. We had most of our meetings in an old building we called the whare. We often took food over there, so we could have feasts and celebrations. But we spent as much time as possible outside, sometimes rolling round the paddock in an old corrugated iron tank, sometimes lighting camp fires and cooking sausages – and damper – down by the river, or building a hut in the pine trees near the house. We filled sacks with dry pine needles and used them for seats. We had boxes for a table and a cupboard where we kept a pack of cards, knife and string, notebooks and pencils. We thought that if New Zealand was ever bombed or invaded we would hide in our hut. We sometimes had concerts and we all had bicycles, so we worked out tests we had to pass before we could have a license and we often rode our bikes to Okoroire Hot Springs for a swim, and spent hours searching the banks of our river for a hot spring of our own.

Below is the programme of one of our concerts. The Watkinses seem to have played a much larger part than the Harrops, but I'm sure a good time was had by all. I have no idea why the dance was cancelled. When the page is turned over, item 16 is seen to be a second singing of the National Anthem. We were all very patriotic in those days.

Widespread hopes that 1944 would be the Year of Victory had now been dashed, but in September I was able to write, 'Isn't the war news super. Anytime anybody mentions it I feel awfully excited.' Paris had been liberated; the first American troops were on German soil. We were now writing airgraphs – a clever innovation operated by Kodak for the Post Office, mainly for the Forces. The original form was photographed and reduced to a tiny negative so that hundreds of letters could be sent in a very small packet.

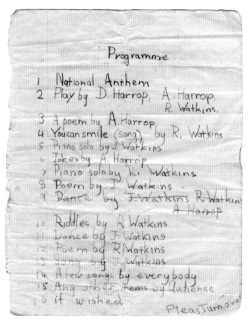

Apparently a roll of film with 1500 airgraphs on it weighed only six ounces. And if it happened that the plane carrying the films was shot down, the original messages could be photographed again. The forms were only destroyed when the airgraphs had been safely enlarged at the other end. During the two and a half years the service existed, nearly eight million airgraphs were sent to and from New Zealand. Here is one I wrote in September 1944.

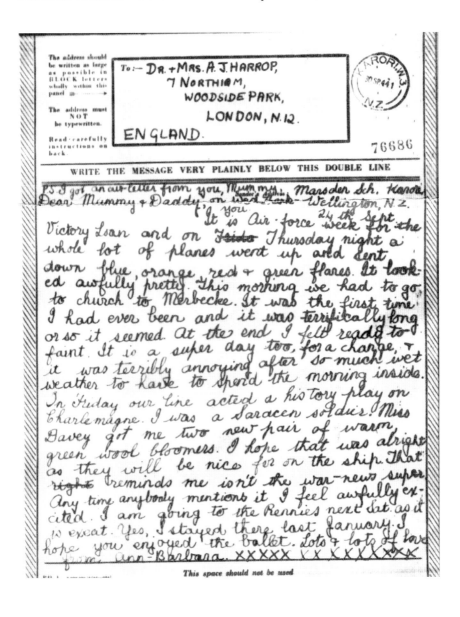

With the end of the war in sight, my father was able to 'wangle' (as he would have put it) a visit to Australia and New Zealand. The official story was that he had been 'summoned to Sydney on business' – to familiarise himself with conditions in Australia. After five years and two months in wartime London, the summons was very welcome. He was, of course, very keen to collect us – and, as it was ten years since he had been in New Zealand, it was high time he took a look at what was going on there. As things turned out, he was away from England – and Hilda – for eight months.

On 12 November 1944 I wrote to my mother in London: 'I hope you're not too lonely without Daddy, but you will have tons to do as he won't be able to help you with the *New Zealand News*.' Angus had set off a few days earlier to go 'Round the World in Wartime', as he titled a piece for the New Zealand *Listener*. Travel, as he said, was one of the more strictly rationed commodities in wartime. 'Apart from the armed forces and government representatives there is very little contact between people of different nationalities.' His journey to us was eventful – filling nine pages of his passport with visas and travel permits. His plan, approved in Australia, had been to cross America, sending stories to the *Sydney Daily Mirror* as he went. He reached New York on the *Aquitania* in just seven days and, after two weeks, moved on to Washington, Philadelphia, Cleveland, Chicago – flying – and then took the Overland Express to San Francisco, where his old teacher and friend Jack Condliffe was now Professor of Economics at Berkeley. Angus was supposed to fly to Australia from Los Angeles, but when he got there he found the bomber delivery service had been suspended. There was no alternative but to take a train for three days and three nights to Mexico City, and then to fly south to the Panama Canal Zone and wait there for a ship. This involved an 1800-mile flight, calling at every country in Central America, 'bounced up and down in the sky'. 'I wish I was you flying all over the place', I wrote to my father when I heard what he'd been up to. 'I have never been in a plane. Worst luck …. It's going to be corker seeing you after all these years.' When he got to Balboa, Angus found not only that his ship had not yet left England, but that some sort of uprising was taking place in Panama and the revolutionaries kept dodging across the border to seek refuge in his hotel in the Canal Zone. He took his first lessons in Central American politics, duly filing a news story while enjoying a three-week holiday in his tropical suit in the shade of a scarlet bougainvillea.

In Australia Angus had the chance to see his sister and get to know her children. He also did enough to make himself (and his employers) feel that he was earning his living. He eventually reached Wellington on 30 March 1945. He was laden with presents: Slazenger tennis balls and fountain pens for both of us and for me a photograph Deanna Durbin had personally signed in Hollywood and even a perfume called 'Adventure' – a subtle acknowledgment that I was growing up.

I made the short journey down from Marsden in Karori; David made the much longer one on the Lyttelton ferry from Waitaki Boys' High School, where he had started only two months before, soon after the dramatic death of its old headmaster, Frank Milner. In Wellington we stayed at the Waterloo Hotel and marvelled at our bathrooms and at the telephones in every room. We had never seen anything like it before. I looked at my father and wrote to my mother: 'I don't think he has changed a bit', though his eyebrows were even wilder. David wrote: 'He is still witty and he can still get things done in a hurry.' Angus wrote to Hilda: 'I'm delighted with the children. They are both splendid and we've a good deal to thank New Zealand for', adding that 'Events have conspired to give David the idea that his father always meets somebody capable of effecting miracles. I hope I don't let him down.' I would marvel too at the way there were always seats available for us on trains supposed to be full and how cars from the Tourist Board – or the suspect Truth Newspapers Group – would surprisingly appear to take us off to interesting destinations. It would be difficult to get used to ordinary London suburban routines again.

We went back to school while Angus travelled all over both islands, bringing up to date his knowledge of his own country, which meant so much to him, but where he could never live. He wrote to Eric Baume in London: 'The city papers here are pretty hopeless owing to the lack of competition.' On VE Day, 8 May 1945, he thought of London and the Savoy: 'You will be having exciting times in the office and I'm sorry to be out of it.'

Hilda wrote on VE Day, that 'joyous day of thanksgiving for the end of the European war', how lovely it was to have all the lights on again and 'the horrid stuff off all the windows' – that sticky paper that had been unable to stop the glass shattering on the night of the nearest bomb. Flags were flying all over London; Hilda and Moyra drank a toast to 'a lasting peace'. But 'what a mess the world is still in', Hilda wrote as she put together a special Victory issue of the *New Zealand News* with messages from the New Zealand High Commissioner in London, Bill Jordan, and from General Howard Kippenberger. My father would say how clever she was 'to get Kip to write.' Hilda said 'Everyone is worried about Russia', and there was still Japan, of course, to be dealt those final dreadful blows. The Pacific remained far from safe. When we crossed it a few weeks later we would have to observe a blackout and a ban on anything being thrown overboard.

On his travels round New Zealand my father had, typically, managed to go through the new Homer Tunnel – construction of which had involved blasting a way through three quarters of a mile of rock – before it was complete and to write about it, just as he had with the Otira Tunnel in 1923. I think he did not visit Seacliff, the mental hospital where I now know his poor brother, Frederick, was still alive. But perhaps he did and renewed his guilt.

He went shark fishing in Milford Sound, and boiled a billy on a driftwood fire. In Hokitika Angus walked down Fitzherbert Street and paused in front of the little wooden house with the veranda, where his photograph had been taken not long after his mother's death. He did not attempt to go inside.

We joined him when we broke up for the May holidays. We would not go to school again until we were in England in September. In Wellington we had a last chance to go to a Dorothy Davies concert: Judith Alley and Margie Laybourn came with us and Angus gave us all dinner first at the Hotel St George. We paid farewell visits to everyone we knew. 'More goodbyes', I wrote to my mother. 'It seems as if all we do these days is say goodbye.'

We took our cousin Ruth with us to Rotorua for a few days and swam in the Blue Baths. In Orakei Korako the steam rising from the mud pools contributes to the general blur of the black and white photographs and I remember the sound of an old record played on a wind-up gramophone in the great cave: 'When you come to the end of a perfect day.' I was glad to find when I returned years later the gramophone had gone and only the extraordinary natural beauty remained – the tree ferns silhouetted against the sky as you walk up from the bottom of the cave. F.H. Coventry recorded a version of that scene for me when, only two years later, he illustrated my first published story (opposite).

At the farm we had a breaking-up ceremony for the Harwats. We found the roof of the hut we had made the year before had fallen in. So we dismantled

F.H.COVENTRY

it and left the place where we had played so many times looking tidy and not just abandoned. On our last Sunday in Auckland, before church, we went along to the IZB studio to see something called 'Uncle Tom's Choir', which we had often heard on the radio. In my last letter to my mother – posted on the day the *Empire Grace* sailed – I wrote: 'They always announce the names of the visitors from outside Auckland. He made us stand up and he said what a wonderful thing it was to be going home.' David and I smiled vaguely at the word 'wonderful'; we both had mixed feelings about leaving.

David had settled down quickly at Waitaki School since his move from Southwell and Hamilton. He had grown three inches in three months. Not long after he started, he had written to his mother suggesting he should stay and finish his education in New Zealand. Hilda was, of course, appalled. She had lost part of his childhood; how could she lose his adolescence as well? He promised not to mention the idea again. But I had heard of it. I wrote to him, 'You've no idea how glad I am that you've changed your mind about going home.' The possibility of *not* going back had never occurred to me. Hadn't we been looking forward to doing just that all through the long war years? But I knew how much I would miss Marsden and all the familiar people and places I thought I might never see again. I knew that no one in London had the chance to ride bare-back down a hillside – as I had just learnt to do on Jennette Rennie's pony. I thought I would never again have the chance to crest the waves in a canoe at Plimmerton, eat damper hot from the camp fire on Cabbage Tree Flat or swim in hot springs under the stars.

'I hope the chicks aren't too sad at leaving New Zealand', Hilda had added at the end of a long letter to Angus, full of London news. We were no longer 'chicks' and we *were* sad. But we were curious and excited too about what England would mean to us. We faced the future with a reasonable stoicism. There were inevitably some storms ahead but, nourished by all those hundreds of letters, there remained a strong family bond, which would always endure.

Dorothy wrote some months after we left:

When we go walking and climbing round here, which we do a great deal in the summer, I always wear an old Marsden panama hat of Ann's. Today we climbed Mt. Roberts. Coming back we got blackberries in Ann's hat, now slightly dotted with purple stains. It's a comfy hat and keeps the sun out of my eyes and it is greatly cherished.

So there I was by then in London and my hat was in New Zealand. It would not be until 1973, twenty-eight years later, that I would again travel the 12,000 miles, going to stay on David's farm in Taranaki. That time it was by air with my mother, after my father's death, and with my own younger children. Alice was eight, the age I had been when I arrived in New Zealand in 1940, and Lucy was twelve, the age I had been when I left. They reminded me just what it was like to see New Zealand with a child's eyes.

We had reached Liverpool on Thursday, 5 July 1945. It was the day of the General Election. Angus had written to Hilda: 'Vote Labour for me.' An overwhelming majority had done the same. It was a signal of hope for a new and fairer society.

The port was ugly in the sunshine, horribly damaged. Our taxi driver did not spare us as he drove us from the docks to the railway station. 'That was a big one,' he said, over and over again, gesturing to a bomb site, already bright with willow-herb and white convolvulus anxious to cover up the wounds. 'Sixty people killed just there.' The city had suffered, but it was England, the other side of the world. We were back in the place we had left five long years before.

We were both changed forever by those years we had spent away from the country of our birth. We had crossed the seas just as our great-grandparents had done nearly a century earlier. It seems appropriate that eventually I made my home in England and David chose to make his in New Zealand, on the opposite sides of the world.

David carries two passports. I have only a European Union one, which annoys me when I have to queue with the foreigners coming into Auckland airport. How many people in the other queue have four grandparents, all born in New Zealand?

Twelve thousand miles apart, David and I are, of course, able to communicate instantly with each other, whenever we want to, in ways unimaginable to our ancestors, who set out on those long journeys under sail, taking three or four uncomfortable months on their way to an unknown country, leaving everything they knew behind.

I think of my great-grandfathers, the cabinet-maker, the carriage painter, the sailor and the railway guard, and my great-grandmothers, their enterprising wives. Like so many others, they were emigrants who made brave and difficult decisions, confident they would have better lives in New Zealand. They changed their own lives around, so that our lives too have been completely different from what they might otherwise have been.

I feel fortunate to have roots on both sides of this amazing world.

Afternote

It has been suggested that some people will want to know what happened next and, as I have no intention of writing another book, perhaps I should at least tell you that I now feel it was New Zealand – and in particular the three years without our parents – that transformed us from being difficult children into adolescents (I was nearly thirteen; David was fourteen), who had a chance of good lives.

When we grew up, David and I both did what we wanted to do – David as a farmer, myself as a writer. We both made good marriages and produced good children and grandchildren. Hilda, many years after the events in this book, became a devoted grandmother to her seven grandchildren – three in New Zealand and four in England. She lived until she was ninety. Angus, sadly, who would have been a marvellous grandfather, had little chance to enjoy that role. He suffered a devastating stroke on his way to New Zealand at the end of 1960, was in hospital for two and a half years, and died aged only sixty-three, two weeks after being finally taken home to London.

Looking back over what I have written, I must now admit that, while I have tried to be as objective as I am when writing biography, I realise that I have left out some things I find distasteful. My brother asked for only two cuts – both about uncles as it happens – but I see that I have spared our parents more than I intended, having omitted any reference to fur coats or cigarettes. Hilda loved furs and Angus's wedding present to her was a fur coat; later she had one of those fox furs that dangled round women's necks in the 1930s. Angus was almost a chain-smoker at one period until he gave up on the *Empire Grace* in 1945, vowing to devote the money he would save to our stamp collection. These fashions and addictions were commonplace at the time, but I think that the fact that I have unwittingly not mentioned them has some significance.

Mine was not a particularly remarkable family. Yours is very likely to be just as interesting. If you have found yourself thinking that as you read this book, sit down and start writing your own story. It may not be as easy as you think, but it's worth doing. As I said in the Introduction, I will always be interested to hear from readers whose own family histories have something to do with mine.

Notes

INTRODUCTION

p. 11   *women's writing*: Alison Drummond, *Married and Gone to New Zealand. Being Extracts from the Writings of Women Pioneers* (Hamilton: Paul's Book Arcade, 1960), p. 19.

CHAPTER 1: MAINLY ABOUT THE CAMPBELLS AND THE BROWNS

p. 15   *the road at Barrytown*: Arthur Harrop was certainly there but not perhaps the man trudging.

p. 16   *May Celia*: May Celia Harrop (later Cuthbert) at some point – in the 1930s, I think, on moving to Australia – discarded her first name and became my Auntie Celia. I decided she must have only one name in this book.

p. 17   *secure places ... to live*: Michael King, *The Penguin History of New Zealand* (Auckland: Penguin, 2003), p. 10.

p. 17   *melodious wild musick*: Quoted in *Ibid.*, p. 15.

p. 18   *the Far North*: James Belich, *Making Peoples: A History of the New Zealanders, from Polynesian Settlement to the End of the Nineteenth Century* (Auckland: Penguin, 1996), p. 48; *human occupation ... limited*: King, *The Penguin History of New Zealand*, p. 18.

p. 18   *last of such lands*: William Pember Reeves, *The Long White Cloud*, revised by A.J. Harrop (London: Allen & Unwin, 1950), p. 25.

p. 18   *migrations of people*: Te Rangi Hiroa (Dr Peter H. Buck), quoted in A.J. Harrop, *Touring in New Zealand* (London: Allen & Unwin, 1935), p. 17.

p. 18   *the great New Zealand myth*: King, *The Penguin History of New Zealand*, pp. 38–47.

p. 19   *Kotahitanga ... so much about*: *Ibid.*, p. 44.

p. 19   *Kupe's deeds ... foundations*: *Ibid.*, p. 45.

p. 19   *Sutherland ... to Greymouth*: 'The Sutherland Clearances began in 1807 .... In 1809 several hundred were evicted from the parishes of Dornoch, Rogart, Clyne and Golspie, driven in the most merciless and cruel manner from the homes of their fathers.' Some 'were driven by various means to leave the country altogether.' Alexander McKenzie, *The Highland Clearances* (Lanark: Geddes & Grosset Ltd, 2001), pp. 9–11.

p. 21   *those who feared to fall*: Belich, *Making Peoples*, p. 307.

p. 22   *nearly all literate*: Records show that nearly seven out of ten of the emigrants to New Zealand in 1861 could both read and write.

p. 25   *Perth-based ... Oceana Gold*: Part of the Macraes group, Oceana Gold started work in 2004 on the Black Water gold mine shaft and in 2007 they announced their Globe Progress opencut mine, both in Reefton.

p. 27   *Robert Paulin ... the malt*: Robert Paulin, *The Wild West Coast of New Zealand: A Summer Cruise in the 'Rosa'* (London: Thorburn and Co., 1889), p. 6.

p. 28   *There was no royal road to wealth*: A.J. Harrop, *The Romance of Westland: The Story of New Zealand's Golden Coast* (Auckland: Whitcomb and Tombs, 1923), pp. 49–50. Some of my material comes from A.J.H.'s M.A. thesis and is not in the published book.

p. 30   *about £1000 in Bank Notes*: There is a copy of this poster on display at Shantytown, an attraction ten kilometres south of Greymouth, which gives visitors an idea of life in gold rush days.

p. 31   *a pupil teacher*: Pupil teachers had to undergo four years of training for minimal wages. They were taught daily (in theory) outside school hours by the headmaster and were examined each year, with a trained teachers' certificate at the end.

Chapter 2: Mainly about the Harrops

p. 37   *anxiety and partial starvation*: Alfred Russel Wallace, *The Wonderful Century* (New York: Dodd, Mead and Company, 1899), p. 346.

p. 38   *out of work ... their heads*: Henry Mayhew, *London Labour and the London Poor*, Vol. 3 (London: Griffin, Bohn and Co., 1851), pp. 231–41.

p. 40   *Britain of the South*: Charles Hursthouse, *New Zealand or Zealandia, the Britain of the South* (London: Edward Stanford, 1857), pp. 62–75.

p. 41   *diaries ... from fellow passengers*: The originals of the Price and Carr diaries can be found in the Canterbury Museum Library. The diaries of David Carr, Arthur Price and Henry Shepherd ('the dullest'), alongside other information about the *Lancashire Witch*, can be found on-line at: http://www.rootsweb. ancestry.com/~nzlscant/lancashire_witch.htm

p. 41   *Richard Pelvin*: Richard Pelvin's observations, dated 30 October 1899, can be found at: http://www.rootsweb.ancestry.com/~nzlscant/lancashire_witch. htm#pelvin

p. 43   *bell tolled ...*: David Carr, Diary, 19–20 July 1863.

p. 45   *genteel ... vote with their feet*: Belich, *Making Peoples*, p. 339.

p. 45   *Mary Anne ... so very happy*: Lady Barker, *Station Life in New Zealand* (1870), Letter XXV – 'How we lost our horses and had to walk home', *New Zealand Electronic Text Centre*, http://www.nzetc.org/tm/scholarly/tei-BarLife-BarLife-c25.html

p. 46   *Emigration Map*: The 'Emigration Map' can be found on the endpapers of the hardback edition of Rose Tremain's novel *The Colour* (London: Chatto & Windus, 2003).

p. 48   *few women to go around*: Belich, *Making Peoples,* pp. 334–5.

p. 49   *leader of gang's confession*: See Carl Pfaff, *The Diggers' Story, or Tales and Reminiscences of the Golden Coast, from Westland's Earliest Pioneers* (Wellington: West Coasters Association, 1914).

p. 50   *Wakefield … great coloniser*: Belich, *Making Peoples,* p. 122.

p. 50   *absolutely no servility*: Wakefield to R.S. Rintoul (editor of *The Spectator*) 17 April 1853, quoted in A.J. Harrop, *The Amazing Career of Edward Gibbon Wakefield* (London, Allen & Unwin, 1928), p. 175.

p. 50   *Priscilla Wakefield's diary*: Ibid., p. 16.

p. 51   *I think … quietly buried there*: Charlie Douglas, quoted in A.P. Harper's introduction to Graham Langton's edition of *Mr Explorer Douglas* by John Pascoe (Christchurch: Canterbury University Press, 2000), pp. 15–6.

p. 54   *the great colonial game*: Belich, *Making Peoples,* p. 376.

p. 54   *marginally genteel … Surveying*: Ibid. Belich makes much of the words 'genteel' and 'gentility' and of the differences between gentility, respectability and the New Zealand élite. I find it difficult to fit my family into his categories, but my parents, by going to university, obviously did join some sort of élite.

p. 55   *Seddon … romantic New Zealand*: Pember Reeves, *The Long White Cloud*, pp. 295–306.

p. 55   *systematic survey of … South Westland*: Angus J. Harrop, *New Zealand After Five Wars* (London: Jarrolds, 1947), p. 65.

p. 55   *this remarkable man*: Ibid.

p. 56   *bach at the back of the office*: Pascoe and Langton, *Mr Explorer Douglas*, p. 76.

p. 58   *All the trig … landmark*: Nola Easdale, *Kairuri: The Measurer of Land* (Wellington: Highgate/Price Milburn, 1988), pp. 25–6.

p. 59   *surveyor … work is never done*: Quoted in Ibid., p. 38.

p. 60   *eight-hour day … earliest times*: Labour Day commemorates the introduction of the eight-hour day in 1899.

p. 60   *Surveyor's wives … home*: Quoted in Easdale, *Kairuri*, p. 153.

CHAPTER 3: DESPAIR AND HOPE IN HOKITIKA AND WAITAKI

p. 61   *We … no possible pretentions*: Hursthouse, *The Britain of the South*, pp. 201–2.

p. 62   *the fatal syncope*: *The West Coast Times* (15 January 1907) reported that Bertha's death 'caused a painful sensation in the town. Her sudden end was quite unexpected ….' Dr Teichelmann left the next morning for his annual holiday.

p. 63   *Tennyson's younger brother, Edward*: See Ann Thwaite, *Emily Tennyson: The Poet's Wife* (London: Faber, 1996), p. 87.

p. 64   *got as much pleasure as*: A.J. Harrop, *My New Zealand* (London: Jarrolds, 1939), p. 163.

p. 65   *The poem that struck Cynthia*: Philip Larkin, 'This Be the Verse', *Collected Poems*, ed. Anthony Thwaite (London: Faber, 1988), p. 180.

p. 66 *I went camping*: Harrop, *My New Zealand*, p. 171; Harrop, *New Zealand After Five Wars*, p. 66.

p. 67 *inscription on the back*: I thought this (written by A.N.H. on the back of the photo) an odd name, then I realised 'Bang' must be a nickname. The same young man appears in a photo facing p. 129 of *The Romance of Westland* and is identified as A. Hugo, son of Bertha's sister Bessie.

p. 68 *A New Zealander on London Bridge*: Thomas Macaulay (1800–59), in his essay on von Ranke's *History of the Popes*, imagined a New Zealander in the distant future visiting a London in ruins.

p. 69 *the 'spastic' brother*: When, after my father's death, I first heard of Frederick, I asked my mother when he had died. She said, 'Oh, many, many years ago'. David's recent researches showed it was not until 1951, only twelve years before Angus himself.

p. 71 *Treaty of Waitangi … problematic*: King, *The Penguin History of New Zealand*, p. 157.

p. 71 *secondary school … 1917*: Belich, *Paradise Reforged: A History of the New Zealanders from the 1880s to the Year 2000* (Auckland: Penguin, 2001), p. 130.

p. 73 *our modern system*: Truby King, *The Evils of Cram – Reports of a Series of Addresses Bearing on the Need for Reform in Education* (Dunedin: Evening Star, 1906).

p. 76 *Arnoldian principals … 'the Man'*: Belich, *Paradise Reforged*, p. 130.

p. 77 *British Empire … supreme political creation*: See Ian Milner, 'The Imperial Theme', *Milner of Waitaki: Portait of the Man* (Dunedin: Waitaki High School Old Boys' Association/McIndoe, 1983), pp. 133–45. Ian Milner was certainly rebellious but not, I think, 'The Rhodes Scholar Spy' as Richard Hall called him in a book published in Australia in 1991. Milner always denied he was a 'spy' and Hall agreed he was a 'rigidly honourable man', though 'such men can be dangerous'. A.J.H. saw him in Canberra in 1945 and we got to know him in the 1970s.

p. 77 *inner sturdy fibre of … democratic feeling*: Ibid., p. 143.

p. 78 *Waitaki … remarkable boys*: In the official history of the school by A.R. Tyrrell, *Strong to Endure* (1983), a photo of A.J.H. is flanked by photos of Baume and Lochore.

p. 80 *free education*: Primary Education was free from 1877, but Secondary not until the 1935 Labour Government.

p. 80 *war-time certificates*: In *Strong to Endure*, Tyrrell says that during the war 'the boys agreed to forgo all prizes, scholastic and athletic, in order to devote to the war funds money usually spent on their purchase.' In addition the boarders 'gave up half their pocket money'.
       one of his staff: Ian Milner, *Milner of Waitaki*, p. 58. The master was Stewart M. Kinross.

p. 81 *redeemed … from barbarism*: Milner, *Milner of Waitaki*, p. 56.

p. 82 *girls embraced 'evil cram'*: Belich, *Paradise Reforged*, p. 187.

p. 82 *Dickens or Thackeray?*: In her old age, asked by her granddaughter Emily for her favourite writer, Hilda named George Eliot.

p. 85   *Gammack scholarship*: If this had not been offered ('a bird in the hand' her father said), Hilda had intended to go to Otago like her father, not C.U.C. If she had, I'm sure David and I would not exist.

p. 87   *Mr Harrop suddenly collapsed*: Milner, the other father-figure in A.J.H.'s life, died in a similar way, collapsing in public, but not until 1944.

CHAPTER 4: HOGGS, OLIVERS AND JEFCOATES

p. 89   *great works of European Romanticism*: Karl Miller, *Electric Shepherd: A Likeness of James Hogg* (London: Faber, 2003), cover.

p. 93   *Uncle William's fortune*: Another copied letter exists (24 August 1890) setting out the claim of Isabella Dalgliesh of Langholm to a lawyer in Sydney, stating her mother, Jane Oliver, was 'a full cousin' of William Oliver. My great-grandmother was William's niece.

p. 93   *Hoggs ... gone to North America*: A letter survives in Canada written by Janet Jefcoate on 15 January 1895 from Oteramika: 'When we were Home on a visit about 4 years ago, we thought about coming back through America. If we had, we'd have seen you all.'

p. 94   *railway mania*: See Michael Freeman, *Railways and the Victorian Imagination* (New Haven and London: Yale University Press, 1999), *passim*.

p. 96   *The first shock ... improvement*: Charles Dickens, *Dombey and Sons*, ed. Alan Horsman (Oxford: Oxford University Press, 1982), pp. 52–3.

p. 101   *little demand for goods guards*: In New Zealand in 1870 there were only 46 miles of public railways. Christchurch and Dunedin were linked in 1879.

p. 104   *Bricks Wharf ... smaller boat*: It seems incredible that Christchurch could be reached by boat from Lyttelton, but a memorial at Bricks Wharf confirms this was so.

p. 104   *'sod hut' at Spreydon ... no sewers*: See Gloria Heazlewood, *The Journey: 125 Years of Spreydon Baptist Church* (Christchurch: Outreach Press, 1991).

p. 105   *Grandfather ... enthusiastic organiser*: Constance Whyte, daughter of James Jefcoate, Thomas's youngest son, writing to Helen Davidson for her unpublished manuscript 'Discovering the Jefcoates' (1996).

p. 109   *A local history*: John Button, *South of the Burn: The Southburn Story* (Timaru: The Southburn Historical Publication Committee, 1992).

p. 110   *James Jefcoate ... raw deal*: Davidson, 'Discovering the Jefcoates'.

p. 110   *year of his wife's death*: Thomas Jefcoate was buried with his wife, Janet. There was a second marriage to Sarah Ellen Owen, aged thirty-eight, in 1902, which ended in a separation. In 1911 Sarah Jefcoate was in St Clair, Dunedin, and Thomas, two years before his death, in Christchurch.

CHAPTER 5: MAINLY ABOUT THE VALENTINES AND THE MAXWELLS

p. 116   *Thom ... decided to go to sea*: The next generation of Thoms also went to Waikouaiti.

p. 116   *The Jura diary*: The diary is held in the Hocken Library, University of Otago, Dunedin.

p. 117   *his wife, Ellen*: Sometimes known as 'Helen', but 'Ellen' is on her gravestone.

p. 117   *Don't make enquiries … Firth*: Jim Valentine recorded this remark in a letter to his granddaughter, then Ruth Watkins, 29 July 1942.

p. 117   *Parkhead estate*: The estate's name survives only in an Alloa street name.

p. 118   *Alva Hill*: Alva, after which the Maxwell farm my brother inherited was named, is just north of Alloa.

p. 119   *CORSO*: Council for Relief Services Overseas, established in 1944.

p. 120   *driving the Pakeha … sea*: J.C. Firth, *Nation-Making, a Story of New Zealand: Savagism v. Civilisation* (London and New York: Longmans, Green and Co., 1890), p. 93.

p. 121   *In this book … remarkable fact*: A.J. Harrop, *England and the Maori Wars* (London: The New Zealand News, 1937).

p. 122   *prophet-generals*: Belich, *Making Peoples*, p. 220.

p. 122   *Some women … gleefully and with ease*: G.W. Rusden, *History of New Zealand* (London: Chapman and Hall, 1883). The words come from p. 6 of Bryce v Rusden, First Day, Royal Courts of Justice, 4 March 1886 (transcript of short-hand notes).

p. 122   *a school textbook*: *The Land of New Zealand* (1964).

p. 123   *James Livingston … Maxwell's death*: 2 January 1869, from a Livingston diary, a copy of which is in the possession of David Harrop.

p. 123   *The local paper*: Probably the *Wanganui Chronicle*. Copies of cuttings in my brother's possession have no attribution. They came from Wanganui Museum.

p. 124   *named Maxwelltown … in memory of*: E. Feist and H.F. Richardson, *Bush, People and Pasture: The Story of the Waitotara County* (Waitotara: Waitotara County Centennial Committee, 1983), p. 7.

p. 124   *no Maori troubles to speak of*: Pember Reeves, *The Long White Cloud*, p. 177.

p. 124   *Mrs Joanna Cunningham*: Joanna Cunningham's daughter Jean was at Canterbury with my mother and eventually became my godmother.

p. 125   *A wholly unsuccessful miner*: Belich, *Making Peoples*, p. 346.

p. 128   *John Valentine*: My mother once received a letter from a granddaughter (by John Valentine's second marriage) who described him as 'a rotter of the first order'.

p.130   *small oval discs, lead*: We saw similar ones in the museum at Fort William in Scotland. They were said to be given to parishioners as a voucher of fitness to be admitted to communion, and were used in many denominations from the sixteenth century.

p. 132   *Flo was recruited*: Flo Valentine's career is recorded in the R.S.A. *Review*, April 1965.

p. 133   *Win … first memory of her father*: W.A. Valentine, 'The Valentine Saga' (1968).

CHAPTER 6: THE HEADMASTER'S DAUGHTER

p. 142   *holding their certificates*: The Proficiency certificates are too small to be the ones in the photograph. They could have been for music.

p. 146   *the river cold and 'milky'*: The milkiness actually comes from finely ground rock washed down from the glaciers.

p. 147   *Helen Stewart*: my Grandmother's close friend was the great-aunt of our friend Jon Stallworthy, poet and biographer.

p. 149   *eighty-eight per cent casualty rate*: King, *The Penguin History of New Zealand*, p. 299.

p. 153   *women friends*: they included Jean Cunningham Struthers, Muriel Innes Bradshaw, Isobel Aitken McCaskill, Hetty Porter Wild and Marion Haskell Dorrington.

p. 156   *Is not the world's creed ... noticeable*: Hilda was eighteen at the time of writing. This excerpt from her diary is dated 29 January 1919.

p. 158   *with Mr Luke ... dozen others*: Otago and Auckland students met at inter-varsity tournaments. I think Mr Luke may have become the doctor father of Pattie and Raema Luke, at Marsden with me.

p. 159   *Frederick's maintenance*: Arthur Harrop left £1033 in his will, the equivalent of perhaps NZ$80,000 in today's money. Of this, two-thirds was held 'in trust' for Frederick.

p. 160   *Janet Frame*: the writer described her experiences at Seacliff in both fiction, *Faces in the Water*, and in her autobiographical volume, *An Angel at my Table*. The quotations come from a letter from Janet Frame to John Money, 21 January 1948, in Michael King, *Wrestling With the Angel: A Life of Janet Frame* (Auckland and London: Viking, 2000), p. 76.

p. 161   *Bruno Bettelheim*: Bruno Bettelheim, *Freud and Man's Soul* (New York: Knopf, 1983), p. 166.

CHAPTER 7: CHOOSING PARTNERS

p. 165   *Eva Rowe ... Muriel Innes*: All six became teachers. Five eventually married – Muriel Innes to the Professor of Music at C.U.C., becoming, after his death, a notable benefactor of the university. My mother saw this photo hanging in Connon Hall when she visited in 1957.

p. 170   *As Leicester Webb wrote*: New Zealand *Listener*, 5 March 1948.

p. 170   *History papers ... what he chose to write about*: There were twelve questions. A.J.H. answered these six.

p. 172   *George Lockwood*: Hilda actually calls him 'Trevor'.

p. 174   *Savage... most loved Prime Minister*: Belich, *Paradise Reforged*, pp. 259–60.

p. 174   *new Diploma in Journalism*: The course had originally been introduced by Hight in 1909, but lapsed due to a lack of applicants.

p. 176   *eight students ... first class honours*: Five of those eight recipients of first class honours were women.

p. 178   *society ... danger of decline and collapse*: Belich, *Paradise Reforged*, p. 113.

p. 178   *trouble in Paradise*: Belich, *ibid.*, p. 87.

p. 179   *A.G.A. Harmsworth*: Richard Bourne in *Lords of Fleet Street: The Harmsworth Dynasty* (London: Unwin Hyman, 1990) says Geoffrey Harmsworth was homosexual, eccentric and amusing. As a boy he was apparently beaten by his father if he were found with a paintbrush in his hand. Bourne tells of him ordering a live lobster in a Torquay hotel and asking the waiter to go with him to return the lobster (on a silver salver) to the sea. I have a photo of him with A.J.H. on a tennis court. In later life he was co-author with Reginald Pound of the huge biography of his uncle, *Northcliffe* (London: Cassell, 1959).

p. 179   *return ticket to England*: The return ticket was from the Government, the money from C.U.C. (Hight's idea, A.J.H. thought).

p. 180   *her 'good grounding in French'*: Mary Brodie, writing in the New Plymouth Girls High School centennial book.

p. 181   *great South Island floods*: A.J. Harrop, unpublished unfinished autobiography.

p. 181   *long-awaited Otira tunnel*: A.J.H. was able to go on a week's holiday on the West Coast, saying goodbye. He turned down the offer from the *Press* of a senior reporter job at £350 per year.

p. 183   *What … only New Zealand know*: Michael King in *Wrestling with the Angel* says this was a favourite phrase of Frank Sargeson's years later (p. 131).

p. 183   *D.H. Black*: D.H. Black was C.U.C.'s Rhodes candidate but did not get that scholarship.

p. 187   *tentatively selected Thomas Hobbes*: One of the questions on A.J.H.'s History paper had been 'Compare the ideas on religious liberty of Hobbes, Rousseau and J.S. Mill.'

p. 187   *Battle of Jutland*: The Battle of Jutland was disastrous, with huge losses on both sides. Seven British ships were sunk with the loss of 2545 lives.

p. 190   *hospitality for overseas students*: His hosts asked A.J.H. back the following year for ten days, a tribute I feel to his being a perfect guest.

p. 191   *Noeline Bruce*: Hight mentions Noeline Bruce in New York in 1927. She had married Allan Peebles, Lecturer in Economics at Columbia.

p. 192   *Married Love*: Hilda's copy of Dr Marie Stopes' *Married Love* is a 1921 edition (161st thousand). For New Zealand attitudes to sex at the time, see King, *Penguin History of New Zealand*, p. 375–6 and Belich, *Paradise Reforged*, p. 178.

CHAPTER 8: REMEMBERING, NOT FORGETTING, NEW ZEALAND

p. 201   *leading cultural historian*: King, *The Penguin History of New Zealand*, p. 361; *brilliant critic*: Belich, *Paradise Reforged*, p. 337.

p. 201   *A post-graduate scholar … college*: E.H. McCormick, *An Absurd Ambition: Autobiographical Writings* (Auckland: Auckland University Press, 1996), p. 108.

p. 201   *G.H. Scholefield's review*: New Zealand *Listener* 5 March 1947.

p. 202   *old Pakeha myth, deified ancestor*: Belich, *Making Peoples*, pp. 122, 279.

p. 202 *Wakefield … on the side of the poor*: A.J. Harrop, *The Amazing Career of Edward Gibbon Wakefield* (London: George Allen & Unwin, 1928), p. 195.

p. 203 *Wakefield's very elderly nieces … private letters*: Ibid., Preface, p. 6.

p. 203 *I was … disappointed life: Ibid*, Alice Freeman, quoted on p. 187.

p. 205 *how he would … a post at Canterbury College*: J. Hight, letter to A.J.H., 7 November 1927. Hight was aware that A.J.H. was likely to want to 'stick to journalism, having already gone so far'.

p. 206 *women's domestic reputations*: King, *The Penguin History of New Zealand*, p. 375.

p. 208 *Frank Milner … temporary pacificism*: Milner, *Milner of Waitaki*, p. 156.

p. 208 *Baron Hayashi interview: Daily Mail*, 4 August 1925.

p. 209 *Philistine community, backward peoples*: Belich, *Paradise Reforged*, pp. 337, 335.

p. 209 *possible to telephone New Zealand*: In 1931 a short call cost £6.15s, more than many people earned in a week. Even so, 312 calls were made in the first year.

p. 209 *letters coming by ship*: From 1931 trans-Tasman mail steamers connected with flights from Australia to England. New Zealand was not regularly linked by air with Australia or San Francisco until 1940.

p. 209 *Girls didn't work in those days*: Hilda's remark that 'Girls didn't work in those days' is very middle-class. Many married women always had to work, as domestic servants, in the mills and so on. Twenty-nine thousand women worked in the Staffordshire potteries in 1911. It was the same in New Zealand. Farmers' wives were normally part of a team.

p. 212 *Cresswell and Mackay*: King, *The Penguin History of New Zealand*, pp. 376–7. For a rather different version, see *Dear Lady Ginger: An Exchange of Letters between Lady Ottoline Morrell and D'Arcy Cresswell*, ed. Helen Shaw (Auckland and Oxford: Oxford University Press, 1983). Cresswell, rather surprisingly, was totally exonerated.

p. 214 *looking forward to a daughter*: In those days before one could know the sex of a child before birth, Hilda continued to expect 'Ann Barbara' in 1929. Marie Stewart, who had been asked to be my godmother, used my name two weeks before my eventual birth. 'I'm wondering whether this letter will discover her arrived?' 18 September 1932. Both my godmothers were rather remarkable women with impressive careers. Marie Stewart was a poultry farmer and prolific writer on her subject, for fifty years a regular columnist in the *New Zealand Farmer*. Jean Struthers, who died only in 2002 at the age of 102, was a science teacher who took her M.A. from Canterbury with first class honours.

p. 217 *quinine … possible toxic effects*: It is interesting to compare the 1929 situation with that in 1851 when the Tennysons' first son was born dead. See my *Emily Tennyson*, pp. 226–7. My doctor, Stephen Bamber, lent me his *Clinical Pharmacology* (D.R. Laurence et al.), which says 'quinine is now widely known to the general public as an abortifacient.'

p. 218   *small office … McCormick remembered*: McCormick, *An Absurd Ambition*, p. 108.

p. 218   *Rutherford … quickest readers*: A.J. Harrop, 'Calling New Zealand', 1944 BBC broadcast.

p. 219   *Shaw Savill luxury liner … transformation*: *Otago Daily Times* 22 February 1933.

p. 220   *fine publicity*: *Dominion*, 27 July 1934.

p. 224   *Hanmer Springs … finest hotels*: A.J. Harrop, *Touring in New Zealand*, p. 41

p. 224   *It is possible … attempt*: Ibid., p. 40.

p. 224   *state of crisis … declining birthrate*: In 2001, it was calculated at 14 per 1000, compared with 44 in 1868.

CHAPTER 9: A STRENUOUS PAIR

p. 228   *dear octopus … escape*: Dodie Smith, *Dear Octopus* (London: Samuel French, 1939), Act 3, Scene 2, p. 89.

p. 229   *infantile anecdotage*: Virginia Woolf, letter to Ethel Smyth, 11 December 1932. In *The Letters of Virginia Woolf*, ed. Nigel Nicolson (London: Hogarth Press, 1979), p. 135.

p. 231   *The Little One's Log Book*: Eva Erleigh, *The Little One's Log Book: Baby's Record*, illus. E.H. Shepard (London: Library Press, 1930).

p. 234   *A.A. Milne poem*: A.A. Milne, *Now We Are Six* (London: Methuen, 1927), p. 68.

p. 234   *a forgotten boredom*: Philip Larkin, 'Coming', *Collected Poems* (London: Faber, 1988), p. 33.

p. 234   *Stories from the Odyssey*: Jeanie Lang, *Stories from the Odyssey: Told to the Children* (New York: Dutton, n.d.).

p. 235   *As Milne put it … clever*: Ann Thwaite, *A.A. Milne: His Life* (London: Faber, 1990), p. 1.

p. 236   *Frederick Ost … illustrations*: Frederick Ost's illustrations were drawn 'as a return for favours rendered'. A.J.H. had helped to get him and his cellist wife to New Zealand.

p. 236   *Milne's poem 'Rice Pudding'*: A.A. Milne, *When We Were Very Young* (London: Methuen, 1924), p. 48.

p. 239   *John Bowlby … maternal presence*: John Bowlby, *Maternal Care and Mental Health* (Geneva: World Health Organisation, 1952).

p. 240   *increase in his salary*: This was at a time when a British M.P. earned £600 per year, so £400 was excellent for a part-time job.

p. 242   *international language of liberal Jewry*: R.A. Lochore, *From Europe to New Zealand* (Wellington: Reed, in conjunction with the New Zealand Institute of International Affairs, 1951), p. 75.

p. 244   *tribute to my mother*: Harrop, Acknowledgements, *England and the Maori Wars*, p. 7.

p. 247   *We are still … Devonshire*: Harrop, *My New Zealand*, p. 318.

p. 247   *We have set … society*: Ibid., pp. 315–6.

p. 247   *We need more … Nazi machine*: Ibid., pp. 315–8, 318.

p. 248   *New Zealand friends*: The Roberts family. One of the sons became Sir Geoffrey Roberts, general manager of Air New Zealand.

p. 253   *best in his class*: Hilda recorded that, at seven, David was reading the Bible to himself, 'very carefully'.

p. 256   *training with the Red Cross*: A certificate survives, signed by Lord Jellicoe, showing she had qualified to render 'First Aid to the Injured' with the St John Ambulance Association in November 1921.

CHAPTER 10: OUT OF HARM'S WAY

p. 263   *Children exist in a continuous present*: Penelope Lively, *A House Unlocked* (London: Viking, 2001), p. 38.

p. 272   *Marie Plowman's brother*: Claud Plowman's radio factory, Airzone, became a munitions factory during the war and he was knighted for services to the war effort, according to his niece, my cousin Judith.

p. 273   *taken prisoner … Emirau*: See Jessica Mann, *Out of Harm's Way: The Wartime Evacuation of Children from Britain* (London: Headline, 2005), p. 183.

p. 280   *Reuel Lochore*: At Waitaki, Reuel Lochore had been dux two years after A.J.H.

p. 286   '*at the Bay*': 'At the Bay' is the title of one of Katherine Mansfield's best stories.

CHAPTER 11: THE LAST LAP

p. 290   *Holly's too early death*: Barbara Yaldwyn died in 2003.

p. 291   *hymn that became a favourite*: 'Dear Lord and Father of Mankind'.

p. 291   *Barbara Whitman*: Barbara Whitman became Barbara van den Broek, a distinguished landscape architect and town planner in Australia. She died in 2001.

p. 294   *ferry across the harbour*: The Wellington Harbour ferry at this time recorded its highest revenue in a twenty-year period.

p. 296   *Weldon … had not heard of lesbianism*: Fay Weldon, *Auto da Fay* (London: Harper Collins, 2002), p. 119.

p. 296   *Fysh … QANTAS*: Winty's father-in-law was to be Sir Hudson Fysh, founder of the Australian airline, which her husband John would work for.

p. 301   *Eric Baume*: Eric Baume, whatever his faults, remained devoted to A.J.H.. In 1961 Baume wrote of his 'life-long school mate – a man of highest honour, outstanding character, a great Christian, a devoted husband and father … a type far too rare in these days.' A.J.H. visited Baume's family in Australia in 1945 and, to Baume himself, reported on the slanders and 'iniquities' about him that he heard.

p. 301   *New Zealand Truth*: See Belich, *Paradise Reforged*, pp. 179–80.

p. 302   *both men … socialists*: When Milner was persuaded to stand for the National Party, A.J.H. wrote 'that suggests they have more sense than I credited them with'.

p. 304   *Without children themselves*: After we left, the Lochores adopted a son, Mark.

p. 304   *the Alleys*: It has been pointed out that five Alleys of Geoff's generation at one time appeared together in *Who's Who in New Zealand*. My parents had known Gwen in Christchurch.

p. 305   *strange story of Reuel Anson Lochore*: in Michael King, *Tread Softly for You Tread on My Life: New and Collected Writings* (Auckland: Cape Catley Ltd., 2001), pp. 64–86.

p. 305   *posthumous slurs*: R.A. Lochore comes out badly in Belich, *Paradise Reforged*, pp. 225–6, 230. Certainly some of his views (though 'entirely consistent with Cabinet policy') are 'politically incorrect' today and rather embarrassing.

p. 305   *hot clear days ... conversations, music*: King, *Tread Softly for you Tread on my Life*, p. 66.

p. 306   *a section at Porirua*: In April 1952 Dorothy wrote: 'No sign of our house. At least I nagged the book out of him.' Reuel's book, *From Europe to New Zealand*, was inscribed to me in 1951 as 'one of the anonymous research assistants mentioned on page 10'. It is much more sympathetic than Belich's comments would suggest. It ends with a plea to New Zealanders to welcome 'new people of all sorts' and draws attention to the fine record of Jews in the settlement of New Zealand.

p. 308   *'to lead the kind of intellectual and moral life they chose'*: Janet Frame to Frank Sargeson, quoted in King, *Tread Softly for You Tread on My Life*, p. 40. She was suggesting how different America was to New Zealand.

p. 309   *Ruth ... made up all the rules*: Ruth Watkins (later McDonald) kept these and gave me a copy for my sixtieth birthday. All four of us had a Harwat reunion in Norfolk in 1991.

p. 310   *airgraphs*: The service ran from January 1943 to July 1945 according to *The Post Office in New Zealand*.

p. 312   *piece for the ... Listener*: 'Round the World in Wartime', New Zealand *Listener*, 22 June 1945.

p. 313   *dramatic death of ... Frank Milner*: Frank Milner had assured A.J.H. that David would be well looked after, though he was himself retiring. He died making a farewell speech at the school on 2 December 1944.

p. 313   *clever ... to get Kip to write*: Kippenberger was not only the 'most popular of the senior New Zealand officers' but also a good writer. See King, *The Penguin History of New Zealand*, p. 400.

p. 317   *General Election*: The result of the General Election was not declared until 26 July.

Bibliography

Alpers, Anthony. *The Life of Katherine Mansfield*. London: Jonathan Cape, 1980.

Andersen, Johannes. *Jubilee History of South Canterbury*. Auckland: Whitcombe and Tombs, 1916.

Barker, Lady. *Station Life in New Zealand*. London: Macmillan and Co., 1870. Letter XXV – 'How we lost our horses and had to walk home', *New Zealand Electronic Text Centre*, http://www.nzetc.org/tm/scholarly/tei-BarLife-c25.html

Baume, Eric. *I Lived These Years*. London: Harrap, 1941.

Belich, James. *Making Peoples: A History of the New Zealanders from Polynesian Settlement to the End of the Nineteenth Century*. Penguin: Auckland, 1996.

— *Paradise Reforged: A History of the New Zealanders from the 1880s to the Year 2000*. Auckland: Penguin, 2001.

Bettelheim, Bruno. *Freud and Man's Soul*. New York: Knopf, 1983.

Bourne, Richard. *Lords of Fleet Street: The Harmsworth Dynasty*. London: Unwin Hyman, 1990.

Bowlby, John. *Maternal Care and Mental Health*. Geneva: World Health Organisation, 1952.

Bradshaw, Julia. *Gold Rush to Ross – A Short History*. Pamphlet. Ross: Ross Information Centre, 2002.

Button, John. *South of the Burn: The Southburn Story 1892–1992*. Timaru: Southburn Historical Publication Committee, 1992.

Carpenter, Kirsty. *Marsden Women and their World: A History of Marsden School*. Wellington: Samuel Marsden Collegiate School, 2003.

Carr, David. *Lancashire Witch* Diary. 1863. Original in Canterbury Museum Library. http://www.rootsweb.ancestry.com/~nzlscant/lancashire_witch.htm

Cowan, James. *Romance of the Rail: the North Island Main Trunk*. Wellington: New Zealand Railways, 1928.

Dickens, Charles. *Dombey and Son*. Ed. Alan Horsman. Oxford: Oxford University Press, 1982.

Drummond, Alison, ed. *Married and Gone to New Zealand: Extracts from the Writings of Women Pioneers*. Hamilton: Paul's Book Arcade, 1960.

Earp, G.B. *The Emigrant's Guide to New Zealand: Comprising Every Requisite Information for Intending Emigrants, Relative to the Southern Settlements of New Zealand*. London: W.S. Orr, 1848.

Easdale, Nola. *Kairuri: The Measurer of Land*. Wellington: Highgate/Price Milburn, 1988.

Erleigh, Eva. *The Little One's Log Book: Baby's Record*. Illus. E.H. Shepard. London: Library Press, 1930.

Feist, E., and H.F. Richardson. *Bush, People and Pasture: The Story of the Waitotara County*. Waitotara: Waitotara County Centennial Committee, 1983.

Firth, J.C. *Nation-Making, a Story of New Zealand: Savagism v. Civilisation*. London and New York: Longmans, Green and Co., 1890.

Frame, Janet. *An Angel at My Table: An Autobiography*. Vol. 2. London: The Women's Press, 1984.

Freeman, Michael. *Railways and the Victorian Imagination*. London and New Haven: Yale University Press, 1999.

Hall, Richard. *The Rhodes Scholar Spy*. Sydney: Random House, 1991.

Hannam, Mary, ed. *Timaru South School Centenary*. Timaru: Timaru South School, 1981.

Hardyment, Christina. *Dream Babies: Child Care from Locke to Spock*. London: Jonathan Cape, 1983.

Harmsworth, Geoffrey, and Reginald Pound. *Northcliffe*. London: Cassell, 1959.

Harrop, A.J. *The Romance of Westland: The Story of New Zealand's Golden Coast*. Auckland: Whitcomb and Tombs, 1923.

— *England and New Zealand: From Tasman to the Taranaki War*. London: Methuen, 1926.

— *The Amazing Career of Edward Gibbon Wakefield*. London: George Allen & Unwin, 1928.

— *Touring in New Zealand*. London: Allen & Unwin, 1935.

— *England and the Maori Wars*. London: The New Zealand News, 1937.

— *My New Zealand*. London: Jarrolds, 1939.

— *New Zealand after Five Wars*. London: Jarrolds, 1947.

— *Round the World with Willa Webfoot*. London: Watts, 1947.

Harrop, H.M., *The Young Traveller in New Zealand*. London: Phoenix House, 1949.

— *A Privileged Life: The Memoirs of Hilda Mary Harrop*. New Plymouth: David Harrop, 2007.

Heazlewood, Gloria. *The Journey: 125 Years of Spreydon Baptist Church*. Christchurch: Outreach Press, 1991.

Hight, James, ed. Vol. VII, part II: New Zealand. *The Cambridge History of the British Empire*. Gen. ed. J. Holland Rose, A.P. Newton, E.A. Benians. Cambridge: Cambridge University Press, 1933.

Hogg, James. *Tales*. With a Biographical Sketch of the Author by J.T.B. London/ Glasgow: Hamilton, Adams and Co./Thomas D. Morison, 1880.

Hursthouse, Charles. *New Zealand or Zealandia, the Britain of the South*. London: Edward Stanford, 1857.

King, Mary. *Truby King, the Man: A Biography*. London: George Allen & Unwin, 1948.

King, Michael. *Wrestling with the Angel: A Life of Janet Frame*. Viking: Auckland and London, 2000.

— *Tread Softly for You Tread on my Life: New and Collected Writings*. Auckland: Cape Catley, 2001.

— *The Penguin History of New Zealand*. Auckland: Penguin, 2003.

King, Truby. *The Evils of Cram – Reports of a Series of Addresses Bearing on the Need for Reform in Education*. Pamphlet. Dunedin: Evening Star, 1906.

Lang, Jeanie. *Stories from the Odyssey: Told to the Children*. New York: Dutton, n.d.

Larkin, Philip. *Collected Poems*. ed. Anthony Thwaite. London: Faber, 1988.

Lively, Penelope. *A House Unlocked*. London: Viking, 2001.

Lochore, R.A. *From Europe to New Zealand*. Wellington: Reed, in conjunction with the New Zealand Institute of International Affairs, 1951.

MacGibbon, John. *Going Abroad: The MacGibbon Family and Other Early Scottish Emigrants to Otago and Southland*. Wellington: Ngaio Press, 2002.

Mann, Jessica. *Out of Harm's Way: The Wartime Evacuation of Children from Britain*. London: Headline, 2005.

Mansfield, Katherine. *The Garden Party and Other Stories*. London: Constable, 1922.

May, Philip Ross. *Gold Town: Ross, Westland*. Christchurch: Pegasus, 1970.

Mayhew, Henry. *London Labour and the London Poor*. Vol. 3. London: Griffin, Bohn and Co., 1851.

McCormick, Eric. *An Absurd Ambition: Autobiographical Writings*. Auckland: Auckland University Press, 1996.

McKenzie, Alexander. *The Highland Clearances*. Lanark: Geddes & Grosset Ltd, 2001.

McNeish, James. *Dance of the Peacocks: New Zealanders in Exile*. Auckland: Vintage, 2003.

Miller, Karl. *The Electric Shepherd: A Likeness of James Hogg*. London: Faber, 2003.

Milne, A.A. *When We Were Very Young*. London: Methuen, 1924.

— *Now We Are Six*. London: Methuen, 1927.

Milner, Ian. *Milner of Waitaki: Portrait of the Man*. Dunedin: Waitaki High School Old Boys Association/McIndoe, 1983

Nicol, Jean. *Meet me at the Savoy*. London: Museum Press, 1952.

Pascoe, John, and Graham Langton. *Mr Explorer Douglas*. Christchurch: Canterbury University Press, 2000.

Paulin, Robert. *The Wild West Coast of New Zealand: A Summer Cruise in the 'Rosa'*. London: Thorburn and Co., 1889.

Pelvin, Richard. Account of a Voyage on the *Lancashire Witch* (1863). Autobiography. 30 October 1889. http://www.rootsweb.ancestry.com/~nzlscant/lancashire_witch.htm#pelvin

Pfaff, Carl. *The Diggers' Story, or, Tales and Reminiscences of the Golden Coast, from Westland's Earliest Pioneers*. Wellington: West Coasters' Association, 1914.

Price, Arthur. *Lancashire Witch* Diary. 1863. Original in Canterbury Museum Library. http://www.rootsweb.ancestry.com/~nzlscant/lancashire_witch.htm

Reeves, William Pember. *The Long White Cloud*. Revised with additional chapters by A.J. Harrop. London: Allen & Unwin, 1950.

Rusden, G.W. *History of New Zealand*. London: Chapman and Hall, 1883.

Shaw, Helen, ed. *Dear Lady Ginger: Letters between Lady Ottoline Morrell and D'Arcy Cresswell*. Auckland and Oxford: Oxford University Press, 1983.

Shepherd, Henry. *Lancashire Witch* Diary. 1863. Original in Canterbury Museum

Library. http://www.rootsweb.ancestry.com/~nzlscant/lancashire_witch.htm

Simpson, Tony. *The Immigrants: The Great Migration from Britain to New Zealand.* Auckland: Godwit, 1997.

Smith, Dodie. *Dear Octopus.* London: Samuel French, 1939.

Temple, Philip. *Coaching Yesterday.* Dunedin: John McIndoe, 1980.

Thwaite, Ann. *Edmund Gosse: A Literary Landscape.* London: Secker and Warburg, 1984.

— *A.A. Milne: His Life.* London: Faber, 1990.

— *Emily Tennyson: The Poet's Wife.* London: Faber, 1996.

— *Glimpses of the Wonderful: the life of Philip Henry Gosse.* London: Faber, 2002.

Tremain, Rose. *The Colour.* London: Chatto & Windus, 2003.

Turnbull, Michael and Ian A. McLaren. *The Land of New Zealand: Being a Companion Volume to The Changing Land: A Short History of New Zealand.* London: Longmans, Green, 1964.

Tyrrell, A.R. *Strong to Endure: Waitaki Boys High School.* Oamaru: Waitaki High School Old Boys Association, 1983.

Wallace, Alfred Russel. *The Wonderful Century.* New York: Dodd, Mead and Company, 1898.

Wilford, John Russell. *Southern Cross and Evening Star: Reflections and Recollections.* London: Martini Publications, 1949.

Wood, Sydney. *The Railway Revolution.* London: Macmillan Children's Books, 1981.

Woolf, Virginia. *The Letters of Virginia Woolf.* ed. Nigel Nicolson. 6 Vol. London: Hogarth Press, 1979.

Unpublished

Davidson, Helen. 'Discovering the Jefcoates'. 1996.

Valentine, J.A. 'Autobiographical Notes and Reminiscences'. 1947.

Valentine, W.A. 'The Valentine Saga'. 1968.

List of Illustrations

✿

page

15 The house in Fitzherbert Street, Hokitika, with my father, Angus Harrop, 1907

16 May Celia and Angus John, Hokitika, 1904

20 Ships lined up at Hokitika quay, c. 1870

20 Edmonston Castle, where Adam Brown, my great-great-grandfather, grew up

29 Cliff Street, Lyell, 19th century

31 Bertha Jane Campbell, later Harrop, my grandmother, Reefton, 1899

31 My father, Angus Harrop, Reefton, 1900

36 The Pool of London, 19th century

39 *The Emigrant's Guide to New Zealand*, 1848

42 Emigrants' quarters on board the *Aurora. Illustrated London News,* 13 April 1844

50 1884 copy of Arthur Harrop's certificate of baptism, 1869

52 Group photo of members of the Lands and Survey Department, Hokitika, 1895

53 Canterbury College examination fee receipt, 1892

56 Cover of one of Arthur Harrop's field books

57, 58 Pages from one of the field books, Taipo and Hohonu Rivers

59 Photographs of surveying gangs, c. 1908

66 Arthur Harrop and Angus Hugo, his nephew, 1906

67 Hokitika Free Public Library, now the West Coast Historical Museum

72 Postcard from Arthur Harrop to his son, Angus, 1912

74 Junior National Scholarship Board, Hokitika School, 1903–1915

74 Cobb and Co's coaches, Otira, c. 1910

76 Waitaki Boys' High School, Oamaru, 1913

79 Letter from Arthur Harrop to his son, Angus, 1916

80 Waitaki War Certificates for fives and tennis, 1917 and 1918

81 Sixth Form Boarders, Waitaki, 1918

83 Hilda Valentine, my mother, and her sister Lottie on Arthur Lascelles' motorbike, 1916

86 Waitaki War Certificate, Dux of School, 1918

87 Note of sympathy from Hilda Valentine to Angus Harrop, 1919

91 James Hogg, writer, statue by St Mary's Loch, Scotland

95 Map of the new railway coming into London

97   L for Lampman, from Warne's *Railway Alphabet*
99   Cover of song-sheet: *The Railway Guard* or the Mail Train to the North
101   Lithograph of steam train passing over the Stockport Viaduct, 19th century
106   Stock and workers at Prospect Farm, Pareora, 1880s
107   The Jefcoate family (including my grandmother), Pareora, Christmas, 1888
108   My grandfather, J.A. Valentine, graduating from Otago University, 1886
111   Memorial card for my great-grandmother, Janet Jefcoate, 1900
125   Newspaper advertisement offering reward for capture of deserting seamen, 1858
126   Marriage certificate of my Valentine great-grandparents, Otago, 1862
135   Four generation photograph, Maxwells and Valentines, 1893
138   My mother, Hilda Valentine, 1901
138   Hilda and her sisters, Lottie and Nettie, 1905 and 1910
139   Coronation celebrations, Timaru, 1902
140   My great-grandmother, Mary Maxwell Valentine
141   Photographs of Caroline Bay, Timaru, c. 1911
142   Hilda Valentine with her cousins, Win Bardsley and Ivy Clay
142   N.Z. Education Dept. Certificate of Proficiency, 1912
143   The group photograph at the School House, Timaru South, includes from the left two of my mother's cousins, Will and May Johnson, my Valentine grandparents, my great-grandfather, Thomas Jefcoate, and four of my mother's siblings: Jeff and Graham in the back row, Max and Lottie in the front
148   Timaru Girls' High School
149   My mother's family at the time of her parents' silver wedding, 1914
        From left: Nettie, Max, Nellie (my grandmother), Jeff, Lottie, Graham, Jim Valentine (my grandfather) and Hilda herself
154   Tennis Court at Caroline Bay, Timaru, 1914
157   The Franz Josef Glacier
159   Bishopscourt tea party, Christchurch, 1920
161   Seacliff Mental Hospital, Otago
164   Postcard sent by Angus to Hilda, 1919
166   Connon Hall students, 1919
166   Wedding group. Nettie Valentine to Lewis Watkins in St Aubyn Street, New Plymouth, 1923
167   College House rugby team, Canterbury University College
168   Canterbury University College's victorious tennis team, 1922
169   Canterbury University College, Christchurch
171   C.U.C. Drama Society programme: *The Two Mr Wetherbys*
174   University of New Zealand B.A. certificate, 1922
178   C.U.C. graduates, 1922/1923
181   Otira station, 1923. Angus is second on the left
182   Hilda Valentine, 1923
182   Fred, Louisa, John and Marion Godber, with Angus, 1923
184   D.H. Black and A.J. Harrop accepting their Cambridge doctorates, 1926
187   Gonville and Caius College, Cambridge, postcard

188   Gonville and Caius College Lawn Tennis Club invitation
189   A.J. Harrop, Cambridge visiting cards
193   Tailors and Robe Makers receipt, King's Parade, Cambridge
193   Imperial cablegram, 1926
194   s.s. *Beltana*
195   Typewritten note, Bloomsbury, August, 1926
196   Angus flanked by his sister and his wife, 1927
197   St Martin-in-the-Fields
197   Marriage certificate of my parents, London, 1926
198   The bride and groom
207   Nice in the south of France, postcard, 1927
213   43 Highfield Avenue, London, N.W.11
214   Angus at his typewriter, his mother-in-law and the garden fence
219   Menu for dinner for New Zealand University graduates in London, 1932
220   Flier advertising *Touring in New Zealand*
221   The Harrop family arriving in N.Z., 1934
222   Dr Harrop and Dr Hight, C.U.C., 1934
223   Hilda with her parents and sisters, Wellington, 1934
225   Ann and David with the Valentine grandparents, 1934
227   Hilda enjoying a picnic with the Todd sisters
229   The Harrop family, 1934
233   David and Ann, 1936
233   Up a tree in Highfield Avenue, 1937
235   The children's book plate
236   Illustration for *Round the World with Willa Webfoot* by A.J. Harrop
238   Family gathering: from left to right: Back row: Patricia Valentine, Lottie Elliot, Evelyn Valentine (Jeff's wife), Murray Valentine in his father Jeff's arms, Ruth Watkins in her mother, Nettie's, arms, Lewis Watkins. Front row: Helen Watkins, Jim Valentine, Ian Valentine, Nellie Valentine, Valentine Watkins
238   The Watkins family, 1936, Val, Nettie, Janet, Ruth, Helen, Lewis
243   Invitation to the Coronation, 1937
245   Jacket of *England and the Maori Wars*
249   Postcard showing route to 7 Northiam, Woodside Park
249   The Harrop family, 1938
252   David, Bruno, Hilda, Ann with Moyra Todd in South Square, London, N.W.
253   The Dollis Brook. Left to right: Andrew Reynolds, David Harrop, David Reynolds, Ann
253   In the wigwam, Woodside Park
254   Postcard from Moyra and David to Ann
255   Portreath, Cornwall, 1939, playing in the caves
255   Portreath, Cornwall, 1939, filling sand bags
257   War Office and Ministry of Home Security leaflet
259   s.s. *Ceramic*
262   7 Northiam, Woodside Park, 1941

262   Angus with Ivy and John Moore
265   Letter from Ann to her father, 1940
266   On the beach in Cape Town, South Africa: Ann, Jennifer Hyde, Donald
       Hopkins, Valerie, Deirdre and Pixie Campbell, David
267   Rickshaw rides for my 8th birthday, Durban
272   Leaving Sydney, 1940:   Hilda, Ann, Judy Valentine, David, Aunt Marie
       Valentine
277   At the Waikato farm: Ann with Ruth and Janet Watkins
277   Note from Ann to her mother
280   Dorothy Davies (Lochore) with Marie Vanderwart and Erika Schorss, 1946
283   Marjorie Grieve with Ann, David and Helen Grieve, Christmas, 1941
289   Marsden School on my book plate
291   Report on Carol Concert by Barbara Haldane
294   'Diagrams' illustrating one of my letters, 1943
297   School photo, Marsden, 1943
298   IVB Boarders, Marsden, 1944
299   Wartime visiting cards
301   Eric Baume
307   Ann and David on the Lochores' section, 1944
309   Ann and David, Auckland, 1943
310   Concert programme at Tirau
311   Airgraph to England, 1944
314   Angus in Milford Sound with fishing companion
315   Illustration by F.H. Coventry to a later story

Index

Agar, Winty, later Fysh: 294, 296, 297(illus), 298(illus); n.330

Aitken, Grace, later Maxwell: 83, 165

Aitken, Isobel, later McCaskill: 83, 84

Akaroa (liner): 219-220, 223, 286, 299

alcohol, drunken behaviour: 27; in Ross 47, 49, 51; in Scotland 93; in Stony Stratford 95; in Timaru 108; disgraceful Valentines, temperance 114-115; in Taranaki 121; 153; 'all pleasure not alcoholic' 173

Alhambra (ship): 23

Alice in Wonderland (Carroll): 235

All Blacks: 189, 221, 304

Allen and Unwin (publisher): 202, 220

Alley, Geoff: 304; n.330

Alley, Judith, later Tait: 304-305, 314

Alley, Patrick: 304

Alley, Roderick (Rockie): 304-305

Alley, Ruth, later Craft: 304-305

Alloa, Clackmannanshire: 117, 118; n.325

Alva Hill, farm: 118-121; house burnt down 122; 124; n.325

The Amazing Career of Edward Gibbon Wakefield (AJH): 202-203, 205, 246

Americans in NZ: 294

Anderson's Bay cemetery: 17

Anglicans, see religion

Angus Lost (Flack): 235

Anzac Cove: 78, 149

Aorangi (ship): 273

Aotearoa: 18

Archey, Thomas: 159

Arahura (ferry): 70

Arandora Star (liner): sunk 258

Arthur's Pass: 75-76, 84, 150, 151

Atherton, Cynthia, see Cuthbert, Cynthia

Auckland: 1851 exhibits 37; George, Win Valentine there 131, 132; Will Johnson there 143, 243; university Easter tournament 173, 176; Todds there 227(illus); 1940 arrival 273; Nettie in hospital there 280-281; Japanese submarines? 286; 301,

303; holidays there 308-309(illus); 1945 departure 315-316; return 317

Auckland Star, newspaper: 202, 206, 245

Australia: family connections 16, 19-23, 40, 115, 210, 212, 266, 268; we visit 1940 268, 271, 272(illus), 273; and Winty 296-298; *Sydney Daily Mirror* cable service 301-303; AJH visits 312

Australian Associated Press: 301

Bakewell, Dr Helen (Tui): 195

Balclutha: 137

Ball, Mary and Edward: 101

Banks, banking: 24, 29-30, 54

Banks, Joseph: 17

Bannan, George: 24-25

Baptists, see religion

Bardsley, Lucy Jane, née Jefcoate: 106, 107(illus), 110, 140, 214

Bardsley, Trina, later Speight: 142

Bardsley, Win, later Nicol: 140-142(illus)

Bardsley, William: 141

Barker, Lady, *Station Life in NZ*: 45

Barrytown: 15, 150, 152-153

Batten, Jean: 240-241

Battleships (game): 268, 306

Baume, Eric: 78, 301-303, 313; n.324, n.330

Bax, Clifford, *Square Pegs*: 172

Beaglehole, John: 206

Beauchamp, Mr & Mrs Hal: 70-71

Beauchamp, Kathleen, see Mansfield, Katherine

Beauchamp, Leslie: 77

Beeby, Clarence: 206

Begg, Jean: 132

Belich, James: quoted on immigrants 18, 21, 45; on Wakefield 50, 202; 54, 71, 82, 120, 138; on Savage 174; 'trouble in Paradise' 178; on McCormick 201; n.323

Bell, Myrtle, later Evans: 165

Belloc, Hilaire: *Cautionary Tales* quoted 237

Beltana (liner): 193-194
Belturbet, Cavan, Ireland: 118
Bendigo (liner): 212
Benians, E.A.: 187
Best, Jimmy: 278
Bettelheim, Bruno: quoted 161
bigamy: 55
Binnings, Mr (Pareora head): 108
birth rate, decline: 224, n.329
Bishopscourt, Christchurch hostel for women
  students: 159(illus)
Black, Dr D.H.: 183-184(illus); n.327
Black, Maida: 184
Black's Point Museum, Reefton: 25-26, 31
Bledisloe, Lord: quoted 202; 203
Blunt, Roger: 207
Bogle, Sukie, later Fetherston: 293; quoted
  297; 298(illus)
Bolitho, Hector: 303
Booth, Helen, née Bannan: 24
Bowlby, John: quoted 239
Bracken, Brendan: quoted 303
Bradshaw, Muriel, see Innes, Muriel
Bricks Wharf, Christchurch: 104; n.325
Bridge (game): 193, 204, 218, 224, 271
The Britain of the South (Hursthouse): quoted
  40, 61
British and Inter-Colonial Exhibition, 1923:
  27
Brown, Adam: 20; impressive ancestry 21;
  23
Brown, Bethia, see Campbell, Bethia Jane
Brown, Professor John Macmillan: 165, 182,
  188, 219
Bruce Bay: 150, 151
Bruce, Noeline, later Peebles: 191; n.328
Brunner, Lake: 15, 46
Bryce, John: 122
Bryce & Rusden, libel action: 122
Buck, Peter (Te Rangi Hiroa): 18
Buller River: 29-30
Burnett, Frances Hodgson: 17
Burns, Alexander (Alec): 175, 179

Caerthillian Nursing Home: 215-216
Cahill, David: 122
Cambridge University: CUC teachers there
  168-170; 175, 179; AJH goes 183-184;
  at Caius College 187(illus)-189; PhD
  184(illus) and 192-193; Congress 240
Cambridge History of the British Empire: 187-
  188, 202
The Camelthorn Papers (Thwaite): 284
Campbell, Angus, 1828-1910: marriage 21;

to NZ 22; Ikamatua, Reefton 23-27; 30;
  rise and fall 32; 63, 210
Campbell, Angus James, 1867-1944: 23;
  joins Bank of NZ 29; 30
Campbell, Barbara Ann, later Patterson: 23,
  27, 33, 63, 69
Campbell, Bertha, see Harrop, Bertha Jane
Campbell, Bethia Jane, née Brown: 20;
  marriage 21; 22, 23, 24; death 26-27
Campbell, Elizabeth (Bessie), later Hugo: 23,
  27, 30, 306
Campbell family (on 1940 voyages):
  266(illus), 268
Campbell, John, 1789-1870: 20
Campbell, John Adam, 1864-1919: 21, 23,
  32
Campbell, John Clifton, 1937- : 21, 22, 23
Campbell, Louisa, see Godber, Louisa
Campbell, Margaret Jane, later Perry: 22
Canterbury Museum: 102
Canterbury University College: Arthur
  Harrop's exams 53(illus); 77, 82; Hilda
  goes 85; 87; Hilda and AJH there 163,
  165-178 (169 illus); 183; invitation to
  return 205; AJH represents in UK 218;
  addresses graduates 221-222; n.327
Carlyle, Thomas: quoted on Wakefield 202
Carlton, Lulu: 153
Carnegie, Andrew: 67
Caroline Bay, Timaru: 85, 106, 141(illus),
  154(illus)
Carr, David (diarist): 41; quoted 42; 43-45
Cartwrights (farmers): 146
Castle, Gaye, later Law: 296-297(illus)
Ceramic (liner): 258-259(illus), 263-266
cerebral palsy: 160
Chamberlain, Neville: 246, 252, 255
Chambers's Information for the People: 129
Chesterton, G.K.: 207
Christchurch, see also Canterbury University
  College: 32, 50; LINZ 54; 64, 72; *Press* see
  separate entry; 89, 100, 102; Jefcoates arrive
  104-105; 152, 159, 180, 194, 211, 296
Christchurch Girls' High School: 165, 171,
  296
City of Benares (liner): sunk 267-268
Clarke, William: 122
Clay, Ivy: 142(illus)
Clay, Susan Warner, née Jefcoate: 106,
  107(illus), 142
Clutha River: 126
Coal Creek Falls: 54

Coates, Gordon, (PM): 208

Cobb & Co's coaches: 74(illus), 75, 151, 181

Cobham, Sir Alan: quoted 208

Coleridge, S.T.: 'Ancient Mariner' quoted 44, 102

College House, CUC: 86, 165, rugby team 167(illus), 168

Confessions of a Justified Sinner (Hogg): 89, 90

Condliffe, Professor J.B. (Jack): 168-169, 177, 188, 191; at League of Nations 239; in USA 284, 312

Connon Hall, CUC: 165-166, 177; n.327

Connon, Helen, later Brown: 165

Cook, Captain: 17, 19, 35, 176

Cook Islands: 180, 196

Cook, Mt.: 19, 145

Corbett family (Westland): 66

coronations: Edward VII 139; George VI 243-244(illus)

Cornwall: Portreath holiday 1939 254-255(illus)

corporal punishment: 144-145; Graham thrashed 146

Correspondence School, Wellington: 150, 279

Coventry, F.H.: 244-245(illus), 314-315(illus)

Cowan, James: 245, 246

Coward, Noel: 303

Crabb, James: 118, 124

Crabb, Mary, née Maxwell, 1853-1940: 113, 118, 119, 124

Crabb, Mary, 1889-1955: 118-120, 124

Cresswell, D'Arcy: 211-212; n.328

cricket: in Hokitika 68; in Balclutha 137; 168, 175; at Lord's 185, 241; 206-207

Cron, Jack: 151-152

Croomlea, Timaru hostel: 153

Cunningham, Jean, see Struthers, Jean

Cunningham, Joanna: 124

Cunningham, Mr: 135

Curnow, Allen: quoted 201-202

Curnow, Tremayne: quoted 75

Cuthbert, Cynthia, later Atherton: quoted 64-65; 224, 271, 312

Cuthbert, May, see Harrop, May Celia

Cuthbert, Geoffrey: 64-65, 69, 159(illus), 183, 190; in England 196-197; 224, 271

Cuthbert, Gill, later Poulier: 64, 65, 271, 312

Daily Mail (London): 179, 186; AJH works for 189-192, 204, 205, total eclipse 207, 209; AJH leaves 210; Teddy Tail 248

Daily Telegraph (London): 256, 260-261, 265, 269; AJH leaves 301; 302

Dairy Division, Dept. of Agriculture: 131

dancing: in Ross 47; 84, 116-117; at CUC 158, 163, 172-173; 191, 193, 205, 219

Dannevirke: 23

Davidson, Helen, see Watkins, Helen

Davies, Dorothy, see Lochore, Dorothy

Day, Eva: 154

Deptford, London: 35-36, 42

Devenney, Michael: 160

Dickens, Charles: *Dombey and Son* quoted 96, 97

Didham, Iris: 24

diggers, see gold

Dominion, newspaper, Wellington: 220, 222, 239, 246, 286

Donald, Eve, later Monteith: 298

Dorrington, Marion, née Haskell: n.326

Douglas, Charlie: quoted 51; 52(illus), 55-56

Drake, Janet, née Jefcoate: 106, 107(illus)

dressmaking: 21, 22, 31, 115, 131, 132, 141, 231

Drew, H.B. (Bert): 210

Druce sisters, Mabel and Violet: 250, 253

Drummond, Alison: *Married and Gone to New Zealand* quoted 11

Dunedin, see also Otago U.: 12, 30; Settlers' Museum 42; Gilkisons arrive 90; Hogg memorabilia 92; JAV teaches NE Valley 109, 137; 115; Maxwells and Archie arrive 116-117, 124; 131; Speights 142; 173, 201; visit to Valentines 284

Dunsany, Lord: 246

Dunstan Rush: 125

Early New Zealand Engineers (Furkert): 48

Easdale, Nola: *Kairuri: the Measurer of Land* quoted 58

Eastern Empire (brig): 101-104

eclipse, total (1927): 207-208

Edmonston, Lanarkshire: 20(illus); castle n.321

education, teaching, see also individual schools and universities: in Reefton 24; extra-mural exams 53-54; pupil teaching 31, 52, 107-108; 71-72; 'evils of cram' 73, 82; 132, 140, 144, 145; JAV's career 148-149, 224, 240; West Coast schools 150-151; 164; Hilda at NPGHS 179-180; women and 82, marriage and 193; Harrop children in UK 250, 251, 253, 256; n.324

Egypt: 132, 138

electricity: lighting Reefton 26; Wellington 70

Eliot, George: *Middlemarch* 82, 156; n.324

Ellingham, Pilot Officer: 270

Elliot, Helen Charlotte (Lottie), née Valentine: 83(illus), 104, 137-138(illus), 143(illus), 145, 147, 149(illus); Nettie's bridesmaid 166-167(illus); 197, 213, 223(illus); quoted 227, 228; 238(illus), 242; wartime contact 273, 306, 308

Elliot, Max: 228

Emigrant's Guide to NZ: 39(illus)

Emigrant Voyagers' Manual: 41

Empire Grace (ship): 315, 319

Endeavour (Cook's barque): 17

England and the Maori Wars (AJH): 68; quoted 120; 223, 244-245(illus), 246, 256

England and New Zealand (AJH): 187, 192, 223, 244

Erleigh, Eva: *The Little One's Log Book* quoted 231

Essikebo (hospital ship): 132

The Ettrick Shepherd's Tales (Hogg): 89, 90

evacuation scheme: 254, 257-8, 266, 268, 273

Evans, Alice: 218, 260, 261, 303

Faber and Faber (publisher): 211

Fairburn, Rex: quoted 209

Father and Son (Edmund Gosse): 12

Fell, Blair: 128

Fell, Margaret, see Valentine, Margaret (Peg)

Fetherston, Sue, see Bogle, Sukie

film critic, AJH as: 175, 178

Fox Glacier: 151

Frame, Janet: 160, 290; n.326

France, French: ancestry 115; 156; Hilda teaches 180; AJH works in Paris 189, 207; colonization possibility 187, 189, 203; Riviera visit 207(illus); 215, 217, 242

Franz Josef Glacier: 157(illus), 163

Fraser, Evelyn: 147

Fraser, Peter, (PM): 284, 306

Freeman, Alice: 50, 203

Freeman, Mary: 203-204

From Europe to NZ (Lochore): n.331

Furkert, Eliza, née Sales: 37, 48, 55

Furkert, Frederick William: 48

Furkert, Geoffrey: 48

Furkert, Ursula: 48

Gabriel's Gully: 45

Gallipoli: 77, 78, 132; Graham wounded 149-150

'The Garden Party' (Mansfield): 71, 286

Garner, Dawn, later Built: 298(illus)

Garnett, David: 246

Garnett, Edward: 203, 246

Gate Pa disaster: 120

General Strike: 192-193

Geneva (League of Nations): 239

Germany, Germans: World War One 77-78, 85, 132, 149; colonization possibility 187; family learns language 217, 241-242; Fräuleins in home 241-242, 248, 253; AJH on Rhine 242; Bruno stays 251-252(illus); at war again 255-313; and Lochore 280, 305-306

Gibbons, Carroll: 303

Gibson, Wilfrid: quoted 77-78

Gilkison, Robert and Harriet: 90, 92

Gisborne: 190, 220; my 2nd birthday 224

Glasgow, Scotland: 18, 116

Glover, Denis: quoted 209

Glen, Margaret, later Valentine: 127

Godber, Frederick: 70-71, 182, 286

Godber, Louisa, née Campbell: 23, 27; leaves school 29, 30; 63; understands AJH 69, he visits in Wellington 70-71, 182(illus)-183; 279, 286, 299, 306

Godber, Marion and John: 182(illus)

Godbers', Wellington confectioners: 70-71, 286

Godley, John Robert: 203

gold, gold rush: 18; West Coast 20, 23-30, 70; in Australia 22; Tuapeka area 40, 45; Ross 46-48; 52, 55; Dunstan Rush 125; Archie as gold digger 125-126; Nenthorn 133; Waihi 143

Goodman family (on *Lancashire Witch*): 43

Gosse, Edmund: 12, 17

Gosse, Philip Henry: 17, 121, 265

Grant, Florence, see Valentine, Florence

Great Exhibition (1851): 37

Green Island: 124, 126, 128

Gregorie, Barbara: 289, 290-291

Greymouth: 19-20, 23, 24, 54, 64, 70

Grey River: 24, 27, 30, 46

Grieve family (Wairoa): 283(illus)

Haast (Pass and River): 49, 150, 151

Haldane, Barbara, later Yaldwyn: 290-291, 296-297(illus), 298(illus)

Hamilton, see Southwell School

Handley, James: 122

Handley's woolshed incident: 122

Hankin, St John (*The Two Mr Wetherbys*): 171(illus)

Hanmer Springs: 223-224

Harmsworth, Hon. A.G.A. (Geoffrey): 179, 185, 186, 189

Harper, Archdeacon Henry: 50, 72

Harrop, Angus John Neville: passim

Harrop, Arthur Neville: 33; born 46; 49; in Ross 50, 51; studies in Kokatahi 52-53; as surveyor 54-60, 65, 66; bereaved 62-63, 67; 69, 74; quoted 72, 79; dies 86-87, 133; 100, 150, 152, 156, 161; n.321, n.326

Harrop, Bertha Emily (pharmacist): 40

Harrop, Bertha Jane, née Campbell: 16, 21; birthplace 23-24; 27, 29, 30, 31(illus); surveyor's wife 32-33, 60; dies 62-63, 67; n.323

Harrop, Christopher Neville: 47, 161, 272, 274

Harrop, David Neville: passim

Harrop, Eva Bertha Sales: 16, 62-63, 64, 161, 216

Harrop, Frederick James, 1871-1923: 46, 49; marries 51, 52(illus), 71

Harrop, Frederick, 1904-1951: 16, 30; disabled 62-63, 64, 82; books for birthday 85, 86; 87, 156; at Special School 159; at Seacliff 159-161; 183, 216, 271, 308, 314; n.323-324, n.326

Harrop, Hilda Mary Florence, née Valentine: passim

Harrop, James: 27, 35-50; disappears 51; 54, 100

Harrop, John (stillborn): 216-217

Harrop, Jonas, m.1836: 35, 37

Harrop, Jonas, 1840-1889: 40

Harrop, Margaret, née Penn: 12, 24, 161

Harrop, May Celia, later Cuthbert: 16(illus), 62-65, 69, 72, 85-87, 159-161, 182-183; marries 190; in England 192, 196(illus) -197; 204, 224; in Melbourne 265-266, 268, 271; AJH visits 312; n.321

Harrop, Robert Henry: born & died 46, 51

Harrop, Sarah, née Sales, later Smyth: 35-52; marries Smyth 54-55; dies 63; 100

Harrop, Stephen Maxwell: 161, 274

Harrop, Susan Margaret: 161

Harwat Club: 309, 314-315

Hawera: 119, 123

Hay, Mary, née Valentine: 132

Heitiki Club, U.K.: 188

Hess, Rudolf: 303

Hight, Dr James, later Sir: his parents 45; 53; Professor of History 169-170, 176, 187-188; in England 205; invites AJH 188, 205, 221-222(illus); 224, 235; quoted 244-245; 279; n.327

Hillary, Sir Edmund: 210, 292

Hillary, June, later Dr Carlile: 292

historian, AJH's status as: 201-202, 244-246

Hobbes, Thomas: 187; n.327

Hogg family (the poet's): 90, 92

Hogg, Helen, see Oliver, Helen

Hogg, James, 1730-1800: 92

Hogg, James, poet, 1770-1835: 89-92, 103

Hogg, James, 1806-1892: 92

Hohonu River: 15, 58(illus), 66

Hokitika: 15-17, 19-20(illus), 27, 33, 46, 48; Harrops arrive 49; 51, 52, 54-56, 58; archival photos 59; AJH's childhood 61-67(illus)-74(illus); Valentines arrive 82-83, 150; 137, 152, 163, 166, 167, 177, 194, 314

Hokitika Free Public Library: 67(illus), 74

Homer Tunnel: 313

Hughes, Gillian: 91-92

Hugo, Angus (Bang): 30, 66(illus), 67; n.323

Hugo, Elizabeth, see Campbell, Elizabeth (Bessie)

Huguenots: 115-116

Hunter, Helen, see Valentine, Helen (Nell)

Hursthouse, Charles: *The Britain of the South* quoted 40, 61

Ikamatua: 23-24

Imperial Conference (1937): 247

Inangahua: 24; *Herald* 26; 29-30

influenza epidemic: 85-86

Innes, Muriel, later Bradshaw: 165; n.327

Innes, Rosa, later Seddon: 165

International Council of Women: 1930 conference 217

invasion, fears of: in Britain 256-258, 261; in NZ 286, 289

Ireland: 117-118, 124

Japan: Tokyo 132, 298; Ambassador 208; Pearl Harbor 282, 284; threat to NZ 286, 289; atom bombing 313

Jefcoate, Charlotte New Zealand, see Johnson, Charlotte

Jefcoate, David: 110

Jefcoate, Edward (c.1720-1800): 94

Jefcoate, Edward (b.1846): 96

Jefcoate, Hannah, née Warner, later Kingdom: 22, 97, 100

Jefcoate, Helen, see Valentine, Helen (Nellie)

Jefcoate, Janet, née Oliver: 89; birth 91, 93; 94, 98-107(illus), 108, 110, 111; n.324

Jefcoate, Janet Oliver, see Drake, Janet
Jefcoate, James Edward: 106, 110
Jefcoate, Leonard Charles: 110
Jefcoate, Lucy Jane, see Bardsley, Lucy
Jefcoate, Richard: 94-95
Jefcoate, Samuel: 95, 99
Jefcoate, Stanley: 110
Jefcoate, Susan Warner, see Clay, Susan
Jefcoate, Thomas, 1814-1854: 95; lampman 96; dies 97
Jefcoate, Thomas, 1839-1913: 89; born 96; joins LNWR 97; goods guard 98-99(illus); marriage 99-100; emigrates 100-102; arrives in Christchurch 104; Prospect Farm, Pareora 105-106(illus), 107(illus), 109; visits England 109-110; Oteramika 110; wife dies 110-111; 210; n.325
Jefcoate, Thomas Eastern Empire (East), 1864-1936:   birth   102;   105-107(illus); marries 110; 144
Jellicoe, Lord: introduction 187; Jutland n.328
Jennings, Millicent: 171
Johnson, Charlotte (Lottie), née Jefcoate: birth 104; 105-107(illus); in Waihi 143, 147; 144
Johnson, William: 143, 147
Johnson, Dr Will: 143, 243
Jordan, W.J. (Bill), later Sir William: 247, 313
Journalism, Diploma in: 174; n.327
Joynt, J.W.: 218
Jura (sailing ship): 116-117, 124, 125
Jude the Obscure (Hardy): 190

Kai Iwi Cavalry, see Wanganui 121-124
Kanawa, Kiri te: 210
Kanieri, Lake: 28, 47, 79
Keane, M.C. (editor): 175-176
Keith, Professor A.B.: 245-246
King, Michael: quoted 17, 18; 120, 149; on McCormick 201; 202; on New Zealanders abroad 206; 290; on Lochores 305; n.321
King, Dr Truby, later Sir: 'evils of cram' 73; Superintendent Seacliff 160; childcare 215, 231-232, 239
Kippenberger, General Howard: 313; n.331
Kirks, Kirkcaldies (department store): 183, 204
Kodak airgraph scheme: 310-311(illus)
Kokatahi: 28, 47, 52-53
Kotahitanga: 19; n.321
kupapa: 120
Kupe: 18-19

Labour Day, eight-hour day: 60; n.323
Lambie, Brian: 21
Lancashire Witch (sailing ship): 41-45
Land Wars, see Maori Wars
Largs Bay (liner): 271-272
Larkin, Philip: quoted 64-65, 224, 234
Lascelles, Arthur: 83
Laybourn, Margie: 294, 296-297(illus), 307, 308, 314
League of Nations: 239, 246-247
Learmont, Mr (student): 158
letters, importance of: 11-12, 22, 206, 209; problems before airmail 186, 196, 228, n.328; HMH's first airmail letter (1937) 243; 'Clipper' letters 268-269; school letters 293, 295; airgraphs 310-311(illus), n.330; 316
Libya: Benghazi 266; 284
LINZ, Land Information, NZ: 54, 56
The Listener (NZ): quoted 169; 201, 312
literacy: 22; n.321
Liverpool, England: 1940 departure 258; 1945 return 316-317
Lively, Penelope: quoted 263, n.330
Livingston, James (diarist): quoted 123; n.326
Lochore, Dorothy, née Davies: career 279-280; 285, 293, 304-308; concert 314; writes to London 316; n.331
Lochore, Reuel: 78, 280, 285, 293, 304-308; n.324, n.330, n.331
Lockwood, George: 172-173; n.327
London, England, see also *Daily Mail*, Savoy Hotel etc: Harrops there, Deptford, Camden Town 35-37; Wallace and Mayhew on conditions 37-38; Euston Station 95(illus); Jefcoates there 96-97, married in Bloomsbury 99-100; AJH arrives 185-186; AJH's first job in Fleet Street 189; Hilda arrives 195; King William Street flat 196, 206; married at St Martin-in-the-Fields 196-198(illus); life in London 205-206; Gower Street office for University of NZ 201, 218, 260; North London houses 213(illus), 249, 262(illus); children born there 216, 217; Blitz 260-261, 269, 270, 303-304
London Labour and the London Poor (Mayhew): 37-38
The Long White Cloud (Reeves): quoted 18, 55, 124; AJH updating 202
Lord of the Rings (film): 175
Lucas, Dr (child psychologist): 253, 285
Luke, Mr (student): 158, 163; n.326
Luke, Pattie, later Reed: 295

Luke, Raema, later Watt: 295
Lyell: 29(illus)-30
Lyttelton: 45, 104, 148; *Times* 177; 313; n.325

Macaulay, Thomas: 68; n.323
Macclesfield, Cheshire: 35, 40
McCaskill, Isobel, see Aitken, Isobel
McCaskill, Lance: 84
McCormick, Eric: in London 201; on AJH 201, 204, 218
McIndoe, Archie, later Sir Archibald: 270
MacKay, Angus: 22-23, 30
MacKay, Charles Ewing: 212
MacKay, Jane: death 22
McKenzie, Clare: 270
McKenzie country: 147
Malfroy, Jules: 74, 83, 84
Malvern, Worcestershire: 203-204
Mander, Jane: quoted 209
Mansfield, Katherine: 70-71; her *Letters* 215; 286
Manutahi: 118-121
Maori: 18-19, 28, 40, 45; trouble in Taranaki 120-124; no trouble in Otago 124 or in Timaru 140; Hilda's CUC thesis on 176; 189; AJH writes on 244-245; land claim 245; culture inadequately supported 247
Maori Wars, Land Wars: 120-124; see also *England and the Maori Wars*
Married and Gone to New Zealand (Drummond): quoted 11
Marsden School (Samuel Marsden Collegiate): 153, 286, 289(illus), 297(illus), 298(illus), 299, 304, 307, letter from 311(illus), 313, 316
Marsden Women and their World (Carpenter): quoted 290
Martin, J.C. (Fred): 59, 66
Mason, Helen (Bili), née Valentine: 132, 284
Mason, Malcolm J.: 284
Massey, William, (PM): 182
Mathieson, John (diarist): quoted 116
Maui: 18
Maxwell (town): 123-124
Maxwell, Allan: 119
Maxwell, Catherine, later Hunter: 118, 119
Maxwell, Ellen, later Hamilton: 118, 119
Maxwell, Ellen (Helen), née Taylor: 117, 124, 128, 134(illus); dies 135; n.325
Maxwell, George, b.1794: 113, 117, 118
Maxwell, George, 1842-1868, Taranaki: 113, 114, 118, 120-124

Maxwell, George, 1849-1924, Waikouaiti: 113, 114, 117, 118, 127; quarrel with Archie 128-130; 135
Maxwell, George, 1879-1965: 113, 119
Maxwell, James, 1818-1904, Waikouaiti: 113, 117-118, 124, 127, 128, 134(illus); dies 135
Maxwell, James, 1840-1860: 117; dies 124
Maxwell, James, 1884-1963: 119
Maxwell, Jane (Jeannie), née Valentine: 114, 115, 127, 135
Maxwell, John, 1815-1895, Wanganui: 113, 118, 124
Maxwell, John, 1853-1938: 113, 117-118, 128, 135
Maxwell, Mary, see Crabb, Mary
Maxwell, Mary, née Jack: 113, 117, 118
Maxwell, Mary, see Valentine, Mary
Maxwell, William: 117, 128, 135
Mayhew, Gladys (Marsden head): 286; quoted 290, 293, 295
Mayhew, Henry: quoted 37-38
Melbourne, see Australia
men, how to behave with: 158
Methuen (London publisher): 192
Metro (magazine): King on Lochore 305
Milford Sound: 314
Miller, Karl: 89, 90, 92
Milne, A.A.: 17; *Winnie-the-Pooh* 204; Christopher Robin 224, 236; 231, 233; quoted 234-237
Milner, Frank (Waitaki headmaster): 74, 76(illus), 77-78, 80; testimonial 85-86; in London 206, 208; quoted on Baume and AJH 302; death 313; n.324, n.331
Milner, Ian: 77; n.324
Moodie, Bedford: 152
Montrose, Scotland: 114, 115-116
Moore family, UK: 262(illus)
Moore, Samuel (headmaster): 108
Moriori: 18
Mount Maunganui: 277
Mulgan, Alan: *Home* 206
Müller, Hella: 248, 253
music: Hilda, piano, singing 82, 139, 157, 171-172, at NPGHS 172, 180, in London 196, 205, 215, 242; Valentines in Waikouaiti 114, 128, 133; in Timaru 148; and Dorothy Davies 279-280, 307; in Tirau 282; at Marsden 291, 294-295
Myers, Dr Bernard: 232, 241, 302
My New Zealand (AJH): 246, 256, 302
myths: 18-19; n.321

Napier: 23, 71, 224, 283
National Patriotic Fund: 269
Nelson: 27, 70, 77, 78, 150, 218
New Plymouth: Valentines move there, Nettie's wedding there 166(illus); Hilda teaches at NPGHS 171-172, 177, 179-180, 191, 193, 194, 217; 1934 visit 224-225(illus); Coronation celebrations 243; Boys' High School 274; our wartime visits 273, 275-276, 285; 286
New Statesman (magazine): 246
New York Times Book Review: 202
HMS *New Zealand* (battlecruiser): 148
New Zealand after Five Wars (AJH): 201
A New Zealander on London Bridge (AJH): 68
NZ Company: 120, 124, 187, 202
NZ Forces' Club, London: 269, 270
New Zealand Government: 120; Education Dept. 132, 142(illus); 174; supporting *NZ News* 209-211, 269; underfunding universities 222; 245, 247; wartime injunctions 278; Dept. of Internal Affairs 305; diplomatic service 306
New Zealand News (London): 201, 204, 205, 209, 210; first publication 211; 212, 213, 215, 217, 218, 239, 240; publishes *England and the Maori Wars* 244; 247, 248, 250, 258; plan in event of AJH's death 260; free copies for troops 269; 270, 300, 301, 312; Victory issue 313
NZ Press Association: 218, 260
NZ Railways: 132
NZ Shipping Company: 210
NZ Society of Accountants: 132
Ngaitahu (Ngai Tahu) land claim: 245
Ngata, Apirana: 53
Nice, the Sunshine Centre (AJH): 207
Norfolk, England: 17, 167, 184
Northcliffe, Lord: 179, 190
Nova Scotia: 19-20, 22
Nukumaru: 122-124

Oamaru, see also Waitaki Boys' High School: 74
Observer (London): 189, 209
Oceana Gold: 25-26; n.321
O'Connor, Irma: 203, 211
Oe, Kenzaburo: 161
Oertel, Bruno: 251-252(illus)
Okoroire Hot Springs: 310
Okuru: 150-151
Oliver, Helen, née Hogg: 89-93, 98
Oliver, Janet, see Jefcoate, Janet

Oliver, John: 93
Oliver, Peter: 92-93
Oliver, Susan, later Little: 93-94, 99, 107
Oliver, William: 93
Opihi River: camping 145-146; n.326
Orakei Korako: 314-315(illus)
O'Regan, Cornelius: quoted 26-27
Ost, Frederick (artist): 236; n.329
Otago Daily Times: quoted 177, 220
Otago Infantry Battalion: 150
Otago Museums: 42, 49, 92
Otago University: JAV graduates 108(illus); medical students 143, 149, 219; 153, 174; Hocken Library 116, 201, n.325; cousin Jim, Chancellor 284; n.324, n.326
Otekaike (special school): 159
Oteramika: 110
Otira, river, gorge, tunnel: 75, 151, 181(illus), 314
Outlook Knots and Puzzles: 277

Palmer, Grace and James: 101
Panama Canal: 181, 185, 284, 299, 312
Pareora: 105, 106(illus), 107(illus), 108-110, 131, 139, 144, 146
Parkhead estate, Stirlingshire: 117
Parkhead farm, NZ: 118, 119
Parr, Norah: 90-92
Parry, Evan: 181
Patterson, Barbara Ann, see Campbell, Barbara
Patterson, Isaac: 32-33
Patterson, Jack: 33
Paulin, Robert: *The Wild West Coast* quoted 27; n.321-322
Pearl Harbor: 282, 284
Pease, Audrey: 298(illus)
Pelvin, Richard: 41
P.E.N. Club: in London 207, 211, 241; in NZ 221
Pennsylvania State Reformatory: Win works there 132
Petterson, Randi: 241, 249, 256
Pfahlert, Denis: 59, 60
Pfahlert, Joe: 59
Pharazyn, Mr (astronomy teacher): 263
Pharazyn, Robert: 123
Plimmerton: 308, 316
Plowman, Sir Claud: 272, n.330
Plunket Society: 215, 231
Porirua: 306-308
Port Chalmers: 116
pottery: 18, 132
Poulier, Gill, see Cuthbert, Gill

Presbyterians, Church of Scotland, see religion

The Press, newspaper, Christchurch: AJH works for 75, 175-181, sends reports from abroad 184-187, All Blacks' tour 189; invited to return 205; 207, 209, 217, 246; n.327

Preston's (sheep station): 147

Price, Arthur (diarist): 41; quoted 43, 44, 45

Pride and Prejudice (Austen): 121, 300

Pringle, John (diarist): quoted 102, 103, 104

prisoners of war: cousins captured 284; receiving books 300-301

Pritchard, Peggy, later Eastwick: 298(illus)

public works (road-making, bridge-building): 76, 106-110, 129-130, 133

pupil teachers: 31, 52, 107-108; n.322

Queen Mary (liner): 272

railways: in U.K., early development 94-95(illus); Jefcoates employed 96-100; 258; in NZ, 106, 180-181(illus); Main Trunk Limited 285, 308; n.325

Rangitane (liner): sunk 272

Rangitata River: 105

Rankine Brown, Professor John: 251

Red Cross: 256, 271, 275, 279; books for prisoners scheme 300-301

Reed, A.H. (publisher): 202

Reefton: 22, 23, 24-33, 60

Reeves, William Pember, see *The Long White Cloud*

religion, churches, faith: devoted Baptists 99-100, 104-105, 110-111; Roman Catholics 173; 212; Presbyterians, Church of Scotland 23, 99, recruiting emigrants 124, church token row 130-131, n.326; JAV writes to Hilda on 154-155; Hilda writes on 155-156, speaks on 178; Anglicans 155, 212; Nellie's faith and Hilda's 237-238; childhood prayers 238-239; house blessing 249-250; at Marsden 292-293

Remuera (liner): 182, 183-185

Rennie family, Wellington: in airgraph 311; 316

Reynolds family, North London: 228, 252-253, 257(illus)

Roberts family, London and NZ: n.330

Rogart, Sutherland: 19

Romance of Westland (AJH): 27, 176-177

Ropata (Maori leader): 121

Ross: 46-51, 151

Ross, Capt. Frederick: 120

Rotorua: 277, 314

Round the World with Willa Webfoot (AJH): 236(illus), 262, 266

Rout, Ettie, *Safe Marriage*: 192

Rowe, Eva: 165

Royal Courts of Justice, London: 122

Rugby, Warwickshire: railway housing 98-101

rugby football: in Hokitika 68; at CUC 167; 185: All Blacks' tour 189

Runanga: 54, 152

Rusden, G.W.: 122

Rutherford, Ernest, later Lord: 53, 77, 184, 210, 218-219, 274

Ryder, Lady Frances: 190

St Martin-in-the-Fields, London: weddings 132, 196, 198(illus); 212

St Mary's, Karori, Wellington: 292; in airgraph, Merbecke 311

St Paul's Cathedral, London: 269

Sales, Eliza, see Furkert, Eliza

Sales, George: 36, 37

Sales, Sarah, née Witchell: 36, 37

Sales, Sarah, see Harrop, Sarah

sanitation: 133

Savage, Michael Joseph (PM): 174, 244, 247

Savoy Hotel, London: 303; VE Day 313

Schnabel, Artur: 279

Scholefield, G.H.: 201-202

Schorss, Erika: 280

Schroder, Erle: 74, 163, 173

Scotland: Campbells of Sutherland leave 19; Browns and Edmonston 20-21; medical studies there 23, 32, 143; Hogg connection 89-92; Olivers and Langholm 92-94, 98; 102-103; Valentines and Montrose 114-116; Maxwell background 117; from Alloa to Wanganui 118; from Alloa to Otago 124; University of Edinburgh 246

Scott, Andrew: 152

Scott, Captain (of the Antarctic): quoted 28

Scott, Sir Walter: 51, 90, 113

Seacliff Mental Hospital: 73, 159-161(illus), 231, 308, 314

Seddon, Richard (King Dick): 55

Sergel, H.G.: 219, 274

Sergel, Ethel, née Rutherford: 219

sex education: 147, 192, 296; n.328

Shaffrey, Mary Ann, later Harrop: 51, 71

Shaffrey, Michael: 59

Shantytown, West Coast: n.322

Shaw, G.B.: 207, 241

Shaw Savill & Co (shipping line): 41, 219, 258, 264

Shelley, Professor James: 170
Shepard, E.H. (artist): 231, 237
Shepherd, Henry (diarist): n.322
Sherlock, W. (photographer): 31
Sherriff, R.C.: *Journey's End* 208
shipboard diaries: quoted from *Lancashire Witch* 41-45; from *Eastern Empire* 102-104; from *Jura* 116; from *Beltana* 194; n.322
Singapore: 208, 284, 286
Six Day War (1967): 266
Smith, C. Fox: quoted 78
Smith, Dodie: quoted 228
Smyth, John Neville: 45-47, 50-52; marries Sarah Harrop 54; 63, 64
South Africa: 43; 194; 1940 in Cape Town 264-266(illus), in Durban 267(illus)
Southburn Story (John Button): 107
Southern Alps: 19, 46, 55, 64; coaches 74(illus); 75-76, 147, 148, 181
Southern Cross and Evening Star (Wilford): 167
Southwell School, Hamilton: 219; David there 274-275, 283, 284, 285, 293, 304, 316
Spectator (London): 209, 246
Speight, Deirdre, later Wilson: 142
sport, see also cricket, rugby football, tennis: in Hokitika 67-68; at Waitaki 79-80; bowling 86-87, 150; basketball 177; croquet 179; at Hanmer 224; in London 241; swimming 51, 84, 265, 285; at Southwell 274
Spreydon, Christchurch: 100, 104-105
Squires, Thomas: 122
Squirrel Goes Skating (Uttley): 235
Standring, Rev. James: 109
Station Life in NZ (Lady Barker): 45
Stewart, Helen: 147; n.326
Stewart, Marie: 197, 215; n.329
Stewart, Rena, later Bell: 197
stillborn child (John Harrop): 216-217
Stockport viaduct: 100-101(illus)
Stony Stratford, then Northamptonshire: 94-96, 98; place of origin 101
Stopes, Marie, *Married Love*: 147, 192, 217
Stories from the Odyssey (Lang): 234-235
Strandon, New Plymouth hostel: 180, 191
Strombom, Kathleen: 292
Struthers, Jean, née Cunningham: 197; n.329
Sturge, Mary: quoted 60
suffrage petitions, women's: 55
Sunday Dispatch (London): 210, 217, 218
Sunshine from Southern Skies (Harrison Lee): 114

surveyors, surveying: 15, 47, 49; examinations 52-53(illus); 54, 55-60, 65-66
Sutherland, Scotland: 19; n.321
Sydney Daily Mirror, see Australia
Sykes, Philip: 218, 228

Taipo River: 57
Taituha, Harry: 301
Tamaroa (liner): 224, 227, 229, 232, 239
Taramakau River: 66
Taranaki, see New Plymouth
Taranaki Herald: quoted 177; 276
Taranaki War: 120-124, 187
Tasman, Mt: 151
Taupo: 283
Tauranga: 193
Tauranga Ika pa: 122
Teachers' Training College, Christchurch: 159, 176, 177
teaching, see education
Te Angina, Uru: 122
Teichelmann, Dr Ebenezer: 62
Te Kanawa, Kiri: 210
Te Kepa: 121
Te Kooti: 120-121, 122, 245
Telegraph, see *Daily Telegraph*
telephoning NZ from U.K.: 209
television, early days: 241
temperance, prohibition: 114-115
tennis: in Hokitika 68-69, 72-73, 84; in Timaru 154(illus); at CUC 163, 168(illus), 172-173, 176, 177; with Harmsworth 179; in Cambridge 188(illus); in London 69, 196, 204, 214-215, 228; at Hanmer Springs 224; children's lessons 241
Tennyson family: 17, 63; n.329
Tennyson's poems: 139
Te Rangi Hiroa (Sir Peter Buck): 18
Testbank (freighter): 264
Themistocles (ship): 267
Thom, Capt. James: 116; n.325
Thompson, John (of Montrose): 114
Thwaite, Alice: 161, 266, 316
Thwaite, Anthony: 3, 64, 150
Thwaite, Caroline, later Leckie: 161, 266
Thwaite, Emily: 161, 266; n.324
Thwaite, Lucy: 147, 161, 266, 316
Timaru: Harrops disembark 45; St Mary's Church 72; 74; Hilda's birthplace 110; JAV head Timaru South 137-142(illus), 143(illus), 144-150; Hilda at Timaru GHS 82, 84, 85, 148(illus), 153, 157; 194, 237, 279; Harbour Board 141
The Times, London: 181, 190, 202, 260, 300

Tirau, Waikato: Watkins' farm 224, 243, 274-275; my year there (1941) 276-278, 280-283, 296; holidays there 308, Harwats 309-310, 314-316

Titokowaru: 121, 122, 123

Tizzard, Nance: 172

Todd, Charles: 206

Todd, Dr Kathleen: 195-196, 206; to America 214; in Auckland 227(illus); return to England 228; 232; helps David 242, 253; he lives with them 253-254; 280

Todd, Moyra: letters to 12, 267, 268, 281, 282; first meeting, instant friendship 195-196; 205, 206; holiday with Hilda 213; stays in Highfield Ave 214-215; in Auckland 227(illus); David lives with them 253-254; 258, 270; quoted 275; 280, 313

Torlesse, Fanny: 203, 204

Touring in New Zealand (AJH): 220(illus), 223, 229

tourism, developing industry: 220

Treaty of Waitangi: 71, 120; centenary 247

Tremain, Rose (novelist): n.322

Trendall, Professor Dale: 273

Truth (NZ): 301-302, 313

Truth and Sportsman group Australia: cable service 301

Tuapeka: 40, 45

Turnovsky, Fred: 305

Twigger, Charlotte: 100, 104-105

Twigger, Joseph: 104-105

United States of America: AJH there 312

Universities Bureau of the British Empire: AJH represents NZ 218, 240

University of New Zealand, see also Auckland, CUC, Victoria: 174; AJH represents 201, 218; London dinner 219; 'seriously underfunded' 221-223; Senate 224, 240, 251; London office 201, 248, bombed 260; AJH doctorate 246; salary n.330

Valentine, Ailsa, née Gold: 306

Valentine, Amy: 113, 128, 132, 140, 273

Valentine, Archibald, 1809-1879: 113; 'drunken tailor' 114-115

Valentine, Archie, 1840-1890: 113, 114-118, 124; deserts ship 125; as gold digger, marries 125-126; as nurse 126-127; quarrels with Maxwells 128-130; a contractor 129, 133; and church tokens 130-131; Win remembers 133; death 133-134

Valentine, (Archibald) Graham, 1892-1956: 110, 134(illus), 137-138, 143(illus),

144; relationship with Hilda 145-147; 149(illus); Gallipoli 149-150; 273, 275

Valentine, Charlotte, née Thompson, 1808-1878: 114, 115, 127

Valentine, Florence (Flo), later Grant: 132, 138

Valentine, George: 130, 131, 134, 135

Valentine, Helen (Bili), see Mason, Helen

Valentine, Helen Charlotte (Lottie), see Elliot, Helen

Valentine, Helen (Nell), later Hunter: 113, 128, 131, 132, 140

Valentine, Helen (Nellie), née Jefcoate: 87, 89, 91, 100; birth 105; in Pareora 106-107(illus), 108, marriage 109; Hilda's birth 110; 113, 131, 134-135(illus); Balclutha to Timaru 137; in Timaru 137-144; camping 145-146; 147, 149(illus); to Hokitika 150; in New Plymouth 179-180, 192, 193, 196, 197, 204; visits England 212-214(illus); 223(illus), 225(illus), 228; sends photos 237-238(illus); death 242-243

Valentine, Henry (Hal): 131-132, 135, 284

Valentine, Hilda Mary Florence, later Harrop: passim

Valentine, James Archibald (Jim), 1863-1948: 12, 82, 87, 91, 105, 108; marriage 109; 110; his family history 113-118, 125; birth 126; in Waikouaiti 127, 128, on farming practices 129, 131, 134-135(illus); in Balclutha 137; Timaru South School head 137, 140, 143(illus), 144-145, 148; camping 145-146; career 148-149(illus), 224; on West Coast 150-155, 157; in New Plymouth 166-167(illus); to Cook Islands 80, 196; visits England 212-214; 223(illus); quoted, proud of Hilda 240; wartime contact 273, 275-276, 284, 285; quoted 299

Valentine, James Archibald, b.1922: 284

Valentine, James Jefcoate (Jeff), 1895-1966: 110, 137, 138, 143(illus); medical training interrupted 149(illus); 193, 216, 238(illus); disconcerting letter 273-274; 281

Valentine, Jane (Jeannie), see Maxwell, Jane

Valentine, Janet Koanui (Nettie), see Watkins, Janet

Valentine, John: 113, 127; n.326

Valentine, Judy, later Mertzlin: 272(illus); n.330

Valentine, Mabel: 128, 132, 273, 299

Valentine, Margaret (Peg), later Fell: 128, 132

Valentine, Marie, née Plowman: 179, 272(illus)

Valentine, Mary, née Maxwell: 113, 116-119, 124, 125; marries, first child 126; family quarrel 128-130; described by Hilda 130; 133-135(illus); funeral 135; Hilda visited 140(illus)

Valentine, Mary, later Hay: 132

Valentine, Shirley, née Williamson: 284

Valentine, William Maxwell (Max), 1903-1984: birth 137, 138, 140; 143(illus), 144, 148, 149(illus), 212; host in Sydney 272

Valentine, Winifred (Win): 12, 113; as family historian 114-119, 125, 128-130; birth 131; her career 132; on her father 133; 230; in Kelburn 287; 306

Vanderwart, Marie: 280

vegetarianism: 276, 294

Viceroy of India (liner): 264-265

Victoria University College, Wellington: 173, 174, 206, 218, 224, 251

Vienna: womens' conference 217

Waihi: Hilda visits 143-144, 147

Waikari: 167

Waikouaiti: 114-115, 126-131, 133-135, 139, 140, 146, 273; n.325

Waimakariri River: 75

Wairoa: 283

Waitaki Boys' High School, Oamaru: 74; AJH begins there 76(illus); 77-82, 85-86, 148, 149, 173, 189; 221; London reunion 269; 'best school' 301; David there 313; n.324

Waitangi, see Treaty of

Wake, Hugh: 68, 69

Wakefield, Alice, later Freeman: 50

Wakefield, Edward Gibbon: 50, 202-204, 246

Wakefield, Priscilla: 204

Wall, Professor Arnold: 170, 177

Wanganui: 123, 212; n.326

Wanganui and Kai Iwi Cavalry: 121-124

Ward, James Allan, VC: 270

Watkins, Helen, later Davidson: as family historian 91, 95, 106; on reivers 117; as baby 180, 192; 238(illus); as adolescent 274, 281-282, 285, 309

Watkins, Janet, later Hanna: 238(illus), 274, 276-277(illus), 278, 309, 310; n.331

Watkins, Lewis: 117; wedding 166(illus)-167; 180, 224, 238(illus); and 'war effort' 275; 281-283, 309

Watkins, Lewis Valentine (Val): as baby 192; 238(illus), teases David 274-275; 283, 284, 309

Watkins Janet Koanui (Nettie), née Valentine: 87, 110, 137-138(illus), 145-147, 149(illus); leaves TGHS 153; 157; wedding 166(illus)-167; types Hilda's thesis 176; first baby 180; 192, 197, 223(illus), 224, 228, 238(illus), 242, 243; quoted 259; wartime contact 273-279; car accident 280-281; 282; returns home 283; 306, 309

Watkins, Ruth, later McDonald: 238(illus), 274; quoted 276; 277(illus), 278, 281-283; quoted 309-310; 314; n.325, n.331

Watson, Win: 153

Watt, Barbara: 157

Waugh, Evelyn: 213, 241

Webb, Leicester: 169

Welch, Norma: 229, 239

Weldon, Fay: quoted 296

Wellington: 45, 50, 63, 69; AJH's first visit 70-71; 110; Maxwells arrive 118; 119, 150, 173, 182-183, 203, 218; 1934 arrival 223; 229(illus); Hilda working there 279-280, 284, 285-286; Marsden 289-299; Hataitai 304, 306; Tinakori Rd 307; AJH arrives 312; ferry traffic n.330

West Coast Historical Museum, Hokitika: 59, 67(illus)

West Coast Times: quoted 46, 47, 71, 79

Westland District Hospital: 62

Whitcombe and Tombs (publisher): 27, 244

Whitman, Barbara, later van den Broek: 291, 294, 296-297(illus), 298(illus)

Whitson, Harold: 20

Whyte, Constance, née Jefcoate: quoted 104, 110

Wild, Hetty, née Porter: 153

Wild West Coast of NZ (Paulin): quoted 27

Wilford, Canon John Russell: 167-169; in Jersey CI 258

William (Richmal Crompton): 295

Winnie-the-Pooh (A.A. Milne): 204

The Wonderful Century (A.R. Wallace): quoted 37

Wright, J.D.: *Reminiscences of Wanganui* quoted 122

Wylde, A.H.: 49

Yaldwyn, Barbara, see Haldane, Barbara

Yaldwyn, John: 290

Y.W.C.A.: 132, 165, 230